The Esse
of Film Noir

The Essence of Film Noir

The Style and Themes of Cinema's Dark Genre

DIANA ROYER

McFarland & Company, Inc., Publishers

Jefferson, North Carolina

This book has undergone peer review.

ISBN (print) 978-1-4766-8419-2
ISBN (ebook) 978-1-4766-4590-2

Library of Congress and British Library
Cataloguing data are available

Library of Congress Control Number 2022020009

Shelley Winters and Robert Mitchum in the 1955 film
The Night of the Hunter (United Artists/Photofest)

Printed in the United States of America

*McFarland & Company, Inc., Publishers
Box 611, Jefferson, North Carolina 28640
www.mcfarlandpub.com*

To my dearest Carl
and, as always,
in memory of Carrie

Table of Contents

Acknowledgments   viii

Preface   1

Introduction   3

One. Lit from Behind: The Genesis and Continuity
of Film Noir   9

Two. All the Guys with Eye Patches: Hard Bitten
Film Noir   64

Three. Commies, Nazis and Fascists: Politics
in Film Noir   84

Four. "Something Further May Follow...": Con Artists
and Scams in Film Noir   129

Five. Double Crosses: Religious Delusion in Film Noir   161

Six. Highways, By-ways and Dislocations: The Self
in Neo-Noir   181

Chapter Notes   205

Filmography   211

Bibliography   217

Index   221

Acknowledgments

The encouragement of friends and colleagues has made this book possible. I thank Moira Casey, Bob Davis, and Whitney Womack Smith of Miami University for their administrative support. I'm very appreciative of the assistance of Miami University's librarians, especially that given by Carrie Girton, Krista McDonald, Carla Myers, and Mark Shores.

I am grateful for the friends who inquired after the manuscript's progress and my well-being: Jim Brannon, Tom Flanigan, Kathleen Fox, Nina Hodoruk, Bernie Hyland, Katie Kickel, Mo and Ana Madani, Santo Mirabella, Sal Randazzo, Guylene Smith, Matthew Smith, and Leslie Vernon.

As well, I am grateful for the loving support of my sister, Marian Wolotkiewicz; my cousins Lisa Marshall, Greg Marshall, and Karen Kelly; my mother-in-law, Mary Lou Royer, and stepmother-in-law, Connie Royer; Carl's siblings and cousins, aunt Joan Knott, and nephew Lukas Royer; and my honorary son, Philip Long.

I give thanks for the memories of the love and interest shown by those who passed during the writing of this book: my mother, Rita Wolotkiewicz; my aunt, Dorothea Marshall; my best male friend, Joe Torcicollo; my and Carl's friend Bill Pencak; my friend Alanna Randazzo; and my father-in-law, Carl Gall Royer.

I am deeply appreciative of the graciousness and insightful guidance of my editor at McFarland & Company, David Alff. Cordial thanks are due to Photofest for finding requested photographs.

Preface

This book was inspired by my beloved late husband, Carl Gall Royer, II. It really began with six conference papers on various aspects of film noir that Carl and I wrote and presented at the annual Popular Culture Association conferences from 2007 to 2012; I thank our area chair, Donald Palumbo, for those opportunities. We had planned to expand upon the papers to create a volume of film noir criticism, as we had done with previous conference papers on horror films that became *The Spectacle of Isolation in Horror Films: Dark Parades* (Haworth Press, 2005). Carl's death and then frequent long-distance trips to visit my physically frail elderly mother kept me from working on the manuscript for several years. When I returned to the project, I had the benefit of having taught a seminar on detective fiction and film noir three times. I had always envisioned including the fiction upon which some of the films had been based in the expanded critical volume and was delighted to venture beyond the handful of novels used in my seminars in doing so for this book.

Previous studies of film noir have dealt with various aspects of the genre, such as its gangster characters, its city setting, or its censorship. Others have focused on individual directors or actors. As well, some studies explored the ways in which German Expressionism, World War II, or the Cold War influenced the genre. Numerous guides, filmographies, and studies of individual films exist. The present work contributes to the scholarship on film noir by discussing the genre's thematic aspects, cultural contexts, and stylistic qualities. Both classic and neo-noir films are analyzed. For those films based upon novels, in-depth analysis of the fiction is provided in comparison and contrast to the film version. It is hoped that such a comprehensive approach provides readers with a richer experience of film noir.

Introduction

Many studies of film noir focus on particular directors or cover the classic period of the genre, from 1941's *The Maltese Falcon* to 1950's *Sunset Boulevard*. This book expands and explores the genre beyond previous boundaries set by time period. An examination of classic noir reveals the stylistic aspects that run through the work of particular directors and carry over into neo-noir, both visually and narratively. These directors—Billy Wilder, Otto Preminger, Howard Hawks, Samuel Fuller, Nicholas Ray, Orson Welles, Fritz Lang—craft a uniquely American visual poetry in their treatment of sex, violence, and betrayal as they bring America's cities and open roads to the screen. Too, there is a continuity of a certain style of noir that reveals its psychological complexity through narrative complications rather than through dialogue or thematic development, however nuanced the latter two may be. Concomitantly, the camera becomes an unreliable narrator, a subjective omnipresence reflecting the characters' internal states while at the same time distancing the viewer.

The narratives of classic films noir and neo-noirs reveal themes both somewhat expected and unexpected. Unsurprisingly, American politics flavor a number of films made before and during the Cold War. Sometimes this is primarily a plot device, such as the microfilm that pickpocket Skip pilfers from Candy in Samuel Fuller's *Pickup on South Street*. It can take the mild form of anti–Nazi sentiment that appears in Fritz Lang's *Ministry of Fear*. Sometimes it is overt propaganda like the Communist paranoia saturating the wartime film *Strange Holiday* by Arch Oboler. Or it can be concern over lingering Fascism in postwar Germany, as in Orson Welles' *The Stranger*. Occasionally it serves as impetus for a truly sui generis creation, as in John Frankenheimer's *The Manchurian Candidate*.

Likewise, one might anticipate that con artists and scams would drive the narratives of a genre so often derisive about human nature, frequently having devastating effects on the protagonist, such as the downfall of Stan from nightclub performer Stanton the Great to carnival Geek in Edmund Goulding's *Nightmare Alley*, or Al Roberts' arrest for two murders at the end of Edgar G. Ulmer's *Detour*. In neo-noir the protagonist upon whom the con is worked might come out alive and relatively undamaged himself, like Joe Ross in David Mamet's *The Spanish Prisoner*, whose best friend has been killed, but who can sell his Process to another corporation; or Customs agent Dave Kujan in Bryan Singer's *The Usual Suspects*, who solves the crime but can't catch the perpetrator, Verbal.

Such films present the post–Calvinist view that everyone is potentially corruptible and most are already corrupt. Thus, one might wonder what role religion could play thematically in a genre so generally cynical about spiritual values and convictions. A distorted one, to be sure. Remnants of the Great Awakening, that last gasp of Puritanism, appear in the pathological, messianic figures that manipulate the lives of innocent and criminal alike, whether this be the murderous, child-stalking Harry Powell in Charles Laughton's *The Night of the Hunter* or the serial killer John Doe in David Fincher's *Se7en*, killing off what he sees as embodiments of the Seven Deadly Sins to save humanity. Then there's Charlie in Martin Scorsese's *Mean Streets*, struggling to reconcile his criminal life with his Catholic faith, endlessly preaching to Johnny Boy to do the right thing and pay his debts.

The novels upon which some films were based are telling about American society—for example, Edward Anderson hoboed during the Great Depression, interviewed prisoners, and drew on Bonnie and Clyde for *Thieves Like Us*, which became *They Live by Night* when Nicholas Ray brought the story to the screen. *The Night of the Hunter* author Davis Grubb based Harry Powell on the real-life West Virginia serial killer of the 1920s, Harry F. Powers. James M. Cain wrote for the tabloids, and his novel *Double Indemnity*, which Billy Wilder would film, was inspired by Ruth Snyder and her lover Judd Gray's murder of her husband. Press coverage of this trial was so sensational it lingered in American consciousness long after the two killers were executed in the electric chair on January 12, 1928. In the 1951 science-fiction film *The Thing from Another World*, the reporter, Scotty, who has been trying to get a photograph of the extraterrestrial creature, is waiting for it to come into the building and be electrocuted by a system the Air Force crew have rigged. He says, "I remember the first execution I ever covered, Ruth Snyder and Judd Gray." "Did you get a picture of that, Scotty?" someone asks. "No, they didn't allow cameras, but one guy—." He's cut off because the creature is coming, but he would have said that one photographer smuggled his camera in and managed to get a photo of a bound and masked Ruth Snyder as she was electrocuted.

While noir undeniably has European roots in German Expressionism, and several of the directors under analysis here were German émigrés (Fritz Lang, Edgar G. Ulmer, Billy Wilder, Otto Preminger), this study unfolds how noir—both classic and neo—metamorphosed into a rich, dark American genre studying humanity from a variety of angles, few of them favorable.

Chapter One, "Lit from Behind: The Genesis and Continuity of Film Noir," discusses the early use of the term *film noir* by French critics Nino Frank and Jean-Pierre Chartier before turning to one of the films both these critics place in this new film category, Billy Wilder's *Double Indemnity* (1944). As analysis of Phyllis Dietrichson's machinations reveals, this has become the iconic femme fatale film. It's based on James M. Cain's 1943 novel of the same name, which in turn, as noted earlier, drew from a real-life murder case, and the interplay of these texts is discussed. Another Wilder film, *Sunset Boulevard* (1950), employs symbolic imagery and interesting camerawork to tell its story of what a rotten and rotting place Hollywood can be. A glamorous film noir with a haunting soundtrack, the story of how Otto Preminger's *Laura* (1944) came to be made is as dramatic as the story it presents onscreen. Its roots in Vera Caspary's novel *Laura* (1942) and its journey through the studio system are discussed, as are Preminger's careful framing techniques.

A film that is set in the classic film noir period and evokes its décor and fashion sense yet looks at them through an updated camera eye is Roman Polanski's *Chinatown* (1974), a study of corruption and deception that holds viewers close to the perspective of its private investigator, Jake Gittes. Analysis of the deceptions Gittes uncovers and his attempts to do the right thing by his city of Los Angeles lead inexorably to the film's grim ending and a near guarantee that Jake will never forget what happened in Chinatown. With *Body Heat* (1981) Lawrence Kasdan resurrected much of classic noir's visual and aural feel while, free from the Hays Code, he could infuse his film with all of the sensuality early noirs had to leave up to their audiences' imaginations. Close examination brings out the film's admiration of classic noir's clever dialogue exchanges and its updating of the femme fatale figure. Lastly, Joel Coen and Ethan Coen took inspiration from hard-boiled detective fiction and made their first feature, *Blood Simple* (1984), containing the shady private detective Loren Visser, whose roots in Dashiell Hammett's figure of the Continental Op are explored. The film's lighting, camera angles, and use of sound that hearken back to classic noir are also analyzed.

Chapter Two, "All the Guys with Eye Patches: Hard Bitten Film Noir," examines the ways in which certain directors create a uniquely American visual poetry in their treatment of sex, violence, and betrayal. Howard Hawks' adaptation of *The Big Sleep* (1946) curbs Raymond Chandler's verbiage yet emphasizes the delirious momentum of his 1939 novel bearing the same name. Steady camerawork and smooth dialogue obscure any plot unclarities. Hawks shot the film mostly in sequence, and viewers watch Humphrey Bogart depict the gradual disintegration of private investigator Philip Marlowe's rational persona. In *Pickup on South Street* (1953), Samuel Fuller brings his background in journalism into play in order to deepen and enlarge his tabloid story through camerawork that demonstrates his keen, often startling, grasp of composition and editing.

Nicholas Ray takes noir out of the city in an atypical teens-on-the-run film noir, *They Live by Night* (1948), making a leitmotif out of the fugitives' car on the rural open road. The film is based on Edward Anderson's Depression Era novel *Thieves Like Us* (1937), and a comparative analysis of protagonist Bowie Bowers and other elements in each text reveals important differences that highlight Ray's achievement. Orson Welles' *Touch of Evil* (1958), a masterful study of the abuse of power and vigilante justice performed by a man of the law, uses dizzying camera angles, long takes, and multiple cuts to portray Hank Quinlan's moral and physical disintegration. Close comparison of the film to the novel it took inspiration from, Whit Masterson's *Badge of Evil* (1956), reveals the strengths of each text.

Chapter Three, "Commies, Nazis and Fascists: Politics in Film Noir," explores the right-wing political aspects of classic noir thrillers, noting how some noir was exploiting right-wing paranoia, if not endorsing it. Fritz Lang's *Ministry of Fear* (1944), developed from a Graham Greene novel the director admired, *The Ministry of Fear* (1943), embodies Lang's anti–Nazi stance. Both film and novel are analyzed in depth to compare their protagonists and delve into the function of a Nazi spy ring in the plots. In Arch Oboler's *Strange Holiday* (1945), a film commissioned by General Motors subsequent to the attack on Pearl Harbor in December 1941, businessman John Stevenson returns from a camping trip in the mountains only to discover that the United States has been invaded, the government is controlled by Fascists, and his family has been taken away. Claude Rains' performance, his monologues, and the soundtrack are assessed in terms of their political messages. Orson Welles' *The Stranger* (1946) echoes sentiments from his *New York Post* columns that Fascism would endure in postwar Germany by presenting War Crimes Commissioner Wilson pursuing a "mastermind" of the Holocaust, Franz Kindler, to the Connecticut home where he lives under a new identity as prep-school teacher Charles Rankin. When the newly-wed Mrs. Rankin claims that she's "never even seen a Nazi," Wilson states, "You might without even realizing it: they look like other people and act like other people." Lighting, camera angles, and symbolic imagery contribute significantly to this nightmarish depiction of a fugitive from justice who wormed his way into a woman's heart and a community's social circles.

Gordon Douglas' *I Was a Communist for the F.B.I.* (1951) is overt in its anti–Soviet, pro–American message from the beginning as it glorifies the real-life undercover agent Matt Cvetic's infiltration of the Communist party in Pittsburgh. Popular first as a series in the *Saturday Evening Post* and as a radio show, that this low-budget, propaganda-riddled film received an Oscar nomination testifies to the contemporary anti–Red paranoia in America. John Frankenheimer's late noir, *The Manchurian Candidate* (1962), features right-wing reactionary Eleanor Shaw Iselin, played with chilling effectiveness by Angela Lansbury, who accuses others of being Communists even as she herself is a Communist agent implicated in brainwashing her son to make him a political assassin as part of a plan to gain Communist control of the United States by securing the presidency for her husband, Senator John Yerkes Iselin—who himself has earned credence by claiming Communists have infiltrated the Defense Department. The byzantine plot is conveyed by subjective camerawork and sets that become as integral as the characters. Richard Condon's 1959 best-selling novel and Jonathan Demme's 2004 remake, both of which share the same title with Frankenheimer's film, are referenced to indicate the endurance of conspiracy theories.

The title of Chapter Four, "'Something Further May Follow…': Con Artists and Scams in Film Noir," quotes from the closing line of Herman Melville's novel *The Confidence-Man* (1857), and the chapter presents the dynamic between con artists and their human prey in American culture, literature, and film noir. Edgar G. Ulmer's *Detour* (1945) follows the hapless descent of Al Roberts from hitchhiker to murderer as the femme fatale Vera draws him further and further into what had been initially a fairly harmless, self-preservation–driven identity assumption. The film tames down the selfish characters that appear in Martin M. Goldsmith's 1939 novel bearing the same name, which a comparative discussion highlights. In *Nightmare Alley* (1947), Edmund Goulding tracks the career of social climbing Stan Carlisle from a carnival barker who steals the mind-reading act of Zeena, dumps her for fellow carny Molly, and finds success as nightclub psychic "Stanton the Great"— until his scam of channeling the dead relatives of upper-class socialites backfires, sending him on the tramp and eventually back to the carnival, this time working as a Geek. The film is based upon William Lindsay Gresham's 1946 novel, *Nightmare Alley*, and its author's personal obsessions with Tarot cards, psychoanalysis, and alcohol figure largely in both texts to convey a story terrifyingly deserving of its title.

Moving forward in time, Bryan Singer's *The Usual Suspects* (1995) is an elaborate thriller spun from the intricate false narrative told by con man Roger "Verbal" Kint. Verbal's deceptive handling of Customs agent Dave Kujan is an elaborate word game played using what Verbal has at hand in the office the two men are in and rendered with dramatic impact by the accompanying visual flashbacks. Written and directed by David Mamet, *The Spanish Prisoner* (1997) unfolds the con that draws in its mark, Joe Ross, who in turn suspects his boss of trying to swindle him out of the Process he's designed that is worth millions. Ross is told early on that he shouldn't trust his eyes and people aren't who they appear to be, so it's all the more fascinating to watch him succumb to the treacherous machinations of con artist Jimmy Dell and his accomplices.

Chapter Five, "Double Crosses: Religious Delusion in Film Noir," looks at how, from the classic period to the present, many noir stories center on a messianic figure with pathological tendencies. These characters and their obsession with religion have roots in the evangelical religious movement known as the Great Awakening. A discussion of this 19th-century phenomenon provides a framework for analyzing the films. Harry Powell, in the only film Charles Laughton directed, *The Night of the Hunter* (1955), is a false preacher who latches onto and marries a widow whose children know where their bank-robber father hid $10,000. Preacher, whose crude knuckle tattoos of LOVE and HATE speak volumes about the deranged simplicity of his evangelism, justifies his murderous greed through undigested scripture. The film is based on Davis Grubb's 1953 novel of the same name, and it translates the book's poetic descriptions into stunning visuals captured by Stanley Cortez's cinematography.

Mean Streets (1973) contains the most overt eschatological symbolism Martin Scorsese has ever employed—even more so than *The Last Temptation of Christ* (1988)—showing a rift between the sublime and the profane that magnifies the connection of the two. The main character Charlie, a numbers runner, staggers into mayhem trying to negotiate between his Catholic fervor and life on the street. Another incarnation is John Doe in David Fincher's *Se7en* (1995), who believes he is saving humanity by killing embodiments of the Seven Deadly Sins. Doe thinks God has chosen him to do important work, to make people take notice and stop overlooking and tolerating deadly sin in their daily lives. As he puts it, "The Lord works in mysterious ways." Horribly gruesome ones too, one might add.

Chapter Six, "Highways, By-ways and Dislocations: The Self in Neo-Noir," examines how neo-noir movies of the early 2000s framed questions about the continuity of self in ways wildly divergent from their classic predecessors. To highlight this difference, close analysis of Fritz Lang's *The Woman in the Window* (1944) and the novel upon which it is based, J.H. Wallis' *Once Off Guard* (1942), reveals how English professor Richard Wanley gives in to the urge to do something out of the norm for him, however natural the impulse may be. The resulting nightmare—figuratively in the novel and literally in the film—demonstrates the snowball effect of murder on one's psyche.

More recent films cage the psyche while broadening the playing—or killing—field. Oddly enough, Leonard Shelby's incessant loss of new memories is the most stable element of Christopher Nolan's *Memento* (2000). The film's unusual narrative structure and the protagonist's methods for remembering things are highlighted as his story is traced. David Cronenberg's *A History of Violence* (2005) and the graphic novel it is based upon, John Wagner and Vince Locke's *A History of Violence* (1997), present Tom Stall and Tom McKenna, respectively, men who have relocated to the Midwest from the East coast, leaving behind their previous criminal identities as Joey. But it's hard to shake off the old self completely, and one day it erupts. A comparative discussion of both texts highlights important distinctions. James Mangold's *Identity* (2003) uses a motel as the setting for sorting out a cast of characters whose individual identities become the puzzle viewers must try to fit together—except that the separate pieces create a whole the first-time viewer would hardly expect.

To lay a firm foundation for the exploration of specific thematic and stylistic aspects of film noir, the origin of the term, some of its early incarnations, and some of its later evolutions will be discussed in the upcoming chapter.

ONE

Lit from Behind

The Genesis and Continuity of Film Noir

While a few critics remain strict about applying the label film noir only to those films made between *The Maltese Falcon* in 1941 and *Sunset Boulevard* in 1950, many have taken a more expansive view, coining the term neo-noir to encompass films made in the 1970s and acknowledging that certain contemporary films are influenced by noir. This study intends to push the latter point by demonstrating the lineage of noir from such films as *Double Indemnity* (1944), *Laura* (1944), and *Sunset Boulevard* (1950) down through *Chinatown* (1974), *Body Heat* (1981), *Blood Simple* (1984), and, as will be discussed in Chapter Six, *Memento* (2000), *Identity* (2003), and *A History of Violence* (2005). There is a continuity of a certain style of noir that reveals its psychological complexity through narrative complications rather than through dialogue or thematic development, however nuanced the latter two may be. Concomitantly, the camera becomes an unreliable narrator, a subjective omnipresence reflecting the characters' internal states while at the same time distancing the viewer. Such films allow a precarious balance between empathy and detached speculation. In classic film noir, camerawork adds to the narratives in varying ways.

Origins of the term *film noir*

The French critics Nino Frank and Jean-Pierre Chartier are credited with first using the term *film noir*. Nino Frank concentrates on four films in "A New Kind of Police Drama: The Criminal Adventure," his August 1946 *L'Écran Français* article in which he applies *noir* to what he sees as a new kind of crime film: John Huston's *The Maltese Falcon* (1941), Edward Dmytryk's *Murder, My Sweet* (1944), Billy Wilder's *Double Indemnity*, and Otto Preminger's *Laura*, although he still classifies this last as a detective film. Frank finds a better term for these *noir* films to be "criminal adventures" or "criminal psychology"[1] because they employ a different method in being "true to life."[2] By way of explaining what is different in these films, he appreciates that viewers know who committed the crime in *Double Indemnity* from the outset and then watch as the perpetrators prepare for and commit the murder, then deal with the repercussions. This focuses viewers' interest on the characters themselves while "the narrative unfolds with a striking clarity that is sustained throughout."[3] He credits Wilder with having gone beyond transposing James M. Cain's narrative structure from the novel to having created "a peremptorily precise script" with his co-writer Raymond Chandler that "deftly details the motives and reactions of its characters," which Wilder's directing renders faithfully.[4] Along with "facial expressions, gestures, utterances" helping to convey "the truth of the characters," Frank observes how employment of the voice-over "permits a fragmentation of the narrative, to quickly gloss over the traditional plot elements and to accentuate the 'true-to-life' side."[5] Sacha Guitry, he points out, was the first to use such a narrative technique in *Le Roman d'un Tricheur* (*The Story of a Cheat* 1936).

Chartier's article, "Americans Also Make Noir Films," appeared in *La Revue du Cinéma* in November 1946 and mentions *Double Indemnity*, *Murder, My Sweet*, and Tay Garnett's *The Postman Always Rings Twice* (1946) to discuss this new type of film. Of the first two, Chartier says "all the characters are more or less venal," but "the females are particularly monstrous," using *Double Indemnity*'s Phyllis Dietrichson as illustration.[6] He sees that film's first-person narration being used "for psychological ends: as the guilty man's telling the story, there is no formal mystery; on the contrary, it is the psychological mechanism by which Walter Neff is dragged unrelentingly to the criminal action that unwinds before our eyes."[7] Hearing about this lends "a verisimilitude that draws us personally into this sordid tale."[8] Chartier praises Wilder's use of voice-over narration, noting the director also employs it effectively in *The Lost Weekend* (1945). These aspects of film noir that Frank and Chartier delineate can readily be seen in the films discussed in this chapter, beginning with *Double Indemnity*.

James M. Cain, Billy Wilder and *Double Indemnity*

Billy Wilder, a Jewish émigré director whose family had moved to Vienna when he was ten years old, worked as a freelance journalist there for the tabloids, then wrote for newspapers in Berlin from 1926 to 1931, covering music, theater, and sports.[9] His familiarity with people working in the German film industry led him to try writing screenplays, and he co-directed one film in Paris in 1933, *Mauvaise Graine* (*Bad Seed*), before going to Hollywood in 1934. In *A Divided World: Hollywood Cinema and Émigré Directors in the Era of Roosevelt and Hitler, 1933–1948*, Nick Smedley explains how Ernst Lubitsch sought input from executives at Paramount to get a new team of writers for *Bluebeard's Eighth Wife* (1938) and selected Wilder and Charles Brackett: "Suddenly the unknown exile was working with two men, one of whom was the great genius Ernst Lubitsch and the other an American writer who was shortly to become president of the Screen Writers' Guild."[10] Wilder would write with Brackett until 1950, his first Hollywood film as director would be *The Major and the Minor* (1942), and Brackett would produce Wilder's films. However, as Robert Horton explains, "The relationship was volatile (Brackett recoiled from producing the sordid subject matter of *Double Indemnity*), and was ended by Wilder after the partners tussled over *Sunset Boulevard*."[11]

James M. Cain appreciated the film version of his novel *Double Indemnity* (1936 serially; 1943). Brackett wouldn't co-write and Cain couldn't because he was working on a project for Fox, so Wilder got Raymond Chandler instead, which created a famously bristling collaboration that nonetheless resulted in a fantastic screenplay. "It's the only picture I ever saw made from my books that had things in it I wish I had thought of," Cain remarked. "Wilder's ending was much better than my ending, and his device for letting the guy tell the story by taking out the office dictating machine—I would have done it if I had thought of it. There are situations in the movie that can make your hands get wet."[12]

Wilder had some challenges in casting his leads. Although Barbara Stanwyck liked the script, she was afraid of playing a cold-blooded killer like Phyllis Dietrichson. She recounts that Wilder asked her, "'Well, are you a mouse or an actress?' And I said 'Well, I hope I'm an actress.' He said, 'Then do the part.' And I did and I'm very grateful to him."[13] Stanwyck's Phyllis Dietrichson is the ultimate femme fatale. As Foster Hirsch puts it, "The character is a misogynist's vision of woman as a male-attracting embodiment of evil," a "contemporary Circe luring unsuspecting men with her siren's song."[14] Stanwyck depicts her as "an undiluted study in greed, cunning and ruthlessness. From her determined heels clicking down the stairs at their first meeting, to her shooting of Walter at their last, she is cool complete control. No pity. No excuses. No nerves."[15] Popular male actors balked at playing a murderer too, but Wilder finally convinced Fred MacMurray to branch out from his usual lighter roles and take the part of Walter Neff. Indeed, it's the gutsiest role of his career.

After the opening credits appear over the silhouette of a hatted man walking towards the viewer using crutches, a car drives recklessly through the city at night, parking in front of the Pacific Building, where Walter Neff's Pacific All Risk Insurance office is located and where he intends to record his message to his colleague Barton Keyes. A bullet hole in the left shoulder of his suit jacket and heavy sweating reveal he's been wounded. Walter states that he killed Dietrichson for money and a woman, and he didn't get either. "Pretty, isn't it?" he asks rhetorically, going on to explain that it all began last May. This opening voice-over owes something to Cain's novel, which begins with the written statement of Walter Huff, although readers don't realize this until the last chapter, which begins, "What you've just read, if you've read it, is the statement."[16] Instead, readers might assume they are dealing with a narrator directly addressing them as some narrators have since Jane Austen's time when Huff says, "That was how I came to this House of Death, that you've been reading about in the papers."[17] Cain's first novel, *The Postman Always Rings Twice* (1934), and *Mildred Pierce* (1941) also would be made into classic films noir. It's well worth noting that Cain, a journalist, took some elements from a real-life murder case and used them in *Double Indemnity*.

In 1927 Ruth Snyder convinced her lover, Judd Gray, to murder her husband for his life insurance payout. As the introduction to the published trial transcript explains, a Prudential Life Insurance Company agent "called at the Snyder home to collect industrial insurance then in force. Ruth was alone and promptly engaged him in discussion about life insurance."[18] Albert Snyder later agreed to take out a $1,000 policy, but the agent had left Ruth with three applications, for $1,000, $5,000, and $45,000, the last having a double indemnity clause actually making it worth $96,000. Ruth "covered the larger policies with the thousand-dollar one, allowing only the spaces for signatures to appear. Then she told Snyder that the three papers were the same policy in triplicate."[19] During the trial, Gray's lawyer, Samuel L. Miller, "while not denying his client's guilt, angled for the jury's sympathy by painting Ruth as an irresistible Circe who bent poor Gray to her will."[20] Press coverage painted her that way as well. Thus, Cain employed the double indemnity insurance policy, the ruse used to get the husband to sign it, and the femme fatale drawing her lover into committing murder from this real-life case.

The action of Wilder's film moves quickly over the course of three months, almost as quickly as the dialogue fired back and forth by Walter and Phyllis on the first day they meet. The extreme low-angle shot of Phyllis at the top of the stairs clad only in a towel because she has been sunbathing, ostensibly nude, has become an iconic image, and here it leads Walter to quip that he's there to renew her husband's car insurance because, as he puts it, "I'd hate to think of your having a smashed fender or something while you're not … fully covered." While Walter waits for Phyllis to get dressed, he strolls around the living room. When the maid Nettie (Betty Farrington) lets Walter into the house she is carrying a feather duster and dust rag, but she's a bit brusque and rough around the edges, the kind of cheap help Mr. Dietrichson would hire, and Walter comments in his voice-over about how the room is still stuffy from last night's cigars and how the sun coming through the Venetian blinds showed up the dust in the air. Wilder credits cinematographer John Seitz with the idea of blowing aluminum powder into the air to create the heavy dust. When asked whether the dramatic lighting was an influence of German Expressionism, Wilder replied, "No. There was some dramatic lighting, yes, but it was newsreel lighting. That was the ideal…. Everything was meant to support the realism of the story. I had worked with the cameraman before and I trusted him. We used a little mezzo light in the apartment when Stanwyck comes to see MacMurray in the apartment—this is when he makes up his mind to commit murder. That's it."[21] Wilder has said he wanted to show that Phyllis wasn't much of a housekeeper. Thus, the dusty living room that the lighting emphasizes is another contribution to the "true to life" quality Nino Frank had admired.

After Phyllis is clothed, the camera—and Walter's gaze—follows her lower legs as she descends the curved staircase, featuring her anklet, which piece of jewelry elicits Walter's remark, "That's a honey of an anklet you're wearing, Mrs. Dietrichson," once they are seated in the living room. Neff is so attracted to Phyllis that he doesn't think anything is amiss when she inquires whether he sells accident insurance during this visit. He's more interested in what's engraved on her anklet, and the two start flirting about whether he likes her name, leading to his remark that he'd have to drive it around the block a couple times before he's sure about that, which sets up their subsequent auto metaphor exchange after she tells him to come back the next evening to speak with her husband. He says he's getting over that idea, leading Phyllis to say, "There's a speed limit in this state, Mr. Neff, 45 miles per hour." "How fast was I going, officer?" Walter asks. "I'd say around 90," Phyllis answers. "Suppose you get down off your motorcycle and give me a ticket?" Walter invites, the two of them standing about a foot apart. "Suppose I let you off with a warning this time?" she counters. "Suppose it doesn't take?" he asks. "Suppose I have to whack you over

Walter Neff (Fred MacMurray) and Phyllis Dietrichson (Barbara Stanwyck) flirt in *Double Indemnity* (1944) (Paramount Pictures/Photofest).

the knuckles?" she queries. "Suppose I bust out crying and put my head on your shoulder?" he asks invitingly. "Suppose you try putting it on my husband's shoulder?" she rebuffs, leading him to end their parley with, "That tears it." At the door he asks her if she'll be there tomorrow evening in the same chair, same perfume, same anklet, and Phyllis says she wonders if she knows what he means, to which he responds, "I wonder if you wonder." The shadow of Walter and his hat on the wall as he leaves is a visual echo of the film's opening image. As he drives away, his voice-over dictation from the future recalls the smell of honeysuckle along the Dietrichsons' street and asks, "How could I have known that murder sometimes smells like honeysuckle?"

When he returns at her request on Thursday afternoon Phyllis opens the door to find him casually leaning against the doorjamb, his body language as much of a come-on as his subsequent offer of "maybe there's something I can do for you" when he learns it's Nettie's day off—which Phyllis unconvincingly tries to pretend she forgot. Phyllis starts talking about how she worries about her husband getting injured in the oil fields and how he should have accident insurance. Walter is game for talking with him about it, then she starts painting a picture of her boring evenings with her husband, him listening to a baseball game while she knits. "Is that what you married him for?" Walter inquires. "Maybe I like the way his thumbs hold up the wool," she responds. "Anytime his thumbs get tired," Walter offers, "only with me around you wouldn't have to knit." "Wouldn't I?" she rejoins. "You bet your life you wouldn't," he assures her. When Phyllis asks if she could get an accident policy on her husband without him knowing about it, Walter catches on to her idea of killing her husband and gets up to leave. "Boy, what a dope you must think I am," he says, drawing her to declare, "I think you're rotten." "I think you're swell, so long as I'm not your husband," he retorts. "Get out of here!" Phyllis orders. "You bet I'll get out of here, baby. I'll get out of here but quick," Walter says, doing just that. His voice-over notes that he knew he had hold of a red-hot poker and the time to drop it was before he burned his hand on it.

That night at his apartment as he sits in the dark and rain, Walter's voice-over observes, "I was all twisted up inside and I was still holding on to that red-hot poker. And right then it came over me that I hadn't walked out on anything at all. That the hook was too strong. That this wasn't the end between her and me. It was only the beginning." So when his doorbell rings he knows it's Phyllis "without having to think, as if it was the most natural thing in the world." Phyllis says she is there because Walter forgot his hat, but she's obviously not holding anything. She suggests he misunderstood her intentions during their conversation about the insurance for her husband and wants him to be nice to her like during their first meeting. "It can't be like the first time. Something's happened," Walter explains. "I know it has," Phyllis replies. "It's happened to us." He walks away from her as she talks about her husband watching her, keeping her on a leash, but since he is out of town, Walter tells her to relax. "Maybe I oughtn't to have come," Phyllis says. "Maybe you oughtn't," Walter agrees. "You want me to go?" Phyllis asks. "If you want to," he says. "Right now?" Phyllis goes on. "Sure, right now," he replies, but when she starts to leave, he pulls her back to him and kisses her. "I'm crazy about you, baby," Walter declares, with her affirming, "I'm crazy about you, Walter." The femme fatale has secured her catch.

As they have drinks Walter talks about insurance cases where the husbands died and the wives didn't get away with it. Phyllis implies that would be better than living with her husband and stepdaughter. "You ever think of divorce?" Walter reasonably asks, but Phyllis says her husband wouldn't give her one. She claims she married him because she was his wife's nurse and after she died, she pitied him. She laments that he doesn't have any money since he went into the oil business, he's so mean to her, and all his life insurance goes to his daughter, Lola. She never wanted to kill him, not even when he gets drunks and slaps her face. "Only sometimes you wish he were dead," Walter fills in, moving close to her on the sofa. "Perhaps I do," Phyllis agrees. "And you wish it were an accident and you had that policy for $50,000," he finishes. "Perhaps that too," Phyllis assents. She says she's thought about letting him die with the car running in the garage after he's passed out drunk, but Walter explains how Keyes would expose that murder quickly. He says he doesn't want her to hang and pulls her toward him in an embrace. "So we just sat there," Walter's voice-over narrates, "and she started crying softly, like the rain on the window, and we didn't say anything."

There is a cut to Walter using the Dictaphone and admitting that he had been thinking of cheating the insurance company long before he met Phyllis, "and suddenly the doorbell rings and the whole set up is right there in the room with you." A cut back to the apartment shows Walter lounging on the dark end of the sofa smoking a cigarette and Phyllis sitting by the table lamp at the other end of the sofa applying lipstick, clear indications that the two have had sex. She says she hates her husband and loathes going back to him. "You believe me, don't you Walter?" she asks desperately, saying she doesn't care if she's hung. "They're not going to hang you because you're going to do it and I'm going to help you!" Walter declares. "Do you know what you're saying?" she asks. Her facial expression as she rises and turns away from Walter toward the camera clearly projects "that went just as I had hoped it would." Phyllis leaves and Walter's voice-over comments, "That was it, Keyes. The machinery had started to move and nothing could stop it."

Walter brings forms to the house to get Mr. Dietrichson (in both novel and film the character has no first name) to sign the accident insurance when he thinks he's signing multiple copies of his car insurance. Dietrichson (Tom Powers) has been drinking and his nasty personality shows. At the door when Walter's leaving he tells Phyllis her husband needs to take the train to his college reunion because a train accident is one of the situations in which a policy pays double and she'll get $100,000; the revelation of satisfied greed on her face as she turns to go back in the house after Walter walks away is telling. Walter was not happy that the daughter, Lola (Jean Heather), was whom Phyllis chose as a witness, and now she's waiting in his car, asking for a ride downtown to see her boyfriend Nino Zachetti (Byron Barr), whereas she had told her father she was going roller skating with a girlfriend. But Walter acts the gentleman and drops her off.

Keyes (Edward G. Robinson) thinks so highly of Walter he asks him to be his assistant, a position that would mean a $50 cut in salary. Keyes' speech about insurance claim work, rapidly delivered by Robinson, indicates his passion for it: "And those papers are not just forms and statistics and claims for compensation. They're alive. They're packed with drama, with twisted hopes and crooked dreams. A claims man, Walter," and here Keyes basically describes himself, "is a doctor and a bloodhound … and a cop and a judge and a jury and a father confessor, all in one."

Walter and Phyllis have decided to commit the murder together "straight down the line," a phrase taken from Cain's novel and used multiple times in the film, the first being when Walter explains to Phyllis in his sales pitch that he offers all kinds of insurance policies. On the evening of the event, Walter carefully establishes his alibi in the same way the character in Cain's novel does, making sure the car attendant at his apartment building knows he's staying in for the night, placing phone calls to a colleague, and putting pieces of cardboard in the phone and door bells so he'll know if they rang during his absence and he can have an excuse ready as to why he didn't answer. He waits on the floor in the back of Dietrichson's car while Phyllis gets her husband settled inside—he's broken his leg, easily necessitating his taking the train to the reunion—and drives him to the station. As prearranged she drives off course so Walter can strangle her husband, offscreen. The light illuminates Phyllis' face during this scene and a close-up reveals her disassociated yet satisfied expression because her eyes look steadily ahead and the slightest hint of a smile appears as Walter kills her husband.

The scenes at the train station are extremely dark because they were shot at night during the blackout of World War II. Walter poses as Dietrichson to get onto the train and back to the observation car where the staged accidental falling off the train is to occur. Tension is raised when someone else is on the platform who engages him in conversation, a man named Jackson (Porter Hall). Walter tries to cut this short by saying he left his cigar case back in his overcoat in his section; Jackson offers to get it. After Walter jumps off the back of the train and Phyllis brings the car close, he drags Dietrichson's body to the train tracks, and Phyllis picks up the crutches to toss them at the scene. In the novel, Walter harnesses Dietrichson's body in rope and hooks an iron rod to this as a handle, and Phyllis is the one who moves her husband's dead body: "That man must have weighted 200 pounds, but she had him on her back, holding him by the handle, and staggering along with him, over the tracks. His head was hanging down beside her head. They looked like something in a horror picture."[22] This superhuman feat is an early sign for readers of Phyllis' psychopathy.

Once they are back in the car, Phyllis in the driver's seat, the engine won't turn over. When the scene was originally shot, the car started immediately and they drove away. After filming this scene, there was a break, and Wilder went to get in his own car to go somewhere. It wouldn't start, and he thought that would be a brilliant alteration to the scene. Subsequent films have used this device to create tension to the point of it becoming a cliché. In the novel, as Phyllis drives the two of them argue: "There we were, after what we had done, snarling at each other like a couple of animals, and neither one of us could stop"—until Phyllis orders Walter out of the car, but since he needs to get to his own car to complete his alibi on time, he yells, "Drive on, or I'll sock you."[23] The film smooths this over, indicating Phyllis' emotional coolness when Walter's voice-over says, "I was afraid she might go to pieces a little, now that we had done it. But she was perfect. No nerves. Not a tear, not even a blink of the eyes." Phyllis drops Walter at his apartment, asking, "Walter, what's the matter? Aren't you going to kiss me?" He does, and she says, "It's straight down the line, isn't it? I love you, Walter." "I love you, baby," he returns. This is far from their parting mood in the novel: "We didn't kiss. We didn't even say good-bye."[24] After he establishes his alibi again with the car attendant, as Walter is walking from his apartment to the drugstore for dinner, his voice-over indicates he thought everything would go wrong and reports that he couldn't hear his own footsteps: "It was the walk of a dead man."

Keyes knows that the insurance claim was worked, he just doesn't know how, and in trying to figure it out he engages Neff in conversations about the case, one of which occurs when he shows up unexpectedly at Walter's apartment. Why didn't Dietrichson put in a claim on the accident insurance when he broke his leg, Keyes wonders? Walter, knowing that Phyllis is on the way to see him, nervously suggests that maybe he didn't have time. Keyes thinks perhaps the husband didn't know about the policy, but quickly dismisses this idea because Walter sold him the policy and he trusts Walter implicitly. He suspects the beneficiary, Phyllis. Keyes exits the apartment but is still talking to Walter in the hallway when Phyllis twists the exterior door's knob Walter has his hand on to let him know that she is hiding behind the door. The suspense builds as Keyes needs a match and walks toward Walter, but ultimately Phyllis remains undiscovered. When asked about the fact that Walter's apartment door opens outward into the hallway rather than inward the way normal doors do, Wilder admitted, "Yeah, that was a mistake that we made and I did not want to correct it. We'd already shot it. It worked and I did not want to reshoot it."[25] The suspense achieved in that scene is so intense many viewers don't even notice the oddity of the door.

After Keyes leaves, Walter informs Phyllis that she'll be shadowed because of the claim investigator's suspicion, so they can't see each other. "Afraid, baby?" he asks, to which she replies, "Yes, I'm afraid. But not of Keyes. I'm afraid of us. We're not the same anymore. We did it so we could be together, but instead of that it's pulling us apart. Isn't it, Walter?" "What are you talking about?" he asks. "And you don't really care whether we see each other or not," she complains. "Shut up, baby," Walter orders, kissing her. The scene dissolves into another where Lola shows up at Walter's office and gives him some backstory on Phyllis that lets him know her true character. Six years before, Lola, her mother, and a nurse were at Lake Arrowhead. Her mother had pneumonia. Lola went into her mother's bedroom one night when she was delirious with fever, declaring, "All the bed covers were on the floor and the windows were wide open!" After she covered her mother, the nurse came in. "The nurse stood there. She didn't say a word, but there was a look in her eyes I'll never forget. Two days later my mother was dead. Do you know who that nurse was?" Lola asks. Learning it was Phyllis takes Walter aback. Six months after that incident Phyllis became the second Mrs. Dietrichson. Lola says she saw her stepmother trying on a hat with a black veil two days before her father's death, with that same look in her eyes. She intends to tell everything she knows so that Phyllis won't get away with it, whereupon Walter takes Lola to dinner and the beach that weekend to distract her from doing this.

Summoned to Keyes' office Monday morning, Walter is distraught when he sees Jackson sitting on a chair outside of it, leaving him unnerved as he listens to Keyes explain how he thinks the Dietrichson case was murder, that Dietrichson was never on the train, that he was killed ahead of time and his body put on the train tracks, and someone else pretended to be him on the train. Saying that the only guy who really got a look at the supposed Dietrichson on the train is sitting right outside the office, he invites Jackson in. Walter stands in the background glaring at the man who could identify him as the imposter while Jackson declares after viewing Dietrichson's photographs that he's not the man he met on the observation deck. Walter keeps his lower face covered by working a match in his mouth, but Jackson persists in asking him questions because he's got a sense he's met him before. The suspense is released when Jackson leaves without having recognized him. But Keyes is sure Phyllis is in on it with somebody else:

He'll show. He's got to show. Some time, somewhere, they've got to meet.

Their emotions are all kicked up. Whether it's love or hate doesn't matter. They can't keep away from each other. They might think it's twice as safe because there are two of them. But it isn't twice as safe. It's ten times twice as dangerous. They've committed a murder and it's not like taking a trolley ride together where they can get off at different stops. They're stuck with each other, and they've got to ride all the way to the end of the line, and it's a one-way trip, and the last stop is the cemetery.

Keyes intends to reject Phyllis' claim and hope she sues. After this speech Walter lights Keyes' cigar with the match he's been playing with, the familiar gesture to his friend whom his act of murder has made his nemesis.

Phyllis and Walter meet at Jerry's Market, where he tells her why Keyes is rejecting the claim. When Phyllis says she must sue if it's rejected, Walter suggests too much will come up to incriminate her, like the first Mrs. Dietrichson's death and her trying on the black hat, which information alerts Phyllis that Walter has been talking with Lola. Walter says Phyllis should not sue in order to save their necks. Phyllis rebuts that they need to hold onto it and not go soft inside. Across a low shelf of canned and boxed goods that separates them, Phyllis threatens, "I loved you Walter, and I hated him. But I wasn't going to do anything about it, not until I met you. You planned the whole thing. I only wanted him dead." Walter responds, "And I'm the one that fixed it so that he was dead. Is that what you're telling me?" Taking off her sunglasses and casting him an icy look, Phyllis orders, "And nobody's pulling out. We went into this together, and we're coming out at the end together. It's straight down the line for both of us, remember?" Then she turns and walks away. A stricken Walter, remembering Keyes' remark about the cemetery being at the end of the line and thinking that cemeteries are a place to put dead people in, gets the idea of Phyllis being dead. He sees Lola several times that week because only when he's with her can he relax and let go a little; likely he's drawn to her because she is the polar opposite of her stepmother. In Cain's novel Walter even claims to be in love with Lola, and she says she's crazy about him. In Wilder's film the relationship, thankfully, feels more avuncular. In one nicely set up scene the two are sitting on the ground with the Hollywood Bowl visible in the background; the soundtrack plays the tense strains of the concert ostensibly being performed. Walter lights his match in the usual fashion, by flicking it with his thumb, and Lola confides in him that she thinks Nino and Phyllis killed her father, but that nonetheless she still loves Nino.

Walter really can't figure out why Nino is with Phyllis, but observes that the real brain twister came the next day when Keyes tells Walter in the lobby of the insurance building that the co-killer showed and Phyllis has sued. Walter lights Keyes' cigar as he had in previous scenes, informing him he can get matches when he buys cigars. Keyes says he doesn't like matches because "they always explode in my pocket," a little foreshadowing of how his close friendship with Walter kept him from realizing he was the killer. Wanting to see whether Keyes is playing cat and mouse with him, Walter goes into Keyes' office and, with the shadows from Venetian blinds on his suit mimicking the stripes of a prison inmate's garb, listens to the Dictaphone, learning that Keyes suspects Nino and Phyllis of the murder and that Keyes has established Walter's alibi. Plus, he's known Walter for eleven years and personally vouches for him without reservation. Walter also learns that Keyes has found no connection between Walter and Phyllis—at the point he hears this Walter is sitting on the desk and the Venetian blind bars are no longer on him. Processing this information, Walter calls Phyllis from his own office and says he needs to see her at 11:00 that night and to leave her door open and have the lights out, signing off with

"Goodbye, baby." The endearment is a well-placed bit of dialogue since viewers know Walter is going to Phyllis' home to kill her, and they will soon know that Phyllis has plans of her own because they will see her put a gun under a chair cushion. Interestingly, viewers see Phyllis from an extreme high-angle shot as she descends the stairs, unlocks the front door, and turns out the lights in anticipation of Walter's arrival—the shot is taken from the same perspective of where she had stood, clad only in a towel, when they first met. As that first low-angle shot of Phyllis had established her dominance in the relationship with Walter, this high-angle shot foreshadows her upcoming demise at his hand.

"Hello, baby," Walter says upon arriving. The darkness recreates the atmosphere of their first meeting in that stuffy living room. Fittingly, a radio up the street plays "Tangerine," a song about an alluring woman whose heart belongs only to herself and whose appearance is deceiving. Walter tells Phyllis he plans to frame Nino Zachetti for her murder since Keyes thinks Nino and she killed Dietrichson. Phyllis reveals she has been seeing Nino to work up his jealousy over Lola seeing another man so that he'd kill her, leaving Phyllis to enjoy the money. "For once I believe you," Walter says, "because it's just rotten enough." "We're both rotten," Phyllis rejoins. "Only you're a little more rotten," Walter flings back. "You got me to take care of your husband for you, and then you get Zachetti to take care of Lola, maybe take care of me, too. Then somebody else would have to come along and take care of Zachetti for you. That's the way you operate, isn't it, baby?" "Suppose it is," Phyllis challenges. "Is what you've got cooked up for tonight any better?" "I don't like that music anymore," Walter says, "mind if I close the window?" After he does and draws the drapes, Phyllis shoots him. "You can do better than that, can't you, baby? Better try again. Maybe if I came a little closer," he invites, doing so. The Venetian blind shadows are squarely behind Phyllis on the wall, suggesting that she is the one about to receive punishment, when he asks, "How's this? Think you can do it now? Why didn't you shoot again? Don't tell me it's because you've been in love with me all this time." "No, I never loved you, Walter, not you or anybody else," Phyllis replies. "I'm rotten to the heart. I used you, just as you said. That's all you ever meant to me. Until a minute ago, when I couldn't fire that second shot. I never thought that could happen to me." "Sorry, baby," Walter says, "I'm not buying." "I'm not asking you to buy. Just hold me close," Phyllis requests as she throws her arms around his shoulders. Then she looks at him in disbelief as she feels what turns out to be a gun pressed against her. "Goodbye, baby," Walter says, shooting her twice and laying her dead body on the sofa. After Walter leaves the house, he hears someone walking up and hides behind shrubbery. It's Nino, and Walter apparently decides not to let him take the fall because he calls his name, gives him a nickel and Lola's phone number, and tells him to call her because she's in love with him.

Coughing from his wound, at 4:30 a.m. Walter is still recording on the Dictaphone, asking Keyes to break the truth to Lola gently and take care of her and Nino so they don't get pushed around too much by the police. Walter turns and sees Keyes has come into the office, the janitor having called him because Walter left a blood trail. "Walter, you're all washed up," Keyes pronounces. He intends to call a doctor, but Walter has no wish to be patched up, tried, and sentenced to the gas chamber. He asks Keyes to wait until morning to call the police so that he can get to Mexico, but when he tries to leave, Walter falls down not far from the office and Keyes calls both for the police and an ambulance. When Keyes kneels by him Walter asks, "You know why you couldn't figure this one, Keyes? I'll tell you. Because the guy you were looking for was too close. He was right across the desk from you." Keyes replies, "Closer than that, Walter." "I love you too," Walter says, pulling out a cigarette that Keyes lights for him in the same manner he had lit Keyes' cigars multiple times throughout the film, by flicking the match alight with his thumb. *Double Indemnity* ends with Neff and Keyes, two unmarried men, expressing their platonic bond for each other.

Events go quite differently at the end of Cain's novel. Phyllis Nirdlinger is a nurse who killed six patients, the first Mrs. Nirdlinger, and her husband by proxy, and she shoots Walter, grazing his lung. As Keyes observes, "She's a pathological case, that's all. The worst I ever heard of."[26] In the scene where she and Walter decide to kill her husband, Phyllis tells him, "Maybe I'm crazy. But there's something in me that loves Death. I think of myself as Death, sometimes. In a scarlet shroud, floating through the night."[27] After Walter agrees to send his confessional statement to Keyes by registered mail to arrive on Friday, Keyes tells him, "There'll be a reservation for you, under a name I'll give you, on a steamer leaving San Pedro Thursday night for Balboa and points south. You take that steamer. Friday I get a statement and at once turn it over to the police. That's the first I knew about it."[28] It turns out Keyes arranges for Phyllis to be on that ship as well, and she tells Walter it's time to meet her bridegroom, Death, by jumping off the stern one night. Knowing Keyes was going to post a reward for their capture and that the captain has recognized them, Walter agrees to jump with her. A shark has been sighted in the water and Walter is bleeding internally from the gunshot wound, spitting up blood. Phyllis says they'll wait to jump until the moon is up because she wants to see the shark's fin, "Cutting the water in the moonlight."[29] Since Phyllis enters Walter's stateroom dressed in her red shroud and the final words of the novel are "The moon," readers assume the two commit suicide by shark.[30]

Hollywood, Billy Wilder and *Sunset Boulevard*

Billy Wilder used the voice-over narration he had employed for *Double Indemnity* again in *Sunset Boulevard*, this time with the protagonist speaking from beyond: at the opening of the film Joe Gillis (William Holden) is already dead and floating in a swimming pool, and refers to himself as "Nobody important, really. Just a movie writer with a couple of B-pictures to his credit. The poor dope. He always wanted a pool. Well, in the end he got himself a pool. Only the price turned out to be a little high. Let's go back about six months and find the day when it all started." As he launches into his story, viewers learn that a tire blowout landed Joe, a broke screenwriter fleeing repo men, in the driveway of the house occupied by faded silent film star Norma Desmond. He thinks it's abandoned and describes it as "a great big white elephant of a place. The kind crazy movie people built in the crazy twenties. A neglected house gets an unhappy look. This one had it in spades. It was like that old woman in *Great Expectations*—that Miss Havisham in her rotting wedding dress and her torn veil, taking it out on the world because she'd been given the go-by." That description is prescient of whom Joe meets within the house. Desmond (Gloria Swanson) and her servant Max von Mayerling (former director Erich von Stroheim) think Joe has come with the coffin for her dead pet monkey, both a foreshadowing of Joe's death and his demotion from an independent (if broke) individual to Norma's newest pet. Told that Madame is waiting for him, he plays along with the situation for a while until he sees the monkey's corpse and reveals he's there because he got a flat tire. After Norma orders him out, he recognizes her, saying, "You're Norma Desmond. You used to be in silent pictures. You used to be big," eliciting her retort, "I am big. It's the pictures that got small." Foster Hirsch describes the character of Norma Desmond in *The Dark Side of the Screen: Film Noir* as "etched in acid; she is the embodiment of Hollywood's rotting foundations, its terminal narcissism, its isolation from reality."[31]

When she learns Joe writes for the pictures, she asks him how long scripts are because she's written one for a movie about Salome she intends to have Cecil B. DeMille direct. Her glee in describing how Salome, rejected by a man, has his head on a tray and kisses his cold, dead lips makes repeat viewers want to warn Joe to get out of there, but of course when Norma orders Joe to sit down and read her script, he does, albeit looking at her warily. The script is awful, but like the mark who thinks he's in control of the con being played on him, Joe notes, "I started concocting a little plot of my own," and tells Norma it's fascinating but needs more dialogue and some editing. She wants him to work on it, but in a ploy to get a good salary he lies that he's working on another, finally assenting to do it for $500 a week. The catch is that Norma won't let the script leave her house, so he has to stay in the room over the garage. Here Norma has gained the first big win in her playing of him, yet Joe is the one to think, "I felt kind of pleased with the way I'd handled the situation. I dropped the hook, and she snapped at it." Shown to his room, Max reveals he had made it up that afternoon, evading Joe's question of how he knew he'd be staying over. "Well, I sure turned into an interesting driveway," Joe observes lightly. "You did, Sir," Max replies. Images of death accumulate as Joe's voice-over describes how "the whole place was stricken with a kind of creeping paralysis. Out of beat with the rest of the world. Crumbling apart in slow motion." Noticing the empty pool, he sees there are rats in it eating something and starts to turn away in disgust when his attention is caught by Max and Norma performing last rites for the monkey like it was her only child. "Was her life really as empty as that?" he muses; "It was all very queer, but queerer things were yet to come." Wilder explained, "I picked up the image of the pool from a Raymond Chandler story: Nothing is emptier than an empty swimming pool."[32] He felt it was "an authentic depiction of the way a woman like Norma, living in the past, would allow her property to slide in to ruin."[33]

That night Joe dreams about an organ grinder and a chimp that was "dancing for pennies," further allusion to his situation as a paid pet. When he awakes he finds all his belongings in the garage room and storms angrily into the house, where Max is ominously playing Bach's "Toccata and Fugue in D Minor" on the massive organ, but Norma assures him, "You'll like it here." Admitting to himself that he wants the job and the dough, also feeling indebted because Norma has paid his three months back rent, he stays. Trying to cut down the massive script he takes out a scene featuring Salome, Norma's role, so she demands he put it back in. "I didn't argue with her," Joe's voice-over says, becoming more aware of her state of mind: "You don't yell at a sleepwalker. He may fall and break his neck. That's it. She was still sleepwalking along the giddy heights of a lost career. Plain crazy when it came to that one subject, her celluloid self." The camera underscores this remark by panning to show all the framed photographs of Norma covering surfaces throughout the first floor of the cavernous house. Accordingly, two or three times a week Norma and Joe watch a movie Max projects on her large home screen. "So much nicer than going out, she'd say," Joe's voice-over reports, assessing, "The plain fact was she was afraid of that world outside. Afraid it would remind her that time had passed." The silent film Max screens for Norma and Joe is *Queen Kelly* (1932), a film Stroheim had directed Swanson in and suggested Wilder use. Of her close-up Norma observes, "Still wonderful, isn't it? And no dialogue. We didn't need dialogue—we had faces."

People using each other is a universal theme in noir. Joe will receive lavish gifts from Norma; she will gain a young lover and companion with whom to watch her old silent movies. Occasionally Norma has friends in to play bridge, a group of silent film colleagues Joe calls Norma's "Waxworks," played by Buster Keaton, H.B. Warner, and Anna Q. Nilsson. During one of these card games, the repo men arrive and tow his car, so Norma has her 1929 Isotta-Fraschini 8A fixed up and starts taking Joe on rides. On one of these she complains about Joe's old clothes and orders Max to drive to the best men's shop. "I don't need any clothes," Joe protests, "and I certainly don't want you buying them for me." "Why begrudge me a little fun," Norma responds, "I just want you to look nice. And must you chew gum?" Joe, placed ever further under her control, throws the gum away. The scene in the clothes store makes Joe's position as a kept man quite clear when a clerk brings both a camel's hair and a vicuna overcoat, noting that the latter was more expensive. When Joe asserts that he'll take the camel's hair, the clerk says quietly, "Well, as long as the lady's paying for it, why not take the vicuna?," which makes Joe look at him sharply, in open recognition of what he has become.

He doesn't much like it, but rain leaking into the apartment he has over the garage leads to Joe moving into the main house, into the bedroom of "the husbands," as Max informs him—Norma's been married three times. When Joe notices there are no locks on the doors Max explains "the doctor suggested it" because "Madame has moments of melancholy," and "There have been some attempts at suicide." When Joe wonders why since Norma had a successful career and still gets fan letters, Max says he wouldn't look too closely at the postmarks, suggesting that he is the one who writes them (another idea Stroheim contributed to the script). Joe looks into Norma's adjoining bedroom, "The perfect setting for a silent movie queen," and thinks, "Poor devil. Still waving proudly to a parade which had long since passed her by."

New Year's Eve finds him dancing to live music with Norma, but there are no other guests. "I felt caught like the cigarette in that contraption on her finger," Joe's voice-over reveals. Norma gets a bit tipsy from the champagne they've been drinking, and lying on the sofa with her legs on Joe's lap she exudes, "What a wonderful next year it's going to be. I'll fill the pool for you, or I'll open my house in Malibu and you can have the whole ocean. And when our picture's finished, I'll buy you a boat and we'll sail to Hawaii and—" Joe, who has been biting his knuckles and looking worried and restless as she spoke, cuts her off and tries to extricate himself from the situation by firmly saying, "Stop it! You're not going to buy me anything more." In answer Norma gives him the solid gold cigarette case and lighter she was going to give him at midnight. "Norma, I can't take it," Joe protests, "you've bought me enough." "Shut up," Norma orders, "I'm richer than all this new Hollywood trash," going on to list what she owns and asking, "What's it for but to buy us anything we want?" Pushed to his limit, Joe stands up suddenly and snaps, "Cut out this 'us' business!" Genuinely surprised, Norma asks, "What's the matter with you?" "What right do you have to take me for granted?" Joe demands. "What right? Do you want me to tell you?" Norma responds, sweeping her hand upward to indicate the clothes he's wearing from feet to head that she's bought for him. "Has it ever occurred to you that I may have a life of my own, that there may be some girl that I'm crazy about?" Joe demands. "Who, some car hop or dress extra?" Norma sneers. "What I'm trying to say is that I'm all wrong for you," Joe persists. "You want a Valentino, somebody with polo ponies, a big shot." Hurt and angry, Norma shoots back, "What you're trying to say is that you don't want me to love you. Say it! Say it!," after which she slaps him and runs upstairs to her bedroom sanctuary. Joe looks at those who witnessed this fight, the still-playing orchestra whose members' eyes are averted and Max, who breaks their glance to polish a champagne glass. Grim-faced, Joe gets his overcoat, throws a look upward toward Norma's room, and tries to leave through the ornate iron-gated front entryway, becoming annoyed that his watch chain gets caught on the door handle, another irking sign of his entrapment. He yanks it free, slams the gate shut, and departs in the pouring rain, his voice-over reporting, "I didn't know where I was going. I just had to get out of there. I had to be with people my own age. I had to hear somebody laugh again."

His pursuit of youth and gaiety leads him to the New Year's Eve party being held by his friend Artie Green (Jack Webb), an assistant director who readily tells him he can sleep on the coach when Joe asks if he can stay there a few weeks. It turns out that Artie's girlfriend is Betty Schaefer (Nancy Olson), a script reader who had rejected one of Joe's stories when he was in dire straits for money. Having felt guilty about this she read some of his other stories and found merit in part of one, so they escape the loud party by going into the bathroom to talk about it, play acting a bit flirtingly. Joe is informed by a partygoer that the phone he wanted to use earlier is now free, so Joe calls Max to ask for his things to be packed up and learns Norma cut her wrists with his razor. Distraught, Joe rushes from the party to Norma's bedroom. As the two talk the camera encompasses both Joe standing facing it and the tri-folding mirrored screen behind him to his right, which reflects Norma lying on the bed. The shot helps establish her detachment. "What kind of a silly thing was that to do?" Joe asks. "To fall in love with you, that was the idiotic thing," she explains, telling him to go away, go to his girl. He says he lied, he doesn't have a girlfriend, but he didn't want to hurt her. "You've been good to me," he admits, "and you're the only person in this stinking town that has been good to me." She tells him to go, but he says he won't until she promises to act like a sensible human being. "I'll do it again," she threatens three times, crying. Joe sits on the chaise lounge, thinking and wringing his hands. When the band plays "Auld Lang Syne" he looks toward the sound of the music, looks at Norma, gets up and slowly walks toward her. Sitting on the bed he gently pulls her arms away from covering her face and says softly, "Happy New Year, Norma." She stops crying, opens her eyes, and, reaching a claw-like hand toward him, replies "Happy New Year, darling," grabs the lapel of his overcoat, and pulls him in for a kiss, the screen fading to black to signify that Joe takes the ultimate step in becoming a kept man.

Not to be deterred from working on a screenplay with Joe, Betty tracks him down and telephones Max, who informs her Joe is not there and tells her not to call again. Overhearing, Norma asks him who called, and Max's answer is telling of Joe's situation: "Nothing, Madame. Somebody inquiring about a stray dog. Our number must be very similar to the number of the pound." From the poolside she asks him to get the car out because they are going to deliver the script to DeMille in person. A dripping Joe gets out of the pool and as she's drying his back she tells him she's never looked better because she's never been as happy in her life. The camera on Joe's face reveals he is obviously not happy. A dissolve shows Max driving him and Norma to one of the Waxworks' home a few evenings later for bridge, and the unhappiness is revealed again when he offers to run into a drugstore for cigarettes since Norma's case is empty: she peels a bill off the wad she has and hands it to Joe without looking at him; he takes it with an expression of dissatisfaction. Ducking into Schwab's Pharmacy he runs into Artie and Betty, Betty asking, "Where've you been keeping yourself?" "I haven't been keeping myself at all, not lately," Joe responds, looking at and fingering the money Norma had just handed him for the cigarettes. Betty's gotten someone interested in Joe's story and wants to work on it with him, but Joe says he's given up writing on spec. Again looking at the money in his hand, he says as a matter of fact he's given up writing altogether. Max appears in the doorway, so he must leave.

Continuing his role as gigolo, Joe has to endure what he calls the Norma Desmond Follies, her costumed performances as a Mack Sennett bathing beauty and Charlie Chaplin. Several phone calls from Gordon Cole at Paramount (Cole was an actual employee of the studio, but is played in the film by Bert Moorhouse) prompt Norma to go to the studio to see Cecil B. DeMille (played by himself) about her script since she thinks Cole was calling on the director's behalf. This studio scene was filmed on the actual set where DeMille was currently making or had just finished shooting (sources vary on this point) *Samson and Delilah* (1949). DeMille greets her graciously and seats her in his director's chair, but he'd worried to his assistant in a previous scene what he was going to say to her about her awful script. A boom microphone tracks along right behind Norma and brushes the peacock feather in her hat, eliciting a nasty look from the former silent film star as she propels it along its way and turns from it, then turns back to give the mic a parting annoyed glance. She's recognized by Hog-eye (John "Skins" Miller), a crew member working a spotlight, who fixes the beam upon her. Actors and crew flock around her, and Norma basks in the glory of their attention. DeMille phones Cole and learns he merely wants to use Norma's car in a movie; when the director tries to explain this to her, she begins crying about how it feels to be back in the studio and he kindly doesn't let Norma discover the truth. As she departs after watching him direct a scene, she's exuberant about their working together again, and rather than dissuade her, DeMille just says, "We'll see what we can do." This launches Norma into a beauty and diet regime designed to make her look as young as possible for the cameras that Joe's voice-over is sure will never turn.

While he'd been waiting for Norma in the car at Paramount, Joe had spied Betty heading to her office and ducked in to tell her she could use his story, but she protested she wasn't good enough to write it alone, proposing they work together evenings on it. Since Norma goes to bed very early as part of her beauty routine, Joe sneaks out to write with Betty. When Norma realizes he went out one night and wants to know where he went, Joe impatiently responds, "Norma, I haven't done anything." "Of course you haven't," she says, clutching the hair on the top of his head tightly, "I wouldn't let you." One night Max is waiting for Joe in the garage when he comes home. The two have a revealing conversation in the darkened structure, faces lit only on one side. When Max admits, "I'm greatly worried about Madame," Joe allows, "Sure you are. And we're not helping her any, feeding her lies and more lies. Getting herself ready for a picture. What happens when she finds out?" Max declares, "She never will. That is my job, and it has been for a long time. You must understand, I discovered her when she was sixteen. I made her a star. And I cannot let her be destroyed.... I directed all her early films." Joe seems disgusted that Max gave up his directing career to become Norma's servant, but Max corrects him and says he had asked to be allowed to come back to her because he found it unendurable after she left him, dropping the bombshell, "I was her first husband." There is a dissolve to Norma pacing in her bedroom, possessive, resentful of Joe's forays to the outside world—to life—bursting into his room while he is sleeping to demand, "Oh Joe, where were you? Is it a woman? I know it's a woman." He doesn't awaken, and Norma finds the manuscript "Untitled Love Story" by Joseph C. Gillis and Betty Schaefer.

The dissolve from a close-up on the manuscript to Betty staring at Joe while he looks at it during one of their evening writing sessions prepares viewers for their conversation. Noticing her stare Joe prompts Betty to tell him what's the matter, asking what she's heard and if it's about him—viewers can see he's concerned that possibly she's become aware of his situation with Norma, since Betty previously had noticed his solid gold cigarette case on which Norma had inscribed "Mad about the Boy—Norma" and he had said something vague about an older woman acquaintance. It turns out Betty is fretting because Artie wants her to come out to Arizona where he's working on a picture and get married, but she's not in love with him anymore. "What happened?" Joe asks. "You did," Betty explains, and they kiss. The long dissolve from their embrace to Joe unlocking the iron gate and entering Norma's house, so that the gate is overlaying their kiss, makes visual commentary on Joe's situation. As he closes the gate behind him his voice-over says, "It wasn't until I got back to that peculiar prison of mine," a well-timed bit of monologue, then continues, as he walks up to his bedroom, "that I started facing the facts." He thinks about Betty being engaged to Artie, "as nice a guy as ever lived, and she was in love with me. *Me*!," his emphasis underscoring his gigolo status and self-disgust. He worries that Betty must suspect his setup, that he'd been a heel not to have told her, but since he's crazy about her he hopes, "Maybe I could get away with it. Get away from Norma, and wipe the whole nasty mess out of my life." But even as he thinks this he hears the telephone being dialed in Norma's bedroom; she is calling Betty to ask her if she knows where Joe lives, how he lives, what he lives on. Joe comes in, takes the phone from Norma, and gives Betty the address, advising she come see for herself. Pleading that he not hate her, Norma says she did it because she needs him. She reveals she bought a revolver but couldn't kill herself. As Norma rants about the revolver Joe simply glares at her with hatred, and when he leaves to answer the door and let Betty in, a shot of Norma rising off of her bed lets viewers see the gun she has been referencing.

Max is shrugging on his uniform jacket as he rushes to answer the door—this scene, a subsequent scene the same night in Joe's bedroom when Max appears because Norma yelled for him, and the scene in which he trots out of the garage after Norma shoots Joe are the only ones in which he isn't wearing the white gloves that clad his hands throughout the rest of the film. Joe beats him to the gated entry and lets Betty in. With self-loathing Joe cruelly enumerates the lavish, large house's amenities and their extravagant lifestyle, saying that Norma called Betty out of jealousy, explaining, "It's lonely here, so she got herself a companion. A very simple setup. Older woman who's well-to-do and a younger man who's not doing too well. Can you figure it out yourself?" When Betty declares "No!" he continues, "All right, I'll give you a few more clues." "No!" Betty interrupts him, willing to sweep this part of Joe's life away by pretending she never got the phone call, never came to the house, hasn't heard what Joe has been telling her. "Now get your things together and let's get out of here," she tells him. Not able to let it go Joe asks, "All my things?" and starts listing all the clothes and accessories Norma has given him as payment for his services. "Come on, Joe!" Betty persists, but he challenges, "Come on where?," to a one-room apartment he can't pay for, a story that could, but probably won't sell? "If you love me, Joe—" Betty starts, but Joe interrupts, "Look sweetie, be practical. I've got a good deal here. A long-term contract with no options. I like it that way. Maybe it's not very admirable. Well, you and Artie can be admirable." "I can't look at you anymore, Joe," Betty says, turning away from him and covering her eyes because she's crying, to which he replies, after glancing upwards toward Norma's bedroom, "How about looking for the exit? This way, Betty," and walks her to the door. "Good luck to you, Betty. You can finish that script on the way to Arizona. When you and Artie get back, if the two of you ever feel like taking a swim"—at this juncture Joe flips on the light in the pool—"here's the pool." Devastated, Betty staggers away from the house. A close-up on Joe's face reveals how much this desecration of innocence has cost him. He pushes Betty away both to punish himself for becoming a kept man and to make her aware of what a rotten place Hollywood can be. Joe destroys his own chance at happiness and will walk away from his cushy existence with Norma in some attempt to exonerate his behavior.

Norma has been watching from the mezzanine—a shot echoing the one when he first saw her on the second-floor exterior mezzanine behind straw blinds—and says, after he strides purposefully up the stairs, "Thank you, darling. Thank you, Joe," but he walks past her into his bedroom. Norma preps herself in the hall mirror for the upcoming scene by fluffing her hair and removing the Frownies she wears to prevent wrinkles; her eyes become wide and crazed. She asks to come into his room, "Joe, tell me you're not cross, tell me everything is just as it was, Joe." But Joe is packing. "You're leaving me!" Norma observes. Joe returns the jewelry, the trinkets she gave him and says he's heading back to his job at the copy desk in Dayton, Ohio. "You know I'm not afraid to die," Norma says. "That's between you and yourself," Joe replies with disinterest, stripping off his cuff links. Norma gets her gun, asking whether he thinks she has the courage. "Oh sure, if it would make a good scene," Joe says wryly. "You don't care, do you?" she asks, "but hundreds of thousands of people will care." "Oh, wake up, Norma," Joe retorts, "You'd be killing yourself to an empty house. The audience left twenty years ago. Now face it." "That's a lie!" Norma protests, "They still want me!" "No, they don't," Joe rejoins. "What about the studio? What about DeMille?" she queries. "He was trying to spare your feelings," he explains. "The studio only wanted to rent your car. DeMille didn't have the heart to tell you. None of us has had the heart." "That's a lie, I get letters every day," she contradicts. When Max appears in the doorway in response to Norma's yelling for him, Joe implores him to tell Norma the truth, that there won't be a picture and that he writes the letters, but Max only declares "Madame is the greatest star of them all!" and glares at Joe as he turns to carry his suitcases outside. "You heard him— I'm a star!" Norma exudes. "Norma, you're a woman of fifty," Joe says in exasperation. "Now grow up. There's nothing tragic about being fifty, not unless you try to be twenty-five." "The greatest star of them all," Norma continues. Seeing she is disassociated, Joe simply says, "Goodbye, Norma," and carries his last suitcase out of the room. Looking after him, in a hushed voice Norma says, "No one ever leaves a star, that's what makes one a star." Then she snaps back to reality and runs after Joe, calling out his name. Catching up to him outside she shoots him twice in the back and once in the stomach when he spins around after the first two shots, whereupon he drops into the swimming pool. Max hurries to see what happened, realizes Joe is beyond help, and runs toward Norma, who is leaning against a pillar and looking upward. Light is shining on her face as she asks, "Stars are ageless, aren't they?," disassociated once again.

A dissolve takes viewers to the daylight scene with Joe's body floating in the pool. Wilder wanted a low-angle shot on Joe's floating corpse, telling associate art director John Meehan, "the shot I want is a fish's viewpoint."[34] Meehan worked with plastic dolls, a mirror, and an aquarium and learned that from "a certain angle, the objects in the water were as clear as the objects above the water."[35] Putting Holden in a water tank, "the shot was actually taken from above the water, the camera pointing down toward a mirror on the floor of the tank."[36] Joe's voice-over returns to say, "Well, this is where you came in. Back at that pool again, the one I always wanted. It's dawn now and they must have photographed me a hundred times. Then they got a couple of pruning hooks from the garden and fished me out, ever so gently. Funny how gentle people get with you once you're dead." Police, reporters, and Paramount newsreel guys are there, "The heartless so-and-so's. What would they do to Norma?" His voice-over speculates that even if she got away with it in court, the headlines would kill her: "Forgotten Star a Slayer," "Aging Actress," "Yesterday's Glamour Queen." The gossip columnist Hedda Hopper (playing herself) is on the scene and won't let the coroner use the telephone line because she's phoning in her story, which she decrees is more important. An unhearing Norma is being badgered with questions from a detective when an officer comes into her bedroom to tell him the newsreel men are there with cameras. Norma has been looking in a hand mirror and primping, and bright light, ostensibly reflected from the hand mirror, illuminates her face as she asks, "Cameras … what is it, Max?" "The cameras have arrived," he announces. "They have? Tell Mr. DeMille I'll be on the set at once," Norma replies. A glance Max gives the detective lets him know that Norma is delusional. "Well, it's one way to get her downstairs," an officer suggests. "Everything will be ready, Madame," Max assures Norma. "Thank you, Max. You'll pardon me, gentlemen, but I must get ready for my scene," Norma says dismissively to the police in the room.

Max "directs" the scene, calling "Quiet everybody! Lights" and, using her name as DeMille would have, asking, "Are you ready, Norma?" "What is the scene? Where am I?" she inquires. Thinking quickly, Max explains, "This is the staircase of the palace." "Oh yes, yes, down below they're waiting for the princess. I'm ready," she responds. "All right, cameras. Action!" Max calls, his face revealing his pain over Norma's mental state and his need to fool her this one last time. Joe's voice-over says, "So they were turning after all. Those cameras. Life, which can be strangely merciful, had taken pity on Norma Desmond. The dream she had clung to so desperately had enfolded her," meaning the psychosis has set in for good. Norma thinks she's on the set of *Salome*. As she descends the stairs, moving her arms as if doing some exotic dance, among the onlookers, Hedda Hopper's face reveals her empathy and sorrow over Norma's mental state, as does a quick cut to Max, who gives just the slightest glance downward with his eyes and then puts them back on Norma. "I can't go on with the scene—I'm too happy!" Norma declares ecstatically. "Mr. DeMille, do you mind if I say a few words? Thank you. I just want to tell you all how happy I am to be back in the studio, making a picture again! You don't know how much I've missed all of you. And I promise you I'll never desert you again. Because after *Salome* we'll make another picture, and another picture! You see, this is my life—it always will be. There's nothing else. Just us, and the cameras. And those wonderful people out there in the dark"—she gestures toward the camera. "All right, Mr. DeMille, I'm ready for my close-up," Norma says, walking toward the camera, which goes hazy while moving in on her face, then fades to black, capping off Wilder's commentary on the Hollywood studio system within which he is working.

Despite its content, *Sunset Boulevard* was nominated for eleven Academy Awards, including Wilder as Best Director and the four mains for Best Actor/Actress and Best Supporting Actor/Actress, but perhaps because of its content it won only three, with Wilder's award being shared with Brackett and D.M. Marshman, Jr., for Best Story and Screenplay. Wilder would have to remain content with his previous Oscar for Best Director for *The Lost Weekend* (1945) until he would win it twice more for *Some Like It Hot* (1959) and *The Apartment* (1960):

Some fifty years later, Wilder's voice-over-from-the-dead approach would be used in *American Beauty* (1999). Although this study is not arguing that Sam Mendes' film is a noir film, it does pay tribute to *Sunset Boulevard* with the protagonist's opening voice-over: "My name is Lester Burnham. This is my neighborhood. This is my street. This is my life. I'm 42 years old; in less than a year I'll be dead. Of course, I don't know that yet, and in a way, I'm dead already." In this satirical American Dream film, Lester (Kevin Spacey) realizes that he's lost something, which his voice-over acknowledges: "I'm not exactly sure what it is, but I know I didn't always feel this … sedated. But you know what? It's never too late to get it back." He tries to get his youth back by running, lifting weights, and coming on to his teenage daughter's precocious friend. Near the end of the film Lester is shot to death by his neighbor, Colonel Frank Fitts (Chris Cooper), a repressed homosexual who had hugged and tried to kiss Lester when he mistakenly thought Lester was gay. As part of his closing voice-over, Lester says, "I guess I could be pretty pissed off about what happened to me, but it's hard to stay mad when there's so much beauty in the world." That sentiment is quite far away from Wilder's vision of Hollywood.

Vera Caspary, Otto Preminger and *Laura*

The making of *Laura* is a drama in its own right. Author Vera Caspary recalls, in her 1971 *The Saturday Review* article "My 'Laura' and Otto's," that her agent, Monica McCall, gave a typescript of her book *Laura* to Otto Preminger, who was directing and producing in Broadway theater. Preminger wanted to revise the play in collaboration with Caspary, but as she explains, he envisioned "a conventional detective story; I saw it as a psychological drama about people involved in a murder. We fell out over this," so Caspary invited George Sklar to work on it with her.[37] Ultimately Caspary offered the story to Hollywood, with only Metro-Goldwyn-Mayer and Twentieth Century–Fox displaying interest, and Preminger, now back in Hollywood, had to work hard to convince Darryl Zanuck to buy the story. There is some history behind this need to convince the studio head.

Preminger had started with Twentieth Century–Fox in 1935, working on B-films, but was banished in 1936 due to a confrontation with Zanuck over a scene Preminger shot for his first A-film, *Kidnapped* (1938). Zanuck didn't like the rushes and claimed Preminger had cut material out of a scene, which he hadn't. Both men held their ground without apologies. After some success as a producer and director on Broadway (he had achieved a strong reputation in theater in Vienna in the 1920s and 30s and Twentieth Century–Fox executive Joseph Schenck had initially invited him to Hollywood after interviewing him in Vienna in 1935[38]), Preminger seized his chance to get back on board with the studio when Zanuck went to supervise training and combat films for the U.S. Army Signal Corps, leaving William Goetz in charge. Goetz contracted Preminger as a director from 1943 to 1953. In his autobiography Preminger explains how Goetz gave him the go-ahead to make *Laura* during Zanuck's absence, but then Zanuck returned: "He was incensed by some of the decisions Goetz had made in his absence, among them signing me as director.

He suspected that Goetz was trying to take the studio away from him."[39] Zanuck said Preminger could produce *Laura*, but he would never let him direct for the studio. Preminger's memory of their interaction has been countered by Foster Hirsch, who notes that Zanuck said at this same time that Preminger could both produce and direct the B-movie *Army Wives*, which was released as *In the Meantime, Darling* (1944).[40]

John Brahm, Walter Lang, and Lewis Milestone were offered the opportunity to direct *Laura* and turned it down; Rouben Mamoulian accepted. The story of how Preminger took over varies depending on who tells it. Preminger writes that Zanuck hated the rushes, especially Dana Andrews' performance, and ordered Mamoulian to reshoot everything "except for Clifton Webb's closeups," but the new rushes "were identical to the first, or maybe worse," so Zanuck asked Preminger whether he should take the director off the picture, and "Without hesitation I said, 'Yes.'"[41] Beyond initially convincing Zanuck to acquire the story, Preminger had persuaded him, over objections from casting director Rufus LeMaire, to cast Clifton Webb in the role of Waldo Lydecker because the audience would be surprised that this witty aesthete was a murderer. Caspary's Waldo weighs over 250 pounds and is described as "fat" several times; ostensibly he is modeled on Wilkie Collins' Count Fosco in *The Woman in White*. Webb is so lean you can practically count his ribs in the film's first scene, where he is writing in his bathtub. Both the corpulent and the thin Waldo work in that he despises detective Mark McPherson as a rival for Laura's affections because Mark is younger and more physically fit. Not to mention Mark is heterosexual, whereas Waldo might well be homosexual (Webb certainly was, and critics have found hints of Waldo's homosexuality in Caspary's novel). His sexual orientation doesn't really matter, for to Waldo, people are like his collectible antiques and art, and he didn't want to lose his protégé Laura, first to her fiancé Shelby Carpenter and later to Mark.

Prior to Mamoulian's attempts to make the film as its first director, Caspary had been invited to work on the screenplay yet turned the opportunity down, writing later that she was "sick and weary of an old passion" from writing and rewriting the various versions of *Laura* and talking with potential directors for its play format; "'Let Laura stay dead in the first act,' I said; 'I'm through with her.'"[42] Preminger invited Caspary to read the first draft of the screenplay, after which she met with him in his office at Twentieth Century–Fox where the two ended up in a shouting match. Caspary objected to Waldo hiding his gun inside a tall clock because his cane being the gun is a Freudian symbol of his "impotence and destructiveness, actually the theme of the novel."[43] In turn Preminger maintained viewers would miss the symbolism, and ballistic experts had said such a small gun wouldn't have caused the physical damage the dead woman sustained. Caspary yelled that her research determined that it would. The two argued over Laura's character even "more vehemently," Caspary believing Preminger had taken the sexy, engaging Laura from the novel and turned her into "a flat, conventional movie heroine," whereas Preminger thought Caspary's Laura had no character or sex, otherwise she wouldn't have to pay a gigolo like Shelby.[44] Nearly all Preminger writes in his autobiography about this encounter is, "When Vera Caspary read the script she wasn't pleased."[45] After the film opened Caspary happened to see Preminger at the Stork Club, where she claims he gloated "that the screenplay I had so severely criticized was the season's sensation."[46] She countered that she had seen the first screenplay, before Sam Hoffenstein and Betty Reinhardt's rewrite, in which Laura's character had been strengthened and other positive changes made. Preminger called her a liar, and a fight almost broke out when the men she was with took off their coats to defend her, whereupon Preminger bowed and said he hadn't meant to insult her. "We have met since and are always urbane," Caspary writes; "The incident has not been mentioned."[47]

Caspary, influenced by the narrative style of Wilkie Collins' novels that had been suggested to her by a friend, wrote the novel *Laura* from the perspective of different characters, one of which is captured in the stenographic transcription of his police interrogation. This structure was altered for the film, although the flavor of it is retained via the opening voice-over of Waldo Lydecker, who was the first narrator in the novel: "I shall never forget the weekend Laura died. A silver sun burned through the sky like a huge magnifying glass. It was the hottest Sunday in my recollection. I felt as if I were the only human being left in New York. For Laura's horrible death, I was alone. I, Waldo Lydecker, was the only one who really knew her." As the camera roams his living quarters, viewers are shown Waldo's art and collectibles, including the tall clock whose twin figures so prominently in the mysterious murder. As Mark McPherson (Dana Andrews) waits to talk with Waldo, the clock chimes the half hour, although its hands are at 11:33, prompting Mark to check his watch. "I noted that his attention was fixed upon my clock," Waldo's voice-over says while watching the detective through the open door of his bathroom; "There was only one other in existence and that was in Laura's apartment, in the very room where she was murdered." Thus Preminger puts a visual clue right in front of viewers at the outset and will make much of that other clock in the film's closing scene.

Mark is amused to find Waldo in the tub, where it is his habit to type his newspaper column, a situation invented for the film. When the writer stands up offscreen to get out of the bath, Andrews, who can convey a great deal in the merest hint of an expression, glances down and gives the slightest smirk, ostensibly Mark's commentary on Waldo's manhood. The detective asks about a column Waldo wrote two years ago in which he shifted the topic from a book review to the Harrington murder case, Waldo noting that the murder weapon was a shotgun loaded with buckshot, which is the way Laura was murdered. Mark is curious because in reality the murder weapon was a sash weight. It's worth noting that a window sash weight was one of the weapons used on Albert Snyder and is not mentioned in the novel, yet a reference to that real-life murder case does come in the last part of Caspary's book when Mark thinks that to Deputy Commissioner Preble, Laura "looked as guilty as Ruth Snyder."[48] Residing in New York City at the time of the murder trial, Caspary obviously was aware of the sensationalist press coverage of it. As their conversation goes on, Mark pulls out a baseball pinball hand game that he will fiddle with at significant moments in various later scenes (another habit invented for the film); here Waldo asks him whether he confiscated it while raiding a kindergarten, to which Mark replies that the game takes a lot of control. When asked whether he and Laura were in love with each other, Waldo answers, "Laura considered me the wisest, the wittiest, the most interesting man she'd ever met, and I was in complete accord with her on that point." Laura also thought him the kindest, gentlest, most sympathetic man in the world, so he tried to become such a man. "Have any luck?" Mark inquires, giving Waldo the opening to make one of his many witticisms: "Let me put it this way. I should be sincerely sorry to see my neighbors' children devoured by wolves."

Waldo accompanies Mark on a visit to Laura's aunt, Ann Treadwell (Judith Anderson). Preminger complicates the romantic relationships in the film. Whereas Caspary's Shelby makes sure the aunt is comfortably seated and has everything she needs, she dismisses him with indifference and says she wouldn't have him on a gold platter. In the film, with the sunlight coming through the curtain folds casting vertical bar shadows suggestive of prison on the apartment wall behind Waldo and then centrally between Waldo and Ann, one of several visual indicators as to who is the murderer, Mark gets right to it and asks Ann about checks she has written to Shelby, wanting to know if she loves him. Ann says Shelby had been helping her by shopping for her. In actuality, Ann essentially picked up Shelby at the Kentucky Derby and brought him back to New York City, where Laura met him at one of Ann's parties, shown in a later flashback scene. Now, Ann admits she lent Shelby money. Shelby (Vincent Price) comes in and Waldo reveals to him that Laura had gone to the country to reconsider their upcoming marriage. Wanting the key to that country home, Mark, accompanied by Shelby and Waldo, goes to Laura's apartment to look for it.

When the men enter, the clock can be heard ticking. Mark opens the Venetian blinds and it is the first time since the opening credits that Laura's portrait is shown, eliciting Mark's comment, "Not bad." Mamoulian's wife had painted a portrait of Laura that Preminger replaced when he took over as director. The new portrait's life-like quality was achieved by enlarging a photograph of Gene Tierney and airbrushing it with paint. It is little wonder that Mark becomes entranced with it. He then plays a record, which is the hauntingly beautiful theme composed especially for the film. Originally Preminger wanted to use Duke Ellington's "Sophisticated Lady" as the film's theme music, but David Raksin thought it wouldn't suit the film, and the director gave the composer a weekend to write a new song. Raksin recollects, "That weekend I watched the movie several times and it inspired me. Coincidentally, that Saturday, I received a letter of farewell from a lady I was in love with…. The melody of our theme song needed to evoke melancholy, and I had just been given a heavy dose."[49] Indeed, the melody is as much a presence in the film as is Laura's portrait, and the two combined reel Mark in, as will be shown in later scenes.

Mark starts looking at Laura's things, opening furniture and picking up objects. In the bedroom he sits on Laura's bed and plays the baseball hand game while Shelby finds the house key in the nightstand, which Mark calmly points out was not there yesterday when the police took inventory. Waldo implies Shelby had something to do with Laura's death and the two almost fight, but Mark prevents this by standing between them with the baseball game in hand. "Will you please stop dawdling with that infernal puzzle?" Waldo asks, "It's getting on my nerves." "I know, but it keeps me calm," Mark quietly replies.

Mark and Waldo have wine at the restaurant Waldo frequented with Laura, sitting at the same table they always shared, which leads to flashbacks that fill in the story of how they met at the Algonquin Hotel and became friends. Laura (Gene Tierney) approaches Waldo while he is eating lunch to seek his endorsement of a pen for her advertising campaign, whereupon he is rude to her and remains intent on his meal. Rethinking his dismissal of her he later seeks her out at her workplace to apologize, but she gives him the same treatment she had received by saying she's busy and continuing to work as he talks. She accepts his apology and says "Goodbye, Mr. Lydecker," which gains his respect in that he agrees to endorse the pen. She in turn agrees to have dinner with him, and a friendship is born. Waldo explains to Mark that he helped Laura secure other endorsements and clients—"I gave her her start"— "but it was her own talent and imagination that enabled her to rise to the top of her profession and stay there. She had an eager mind, always." The two made a habit of spending Tuesday and Friday nights alone together dining at home, listening to music, Waldo reading his column to her. Then Laura started breaking their dates and he felt betrayed. Going to her apartment only the second time she does this— an act that reveals his obsession with Laura—he is glad to see that she is home until he realizes she's with another man when he observes their silhouettes in the window. Waiting until the man leaves, Waldo learns it is Jacoby (John Dexter), the artist who painted Laura's portrait. In typical Waldo jealousy, he tells Mark, "I never liked the man. He was so obviously conscious of looking more like an athlete than an artist. I sat up the rest of the night writing a column about him." In that column he ridicules Jacoby's work so that Laura loses regard for him and doesn't see him again. Waldo is satisfied that Laura keeps other men at a distance, until she gets involved with Shelby.

Another flashback shows Shelby introducing himself to Laura at one of her aunt's parties and asking her to dance, whereupon she says she is with Waldo, who makes a crack about Shelby having come from sharecroppers when he learns Shelby's from Kentucky. In a key composition typical of Preminger's careful blocking, viewers see Shelby and Laura talking on the terrace, Waldo comes out because he wants to leave the party and stands slightly behind them in the middle ground, and Ann is seen talking to a guest in the background inside the room. It is perfectly balanced with Shelby occupying the far left of the screen, Laura the far right, Waldo exactly in the center between them, and Ann halfway between Shelby and Waldo. Shelby and Laura look at each other as she invites him to come to the agency she works for about a job at 10:30 the next morning; Waldo looks at Laura; and Ann looks at her guest, which places her facing in Shelby's direction, left, with her back in Laura's direction. Had Ann been in the foreground with the other characters, she would have been turning her back on Laura and giving her attention to Shelby, which is rather what happens later because as Laura gets interested in Mark, Shelby goes back to Ann.

Shelby and Laura start dating, so Waldo has Shelby investigated in another character assassination attempt like he had done with Jacoby, uncovering that Shelby wrote bad checks and had been accused of stealing jewelry when he was a houseguest. Laura insists that people can change, whereupon Waldo reveals that Shelby has been seeing a model at their advertising firm, Diane Redfern. Laura strikes back by telling Waldo that she and Shelby are getting married in the coming week; not to be undone, Waldo pulls a cigarette case out of his desk drawer that Laura had given Shelby for his last birthday and that he in turn gave to Diane, who pawned it. When she attempts to call Shelby for an explanation, Waldo tells her he's not home because he's dining with Ann. The two go to Ann's apartment and another tableau is visually composed by Preminger as Ann and Shelby rise from their intimate dining table: Shelby is on the far left, Ann is also on the left of the screen, there is a gap in the middle, then Laura is on the right, with Waldo on the far right of the screen. The couples and the division between them visually drive home which characters are in alliance with each other. Shelby smoothly says he's been telling Ann about their marriage, causing Laura to throw down the cigarette case and stalk out of the room and apartment.

Upset over Shelby's apparent involvement with both Diane and her aunt, Laura phones Waldo that Friday to break their dinner plans because she wants to go to her country house and think. A time jump takes viewers back to the restaurant where Mark and Waldo are now the only patrons left. Before parting ways outside the restaurant, Waldo says he should not have let Laura become involved with Shelby, he should have stopped it somehow. Mark thanks Waldo for the wine, and the camera comes in for an extreme close-up of the side of Mark's face as, deep in thought, he watches Waldo walk away, before a fade to black. In the next scene Mark is in Laura's apartment phoning the liquor store she uses to ask about a bottle of Black Pony scotch that seems subpar to Laura's usual libations. When Laura's maid Bessie (Dorothy Adams) comes for her interview and finds out Mark has been reading Laura's letters and diary, she protests that he has been "pawing over them"—an allusion to his sexual interest in Laura that will be echoed in later scenes—and worries that Mark will tell the newspaper reporters that Laura seemingly had been drinking with a man in her bedroom the night she was killed because they would "make up their nasty stories and drag her name through the mud." Mark has sent for Shelby to be interviewed too, and he shows up with Ann and Waldo in tow. Bessie, as asked by Mark, brings in glasses, ice, and seltzer, and the Black Pony scotch is served while Waldo tries to reclaim a vase, fire screen, and the clock, which he claims he had only lent to Laura. Mark says nothing is leaving the apartment but Waldo, downing his drink before they all depart. Mark's attempt to learn who might have brought the Black Pony scotch to Laura's apartment seems to have shown him it was Shelby, since he is the only one who refused a drink, likely because he associates the liquor with the night of the murder.

That night Mark returns to Laura's apartment, telling the police guard outside the building to go get himself something to eat because he'll take over, adding "Take your time." In Caspary's novel, Mark narrates, "I let myself in as coolly as if I'd been entering my own place," explaining how he got a glass of water, removed his coat and loosened his collar, stretched out on a chair, turned off the lamp, and fell asleep.[50] When Laura enters and turns on a lamp, Mark awakens and is speechless at seeing her until she threatens to call the police, so he informs her he is the police and she is supposedly dead. As the two look at each other, Mark narrates his recollection of his grandmother telling him "about meeting in heaven those whom we had lost on earth," an indication of Mark's attachment to what he had assumed to be the dead Laura.[51] The situation is greatly expanded in Preminger's film, emphasizing Mark's obsession with the dead woman.

Viewers see the clock and hear it ticking after Mark enters the apartment, and strains of the theme song intertwine with a more suspenseful melody. He looks at Laura's portrait, takes off his raincoat and hat, and loosens his tie, making himself very much at home. Pouring rain can be seen through the Venetian blinds. Mark removes his suit jacket and gets Laura's letters and diary out of her desk. Stubbing out his cigarette hard, he walks into the bedroom while smacking the bundle of letters on his hand, tossing them on a bureau to start going through Laura's things. Opening the top drawer, he rifles through some of its contents, picks up and drops a sheer handkerchief, and is looking into what viewers assume is her lingerie drawer. He sniffs the perfume on the top of the bureau while viewers see him in the mirror hung over the bureau, although Mark does not look at himself in it. Picking up the letters again, Mark opens and shuts the closet, this time looking at himself in its mirrored doors, after which he leaves the bedroom. He pours himself a drink and casts a look at Laura's portrait, at which point the theme song dominates the soundtrack. Prior to this, all the time Mark had been becoming tangibly acquainted with Laura's possessions, strains of the haunting theme song had been interwoven with the more suspenseful melody.

In a scene absent from the novel, Waldo arrives, having seen the lights on while passing by, and wittily yet barbedly asks whether Mark has sublet Laura's apartment because he's been there often enough to pay rent. He objects to Mark reading his letters to Laura. Waldo also knows Mark has put in a bid for Laura's portrait, Ann having determined to sell the contents of her niece's apartment. To calm himself after this exposure, Mark starts playing with the baseball hand game. "McPherson," Waldo asks, "did it ever strike you that you're acting very strangely? It's a wonder that you don't come here like a suitor with roses and a box of candy. Drugstore candy, of course," a jab at Mark not being refined like he. "Have you ever dreamed of Laura as your wife?" Waldo continues. "By your side at the policeman's ball? Or in the bleachers, or listening to the heroic story of how you got a silver shin bone from a gun battle with a gangster?" During this pointed barrage Mark's jaw is working to indicate Waldo is getting to him, he stops playing the hand game, and even flips it up as further proof that he's not calm. "I see you have," Waldo states, whereupon Mark says, "Why don't you go home; I'm busy." "You better watch out McPherson," Waldo cautions, "or you'll end up in a psychiatric ward. I don't think they've ever had a patient who fell in love with a corpse." The camera moves in on Mark's face as he takes a drink and glares after the departing Waldo. In this shot, Laura's portrait fills the left quarter of the screen and Mark's face fills three-quarters of the right. The film's added encounter with Waldo and this shot with the portrait underscore Mark's obsession with the dead woman.

Left alone in Laura's apartment on this rainy night, Mark continues drinking Laura's liquor, finally settling in a chair by the fireplace. As the theme song plays, unadulterated by other strains, Mark looks at Laura's portrait, which seems to glow, and either falls asleep or passes out. The camera backs away from Mark and viewers

Waldo (Clifton Webb) and Mark (Dana Andrews) discuss Laura (Gene Tierney) before her portrait in *Laura* (1944) (20th Century–Fox/Photofest).

hear the ticking clock and see Laura enter the apartment. When Laura turns on the lights, Mark rubs his eyes in disbelief at seeing her. As in the novel, when she threatens to call the police, he tells her he is the police and that she was thought to have been murdered in her own apartment. He suggests she take off her wet clothes to avoid catching cold and when she goes to her bedroom to do so, the camera moves in for a close-up of Mark's face looking after her, still coming to terms with the woman he's been obsessing over being alive.

Laura finds Diane Redfern's dress in her closet so Mark intends to investigate the possibility that the dead woman had been Diane, whereas in the novel readers know right away that the dead woman was Diane because Laura had lent her the apartment for the weekend. He tells Laura not to go out or call anyone because "If anything should happen to you this time, I wouldn't like it," revealing his interest in the case is quite personal. Mark's eyes roam over her face as he waits for her reply to his question of whether she decided to marry Shelby while she was in the country, then he gives the merest smile at hearing she will not, further indication of his feelings for her. Moments after Mark leaves Laura calls Shelby, who asks to meet her, which they do, after which Mark, having overheard the call from the basement of the building because he's had the line tapped, tails Shelby to Laura's country house, where Shelby is retrieving a shotgun that hangs over the fireplace. Mark extracts from Shelby that he entertained Diane at Laura's apartment, talking for three hours because while Diane was in love with him, Shelby was not in love with her. When the doorbell rang he asked Diane to answer it because anyone would believe that the kindhearted Laura would let Diane stay there while she was out of town. When Diane was killed, Shelby kept quiet to protect Laura in case she had been the murderer. Mark discovers the radio works—Laura had claimed it was broken and thus she hadn't known about her murder—and remarks to Shelby that he had hoped it wouldn't; viewers know he doesn't want to suspect Laura of killing Diane. Mark confiscates the gun to see if it is the murder weapon, which it will turn out it was not.

The next morning when Mark arrives at Laura's apartment with groceries, the clock is prominently onscreen as they enter the kitchen. Declaring he'll fix some bacon and eggs, Mark asks doubtfully whether Laura can make coffee. Amused, Laura says, "Suppose you set the table while I get breakfast. Do you always sound like this in the morning?" "Don't tell me you can cook," Mark says, surprised that this woman he has heard idealized by others, and that he himself seems to have etherealized, could be domestic as well. "My mother always listened sympathetically to my dreams of a career," Laura explains, "then she taught me another recipe." At this juncture Bessie comes to work and shrieks at seeing Laura, who she thinks is a ghost. When Shelby arrives with a corsage, Mark wryly observes, "Oh, it's on again," obviously disappointed they have decided to marry after all. Waldo comes in and collapses when he sees Laura. Left alone to recuperate in the bedroom, he phones his manservant and directs him to call their friends and organize an impromptu party to celebrate Laura's return. During the party Ann proposes to Shelby, who deflects the offer by saying Laura needs him. Shelby reveals to Laura that he thinks she killed Diane, which is why he went to the country home to hide the shotgun. Upset that he could believe her a murderer, she goes into her bedroom and encounters her aunt touching up her makeup, who asks Laura if she is as interested in Mark as he is in her. Laura protests that she just met him last night, causing Ann to say that is more than long enough sometimes and that Mark is better for Laura than Shelby—"anybody is." "Shelby's better for me," Ann goes on, "because I can afford him and I understand him. He's no good but he's what I want. I'm not a nice person, Laura, and neither is he. He knows I know he's … just what he is. He also knows that I don't care. We belong together because we're both weak and can't seem to help it. That's why I know he's capable of murder. He's like me." When Laura looks questioningly at Ann, she answers, "No dear. I didn't." Lowering the veil from her hat over her face, she finishes, "But I thought of it," and walks out of the room. At this horrid revelation, Laura stubs out her cigarette and also leaves the bedroom.

A phone call comes through for Mark, who assures the caller, "Don't worry, I told you I'd bring in the killer today," at which the music that had been playing stops and everyone at the party turns toward him to listen. Mark looks pointedly at Shelby, then Waldo, and finally at Laura, to whom he says, "All right, let's go." A distraught Bessie screams "No!," Waldo pledges to defend Laura, and Shelby tells her he had told her to watch out for Mark. "It's too bad you didn't open that door Friday night, Carpenter," Mark interjects, causing Shelby to say "Wait a minute" and put his hand on Mark's shoulder, whereupon Mark punches him in the stomach. Shelby caves, causing Ann to comfort him, and he kisses her hand.

At the police station Mark turns two extremely bright lamps on Laura to make her uncomfortable during interrogation, but turns them off when she asks him to. Determining that the radio got repaired after Laura left her country home, Mark wants to know why she pulled the switch on marrying Shelby, saying it was off and now it's back on. She says she changed her mind. Mark whips off his hat and gets in her face to ask, "Now did you really decide to call it off, or did you just tell me that because you knew I wanted to hear it?" She looks at him, curious at his emotion, and explains that they kept the engagement on to avoid suspicion being thrown on either of them for Diane's murder. "Are you in love with him?" Mark demands. "I don't see how I ever could have been," Laura responds, causing Mark's body to visibly relax as he sighs. "Come on, you're going home," he tells her. "I was ninety-nine percent certain about you, but I had to get rid of that one percent doubt." "Wasn't there an easier way to make sure?" Laura asks. "I reached a point where I needed official surroundings," Mark explains, revealing further his feelings for her. Smiling, Laura replies, "Then it was worth it, Mark," confirming her feelings for him.

After taking her home, Mark goes to Waldo's apartment and lets himself in when no one answers the doorbell. The tall clock strikes three quarters of an hour and the hands are on time, not fast as they were before. Mark checks his notebook on this point. Unable to open the clock's lower case, he kicks it in, discovers an empty chamber, and seemingly having a moment of revelation, rushes offscreen. The scene cuts to Laura's apartment where Waldo is trying to talk Laura out of caring for Mark. "I don't deny that he's infatuated with you in some warped way of his own. But he isn't capable of any normal, warm, human relationship," he protests. Waldo stops pacing, looks at the clock and says, "He's been dealing with criminals too long," direct commentary upon himself, viewers will learn. Waldo tries to denigrate both Mark and Shelby and win her loyalty back by reasoning, "When you were unattainable, when he thought you were dead, that's when he wanted you most.... Laura, you have one tragic weakness. With you a lean, strong body is the measure of a man, and you always get hurt.... When a man has everything in the world that he wants, except what he wants most, he loses his self-respect. It makes him bitter, Laura. He wants to hurt someone, as he's been hurt. [Soon viewers will realize Waldo is talking about himself here.] You were a long time finding out about Shelby," he says, placing his palm on Laura's cheek. "But that's over now," he continues, patting her cheek, "we'll be back together again." At this juncture Mark lets himself into the apartment. He announces that the shotgun from Laura's country home wasn't the murder weapon, leading Waldo to say this is the real key to Mark's character, in that while he claimed Laura was innocent, he checked up on her to make sure. "It's the same obvious pattern, Laura," Waldo points out. "If McPherson weren't muscular and handsome in a cheap sort of way, you'd see through him in a second." Laura responds, "Waldo, I mean to be as kind about this as I know how. But I must tell you, you're the one who follows the same obvious pattern. First it was Jacoby, then Shelby, and now I suppose—" at which Waldo interrupts, "Well I—," Laura cutting him off with, "I don't think we should see each other again." "You're not yourself, darling," Waldo protests. "Yes I am," she declares firmly. "For the first time in ages I know what I'm doing." As this exchange goes on, Mark plays with the baseball hand game. "Very well," Waldo concedes. "I hope you'll never regret what promises to be a disgustingly earthy relationship." Looking at Mark, Waldo says, "Congratulations, McPherson. Listen to my broadcast in fifteen minutes. I'm discussing great lovers of history."

After he leaves Laura's apartment Waldo pauses on the stairs, somewhat stunned at what just happened, then he casts a look back at her door as his shadow elongates on the wall behind him. Inside the apartment, Mark finds the shotgun hidden on the tall clock's case and theorizes that Waldo mistook Diane for Laura and killed her because he didn't want anyone else to have her. He removes the cartridges while deducing that Waldo had waited outside the apartment, heard Shelby discover Diane's body and leave, then came back in to hide the gun in the clock. Laura admits having suspected Waldo, but that she owed him too much. The scene cuts to Waldo turning on the stairs and going back up. Mark leaves to go arrest Waldo, kissing Laura and making sure her door is securely locked. Laura turns off the lights and goes into her bedroom. Waldo enters from the kitchen, the light falling on him, the kitchen door, and the clock's face. The clock strikes three-quarters of the hour, cueing Laura to turn on the wall radio. Another cut back to Waldo is a high-angle shot showing him kneeling to get the gun out of the clock's case as his voice comes from the radio: "And thus, as history has proved, love is eternal. It has been the strongest motivation for human actions throughout centuries. Love is stronger than life. It reaches beyond the dark shadow of death." A low-angle shot shows Waldo opening the gun and giving a sigh in recognition that because the gun is unloaded, Mark must have discovered it. The radio voice continues, "I close this evening's broadcast with some favorite lines from Dowson." Waldo loads cartridges into the gun, his shadow cast high on the wall behind him as his radio voice recites, "Brief life. They are not long, the weeping and the laughter, love and desire and hate. I think they have no portion in us after we pass the gate." Waldo cracks the gun barrel shut and there is a cut to Mark finding out from the officer on duty that Waldo never left Laura's apartment building, so he goes back in. There is a cut to Laura fixing her hair as Waldo's radio voice says, "They are not long, the days of wine and roses." Waldo walks into the bedroom as his radio voice intones, "Out of a misty dream our path emerges for a while, then closes within a dream." "That's the way it is, isn't it Laura?" the live Waldo says, causing her to jump. "Waldo! You've taken one life. Isn't that enough?" she desperately asks. "The best part of myself, that's what you are," he responds. "Do you think I'm going to leave it to the vulgar pawing of a second-rate detective, who thinks you are a dame? Do you think I could bear the thought of him holding you in his arms, kissing you, loving you?" A cut shows Mark and two officers noisily trying to get into Laura's apartment. Waldo swings the gun up, pointing it at Laura as he says, "There he is now. He'll find us together, Laura. As we always have been, as we always should be, as we always will be." Laura grabs the barrel and pushes it up to avert the shotgun, running out of the bedroom as Mark breaks in through the kitchen door. Standing in the kitchen doorway next to the clock, Mark grabs Laura and shields her by hugging her and turning away from Waldo, who is shot by one of the officers. "Goodbye, Laura," the dying Waldo says, the camera showing her portrait over his right shoulder. The shotgun blast he managed to get off had hit the clock's face, and as Laura and Mark walk toward Waldo and pass out of frame, the camera goes to a tight close-up of the broken clock face and its damaged inner mechanism, commentary on Waldo's psychological state. "Goodbye, my love" is said by an offscreen Waldo just before the theme song swells and "The End" appears over Laura's portrait.

While Caspary objected to the shotgun being the murder weapon rather than Waldo's walking stick, using the tall clock as its hiding place allows Preminger to place visual clues in front of the viewer throughout the film and to draw attention to them by including the clock's ticking in many scenes. In the novel the twin items Waldo and Laura possess were mercury glass globe-and-pedestal vases, which just wouldn't have had the same impact. Caspary did admit of the film, "Its direction is magnificent. No movement, no tone, no nuance is without significance. The clarity, especially in the first half of the picture, is dazzling."[52] Regarding Preminger, she allows, "For the brilliance of his direction, the skill of the flashbacks, the charm of the background, for superb casting, and, most of all, for his appreciation of the story, I shall always be grateful."[53] She believes it to be his best film, and *Laura* to be her best novel.

Fallen Angel (1945) was the second film noir mystery Preminger directed, again starring Dana Andrews, followed a few years later by a third, *Where the Sidewalk Ends* (1950), with Andrews and Gene Tierney, and then *Angel Face* (1953), starring Robert Mitchum and Jean Simmons. Critics argue over Preminger's importance as a director, but beyond the undeniable status of *Laura* as a film noir classic, *Carmen Jones* (1954) is a strong vehicle for Dorothy Dandridge and Harry Belafonte; *The Man with the Golden Arm* (1955) features Frank Sinatra struggling with drug addiction, a topic not usually dealt with in film at that time; and *Anatomy of a Murder* (1959), which some classify as a film noir, continued to push the limits of the Production Code by dealing with rape. Although he was nominated twice for the Academy Award for Best Director, for *Laura* and for *The Cardinal* (1963), the Oscar remained beyond Preminger's grasp.

Roman Polanski and *Chinatown*

Double crosses that evolve into elaborate self-deception carry over from early noir to influence a number of more contemporary films, such as Roman Polanski's

Chinatown, a film that evokes the glamour but emphasizes the grit of classic film noir. Polanski had a harrowing childhood. He was born in Paris in 1933, his family returned to Poland in 1936, and when the Germans invaded in 1939, his family was relocated to the Krakow ghetto. After his parents' arrest his mother and father were sent to Auschwitz and Mauthausen-Gusen, respectively; his mother was killed. Homeless at age 7, Polanski roamed the countryside until the war was over and he and his father found each other. Polanski attended technical school, acted, then studied film at the Lodz National Film School from 1950 to 1955. His first feature was *Knife in the Water* (1962), from his original screenplay, which gained him international attention. *Repulsion* (1965) was co-written with Gerard Brach, made in England, and became an international hit. *Cul-de-sac*, also co-written with Brach, followed in 1966. *Rosemary's Baby* (1968), adapted from the Ira Levin novel of the same name, was his first Hollywood film.

Polanski has written in his autobiography about how he wanted to make *Chinatown*, but did not want to be in Los Angeles because it reminded him of tragedy; his wife Sharon Tate and their unborn child had been murdered by followers of Charles Manson in 1969 and he had been living in Europe since then. *Chinatown* is set in 1937 Los Angeles, and in *Film Noir and the Spaces of Modernity*, Edward Dimendberg points out how this and later neo-noir films betray a "palpable longing for an older image of the metropolis whose existence it simultaneously mourns and resurrects."[54] Polanski notes in his autobiography that he intended it to be "a film about the thirties seen through the camera eye of the seventies," so he "wanted the style of the period conveyed by a scrupulously accurate reconstruction of décor, costume, and idiom—not by a deliberate imitation, in 1973, of thirties film techniques."[55] While he started filming with Stanley Cortez as his cinematographer, Polanski felt Cortez worked too slowly and replaced him with John Alonzo. Working within the confines of Hollywood aesthetics, or, more accurately, playing at the edges of those confines, Polanski employed the straightforward, quasi-journalistic approach of Howard Hawks, perhaps in reference to the screenplay's echoes of *The Big Sleep*. But the objective view is deceptive; virtually every scene revolves obliquely around Jake Gittes' (Jack Nicholson) point of view, creating a claustrophobic sense of entrapment, which in turn expands throughout the world of the characters. To look at Nicholson's piercing blue eyes is to see through those eyes, and the jaundiced vision defies logic: a bitter desert of corruption, incest and murder—to mention just a few of the issues at stake. Screenplay writer Robert Towne employed the real-life scam perpetrated by Los Angeles' mayor Fred Eaton and the head of the city's Water Department, William Mulholland.

Of Towne's story Polanski found it to be "in the best Chandler tradition, yet its private eye hero, J.J. Gittes, was no pale, down-at-the-heel imitation of Marlowe," he was "a new, archetypal detective figure."[56] The film opens with Gittes, who goes by Jake, trying to console his friend Curly (Burt Young) because his wife is cheating on him; such investigations are the bread and butter of Jake's business. He does try to dissuade his next potential client, a woman claiming to be Mrs. Mulwray (Diane Ladd), but ultimately agrees to look into whether her husband is seeing another woman. Since Hollis Mulwray (Darrell Zwerling) is the chief engineer of the Department of Water and Power, Jake listens at a public hearing where he argues against the building of the Atto Vallejo Dam and Reservoir to bring water to the Los Angeles desert community because he is sure the dam will not hold, just as a previous one had not. There is outcry from attending citizens, including a sheep rancher who has brought part of his flock and accuses Mulwray of stealing water from the valley. Jake follows Mulwray when he visits the dry Los Angeles River's bed, where the engineer speaks to a boy on a horse (Claudio Martinez), then takes out a large book and writes in it. Next Jake follows the engineer to the seaside, remaining until after dark when water comes pouring out of a pipe protruding from the hillside. Returning to his car Jake finds a flyer on it that says "Save our city!!! Los Angeles is dying of thirst. Vote yes Nov. 6th," sponsored by the Citizens Committee to Save presumably Los Angeles, although the last words are out of frame.

Speaking with his operatives back at the office Jake learns that Mulwray had visited three reservoirs the day before and Walsh (Joe Mantell) shows him photographs of the engineer having a public argument with a man named Noah Cross (John Huston). Learning that today Mulwray is at Echo Park in a rowboat with a woman who is not his wife, Jake goes there and photographs the couple in the boat and later outside an apartment Mulwray rents, then leaks the story to the press. This brings the real Evelyn Mulwray (Faye Dunaway) to his office with her lawyer to sue him. Jake's still curious about the water angle of the case, so he goes to Mulwray's office and, finding he's not in, tells the secretary he'll wait in the engineer's office. Here he finds the book of plans Mulwray had at the riverbed, with the handwritten notation "Tues. night—Oak Pass Res.—7 channels used." Going next to the Mulwrays' residence, he notes a pair of eyeglasses with a broken lens in the backyard pond and, since Hollis is not there, informs Evelyn he wants to help her husband because whoever hired him is out to get Hollis. She tells him about two reservoirs Hollis habitually walks around during his lunch breaks. Jack goes to the Oak Pass Reservoir to find police guards telling him it's closed to the public, so he uses one of the business cards he took from the deputy chief of the Water and Power Department, Russ Yelburton (John Hillerman), to gain entry. He finds Lt. Escobar (Perry Lopez) on the scene and witnesses Mulwray being pulled out of the reservoir, his dead body rather beaten up since it looks like he was washed down the entire length of a runoff channel. At the morgue Jake learns that a local drunk drowned in the dry Los Angeles River's bed he made his home in. Visiting that site Jake sees the same boy on horseback Mulwray had spoken with and finds out they had talked about when the water comes, which is in different parts of the river every night.

That night Jake returns to the Oak Pass Reservoir and climbs the fence to get in. When he is shot at he takes cover in a runoff channel right before water rushes into it and slams him against a chain link fence. In writing about this scene in his autobiography, Polanski explained that because he wanted to do it in a single shot, a stunt double couldn't be used. When filming Nicholson held up a finger and called "One!" to him before the water gushed, hoping for one take, which indeed was all it took. It was a dangerous scene to film, so as Polanski notes, it was the last scene they filmed, "in case something happened."[57] Jake manages to climb over the fence and this natty dresser is annoyed that he's lost one of his Florsheim shoes, but worse is to come as a man in a white suit with bow tie and hat (Roman Polanski) calls out "Hold it there, kitty cat, hold it!" as he approaches, accompanied by Claude Mulvihill (Roy Jenson). With his usual smart-aleck attitude, Jake says, "Hello Claude, where'd you get the midget?" Claude punches him in the gut and the short man observes, "You're a very nosy fellow, kitty cat, huh? You know what happens to nosy fellows? Huh? No? Want to guess? Huh? No? Okay, they lose their noses," upon which he slits Jake's left nostril. "Next time you lose the whole thing," the man says, wiping off his knife, "cut it off and feed it to my goldfish. Understand?" Polanski explains that for this illusion he used "a hinge-tipped knife with a concealed tube down one side connected to a bulbful of blood" that he squeezed when he slashed.[58]

Jake gets a call from the woman who had posed as Evelyn, Ida Sessions, who gives him the tip to look in the obituary column of that day's *Los Angeles Post-Record* for the name of one of her employers. When Jake is in a restaurant perusing the newspaper, viewers see that the front page headline reads "Water Bond Issue Passes Council." He's invited Evelyn for lunch and says he thinks she's hiding something; when they leave the restaurant he wants to take her somewhere to continue talking, but she wants to go home. Informing her that her husband was murdered, he goes on angrily, "Somebody's been dumping thousands of tons of water from the city's reservoirs, and we're supposed to be in the middle of a drought. He found out about it and he was killed. There's a waterlogged drunk in the morgue—involuntary manslaughter if anybody wants to take the trouble, which they don't, it seems like half the city is trying to cover it up, which is fine by me. But Mrs. Mulwray, I goddamn near lost my nose, and I like it. I like breathing through it. And I still think that you're hiding something." Slamming shut the passenger door of his car that she wouldn't get into, he strides around to the driver's side and pulls away quickly.

He pays a call on Yelburton, whose secretary (Fritzi Burr) says he's busy, and he notices a photograph of Noah Cross on the outer office wall—he's recently learned that Evelyn's maiden name is Cross, so he's intrigued to learn more about the man. Jake parks himself in a chair and sets out to wear down the secretary by tapping a cigarette on its metal case, smoking, whistling, humming, then strolling around the office looking at photographs. Spotting one of Cross and Mulwray together, he learns from the secretary that Cross didn't work for the Water Department, he owned it. "You mean he owned the entire water supply for the city?" Jake asks incredulously. When affirmed, he asks, "How'd they get it away from him?" "Mr. Mulwray felt the public should own the water," she responds. "Mr. Mulwray?" he follows up. "I thought you said Cross owned it." "Along with Mr. Mulwray," she explains. "They were partners?" he pursues. "Yes, yes, they were partners," she explains annoyedly, then goes into Yelburton's office, coming out a few moments later to say he'll see Jake now.

Jake accuses Yelburton of hiring him to investigate Mulwray because the engineer opposed the dam. "He had a reputation that was hard to get around, you decided to ruin it," Jake postulates. "Then he found out that you were dumping water at night. Then he was, eh, drowned." Suggesting he'll go to the *Los Angeles Times* about the water dumping causes Yelburton to say Jake is making an outrageous accusation. He allows they have been diverting a little bit of water to irrigate orange groves in the Northwest Valley. Trying to come off like a good guy, he points out that the farmers have no legal right to their water, but they've been trying to help some of them out to keep them from going under, and naturally when water is diverted there's a little runoff. "Yeah, a little runoff," Jake says with sarcasm. He asks Yelburton whether he's a married man, is hard working, has a wife and kids, and says, "I don't want to nail you. I want to find out who put ya up to it. I'll give you a few days to think about it. Call me, I can help. Who knows, maybe we can put the whole thing off on a few big shots and you can stay the head of the department for the next twenty years." Taking his leave, he returns to his office to find Evelyn waiting for him. She wants to know why Hollis was killed. Money is the reason, Jake replies, but how they plan to make it out of empty reservoirs he doesn't know. Evelyn wants him to investigate for her. Jake asks a few questions to fill in some background and learns that she married Hollis after he and Cross sold the Water Department; she had just been in grade school when they did that. When Hollis and her father had a falling out over the dam that broke, they never spoke from that point on.

Jake meets a man at the Albacore Club and is taken to Cross' residence for a meal. "You've got a nasty reputation, Mr. Gittes. I like that," he says with gusto. Indeed, John Huston, director of what many critics consider the first film noir, *The Maltese Falcon*, is a fitting choice for this neo-noir and performs the role of a lifetime as Noah Cross, whose name is a veritable biblical word puzzle (the flood/water scam; the ark to keep the breeds going/incest with daughter; Christ on the cross/double cross/don't cross me). Cross continuously mispronounces the name as "Gits" despite Jake's correcting him, which says a lot about Cross' belief that his view of things should be the prevailing one. They discuss the murder case but Jake gets up to leave after Cross asks him if he's sleeping with his daughter. "You may think you know what you're dealing with, but believe me, you don't," Cross observes, causing Jake to smile. "Why's that funny?" Cross asks, and Jake explains, "It's what the D.A. used to tell me in Chinatown." "Yeah, was he right? Exactly what do you know about me? Sit down," Cross requests, which Jake does. Cross wants him to find Hollis' girlfriend, while Jake wants to know what he and Mulwray were arguing about in the photographs taken five days earlier. Cross claims it was about his daughter, again saying he wants Jake to fined Hollis' "girl." "Hollis Mulwray made this city, and he made me a fortune. We were a lot closer than Evelyn realized," Cross notes. Unsatisfied, Jake still wants to know what the argument was about. "Just find the girl," Cross reiterates, so Jake says he'll look into it after he checks out some orange groves.

At the County of Los Angeles Hall of Records' Real Estate Section, Jake discovers that most of the valley sold in the last few months. In an orange grove, Jake is shot at and pursued by the owner on horseback so he drives through the grove to escape, but his radiator and tire are shot and he crashes into a tree. Farm workers beat him up and the owner demands to know whether he's with the Water Department or the real estate office. Jake explains that he's a private investigator and a client hired him to see if the Water Department was irrigating his land. With disdain the owner says the Water Department has been sending people to blow up his water tanks and put poison down three of his wells. Jake shows him Evelyn's contract and gets into a fight with the farm workers. When he comes to Evelyn is there and the owner says they called his employer because he didn't look too good. As Evelyn drives Jake says, "That dam's a con job," explaining that they are conning Los Angeles to build it but the water is going to the valley, not the city. The farmers are being forced to sell their land at a low price. "Do you have any idea of what this land would be worth with a steady water supply? About thirty million more than they paid for it," Jake states. He's put together that one man named in the obituary column, Jasper Lamar Crabb, died two weeks ago, but he bought land one week ago. Following up his hunch, Jake and Evelyn go to the Mar Vista Rest Home and pretend to be looking for a residence for Jake's father in order to snoop around. Jake spots residents' names on the activity board and realizes their identities are being used to purchase land. In the activity room Jake notices a woman working on a quilt that has a piece of cloth from the Albacore Club's flag; her grandson is a member of the club. At this point the director of the rest home comes in to say, "We're a sort of unofficial charity of theirs, Mr. Gittes. Would you care to come with me, please? Someone wants to talk with you." Jake insists Evelyn go wait in the car. When Jake gets to the entrance he finds Mulvihill waiting for him, but Jake gets the jump on him and beats him up badly, then smoothly retrieves his hat before escaping from the man who slit his nose and other henchmen who shoot after them when Evelyn pulls up in her car, he jumps in, and they drive off.

At Evelyn's house they have drinks, she dabs his nose with peroxide, and the two end up in bed. During pillow talk, Jake, who used to be a police officer, says that Chinatown bothers everybody who works there because you can't always tell what's going on—Jake doesn't say it, but viewers know this is precisely the situation with the city's water supply. Jake said he had bad luck there: "I was trying to keep someone from being hurt, and I ended up making sure she was hurt." When Evelyn asks whether a woman was involved, Jake says, "Of course." "Dead?" she inquires, but the phone rings and he doesn't say. This conversation will have resonance for viewers at the end of the film. After the call Evelyn says she has to go but won't tell him where since she maintains it has nothing to do with all of this. Jake learns that Cross owns the Albacore Club and Evelyn says it's possible her father is behind all of this, even Hollis' death. Unbeknownst to her Jake breaks the taillight on Evelyn's car so that he can follow her easily in traffic. She drives to a house whose door is opened by the same butler, Kahn (James Hong), who works at the Mulwrays' home. Spying through the window Jake sees Evelyn giving medication to the young woman he knows as Hollis' girlfriend. When Evelyn comes out of the house she explains to Jake that the girl is her sister and she wanted Hollis to be happy. Tired, Jake goes home and tries to sleep but gets a phone call telling him Ida Sessions wants to see him; he says she can call him at his office. He's rung up again and given her address, told she's waiting. He goes first thing in the morning only to find her house has been broken into and she's dead on her kitchen floor. Lt. Escobar is there, Ida had photographs of Mulwray in the rowboat, and Jake tells him Mulwray was killed because they were dumping water in the ocean.

Jake goes to the Mulwrays' to find the maid (Beulah Quo) covering the furniture and Evelyn's luggage in the front hall. The gardener (Jerry Fujikawa) out back is complaining that the salt water in the pond is very bad for the grass, causing Jake to point out the broken lens he saw on his previous visit; the gardener retrieves a pair of eyeglasses that Jake assumes to be Hollis.' He next goes to the house where the girl is, finding luggage is being packed there too. Evelyn says they are leaving on the 5:30 p.m. train. Because he thinks she killed her husband he calls Lt. Escobar to come. Insisting he wants the truth, Jake demands, "Who is the girl?" Evelyn says her name is Katherine (Belinda Palmer). "Katherine who," Jake asks. When Evelyn responds, "She's my daughter," he slaps her and angrily says, "I said I want the truth." "She's my sister" earns her another slap, as does "She's my daughter"; "She's my sister, my daughter" causes Jake to slap her twice and push her roughly down on the sofa, where Evelyn finishes, "She's my sister and my daughter." Looking up at him tearfully she says, "My father and I ... understand? Or is it too tough for you?" "He raped you?" Jake asks, but she shakes her head no, and when he wants to know what happened after, she explains that she ran away to Mexico and Hollis came and took care of her. (That she later marries her father's business partner is another kind of incestuous relationship for viewers to consider, as well as Hollis' involvement with Katherine.) "I couldn't see her," she says; she was 15 and allows, "I wanted to but I couldn't. Now I want to be with her and take care of her." She plans for them to go back to Mexico. Jake tells her she can't take the train because Escobar will be looking for her. Trying to work out a plan for her escape, he suggests she go to Kahn's home in Chinatown. Before she goes upstairs to prepare, she informs him the eyeglasses he brought aren't Hollis' because he didn't wear bifocals.

After Evelyn and Katherine depart Lt. Escobar arrives and Jake says it looks like they were both too late and he thinks Evelyn's gone to her maid's house. Not trusting Jake, Escobar insists he come with them, but once there, Jake asks for a moment with Evelyn; Escobar agrees to three minutes. As a ruse Jake has brought them to Curly's house. He makes a deal with Curly to take him to Evelyn's for her luggage, then sends him to Kahn's in order to accompany Evelyn and Katherine to Ensenada. As another ruse Jake calls Cross to tell him he has the girl with him at the Mulwray house. When Cross arrives Jake informs him the girl is with her mother, shows him the obituary column, and accuses Cross of killing Hollis in the pond because he found Cross' bifocals in the pond. Cross explains to Jake and viewers what the private investigator has been trying to figure out. Mulwray knew that if you put water in sand and let it percolate down to the bedrock it would stay there instead of evaporate the way it does in reservoirs, so you'd only lose twenty percent instead of seventy or eighty. "He made this city," Cross says. "That's what you were going to do in the valley," Jake states. Cross corrects, "It's what I am doing." If the bond issue passes there will be eight million dollars to build an aqueduct to the reservoir. Jake observes that there are going to be a lot of irate citizens when they find out they're paying for water they're not going to get. "Oh, that's all taken care of," Cross waves this away. "Either you bring the water to L.A., or you bring L.A. to the water." "How you going to do that?" Jake wonders. "By incorporating the valley into the city. Simple as that," Cross concludes. Since Cross is already worth well over ten million dollars, Jake wants to know why he needs more money, what more can Cross buy? "The future!" Cross responds optimistically. "Now where's the girl? I want the only daughter I've got left. You found out Evelyn was lost to me a long time ago." "Who do you blame for that, her?" Jake asks barbedly. In what has to be one of the most repellant responses film viewers had to endure up to that point in cinema history, Cross responds, "I don't blame myself. See Mr. Gittes, most people never have to face the fact that, the right time and the right place, they're capable of anything. Claude, take those glasses from him, will ya?" Jake doesn't want to give them up, but Cross maintains, "It's not worth it, Mr. Gittes, it's really not worth it," and because Claude is holding a gun in his ear, Jake gives up the glasses. "Now where's the girl?" Cross asks unctuously.

With an abrupt cut viewers are taken to Chinatown. Jake is driving, with Cross in the passenger seat and Claude in the back seat, when they see Evelyn's Packard parked on the street. Jake's two operatives are waiting outside Kahn's, and Jake quickly sees they're handcuffed together right before Lt. Escobar walks up and tells Jake he's under arrest. "Good news," Jake says brightly, offering his right arm to be cuffed and telling Escobar that Cross is the bird he's after and he can explain everything if he's given five minutes. "He's rich and he thinks he can get away with anything," Jake begins. The two men try to talk over each other as Cross acknowledges who he is and that he's rich and Jake emphasizes, "He's crazy, Lou, he killed Mulwray because of the water thing." Not having it, Escobar instructs an officer to lock Jake to the wheel of the car. The maid, Kahn and Katherine come out to Evelyn's car and Cross approaches Katherine and tells her he's her grandfather, but Evelyn comes out and ushers Katherine into the front seat, telling her maid and Kahn to go with Curly and she'll follow them. "Get away from her!" she yells as she pushes Cross away from her car. "Evelyn please, please, be reasonable … how many years have I got? She's mine too," Cross oozes. "She's never going to know that," Evelyn declares, pointing her pistol at him to hold him at bay. Performing for the audience of police officers, Cross says, "Evelyn, you're a disturbed woman and you cannot hope to provide—," and Jake calls to her, "Evelyn, put that gun away, let the police handle this," eliciting Evelyn's response, "He *owns* the police. Get away from her!," the latter directed at Cross, who is at the passenger door, where Katherine is looking afraid of him. "You'll have to kill me first," he insists, causing Evelyn to shoot him in the shoulder. As she starts driving away Escobar commands "Halt!" and shoots twice into the air, then takes a low shot as if at a tire, but when he starts to aim a fourth shot higher, Jake springs forward and prevents him. The officer Jake is handcuffed to (one to whom Jake had made a rude sexual remark regarding his wife in an earlier scene) takes aim and fires three times at the car. A car horn sounds steadily and the car rolls slowly rather than accelerates. They all walk toward Evelyn's car, and Katherine is heard screaming. Jake opens the driver's door and Evelyn's body lolls out; she's been shot through the left eye from the back of the head. "Lord, oh Lord," Cross says, then covers Katherine's eyes, although she struggles to get away from him. Jake murmurs, "It still is possible." Escobar asks, "What's that? What's that?," then, to Jake's operatives, "You want to do your partner a big favor? Take him home. Take him home!" To Jake he insists, "I'm doing you a big favor…. Go home, Jake." Walsh speaks what has become a quintessential cinematic quotation, "Forget it Jake, it's Chinatown." Jake's look is fixed, unblinkingly, on Evelyn's dead body, but finally his operatives walk him off, one on either side of him. Escobar disperses the crowd of onlookers that has gathered around the car and two police cars drive up, bringing the film to its grim close.

Robert Towne's screenplay had ended with Evelyn killing her father and leaving with their daughter; Polanski came up with the ending viewers have. He didn't want good to triumph, feeling the film's "dramatic impact would be lost unless audiences left their seats with a sense of outrage at the injustice of it all."[59] Towne won an Academy Award for his screenplay, the only one *Chinatown* garnered out of eleven nominations. Polanski has gone on to make numerous films as an international director, including the acclaimed adaptation of Thomas Hardy's *Tess of the D'Urbervilles, Tess* (1979); *Death and the Maiden* (1994); *The Pianist* (2002), which he considers his best film, just ahead of *Chinatown*; and most recently, *An Officer and a Spy* (2019).

Lawrence Kasdan and *Body Heat*

Lawrence Kasdan's directorial debut, *Body Heat*, has a two-word, punch-hit of a title that evokes and brings to the foreground so much of the sultriness that bubbled below the surface of a classic noir like *Double Indemnity*, with which *Body Heat* shares the basic plot of a married woman seducing a single man in order to have him kill her husband so that she gets all of his money. However, designating *Body Heat* as a remake of *Double Indemnity*, as some critics have, diminishes Kasdan's achievement. He has said he likes film noir because of its extravagant language and the baroque freedom of the camera, and he finesses both in this film. Kasdan started as a screenplay writer; in fact, his work on *Star Wars: Episode V—The Empire Strikes Back* (1980) led to George Lukas sponsoring the script for his neo-noir project. Originally the setting was to be the Jersey shore, but a Screen Actors Guild strike caused shooting to be postponed so long that it was going to be winter, thus the story was reset in Florida, specifically the Lake Worth area. That year turned out to be the coldest winter on record in Florida, so the actors were sprayed down for scenes where they were supposed to be sweating heavily, much to their physical discomfort when these were exterior scenes.

As Ronald Schwartz notes in *Film Noir, Now and Then*, "One decided advantage to neo-noir ... is the revelation of sexuality as the true core of the motives for the protagonists to commit their crimes,"[60] and indeed, from the moment viewers meet Ned Racine (William Hurt), they know him for a man guided by his sexual drive. He's standing in his boxer shorts watching the Seawater Inn burn down from his apartment's balcony while the woman he's just had sex with is getting dressed and preparing to leave, but Ned approaches her for another go round, offscreen. Later scenes will be much more explicit. Kasdan has said that he wanted a woman editor, who turned out to be Carol Littleton, because he didn't want this highly sexual film to be a male fantasy, and Littleton's work conveys the sensuality of the film without being exploitative of either main actor.

Another thing viewers learn very early about Ned is that as a lawyer he isn't scrupulous about the clients he defends. He jokes in the opening scene that whoever torched the Seawater Inn was probably one of his clients, and in the next scene he's in court being admonished by the judge because his client was attempting to defraud the county. Later, he will meet with an older woman he's suing on behalf of for physical injury, a case viewers intuit is overstated. Ned's willingness to represent people who are, essentially, criminals is what leads to his being targeted by the film's femme fatale, Matty Walker (Kathleen Turner, cast partially for her vocal similarity to Lauren Bacall), whom Ned meets when he's listening to an outdoor evening concert at the Miranda Beach boardwalk. He watches as a woman in a white dress (that falls just below her knees and is reminiscent of 1940s fashion, only one of this film's many visual elements that evokes the glamour of classic film noir) gets up from the audience and walks toward where he is standing, but passes by without glancing at him. He follows her to the railing of the boardwalk where she is smoking and looking out at the ocean, and Ned tries to strike up conversation by saying she can stand there with him if she agrees not to talk about the heat. Her response is that she's a married woman and not looking for company. Ned replies that she should have qualified that she was happily married, and after a few more exchanges she asks, "You're not too smart, are you?" and starts walking. When Ned laughs and follows her, she states, "I like that in a man," revealing for viewers, in hindsight, that she intends to use him without his knowledge. "What else do you like?" the accommodating Ned inquires, "Lazy? Ugly? Horny? I got 'em all." After some banter, the dialogue settles into a classic noir come-on scene: "How 'bout I buy you a drink?" Ned offers, garnering, "I told you, I've got a husband," from her in return. "I'll buy him one too," Ned says quickly. The response "He's out of town" from Matty gains an immediate, "My favorite kind. We'll drink to him," from Ned. "He only comes up on the weekends," Matty says, unnecessary information unless she wants to entice him, which of course she does, and sure enough Ned replies, "I'm liking him better all the time. You better take me up on this quick. In another forty-five minutes I'm going to give up and walk away." Eschewing the drink, Matty consents to his buying her a cherry snow cone, which she spills on her dress after laughing at his joke that he only needs tending from a woman that night, not to get married, and when Ned heads off to get a paper towel for her, saying he'll even wipe it off, she asks, "You don't want to lick it?" Of course, Matty's gone when he returns from the men's room, but he's hooked from their flirting.

Having learned Matty lives in Pinehaven, he drives there the next day and returns to the bandstand the next night, but doesn't see her. Finally he tracks her down at the Pinehaven Tavern and after some conversation, Matty agrees that he can come to her house, but only to hear the wind chimes. When she slides her long legs out of her car in the driveway under Ned's watchful gaze, she deliberately grinds out her cigarette using the front part of her high-heeled shoe, silent enticement. They go into the house and up to the second-floor porch where multiple sets of wind chimes are hanging, and when Ned touches her neck she closes her eyes responsively, but moves away and asks him to go. Outside the front door, when she says she shouldn't have let him come, Ned asks, "You're not so tough after all, are you?," and she admits, "No, I'm weak," after which she kisses him on the lips and goes back in the house, closing the door and looking at him through its windows, then stepping back. He starts to leave but returns to the front door. When he looks in the windows of the

Ned (William Hurt) and Matty (Kathleen Turner) cool off on a hot night together in *Body Heat* (1981) (Photofest).

door to see Matty standing at the bottom of the stairs looking at him, one of cine-matographer Richard H. Kline's many beautiful shots has her image also reflected in the beveled glass of two of the central window panes' sides, so viewers see her full image in those central panes and two halves of her on either side, a triple temptress. The door is locked, as are the full-length windows Ned tries to open before pick-ing up a chair from the porch and shattering their glass. Once inside Ned rushes to Matty, and the two kiss and run their hands over each other, ultimately having sex on the stairs, and again in Matty's bedroom. And again another day in the boat-house. And another night in her bedroom, so many times they need to relieve their aching parts in a claw-foot bathtub to which they add ice.

One evening Ned arrives at Matty's and sees a woman from the back in the gazebo wearing a white dress similar to the one Matty had on the night they met. As he approaches the gazebo he calls out, "Hey lady, you want to fuck?" and the woman turns, revealing it's not Matty, to say, "Gee, I don't know. Maybe." Flustered, Ned apologizes, and shortly Matty arrives to hand a thick white envelope to her old friend Mary Ann (Kim Zimmer), who quickly departs.

Another night Matty and Ned are talking on the second-floor porch about all her husband's financial assets. Fog fills the screen, an appropriate cloak for their conversation because Matty admits she wishes her husband would die: "That's really what I want. It's horrible and it's ugly and it's what I most want." "That's where we're at, isn't it?" Ned poses, and when Matty asks, "What do you mean?," he replies,

"That's what we're both thinking—how good it'd be for us if he was gone. It'd be real sweet for us." Matty protests, "No, Ned, please don't, don't talk about it. Talk is dangerous. Sometimes it makes things happen, it makes them real." Ned assures her there's no reason to think her husband is just going to die, "It's not gonna just happen to make things nice for us. It won't just happen." He looks down, contemplative, obviously thinking about murder. There is an abrupt cut to the next scene where Ned is taking leave of one of his clients in prison. As the guard slams the bars shut while Ned is walking away he flinches at the harsh sound, no doubt thinking about himself being in prison if he murders Matty's husband. At the exact moment Ned flinches, the frame shows him surrounded by bars: the barred prison gate behind him to the left, a wall of barred shadows to his far left, the barred windows casting those shadows to his upper right, even the bars of a radiator are to his lower right in the foreground. In a nice noir touch, dust motes are evident in the angled sunlight coming into the corridor through the windows.

There is a dissolve to a shot of the ocean at night, then a jump cut to Ned and Matty on the beach, Ned observing that if Matty leaves her husband she will come out of the divorce all right since her husband is "ripe," but Matty reveals she signed a pre-nuptial agreement and after a year she won't get any money, and she wants to know if that matters to Ned. "The truth? I wish you were going to be loaded. Does it matter? No, *no*," he emphasizes. At this juncture Matty gives him a Fedora for a present. Ned puts the hat on at a jaunty angle and says he wants to see, so Matty offers "Here" and rolls up his car's window. His reflected face in the window as it rolls up replaces her actual one inside the car, a clever shot that Kasdan is rightly proud of.

On one of Matty's husband's returns home he brings his niece, Heather (Carola McGuinness), for a visit, leaving her to stay with Matty when he departs, so Ned and Matty can't be together. Unable to stay away, Ned shows up on Matty's porch at night wearing only jeans. Matty falls to her knees and unzips his pants, at which point Heather comes looking for her aunt and, shocked at seeing Matty with a strange man, runs off. The next morning Heather's mother comes to collect her.

Going to a restaurant for dinner Ned runs into Matty and her husband, Edmund (Richard Crenna), in the lobby. Matty pretends she doesn't know Ned's first name and fabricates that Ned had a client who wanted to buy their house. Edmund insists Ned join them for dinner; during conversation it's confirmed that Edmund is invested in The Breakers and other beachfront property for future development. When Matty goes to the ladies' room Edmund talks derogatorily about businessmen who want to get rich quickly without doing what's necessary, "Whatever's necessary," at which point the camera pans slowly from Edmund across Matty's empty chair and onto Ned as he replies, "Yeah, I know that kind of guy. I hate that. It makes me sick." When Edmund agrees "Me too," Ned emphasizes, "*I'm* a lot like that," and laughs, Edmund joining in so they are both laughing. When Ned looks at Edmund, Hurt briefly gets a maniacal look in his right eye before fastening his gaze contemplatively on the other actor. The next morning Ned runs on the beach and ends up at The Breakers, sitting to study it, hatching a plan as he has a smoke. In all the scenes where Ned runs he ends his workout by smoking a cigarette, commentary on his conflicted character, who has both preservational and destructive tendencies.

Matty is waiting in Ned's office when he returns at lunchtime one afternoon, and he closes the Venetian blinds to the outer reception area so anyone entering will not see them. Assuring him his secretary didn't see her Matty urges, "Ned, hold me. Please, just hold me. Oh God, I love you." She explains she was afraid to call him, and Ned emphasizes that she should never call him because the phone company keeps records. As they are talking Ned continues mentioning the need to be careful about the phones until Matty asks, "Why, Ned? What's happened?" "Because we're going to kill him. We both know that." While Matty stares at him, he asks, "It's what you want, isn't it? We knew it was coming! It's the only way we can have everything we want, isn't it?" Ned closes his eyes, his expression displaying an entranced rapture at holding Matty so closely. Then he says, "A man is going to die for no reason but we want him dead." When he asks if Edmund's will says she'll inherit half of everything, she mouths "Right." Suddenly, the office goes darker, and since neither of them has moved out of the proximity of the other long enough to close the blinds on the street windows, this was staged by a crew member to symbolize the darkness of their decision to murder Edmund. "Well, that's it then. That's it. We're gonna kill him. And I think I know how," Ned says. "It's real, then?" Matty asks, alluding to wording used in their previous discussion on the porch of Edmund's dying. "It's real all right, and if we're not careful, it's gonna be the last real thing we do," Ned replies firmly. At this point the camera backs away from the close-up on their embrace and keeps backing away and then up to the ceiling for a high-angle shot looking down on them, a perspective Kasdan has said represents God's point of view on their intended actions.

One night at Matty's she tries to convince Ned that the niece Heather should be cut out of Edmund's will, but Ned argues that nothing strange or out of the ordinary can happen in Edmund's life now because if it does it doubles the chance they will get caught. "You'll get half of everything he owns; it'll be plenty. No matter what it is, we're going to be satisfied," he reasons. "We're not going to get greedy. If we do we'll get burned." "You're right, darling," Matty seemingly assents. "I'm sorry. I know you're right." Because she claims she wants to take the risk with him, they're both doing this, Matty accompanies Ned when he goes to see one of his clients, arsonist Teddy Lewis (Mickey Rourke), but waits in the car. Repeat viewers realize Matty wants to know how to find Teddy to get another incendiary device for her scheme. Kasdan's script calls for Teddy to be listening to Bruce Springsteen, but the film uses Bob Seger's "Feel Like a Number," which makes commentary equally on Ned's situation as just another working drone who wants recognition as a man, his being a tool for Matty, and Edmund's being more than a statistic on a sheet, which is how he and Matty have been viewing him financially. Teddy tries to talk Ned out of committing arson, and as Ned sits on a sofa the camera settles on him at the end of the scene to reveal his trepidation about what he intends to do.

Ned and Matty plan for her to make sure Edmund goes downstairs at 2:30 a.m. on the night they intend to kill him. The day of the murder Ned goes to Miami to establish his alibi. He meets with a real estate agent about buying an empty lot and rents a car, parking it on the street. Right after, a clown driving a red car, the color of his own sports car, passes him; Ned stares at what will become, as revealed in his final scene of the movie, this symbolic image of himself. He valet parks his car at the hotel he checks into, further establishing his alibi. A jump cut to a close-up of a large spider web on the foggy grounds of Matty's house only accentuates Ned's situation. When Edmund says at 1:15 a.m. that he can't sleep and is going downstairs to get something to drink, Matty invites him back to bed by saying she can't sleep either, and delays him until 2:05 a.m. by having sex with him. "Are you trying to kill me?" he asks afterward, the irony of his question clear to Matty and viewers. He hears a noise downstairs, so gets a revolver Matty didn't know he had and heads there in his boxers, creeping slowly around the front hall entryway. When Edmund turns on a lamp Matty calls out "He's got a gun!" to warn Ned, but of course Edmund thinks she has seen the intruder and is warning him, so he asks "Where?" right before Ned bursts out of the closet and knocks the gun out of his hand. The two men struggle mightily; the plank Ned brought as a weapon has fallen just out of his reach, but he finally grasps it and hits Edmund fatally. A hand stretching towards something just out of reach is a classic element of Alfred Hitchcock's films noir, such as Bruno Antony (Robert Walker) trying to retrieve Guy Haines' (Farley Granger) lighter from a storm drain in *Strangers on a Train* (1951).

With Edmund's now-dressed body wrapped in plastic in the trunk of Edmund's car, Ned intends to take it to The Breakers and Matty is to follow after cleaning up the scene of the crime. There's a very heavy fog that causes Ned to run into some low tree branches he can't see in the driveway, accidentally hitting the horn and drawing unwanted attention to his vehicle. He almost plows into a passing car when leaving the driveway and then nearly gets hit by a truck he pulls in front of, two near accidents that would not be good to have with a dead body in one's trunk. At The Breakers, Ned leaves Edmund's unwrapped body, the bloody plastic, the plank, and a blanket he had covering the body in the trunk, sets the incendiary device, and drops a partially-down ceiling beam on Edmund's head to make it look as if that's the blow that killed him. Matty is waiting in the rental car and when Ned joins her tension about the getaway is raised when a patrol car comes by because the police are on time according to the nightly checks Ned has been making, but he is running late. He drops Matty off back at her house and reiterates, "We won't talk for a long time." As Ned drives off he looks at himself in the rearview mirror, thinking about what he's done, seeing himself as a murderer. There is a jump cut to The Breakers and the explosion, then a dissolve from that fire to Matty, standing on her porch in the fog, becoming alert to sirens in the distance; the scene ends with the slightest of smiles appearing on her lips.

At work Ned is trying to read a document but can't concentrate when he gets a call from a Miami lawyer, Miles Hardin (Michael Ryan), informing him that Mrs. Walker submitted a new will up there that Ned ostensibly wrote, and the camera on his face shows viewers that Ned knows he's screwed. After the other lawyer hangs up, Ned sits listening to the dial tone and staring into space for quite a while as he takes in what Matty has done. He asks his secretary to get her on the line, the camera settles on the Fedora Matty had given him on the hat stand, and he's told there is no answer at Matty's house.

Hardin has arranged a meeting among himself, Ned, Matty, and Edmund's sister, Roz Kraft (Lanna Saunders). To Ned's surprise, his lawyer friend Peter Lowenstein (Ted Danson) is there as well because he's handling the inquiry into Edmund's death on behalf of the County Prosecutor's office. The new will splits the estate equally between Heather and Matty, and it was witnessed by Mary Ann Simpson, who is now in Europe. Everyone save Lowenstein starts smoking when Hardin does, and the camera shows the cloud of smoke rising to the vaulted ceiling as the session continues. The problem lies with the way Heather's bequest is worded. "In writing the will," Hardin explains, "I'm afraid Mr. Racine violated what's known as 'the rule against perpetuities,'" which forbids an inheritance being passed down for generations indefinitely. Even though the will is technically incorrect, Hardin understood Edmund's intent, so he tried to enter it into probate, hoping the judge would not know much about estate law. The problem was, the judge Hardin encountered remembered problems with another will Ned had drawn up a few years prior and ruled this new one invalid, so Edmund died intestate. When Matty asks what happens now, the camera has her profile in a close-up shot, with Lowenstein out of focus in the background looking at her. Hardin asks, "You don't know?," and when she replies, "No, I don't," the camera goes out of focus on her and in focus on Lowenstein, scrutinizing her. Hardin suggests Ned explain it to her. "In the state of Florida," Ned lays out, "when a person dies without a will, and there are no children or surviving parents, then the spouse inherits everything." "My god," Matty says in awe, "You mean … it's all mine?" After Hardin notes that Edmund's intention was for Heather to benefit and Matty assents "Of course," Lowenstein swivels his chair away from her, mulling over the whole situation and giving a slight, enigmatic smile.

Outside Ned walks Matty to her car, telling her she looks good in black, then complaining, "You have really done it, Matty. You really have." She asks him to come to her house that night because she wants him more than ever, to which he replies, "I hope you haven't done us in." In the far background, Lowenstein executes one of the Fred Astaire dance moves he has performed in earlier scenes. Later that day Ned arrives home to find Lowenstein and another friend, Detective Oscar Grace (J.A. Preston), waiting for him. Grace wants to know how he got involved with Matty because she's poison, asking him too what he knows about Edmund's death. Ned replies only what he read in the paper, that it looked like arson, and Lowenstein says it was arson. Grace says he's more "interested in the grieving widow" as a suspect rather than Edmund's business associates, and Lowenstein notes Edmund's sister Roz is too. Both advise Ned to stay away from Matty, but Ned says he won't because she came on to him today and is about to come into a great deal of money, so he's going to accept her invitation to her place that night and intends to keep going there as long as she'll have him. "Ned," Lowenstein warns him, "someday your dick is going to lead you into a very big hassle. That lady may have just killed her husband." "Peter," Ned replies, "she's not going to inherit anything by killing me. Besides," he tries to joke, "maybe she'll try to fuck me to death." Lowenstein leaves, but Grace gives him a cautionary speech: "Ned, you've messed up before, and you'll mess up again, it's your nature. But they've always been small time. But this might not be. She's trouble, Ned, the real thing. Big time, major league trouble. Watch yourself."

The scene cuts to Ned and Matty on her bed, she revealing her past with drugs and how a lawyer got her clean; working for him is how she learned about invalid wills. She swears she wouldn't have used it if she had known about Ned's past case. Admitting she is greedy, crawling up on his naked body with hers, she continues, "I don't blame you for thinking I'm bad. I am. I know it. I'd understand if you cut me off right now. If you never trusted me again, you'd probably be smart. But you must believe one thing. I love you. I love you and I need you and I want to be with you forever." She's giving him direct warning to avoid her at the same time that she's luring him to stay with her. "They already think you're involved," Ned informs her. Reasoning there's nothing they can do, either they'll have the money or not, it's out of their hands, Matty tells him she fired the housekeeper so they can stay together as long as they want. Throughout the entire scene Ned looks at the ceiling rather than at Matty, despairing over the situation Matty has created with the new will. There is a jump cut to the waiting room of the police station, where Lowenstein settles Heather and her mother Roz in some chairs, then goes into Grace's office, where an angry Ned is speaking. He's upset that Grace is asking about his whereabouts on the night of Edmund's murder, but Grace says Ned's being at Matty's every night is drawing attention to him. Lowenstein reports that Edmund's glasses weren't at the arson site, whereas the man was a fanatic about having them with him, so it's looking like he was killed elsewhere. Grace notes that Heather caught Matty with another man and will be coming to tell her story. When Lowenstein says she's waiting outside, Grace offers Ned the chance to escape the aunt by slipping out the back way, but he says he'll go out the front way. Lowenstein watches as Ned speaks to Roz and Heather, the latter of whom appears to have no recognition of having seen Ned before. During their subsequent lunch at their usual hangout, Stella's Coffee Shop, Lowenstein reports to Ned that when Heather interrupted Matty and the man, his pants were down so he was mooning the girl, and she was so disturbed by the sight of the man's erection when he turned toward her that she didn't remember anything else about him except that his hair was slicked back, which Ned's was that night because he'd been in the ocean, but it's not his usual style, so he's relieved that Heather can't identify him.

The scene jump cuts to Ned banging his fist on the inside of the front door at Matty's, angrily confronting her about Edmund's glasses, worried that his fingerprints are on them and insisting she must have found them when she was cleaning up the murder site. But she swears she didn't and casts suspicion on the housekeeper, saying the woman had been acting strangely after Edmund's death, watching Matty and listening to her phone calls. She says she's worried about the two of them because Ned's first reaction was to accuse her, yet also informs him she'll be getting the money soon. "Soon it will be all ours. That's why we've got to stay together, Ned. It won't be long, and then we can get away from here, out from under all of this. All we have is each other. I'd kill myself if I thought this thing would destroy us. I couldn't take it," she claims. Ned walks over and hugs her to comfort her, pulling her tightly to him in the embrace.

A jump cut goes to Grace piecing together Ned's alibi in Miami by visiting the hotel and car rental place. The next scene shows Lowenstein performing one of his Fred Astaire routines at night on the pier, waiting for Ned to come along on one of his runs, and when he does, he lets Ned know that while he doesn't care who killed the unscrupulous businessman Edmund or gets rich because of it, Grace will feel compelled to do the right thing. He informs Ned someone repeatedly tried to call his Miami hotel room from 3:30 to 5:00 a.m. on the night Edmund was killed, but there was no answer. He also says someone is trying to give the County Attorney's office Edmund's glasses. After Lowenstein leaves, Ned continues smoking and looking over the pier railing despondently. By accident when he is in Miami the next day, Ned runs into the lawyer who had to sue him in the case where he wrote a bad will. The lawyer said he tried to make it up to Ned by referring Matty Walker to him, and Ned forcefully extracts from him that maybe he had told Matty they met because of that case. From these two encounters Ned knows for certain that Matty targeted him to use him and has been accumulating evidence against him for Edmund's murder.

Teddy Lewis, in jail, lets him know that a woman came to him saying Ned wanted another bomb and had him show her how to rig it to a door with a little delay. Since all of this is news to Ned, Teddy warns him to watch his step, who thanks him. "Racine, man, don't thank me yet," Teddy replies, "'cause, uh, these guys have been asking me about The Breakers. Hey, I ain't told 'em shit, but I don't like the look on their faces." From Miami Matty phones Ned at his office to tell him she's gotten the money, it's somewhere safe, and she negotiated to get Edmund's glasses back from the housemaid, who has left them in the boathouse, and Ned should retrieve them right away. A close-up on Ned as he receives this information, knowing Matty was the woman who went to Teddy for an incendiary device, reveals his stunned sadness. That night, Ned hesitates to open the boathouse door, leans agitatedly against its porch railing, then peers in the window and spies the wire of the device. He returns to the railing and leans over, taking in the realization that Matty truly intended to kill him.

A series of abrupt cuts elevates the tension as the film moves toward its denouement. Lowenstein sighs in Grace's office when Grace gets his gun out of the desk drawer and says, "Better go get him." At Matty's, Ned parks his car out back so it won't be seen and observes that Matty's car is hidden there too. He goes into the bedroom closet to get Edmund's gun. Grace is shown leaving the house Ned's apartment is in. Ned sits in the gazebo, smoking and drinking. Grace is delayed by a raised drawbridge along the Intracoastal Waterway. In the gazebo, Ned looks at his watch at 10:12 p.m., then Matty drives up in Edmund's car. She is wearing the same white dress as when they first met, and seeing that the main house is dark, she walks past the gazebo toward the boathouse, but when Ned appears in an arch of the gazebo, she walks up to him and says, "Hello, darling." "Hello, Matty," he replies. "Why didn't you turn the lights on?" she inquires; "I could see," he states simply. "It's all ours now," Matty assures him. "We could leave tonight if we wanted to. It's all over." "Yes, it is," Ned agrees, meaning something quite different. Just as he says this, her hand, which has been running down his arm in a caress, feels the gun in his hand, so she steps away from him. "Ned, what is that?" she asks. "It's Edmund's gun, you remember it, don't you?" he replies. "What is it, Ned? What's happened?" she asks, feigning innocence. "I think you know," he responds. Matty protests, "No, I swear I don't." "It's the glasses, Matty," he informs her. "Weren't they there? Didn't she bring them?" Matty queries. Ned says he didn't see them, pointedly suggesting maybe he missed them the way she had that night Edmund was killed. "Ned, I don't know what you're thinking, but you're wrong. I could never do anything to hurt you," Matty assures him. "I love you, you've got to believe that." Acerbically, Ned says, "Keep talking, Matty. Experience shows I can be convinced of *anything*." A cut shows Grace's car turning into the driveway. Matty admits, as Ned walks toward her and she backs up, "I did arrange to meet you, Ned. But that all changed. You changed it. I fell in love with you. I didn't plan that." Ned responds in amazement, "You never quit, do you? You just keep on coming." Matty implores, "How can I prove it to you? What can I say?" "The glasses, Matty," Ned suggests. "Why don't you go down there and get them?" "You said they weren't there," she objects. "I said I didn't see them," Ned corrects. Grace gets out of his car and spots them in the distance on the lawn, the light on Matty's dress and Nick's shirt making them glow in the darkness. "I'll go, Ned. I'll go and look for them," Matty says, turning and walking toward the boathouse, but just before the darkness would have swallowed her up, she turns back to him and says, "Ned, no matter what you think, I do love you," then she turns away and the light on her goes out as she disappears. The camera shows Ned in the foreground, light on the right half of him, and Grace in the extreme background, his full figure lit. Next a close-up shows Ned's torn expression, then he drops the gun and yells, "No! Matty!" and runs after her. The boathouse explodes and Ned drops to the ground, rolls, gets up, and runs, then walks, toward the burning boathouse.

There is a dissolve to an overhead shot tracking along a prison cell block at night. Just before the camera gets to a cell and looks down on a sleeping Ned, a slamming prison door is heard, hearkening back to the earlier scene before the murder when Ned had jumped at that sound. Ned suddenly opens his eyes, draws in a sharp breath, and exclaims, "She's alive." Grace visits him and Ned posits that Matty had been using Mary Ann's identity to land Edmund since her own past was sordid, and when Mary Ann found out, Matty had to pay her to keep quiet. Then she killed Mary Ann, put her body in the boathouse, and planned for Ned to die there too, so she would have no one looking for her. "It was so *perfect* and so *clean*," Ned says admiringly. "You find two bodies, me and this girl. Two killers dead. Case closed." "Do you hear what you're saying?" Grace asks. "It's crazy. This Matty would have to be one quick, smart brawd." "Oscar, don't you understand? That was her special gift. She was *relentless*," Ned says, laughing a little in amazement at her talent. "Matty was the kind of person who could do what was necessary. Whatever was necessary," he stresses, using the line Edmund had during their restaurant dinner together.

Time passes and a now-bearded Ned is handed his mail, a manila envelope holding a 1968 Wheaton High School yearbook. He finds the photograph of Matty Tyler; it's the woman he knew as Matty's friend Mary Ann. He turns pages and finds Mary Ann Simpson, nicknamed "The Vamp," who was on the swim team for two years (explaining how she escaped the grounds after triggering the boathouse explosion), and whose ambition was "To be rich and live in an exotic land." The camera pans up to her photograph, and the sound of wind chimes intertwine with the music as Ned looks at the face of the woman he loved and killed for. Her beaming photograph becomes superimposed in a dissolve to Matty's real, unsmiling face as she lies in a chaise lounge on a beach, palm trees and tropical flowers behind her. The camera revolves to show her in profile against the tropical mountains in the background. A male head and shoulder come into the lower left corner of the frame as he picks up a tropical cocktail and his voice says something in a foreign language. "What?" Matty asks. "It is hot," the voice translates. Likely the conversation takes her back to the night she met Ned and that subsequent hot summer together, for she sighs and replies, "Yes." Putting on her sunglasses, she sighs again and the camera moves in for an extreme close-up, still in profile, to show her blinking rapidly several times behind the glasses—perhaps to stop tears? Then the camera pans up to blue sky containing wispy clouds as the credits roll and John Barry's theme music continues, seeing the film out. The composer says he thought back to films of the 1930s and 40s, specifically Humphrey Bogart vehicles, as he devised it, and it works beautifully throughout the film, as does the intense theme used during tense scenes. In this final scene, which was filmed on Maui, according to Kasdan, Matty's expression is supposed to convey her ambivalence rather than triumph because she unexpectedly had developed feelings for Ned.

Body Heat redefines the femme fatale: the male protagonist clearly admires her skill in orchestrating her plans, and she gets away with her crime unpunished. At least, unpunished by the law. Viewers can take the stance that Matty is unsatisfied because she could not have both Ned and the money, if they choose to believe her when she tells Ned just before going to the boathouse that she does love him. It's certainly easier to believe her than to believe that Phyllis Dietrichson can't shoot Walter a second time because she suddenly realizes that she really does love him. Then again, even if Matty truly loved Ned, she did try to blow him up.

Kasdan has gone on to direct a number of memorable films, including his second feature, *The Big Chill* (1983), in which he cast Hurt as Nick, a character that could have been the slightly older and jaded Ned Racine, had he not gone to prison and had he served in Vietnam. Kasdan's subsequent films range in genre and include the Western *Silverado* (1985), the drama *Grand Canyon* (1991), and the romantic comedy *French Kiss* (1995), just to name a few.

Joel and Ethan Coen and *Blood Simple*

Ten years later, Joel and Ethan Coen's first feature film, *Blood Simple*, also would owe something to *Double Indemnity* and *Sunset Boulevard*. It opens with a voice-over by private detective Loren Visser (M. Emmet Walsh), who is dead, noting that down here in Texas, "you're on your own." Reaching back beyond Wilder's film *Double Indemnity*, the Coens made some use of James M. Cain's novel by the same name, as well as his first novel, *The Postman Always Rings Twice*. In interviews they readily credit hard-boiled detective fiction as inspiration, specifically mentioning authors Cain, Raymond Chandler, and Dashiell Hammett. When asked if they set out to create a film noir atmosphere in *Blood Simple*, Joel responded, "Not really. We didn't want to make a Venetian-blind movie."[61] Ethan added, "When people call *Blood Simple* a film noir, they're correct to the extent that we like the same kind of stories that the people who made those movies liked. We tried to emulate the source that those movies came from rather than the movies themselves."[62] And while the Coens were aware of the neo-noir films *Chinatown*, *The Postman Always Rings Twice* (1981), and *Body Heat* (1981),[63] Joel stipulates that their film merely uses movie conventions, so in that way it is about other films, "but no more so than any other film that uses the medium in a way that's aware that there's a history of movies behind it."[64] This is certainly an outlook any student in an Introduction to Film course learns: every movie made is influenced in some way by the movies that were made before it.

In *Blood Simple* the opening credits get wiped off the screen by windshield wipers on a car containing two people, a married woman and an unmarried man, about to become lovers (can any viewer see windshield wipers at night without thinking of Marion Crane driving away from her crime in *Psycho*?). The woman, Abby (Frances McDormand), says that her husband gave her a pearl handled revolver for their first anniversary and notes that she figured she'd better leave or she'd use it on him; thus the man, Ray (John Getz), is driving her to Houston. Suddenly Abby tells Ray to stop the car; a car stops behind them, then slowly pulls around them and passes. The rain, the contrast of light and shadows in this night scene, and a strange encounter on a lonely road are all features of classic noir. The Coens' use of lighting and washed-out color throughout the film gives it a black and white feel, while the camera angles and use of sound—such as ceiling fans over Marty's desk and in Ray's living room— also pull the film back toward the noir period. Abby is no Phyllis Dietrichson, but she does seem to stumble into an affair with one of her husband's bartenders, Ray, out of boredom and circumstance. One early review of the film criticizes Getz's and McDormand's performances, finding their physical relationship lacks electricity and passion, saying that "it's a tepid affair, and neither character has enough vitality to engage us" and that "Their low-watt rapport leaves a dark, empty space at the center of the film."[65] Certainly Ray's bland remark, "I've always liked you," when driving Abby toward Houston isn't a seductive declaration of love, or even attraction, yet this is exactly the point. That these two are not desperate to be together, not driven by unparalleled physical attraction and passion is what tweaks this neo-noir into a Coen brothers' original.

Unbeknownst to these two, Abby's husband, Julian Marty (Dan Hedaya), has hired a private detective to keep an eye on her infidelities, and after he finds her staying at Ray's house he contracts Loren Visser to kill them, who takes advantage of this secret employment by doctoring a photograph of the sleeping lovers to look like he has shot them, then shooting Marty once in the chest with Abby's revolver and making off with his "salary." Jeffrey Adams, in *The Cinema of the Coen Brothers: Hard-boiled Entertainments*, finds Hammett's figure of the Continental Detective Agency operative to have inspired the Coens' development of Visser's character. In contrast to noir detectives like Philip Marlowe, the hero of Raymond Chandler's fiction, "the Continental Op presents a much shadier, morally ambiguous figure operating on a porous boundary between crime and legality."[66] While pursuing criminals "he is not above certain kinds of misconduct, including illicit sexual affairs with clients, excessive alcohol consumption and, if necessary, occasional blunt, brutal violence, even murder—whatever it takes to crack the case."[67] Adams rightly points out that Visser "embodies an even more pathological version of Hammett's hard-boiled operator" who "shows no hint of conscience."[68] After Marty pays him for the "murder" of Abby and Ray, and right before Visser shoots Marty, he says that to have committed this kind of risky murder "I must've gone money simple," a play on the phrase "blood simple" that appears in Hammett's novel *Red Harvest* and that the Coens took for the title of their film. Several critics have interpreted Hammett's "blood simple" to mean the fear, panic, and/or foolish behavior that killers exhibit after they've murdered and applied it thusly to their interpretation of the Coens' film, which does indeed work. However, the nameless Continental Op in *Red Harvest* says about Personville, the town known euphemistically as Poisonville that he's taken upon himself to end the most recent eruption of violence in, "This damn burg's getting me. If I don't get away soon I'll be going blood-simple like the natives."[69] While he's had to kill before, he continues, "this is the first time I've ever got the fever. It's this damned burg. You can't go straight here…. Play with murder enough and it gets you one of two ways. It makes you sick, or you get to like it."[70] He goes on to say that getting enjoyment out of planning people's murders isn't natural to him, it's what Personville has done to him. Therefore "blood simple" can be taken to mean Marty's intent vengeance to have Abby and Ray killed (and their bodies destroyed in the incinerator out back of his bar, something that makes even Visser say, "Sweet Jesus, you are disgusting"); Visser's trying to clean up loose ends by killing Ray and attempting to kill Abby not when Marty pays him to, but subsequently when he thinks they have evidence to tie him to Marty's murder; and Abby's pinning Visser's hand to the windowsill with Ray's knife and later shooting at him through the bathroom door.

Viewers see that Visser has unwittingly left his engraved lighter on Marty's desk under the fish Marty had caught while out of town lying low while the "murders" were committed. As the ceiling fan slowly revolves the camera rises above it, giving viewers glimpses of Marty in between the rotating blades—ceiling fans in this film are essentially a stand-in for Venetian blinds. Having been unsuccessful at getting his two weeks back pay from Marty earlier, Ray lets himself into the bar and then into Marty's office after discovering the cash register is empty. He finds Marty and the revolver, accidentally kicking the latter and causing it to go off—making both himself and viewers jump—and immediately thinks Abby is the murderer, so he cleans up the bloody scene with comical ineptitude as a muffled version of "It's the Same Old Song" plays on the jukebox out in the bar, Ray's coworker Meurice (Samm-Art Williams) having come after hours with a date to entertain her. In the VHS release this song was changed out for "I'm a Believer." Both songs are wry commentary on Ray's relationship with Abby.

Another shot of the ceiling fan and Marty shows blood dripping out of his nose. Ray puts Abby's revolver in Marty's pocket, drags his body into the back seat of his car, and drives out of town to some fields for a secret night burial. His feelings at what he thinks Abby has done cause him to change the station to silence the radio evangelist to whom he had been listening.

Problem is, Marty isn't quite dead. Ray suddenly stops the car and bolts into a field, stopping to look back at the car, around him, then back at the car again—according to the screenplay, he had heard "faint, labored breathing" coming from the back seat.[71] When Ray returns to the car, he realizes Marty is still alive and has managed to get out of the car and start crawling along the road. Ray backs up his car but can't bring himself to run over Marty; he grabs a shovel but can't hit him with that either. Marty seizes Ray's ankle, and oncoming headlights force Ray to stuff Marty back into the car just before a truck passes—but not before Marty spews blood from his mouth over Ray's shoulder. Once Ray gets Marty into the shallow grave he's quickly dug, he shovels dirt onto him; yet again he can't bear to kill Marty directly, hoping instead he'll suffocate. When Marty, who had been squirming about, pulls the revolver out of his pocket and points it at Ray, Ray just stands there. Marty squeezes the trigger, but the gun only clicks. Ray takes the gun from him and frantically shovels dirt onto Marty as the latter slightly shakes his head "no" twice and puts up his hand to block the falling dirt. After packing the earth down over the grave, Ray waits until dawn to be sure Marty really is dead this time. His car won't start for several tries, another bit of tension borrowed from *Double Indemnity*'s post-murder scene. Driving back into town an oncoming car flashes its lights at Ray to alert him that his are unnecessarily on; when he passes it the driver cocks a finger at him like a handgun—maybe a typical Texan gesture of "on the mark, you got it," but certainly a grim reminder of Marty's leveling Abby's pistol at him graveside, as well as what he believes was Abby's attempted murder of her husband.

While Visser is destroying his doctored and regular photographs of Ray and Abby sleeping, he discovers Marty has kept a doctored one and that his lighter is missing. A ceiling fan revolves above his head as he looks for the lighter at Ray's house. The scene cuts to Ray sitting with one leg up on a table in the loft apartment Abby has rented. These two visual elements connect back to scenes where Marty had had his leg up on his office desk while the ceiling fan rotated, tying the three male characters together. Ray couldn't sleep and is surprised Abby could, telling her he knows what happened and acknowledging that they both did it for each other. Abby has no idea Marty is dead, confusing Ray when she gets a phone caller who says nothing, then hangs up on her, and she reports to Ray that it was Marty (it was Visser, calling from Ray's house). He thinks she's two-timing him and says he'll get out of her way, putting her revolver down before he leaves and noting that she left her weapon behind, meaning at the scene of the crime, but this only further confuses Abby. Such mistrust and lack of proper communication will continue to cause problems for these two.

After listening to a message from Marty on his answering machine saying a whole lot of money was missing from the bar safe—Marty's way of covering the $10,000 he paid Visser—Meurice suspects Ray and goes to confront him. Ray had quickly thrown a blanket over the back seat of his car as Meurice pulled up to his house and Marty's blood now seeps through it. Meanwhile Visser is trying to get into Marty's safe with a hammer when Abby arrives, so he hides in the bathroom while she observes the ransacked office. With the camera tight on her face the scene moves from the office to her lying back on her bed at night, a nice bit of disorientation for the viewer. She wakes, goes to the bathroom to wash her face, and hears someone enter her apartment. Calling "Ray?" she steps out of the bathroom and sees

Marty sitting on her bed. "Lover boy ought to lock the door," he says. "I love you. That's a stupid thing to say, right?" "I love you too," Abby says. "No," Marty replies, "You're just saying that because you're scared. You left your weapon behind," tossing Abby her scallop shell compact mirror. "He'll kill you too," Marty says before puking up lots of blood, at which Abby wakes for real. Viewers realize it had been a dream sequence, although given Marty's survival when Visser shot him, his tenacity at crawling along the road trying to escape Ray, and Ray's inability to kill him outright, it would not have been impossible to believe Marty had dug himself out of his shallow grave, which is why it's one of the more effective dream sequences in film.

Rushing to Ray's house the next morning Abby finds him packed and ready to leave town because he thinks that's what she wants. After she indicates she doesn't, he asks Abby if she wants to come with him. Thinking he's the one who ransacked Marty's office, she insists she needs to know what happened first, to which he replies he's been feeling sick, can't sleep or eat—"Abby, truth is, he was alive when I buried him." Ray means that Abby didn't quite kill Marty when she shot him; Abby thinks Ray fought with Marty at the bar and injured him. Each thinks the other is guilty of violence toward Marty. The two are standing on either side of Ray's screened front door during this discourse, and after Ray's last remark the morning paper hits the screen like a gunshot—a brilliant echoing of the shot Visser fired at Marty and the shot that went off when Ray kicked Abby's revolver when he found Marty's body. Ray doesn't even flinch, but Abby does, running out of the house only to see the blood-stained blanket on the back seat of Ray's car as she departs for Meurice's. Meurice assures her Marty is alive, that Ray stole money from him, and she should stay away from Ray because "the guy's gone nuts."

Ray returns to the bar's office, possibly looking for answers to Meurice's accusation of his stealing money from the safe. What he finds in the safe is the doctored photo of him and Abby looking like they've been shot to death. Viewers are shown that Visser's lighter is still under the fish on the desk. Ray spies Visser's car down the street when he leaves the bar, which had been the car that had passed him and Abby the night he was to drive her to Houston but instead took her to a motel to begin their affair, a night Visser had chronicled photographically for Marty.

Blood Simple is anything but a simple film, and it comes to a close worthy of Hitchcock. Ray is looking out of Abby's loft window in the dark when she returns home and turns on a light, which he orders her to turn off because there are no curtains. "What will people see?" Abby asks suspiciously. "If you do anything the neighbors'll hear." "You think—" Ray begins, surprised she thinks he means to do her harm. "Abby, I meant it when I called," he assures her, referring to the "I love you" he had expressed when calling from a phone booth the morning after he buried Marty. "I love you too," she replies. "You're scared," Ray says, walking toward her, whereupon a shotgun blast through the window kills him. She jumps out of the way and a second shot is fired, then she uses a shoe to break the light bulb suspended from the ceiling, plunging the room into darkness as protection. There's a scene in Hammett's *Red Harvest* that bears a striking resemblance, when the Continental Op enters his hotel room, snaps on the light, and is shot at from the office building across the street, the bullet hitting the door frame. More bullets riddle the frame, door, and wall after he retreats to a corner, so, he explains, "I looked around for something to chuck at the light globe, found a Gideon Bible, and chucked it. The bulb popped apart, giving me darkness."[72] The Coens might have taken inspiration from this, including the bullet riddling of the wall and door about to come in their final scenes.

As footsteps are heard slowly climbing the stairs toward her apartment, Abby gets Ray's knife from his pocket and goes into the bathroom. Viewers watch as Visser enters the apartment, searches Ray fruitlessly for his lighter, and enters the bathroom to discover Abby has crawled out its window and into the apartment next door. Visser reaches his arm out of the bathroom window across to the other window. In a tour de force sequence, Abby slams down the window and puts Ray's knife through his hand, pinning it to the windowsill; Visser punches the wall, shoots holes in it until he is out of bullets, then punches through the wall to take the knife out of his own hand. Returning to her apartment Abby picks up her revolver that Ray had left and moves toward the bathroom; creaking floorboards alert Visser to her presence. While the bathroom sink drips as it had in every previous scene including it, he puts his hat on. Abby looks at Ray's body; Visser walks toward the bathroom door. Abby shoots Visser through the bathroom door and shouts, "I'm not afraid of you, Marty!" Visser laughs and replies, "Well, ma'am, if I see him, I'll sure give him the message." The last shot is from Visser's perspective lying on the bathroom floor—a drop of water beads up and falls toward him from under the sink; the screen goes black and the credits begin to roll. *Blood Simple* is convincingly seedy and gritty, but also highly theatrical. While there are noir aspects to several subsequent Coen brothers' films—*Miller's Crossing* (1990), *Barton Fink* (1991), *Fargo* (1996), *The Big Lebowski* (1998)—*Blood Simple* is their first foray into the genre, and a roundly successful one at that.

Like dada, film noir is a free-floating entity, its own sovereign self, open to use by all. Everyone—the common schnook, whether portrayed by Fred MacMurray, Jack Nicholson, or William Hurt—gets entangled in webs of perversion, a black widow clinging to his cheek. The camera both celebrates and subverts the narration, complicating the situation even as it documents. From its roots in German Expressionistic cinema to some of today's postmodern murder mysteries, noir embodies a leather-bound frailty, hard-boiled but soft-shelled. The next chapter will delve into particular directors who craft the essential elements of film noir into poetry on the big screen.

Two

All the Guys with Eye Patches

Hard Bitten Film Noir

Film noir is by nature coarse, even harsh, but this chapter will look at how certain directors unearth a uniquely American visual poetry in their treatment of sex, violence, and betrayal. Howard Hawks' adaptation of *The Big Sleep* (1946) curbs Raymond Chandler's verbiage while emphasizing its delirious momentum. In *Pickup on South Street* (1953), Samuel Fuller deepens and enlarges his tabloid story through a keen, often startling, grasp of composition and editing, as when the camera pans to a Victrola during a murder and a ballad plays, punctuated by a pistol shot. Noir goes out of the city in *They Live by Night* (1948), with Nicholas Ray making a leitmotif out of the fugitives' car on the rural open road. Orson Welles' *Touch of Evil* (1958) uses dizzying angles and multiple cuts to convey moral and physical degeneration in his most complicated tirade on the abuses of power.

Raymond Chandler, Howard Hawks and *The Big Sleep*

In his 1944 essay "The Simple Art of Murder," Raymond Chandler observes that "classic" English detective stories (those written by Dorothy Sayers and Agatha Christie in particular) don't "really come off intellectually as problems, and they do not come off artistically as fiction. They are too contrived, and too little aware of what goes on in the world."[1] In contrast, American writer Dashiell Hammett "gave murder back to the kind of people that commit it for reasons, not just to provide a corpse; and with the means at hand, not with hand-wrought dueling pistols, curare and tropical fish."[2] Of key importance, Hammett captured the way these people spoke. Chandler prefers a realistic portrayal of a flawed world, and conceives a detective figure he describes in terms that are readily applicable to his own Philip Marlowe, writing, "down these mean streets a man must go who is not himself mean, who is neither tarnished nor afraid," a common yet unusual, honorable man who earns his money honestly, will not suffer insolence from others, and speaks like a man of the times.[3]

Chandler was American-born and English-educated, had worked as a journalist, and held an executive position with an oil company before turning to the writing of detective fiction. After publishing short pieces, his first novel was *The Big Sleep* (1939), which was crafted out of two of his short stories, "Killer in the Rain" (published in *Black Mask* in January 1935) and "The Curtain" (published in *Black Mask* in September 1936). His notable contributions to the crime novel were the urban setting, specifically Los Angeles; tough, pithy, colloquial dialogue; melodramatic action; double plots, described by Stephen Knight as consisting of an outer plot of corruption and crime and an inner plot of betrayal and personal threat to private investigator Philip Marlowe[4]; Philip Marlowe himself, a loner who is moral, cynical, and ironic; and depiction of the modern "mechanised urban anomie," whereby society provides little moral guidance to individuals.[5]

Philip Marlowe is one of Chandler's greatest contributions to the genre. Knight observes that no matter what, Marlowe "still pulls himself together and acts when he must."[6] Mostly this is pedestrian, as when the P.I. goes to bed after drinking too much whiskey and must overcome a hangover to appear at the Hall of Justice. He's a smart-aleck, responding to Vivian Regan's (nee Sternwood) criticism of his manners by agreeing that they are bad and noting, "I grieve over them during the long winter evenings."[7] He's droll: upon finding Arthur Gwynn Geiger's lifeless body and a doped-up, naked Carmen Sternwood whom Gieger had been photographing, he thinks that shooting Gieger was someone's "idea of how the proceedings might be given a new twist," specifically that of the person he had heard fleeing the scene, and of that exit he thinks, "I could see merit in his point of view."[8] He has integrity—when General Sternwood notes he's revealing family secrets, Marlowe assures him they will remain secrets.

In the context of discussing the racist, murderous, criminal character Moose Molloy in Chandler's second novel, *Farewell, My Lovely* (1940), Fredric Jameson allows, in an assessment he places in parentheses, that "Chandler faithfully gives vent to everything racist, sexist, homophobic and otherwise socially resentful and reactionary in the American collective unconscious, enhancing these unlovely feelings—which are, however, almost exclusively mobilized for striking and essentially visual purposes, ... for aesthetic rather than political ones—by a homosexual and malebonding sentimentalism that is aroused by honest cops and gangsters with hearts of gold...."[9] Whereas Jameson sees Chandler's purpose as aesthetic, Chandler's most recent biographer, Tom Williams, looks at charges of the writer's racism, homophobia, repressed homosexuality, and misogyny and provides "ample material upon which to build a case for all of these," yet "decided to resist the temptation to interrogate such attitudes," nor has Williams "spent time on the excuse that they are merely the product of a particular era," choosing to let readers make up their minds on these matters.[10] Certainly, to this reader today, Marlowe—and Chandler—exhibits a homophobia that is rather off-putting. He exploits the stereotype, using a high-pitched, twittering voice and donning horn-rimmed glasses in Gieger's bookstore to pretend he's gay while investigating: "If you can weigh a hundred and ninety pounds and look like a fairy, I was doing my best."[11] He marks Gieger as a homosexual because of his home's décor, which "had a stealthy nastiness, like a fag party"; calls Gieger a "queen" and a "fag" to Carol Lundgren, Gieger's lover; and says of Lundgren's punch, "a pansy has no iron in his bones."[12]

Marlowe's interactions with straight men bear analysis as well. He has a professional relationship with the chief investigator for the District Attorney, Bernie

Ohls, who throws work Marlowe's way and invites him to the scene when the Stern-woods' chauffer Owen Taylor turns up dead in their car, which had been driven off a pier. Ohls doesn't want to pry into what Marlowe is investigating for General Stern-wood, merely asking whether it involved Taylor, and in return Marlowe requests that Ohls leave the General out of his case if possible. Marlowe's relationship with D.A. Taggart Wilde is professionally amiable as well, although Wilde will stand up for his police officers when Marlowe makes a general crack about their being quick on the trigger. Captain Cronjager is another matter: Marlowe takes an instant dislike to him. Whereas Wilde's expressionless eyes somehow convey friendliness, Cronjager is "a cold-eyed hatched-faced man … as hard as the manager of a loan office" who "looked ready for a fight."[13] Ohls, Marlowe, and Cronjager spar throughout their scene together trying to sort out the recent deaths and their possible relation to the Sternwoods. After Ohls and Cronjager leave the D.A.'s office, Wilde and Marlowe have a respectful, supportive conversation about the case, with Wilde commenting on their now speaking man-to-man without him having to growl at Marlowe, sug-gesting some of his performance in front of Cronjager was just that.

Not surprisingly, Marlowe doesn't care much for the criminals he encounters, such as Joe Brody, who pinched Gieger's for-rent pornographic books after his mur-der and waves a gun in Marlowe's face, but he realizes he can manipulate Brody into giving up the photographs of Carmen. In fact, after an acrobatic scene in Bro-dy's apartment in which Carmen, Brody, Geiger's bookstore clerk Agnes, and Mar-lowe tussle in various combinations, Marlowe ends up with everyone else's gun, the photographic plate, and the prints made from it. He even feels a bit sorry for Brody, telling him he's dumb and only thinks he's smart. But Marlowe feels genuine pity for Harry Jones, a self-labeled grifter connected to Brody who follows Marlowe and tries to sell him the information that Mars had Regan killed. Marlowe takes note of Jones' small stature and how he tries to make his eyes look hard but can't, thinking he could toss him like a baseball; Jones is "A small man in a big man's world. There was something I liked about him."[14] When Marlowe goes to meet Jones in order to be taken to Agnes, who will tell her story about Mona Mars' whereabouts, he overhears a hit man talking to Jones and extracting Agnes' address from him; after the hit man leaves Marlowe enters the office and finds Jones poisoned. "You died like a poisoned rat, Harry, but you're no rat to me," he says to the corpse, having discovered Jones gave a false address to protect Agnes.[15]

Racketeer Eddie Mars is more of a force to be reckoned with than Brody or Jones, definitely one of the big men in a big man's world. Marlowe's first sight of him causes him to think how hard he looked. The two of them exchange rapid-fire ques-tions when Mars shows up at Gieger's house while Marlowe is looking for the pho-tos of Carmen, Marlowe holding his own even as Mars holds a Luger. When Mars orders him to open the door and admit his henchmen, Marlowe tells him to open it himself because he doesn't take orders from him. Marlowe shares some of his spec-ulations as to Geiger's murder, but he's not offering up information on the missing books because he's still protecting the Sternwood family as his clients. He even gets in a barb about Mars' missing wife Mona, possibly run off with Regan, by asking him how Mrs. Mars is doing.

But the real menace, Marlowe comes to realize, turns out to be Lash Canino, a man whom Mars hires for his dirty work, such as hiding Regan's body when Vivian asks Mars for help after her sister Carmen killed Regan (Carmen turns out to be mentally unstable in all sorts of ways, attempting to murder men who turn down her sexual advances being one. She tries this with Marlowe near the end of the novel, although he wittingly loaded her gun with blanks). Marlowe first comes face-to-face with Canino after he's witnessed him kill Harry Jones, so he's alert when he follows Jones' information and goes into the auto repair shop next to the house where Mona Mars is being hidden to see about getting two fortuitously occurring flat tires repaired. (In the film, Marlowe [Humphrey Bogart] lets air out of the tires' inner tubes to fake flats, making him a more resourceful sleuth.) He pretends to be an out-of-towner, but Canino and the mechanic jump him, and Marlowe comes to in the house alone with Mona, whom Eddie hid to make the police think she ran off with Regan rather than Eddie having killed Regan. (Both Mona [Peggy Knudsen] and Vivian [Lauren Bacall] are at the hideaway house in the film, affording the romantic relationship between Vivian and Marlowe opportunity to grow.) Mona unties Marlowe, who waits outside to ambush Canino when he comes out looking for him after Canino shoots from a window and Marlowe fakes being hit and dying. Canino uses Mona as a shield when he approaches the car he suspects Marlowe had been in, she screams that she can see him behind the wheel, and Canino thrusts her aside and shoots into the vehicle. But Marlowe had been crouching behind the car and asks whether Canino is done, whereupon Canino turns toward him and Marlowe shoots him fatally four times. In the film, Vivian is the human shield and she and Marlowe drive off together in Canino's (Bob Steele) car, permitting a scene in which Marlowe thanks her for helping him escape, to which she replies, "I guess I'm in love with you," eliciting the same line from Marlowe after she has said she can't go to the police with him because she'd have to tell them she killed Regan. Still trying to protect the Sternwoods, Marlowe wants answers from Mars (John Ridgely), so the two go to Geiger's (Theodore von Eltz) and lure Mars there. It's revealed that Carmen (Martha Vickers) killed Regan because she liked him, but Regan had refused her because he liked Mona Mars. Eddie Mars had Regan's body hidden and blackmailed Vivian for silence about Carmen's murder. Knowing Mars' men are waiting outside, Marlowe shoots off his gun a few times and forces him out the front door; his own men gun him down without realizing who he is. Marlowe wraps things up by calling Ohls (Regis Toomey) to inform him Mars killed Regan, telling Vivian she has to send Carmen away to be cured, and advising her to tell her father the truth about Regan's disappearance. "You've forgotten one thing," Vivian reminds him, "Me." "What's wrong with you?" Marlowe asks, to which she rejoins, "Nothing you can't fix," as police sirens are heard approaching and "The End" flashes on the screen.

Unlike Bogart's Marlowe, the encounters Chandler's Marlowe has with women have caused some speculation as to his concepts of femininity and masculinity, his comfort or discomfort with sexuality. Knight finds Marlowe "quite likes professional, competent women with an apparently reduced sexuality," "feels tenderly toward downtrodden mousy girls," and "is distinctly bothered by overt sexual advances."[16] Regardless of the woman (or man, for that matter), Chandler

Marlowe (Humphrey Bogart) affects homosexuality in front of bookstore clerk Agnes (Sonia Darrin) in *The Big Sleep* (1946) (Warner Bros./Photofest).

has Marlowe catalogue the character's physical appearance, and an appraisal always accompanies this description. When Marlowe first sees Carmen, he notes that she looks good in the light blue pants she's wearing; Vivian's silk-stocking-clad legs invite being stared at because of their long, slim ankles and beautiful calves; and Geiger's bookstore clerk, Agnes, has elongated thighs and approaches Marlowe "with enough sex appeal to stampede a businessmen's lunch"[17]—and this is precisely when Marlowe starts lisping in his gay affectation.

Seeking information about Gieger from the clerk of a nearby bookstore, Marlowe appraises this woman as having delicate, intelligent facial features. She looks up information in a reference book that confirms Marlowe's suspicion that Gieger's clerk is no book specialist because it contradicts what she had told him, and she provides a detailed description of Gieger, which leads Marlowe to assess she'd be a good cop. He thanks her and leaves the store as rain begins. But in Hawks' movie, this clerk is flirtatious, pulls out a bottle of rye and closes the shop in the rainstorm, leading Marlowe to say, "I'd a lot rather get wet in here." End of scene, and when it resumes, Marlowe is departing from the shop with a "So long, pal." Clearly the viewer is to fill in the missing frames with a dalliance. Todd McCarthy claims, "Hawks decided that one of the ways his Philip Marlowe would differ from Chandler's was that … he would be more sexually aware and available."[18] This is apparent in Marlowe's encounters with this clerk in the Acme Bookstore (Dorothy Malone), Carmen, a librarian (Carole Douglas), Agnes (Sonia Darrin), a woman taxi driver

(Joy Barlow), hatcheck and cigarette girls at Eddie Mars' joint (Lorraine Miller and Shelby Payne), Mona Mars, and of course, the divorced Vivian Rutledge.

In the novel Marlowe returns to his apartment one evening to find a naked, giggling Carmen in his bed. (In the film, she's fully clothed and sitting in a chair—Hays Code alterations.) The scene goes on for several pages, but basically Marlowe tells her to get dressed and leave what he reviews in his mind as his private sanctum; when she finally does he rips apart the bedclothes, waking the next morning to think that hangovers can be caused by more than alcohol, such as women, who make him sick. Besides Carmen, Marlowe had had to contend with Vivian the night before, parking by the sea for a while when bringing her home from Eddie Mars' Cypress Club. He sits with his hands on the steering wheel and it is Vivian who calls him a beast and instructs him to embrace her. She more or less invites herself to his apartment, but Marlowe says while he likes kissing her, he wasn't hired by her father to sleep with her, so he keeps asking her what Eddie Mars has on her. Vivian retorts that he's a son of a bitch, and although Marlowe declares he's as warm blooded as any man and isn't blind to her appearance, he maintains that he's working as a detective, not playing. Before they part, though, he tells her twice that he liked kissing her. In Hawks' film, Marlowe is the instigator in the parking scene. He tells Vivian he likes her father and another Sternwood. "I wish you'd show it," Vivian invites. After he kisses her she says, "I like this. I'd like more," and after he obliges, she says, "That's even better." As in the novel, Marlowe still wants to know what Mars has on her, and when she refuses to say, he drives her home as she requests.

A more puzzling encounter in the novel is that with Mona Mars. When he first sees her Marlowe's description is perfunctory, fact-filled about where she is sitting, what she is wearing, and what she is smoking and drinking. No assessment of her looks, as with the other women he meets. When he gets around to this, the first thing he admires is her hand, which is shapely and small. He's been beaten and tied up by Canino, so he asks Mona for some of her drink; as she bends over him he thinks, "Her breath was as delicate as the eyes of a fawn," a really nice mixed sensory description on Chandler's part.[19] As she bends over him again, his blood begins to stir, possibly from her nearness, possibly from the stimulating alcohol, but whichever the cause, he flirts. They converse as Marlowe tries to fill in details of his investigation and Mona defends her husband, Eddie. For whatever reason, she cuts Marlowe's ropes and he's able to stand up, but is still handcuffed, so he stands near her and asks her to light him a cigarette; inches apart, he softly says, "Hello, Silver-Wig," the name he will continue to call her because she is wearing a platinum blonde wig to alter her looks while hiding.[20] For their last "conversation," Marlowe presses his body against hers as her back is against a wall and kisses her hard. (In the film Vivian is the lighter of Marlowe's cigarette and his kissing partner, after which she fulfills his request that she get a knife and cut the ropes binding him.) The rest of the book explains away the mystery surrounding Regan's disappearance, with Marlowe thinking what did it matter whether his body had been in a dirty oil sump, "You just slept the big sleep," uncaring about what killed you or where your body was.[21] Marlowe has no thoughts of Mona until the final paragraph, when he stops for drinks at a bar and starts thinking of her, then the book ends with him saying he never saw her again. Perhaps Mona's allure for Marlowe is her unavailability, her steadfast devotion and loyalty to her husband, and that she is what Captain Gregory of the Missing Persons Bureau describes as a nice girl who wouldn't play games, with which Marlowe agrees. Mostly though, readers are puzzled by Marlowe's sudden and unshakable obsession with Mona.

The plots of three of the movies treated in this chapter—*The Big Sleep*, *Pickup on South Street*, and *Touch of Evil*—make little sense, but that's compensated for through the filmmaking. For instance, working on *The Big Sleep*, the screenwriters (William Faulkner, Leigh Brackett, and Jules Furthman) got so confused that they contacted Chandler to ask who killed the Sternwoods' chauffer, Owen Taylor (Dan Wallace), and he couldn't say. Howard Hawks dealt with that murkiness through the steadiness of his editing—if the camera was sure, the story must follow. He shot largely in sequence, making Humphrey Bogart a special effect unto himself. Bogart shapes his characterization of Philip Marlowe as he might have a stage performance, building from an edgy but accommodating shamus, a guy trained to expect the worst in everyone, to a desperate man unhinged by the betrayals closing in around him. Likewise, Marlowe's disarming wit, capable of seducing women in sixty seconds or your money back, gradually sours and curls inward; by the third act, he's biting his lines short as if the words are poisoning him. In the course of this transformation, the camera serves as a kind of disinterested observer, a second shamus waiting to see how all the sordid details play out. Throughout the film we see a gradual disintegration of Marlowe's rational persona. It begins with him pulling on his earlobe and progresses to him holding his aching back, especially toward the end, when Bogart clearly is changing his physical mannerisms.

Hawks directed films in a variety of genres—indeed, as Gerald Mast writes in *Howard Hawks, Storyteller*, "It is impossible to discuss the power, value, richness, and importance of American genre film and American film genres without reference to at least a half-dozen of Hawks's films, which seem the ultimate embodiments of those genre aspirations and that same tradition...."[22] *Barbary Coast* (1935) presents an historical drama, *Bringing Up Baby* (1938) is the ultimate screwball comedy, *Sergeant York* (1941) is an acclaimed biographical war drama, and *Gentlemen Prefer Blondes* (1953) delivers a light romantic comedy, to name a few genres and films. There are Hawksian touches on his films noir. When Marlowe goes to the offices of Walgreens Insurance, he enters the establishment's outer office and sees Harry Jones—"Jonesy"—(Elisha Cook, Jr.) and Eddy Mars' hit man Canino talking in an inner office. They are silhouettes on a frosted glass window; their muffled speech gradually grows louder and clearer as Marlowe steps closer to the inner office door. Hawks had previously used frosted glass in *Scarface* (1932). Here, the effect emphasizes Marlowe's challenge to figure out what is occurring between the two men, which turns out to be Canino's trying to extract Jonesy's girlfriend Agnes' whereabouts. Hawks moves from having the camera offer Marlowe's perspective to letting viewers witness their conversation firsthand. Canino draws a gun on Jonesy, remarking about his startled expression, "What's the matter, Jonesy, ain't you never seen a gun before? You want me to count to three or something, like in a movie?" Jonesy gives up Agnes' address (actually, a false one), after which Canino says, "You're nervous, ain't you? Maybe you need a drink…. You got a glass?" "Yeah, there at the water cooler," Jonesy tells him, and as Canino walks toward the cooler to get it, viewers see Marlowe peering around a file cabinet to get a look at him. Then the camera returns to Marlowe's perspective as Canino's silhouette moves from the frosted glass, Marlowe sees him clearly through the unfrosted glass of another of the inner office's windows, Canino takes the glass from the cooler, then walks back across the office and is transformed into a silhouette again. At this point Hawks has the camera reenter the inner office and viewers watch Canino hand Jonesy the glass, saying, "Well, drink it. What do you think it is, poison? I'll bet that Agnes of yours wouldn't turn it down." "No, I guess she wouldn't," Jonesy admits, downing the liquor and laughing. "What's funny?" Canino asks; "Nothing's funny," Jonesy replies. With a "So long, Jonesy," Canino leaves, and Marlowe rushes into the room as Jonesy drops the glass and slowly falls out of his chair to the floor dead, poisoned. Hawks' changing of the camera's perspective and the layering of offices adds mystery and tension to the entire sequence. Other interior scenes emphasize claustrophobia, such as Geiger's overly-decorated house or the steamy greenhouse in which Marlowe first meets General Sternwood (Charles Waldron). Most exterior scenes occur at night and contain fog, suggesting a closed-in world that is shrouded in mystery. Rain might pour down, adding another element Marlowe has to deal with in his pursuit of truth. Notwithstanding its flaws, *The Big Sleep* contains some poetic visuals and is an important film in the canons of Hawks and film noir.

Samuel Fuller and *Pickup on South Street*

One of the crucial things about Samuel Fuller's movies is his own, unique hyperactive camera style, a cinematic equivalent of the pulp fiction of the time by Mickey Spillane and Jim Thompson. Martin Scorsese observes that Fuller's films contain "a great deal of sophistication," which is "all at the service of rendering emotion. When you appreciate a Fuller film, what you're responding to is cinema at its very essence. Motion as emotion. Sam's pictures move convulsively, violently. Just like life when it's being lived with real passion."[23] Fuller himself has remarked that a director must have a feeling of visual emotion. That Fuller has this feeling is apparent in *Pickup on South Street*, made from Fuller's original script. The scene on the subway where Skip McCoy (Richard Widmark) picks Candy's (Jean Peters) purse is Hitchcockian in its creepy intimacy: The two keep glancing at each other while two male passengers in the background—FBI agents—observe the pair and notice the lift Skip makes. Fuller shoots the scene in close-ups with no dialogue, and the way Fuller films the lift suggests a molestation, with Skip's fingers fluttering in Candy's purse. To underscore this, she later asks him, "How many times you been caught with your hand where it didn't belong?" Candy only discovers later that she was pick-pocketed while unwittingly passing information to a Communist spy ring via her former boyfriend Joey. Skip too doesn't know what he's harvested on this pick: microfilm of a new patent for a chemical formula. This launches the archetypal search-for-a-valuable-item noir plot.

Candy tracks Skip down to his riverside shack to retrieve the microfilm and is welcomed by his fist to her chin, knocking her out cold. He had heard an intruder as he returned home but hadn't realized it was a woman—yet viewers suspect Skip wouldn't have pulled his punch even had he known. He brings her to by splashing beer on her face as she lies on the floor. As Skip negotiates how much money he wants for the microfilm, the two banter caustically, Candy's inquiry, "How'd you get to be a pickpocket?" drawing Skip's rapid, slap-in-the-face retort, "How'd you get to be what you are?" As with their proximity during the subway scene, again Fuller's use of close-ups makes their exchange sexually charged.

Fuller says that a director is essentially writing with his camera and that the camera's power is like boldface type. Indeed, *Pickup on South Street* is full of energetic camera work, which makes all the more impressive the slow build up in the death scene of the stoolie Moe (Thelma Ritter). All she's been working for is enough money to save her from the plight of being buried in Potter's Field. Fuller has her enter her dark rented room over a tattoo shop in the Bowery, turning on lights and a Victrola, which plays what sounds like a French ballad. She lies on her bed, tired and restless, taking out the book in which she tallies her earnings and living expenses, to discover Joey (Richard Kiley), a Communist agent, is in her apartment. "When I come in here tonight," Moe tells him, "you seen an old clock running down. I'm tired." Fuller holds the camera on her as she delivers a monologue about how difficult going on is, stating, "I have to go on living so I can die. But even a fancy funeral ain't worth it if I have to deal with crumbs like you." When Joey pulls a gun on her, Moe says resignedly, her lower lip trembling, "So I don't get to have a fancy funeral after all. Well, I tried. Look mister, I'm so tired, you'd be doing me a big favor if you blew my head off." Fuller pans to the still-playing Victrola, and a pistol shot punctuates its music.

Fuller notes in his autobiography, "I hate violence. That has never prevented me from using it in my films. It's part of human nature."[24] He qualifies this by remarking elsewhere that he doesn't prefer to have a lot of violence since he wants its use to be emotional. An excellent example of this is the scene in which Candy gives Joey the recovered microfilm, from which Skip has removed a frame. Joey beats Candy up in an incredibly violent scene. In Fuller's lyrical interpretation of brutality, Joey shakes her, hard; as the two struggle they knock over a lamp and fall into an upholstered chair, rolling it over. Candy breaks away and takes time to make a side dash for her purse before making for the door, where Joey shoots her.

Later, as revenge for Moe's death and Candy's beating, Skip beats up Joey in a subway station. The prelude to this, though, is another subway encounter. This time Skip uses his newspaper move to steal Joey's gun. Joey doesn't know who Skip is and wears an expression of indifference as the two sway with the car's movement, quite different from the opening subway encounter in which Candy had been intrigued with Skip. Once the two men deboard, viewers catch a glimpse of nuns going by a turnstile before the fight between Skip and Joey begins in a men's room and progresses, as Joey tries to escape, to the platform, over a turnstile, up and down the subway steps (Joey thumping down the latter as Skip drags him along), and out onto the tracks. Fuller has explained that the choreography of fight scenes must be right

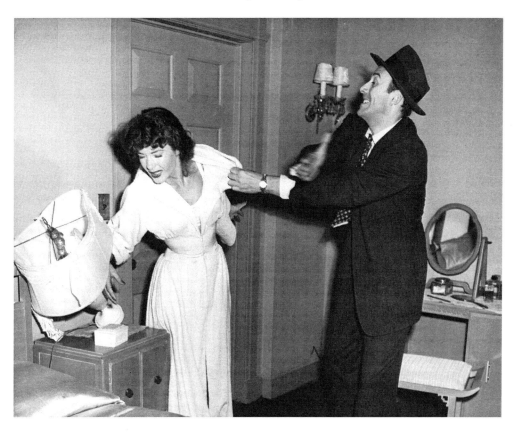

Candy (Jean Peters) suffers Joey's (Richard Kiley) wrath in *Pickup on South Street* (1953) (20th Century–Fox/Photofest).

to be believable, which is why the stuntmen must be really good. He prefers to use a high-angle shot on fight scenes because then viewers will believe the intercut close-ups of the real actors fighting.

Although *Pickup on South Street* was shot in studio, the film shows the gritty realism of the city streets as Fuller had hoped it would; even when it's daylight it seems dark. Fuller's family had moved to New York when he was 11 years old; soon he was hawking papers and breaking into journalism as a copy boy (age 13) and then crime reporter (age 16). While he made journalism per se the subject of his film *Park Row* (1952), he brought the larger—or smaller—world of the streets he got to know as a journalist into *Pickup on South Street*. Fuller made sketches for the sets, going for a look he called "primordial. How could you tell a story about petty thieves, informers, and spy rings without a realistic portrayal of their dilapidated, predatory world?"[25] The movie's art director, Lyle Wheeler, created Skip's shack from Fuller's specifications, and it suggests quite well the basic, precarious existence the pickpocket lives. Likewise, the sets of *Shock Corridor* (1963) help contribute to the nightmarish depiction of the psychological damage a journalist suffers after getting himself committed to a mental hospital in order to solve a murder that had occurred there; and, as its trailer promises, *The Naked Kiss* (1964) gives "reality in the raw" as ex-prostitute Kelly learns that the veneer of small-town life covers ugly secrets. Both films unfold their storylines with Fuller's usual visual grace, however gritty their content.

Edward Anderson, Nicholas Ray and *They Live by Night*

The Big Sleep, Pickup on South Street, and the yet-to-be-discussed *Touch of Evil*, for all their melodramatic implosions, are cynical, even nihilistic films. Not so Nicholas Ray's first feature film, *They Live by Night*, which veers into actual sentimentality in presenting the developing love between Bowie Bowers and Keechie Mobley. In fact, before the opening credits, viewers listen to romantic music while watching Bowie (Farley Granger) and Keechie (Cathy O'Donnell) kissing by firelight, gazing into each other's eyes tenderly as the subtitles read, "This boy … and this girl … were never properly introduced to the world we live in…. To tell their story…," whereupon the music strikes a dramatic note and the two glance in surprised fear toward but above the camera, and the title "They Live by Night" appears on the screen. Ray would go on to be best remembered for directing *Rebel Without a Cause* (1955), another film portraying his sympathetic view of the reoccurring theme of society's youthful outsiders.

Although *They Live by Night* is Ray's directorial debut, as Geoff Andrew points out in *The Films of Nicholas Ray: The Poet of Nightfall*, in theme and style it "prefigures the best of his later work, while his highly expressive use of the medium is remarkably assured and complete. Meaning is conveyed through a comprehensive grasp of cinema's various signifying properties—script, acting, imagery, movement, light and sound—and one never feels that Ray is stressing style simply for style's sake: form, throughout, is at the service of content."[26] This will be discussed below throughout the film's analysis, but it is worth pointing out here that the opening scene of the speeding getaway car on the open country road was filmed in part from a helicopter, an uncommon tactic in those days. It establishes the simultaneous freedom and desperation of the fugitives that will be sustained throughout the film.

The film is largely faithful to the novel upon which it is based, Edward Anderson's *Thieves Like Us* (1937). Anderson wrote for newspapers before settling down to work on hobo stories and novels about wanderers for which he drew on his own experience roaming during the Great Depression, as in his first novel, *Hungry Men* (1935). *Thieves Like Us* is informed also by Anderson's interview of his cousin, Roy Johnson, who was serving a life sentence for armed robbery in the Huntsville State Penitentiary, whose inmates included Charlie Frazier and Roy Thornton—the latter being the estranged husband of Bonnie Parker. The novel uses contemporary slang and criminal lingo: law-abiding citizens are "Square-Johns," a lawyer is a "mouthpiece," a loser is a "gink."[27] Anderson's unusual metaphors and similes have a raw imagery that is often physically felt by the reader, as when Bowie peruses a newspaper and "saw the thing that seized his eyes like a fish-hook."[28] His terse dialogue is a move toward the rapid-fire dialogue exchanged in classic crime novels and films noir, and the fatalism of his young-love-on-the-run plot would become cliché. In the vein of John Dos Passos' *U.S.A.* trilogy written earlier in the 1930s (*The 42nd*

Parallel, 1919, The Big Money), Anderson folds excerpts from newspaper stories in with the narrative, which lends a sense of urgency as the bank robbers read about their escapades. Unfortunately, these praiseworthy qualities of the book are marred by racist, anti–Semitic, and homophobic slurs.

The character of Bowie in the novel is of a much more violent nature than his film counterpart, thinking, as he is about to sleep with Keechie for the first time, "I can snap her little body in my hands. I can break her little body in my grip," and later boasting to her about releasing Chicamaw from the Bingham Prison Farm, "I could go down there with one man to drive a car and take a machine gun and clean out that whole goddamned farm."[29] In the book Bowie is jailed when he's 18 years old for killing a storekeeper during an attempted robbery; he's 27 when he breaks out with two hardened criminals, T-Dub and Chicamaw. In the film, Bowie is jailed at age 16 for a murder he did not commit, and he's 23 when he escapes. T-Dub (Jay C. Flippen) and Chicamaw (Howard Da Silva) take Bowie to the home of Chicamaw's brother, Dee Mobley (Will Wright), where he meets Keechie, Dee's daughter. Bowie is socially awkward with women; Keechie has "never had a fella." He has an obsessive belief that a lawyer in Tulsa can clear his name, but she is shrewd enough to advise Bowie against keeping bad company with T-Dub and Chicamaw. Just as the safecrackers he had known in the carnival resulted in Bowie's arrest for murder, the upcoming bank robbery T-Dub and Chicamaw have coerced him into joining will go awry: Bowie sees a sign in a jeweler's window that reads "For Her?" and subsequently buys a watch for Keechie; that same jeweler (Will Lee) recognizes him when he is sitting at the wheel of the getaway car waiting for T-Dub and Chicamaw to emerge from the Zelton National Bank with their loot. Pushing the jeweler away from his car window and onto the ground, Bowie picks up the two men and they make a clean getaway, but his face is known.

Not too long after, Chicamaw and Bowie are driving too fast, each in their own car, when a car pulls in front of Bowie and he T-bones it. Chicamaw pulls Bowie into his own car and tries to drive away when a police officer arrives on the scene and attempts to take them both in for speeding, so Chicamaw shoots the officer dead and takes Bowie back to Mobley's house to be nursed back to health by Keechie. When Bowie and Keechie are alone Ray has the poetic whipping of the trees and singing of telephone wires in the wind backdrop the scene. Bowie gives her the watch and again expresses faith that the lawyer in Tulsa can clear his name. He then learns he's been framed for the cop's murder, and finally admits, "I guess I can forget that Tulsa lawyer." Keechie hands him a glass of milk, one of the last vestiges of their innocence. Things careen downward as they leave town on a bus, unable to sit together. At one of the stops they deboard and are married by an unjust Justice of the Peace Hawkins (Ian Wolfe), who gets them a used convertible for $3,700 and a $500 finder's fee (Bowie had been outraged at the $1,500 price of a previous getaway car). On the road with the car's top down, a prominent symbol of the freedom they so desperately seek, the two drink soda and Keechie feeds Bowie a sandwich as he drives, each confessing that they don't know much about kissing, but will learn about it together. At last they land in the domesticated space of a rental cabin they decorate for Christmas. Ray films a tender scene of the young lovers lying before the fireplace, talking quietly about whether Keechie would wait for him if he had to go back to prison; light and shadows caress their faces in the darkened room lit only by the flickering flames of the fire.

Chicamaw and T-Dub draw Bowie into another bank robbery because he is indebted to them for his escape from prison. T-Dub gets killed by police during the heist, Chicamaw's craving for alcohol gets him shot trying to break into a liquor store, and Bowie returns to the cabin to find it flooded by a burst pipe. "O Come, All Ye Faithful" and "Tidings of Comfort and Joy" are heard in the background coming from a radio as Keechie tells Bowie she is pregnant, then implies she will have an abortion. When a plumber (Guy Beach) sees the Zelton Jewelers box and hastily leaves, they know they've been made and, quickly packing only their essential belongings, have to race away in their car. Rain streaks beautifully across the driver's side window as Bowie talks about getting to a large city because Chicamaw said people don't "big eye" you so much in them. Keechie tells Bowie she's decided to have the baby, and he assents, noting, "That's right, he'll just have to take his chances, same as us." Ray again uses an aerial shot to show billowing dust clouds trailing from the four tires of their car as they speed along the road, artfully symbolizing their desperation. In one scene they drink Coke from glass bottles as they drive, a teenage ritual that makes viewers wish the two could be a pair dating in a diner. The tender theme music associated with the couple throughout the film plays in a morning scene when Keechie tells Bowie to try to sleep, she settling in the back seat while he beds down in the front. They continue sleeping by day, driving at night, taking turns at the wheel, until Bowie wakes Keechie one night as they are driving by the Mississippi River toward New Orleans. Bowie remarks that he'd like to see some of the country they've been traveling through, Keechie asking, "By daylight, you mean? That'd be nice," underscoring the film's title about how they've been living. In New Orleans, they get a room in a boarding house, and the next morning plan to spend a day outside, "just like other people," going for a stroll in the park. In a nightclub at the end of the day, they share a bottle of soda as Bowie reveals his decision that they will go to Mexico where they can "live like real people." A drunk falls into their table and they leave to avoid drawing attention to themselves, but Keechie wants a cigarette, and as Bowie buys a pack from the vending machine in the men's room, the camera reveals a man (uncredited) sitting in a shoeshine chair in the background. "Bowie the Kid," he says slowly, then swoops in to grab the gun Bowie draws. He tells Bowie he doesn't want trouble in his town and gives him less than an hour to get out of it.

The couple are once more on the road after dark, and, significantly, run into a detour that Bowie fears might be a roadblock to catch them, so rather than take a chance they shift course and go to Mattie's (Helen Craig) Prairie Plaza Motel, which fittingly advertises that it is an auto camp. Initially Mattie, who is married to T-Dub's incarcerated brother, refuses to take them in, but Bowie insists, reminding her she is a thief like them. Mattie cuts a deal to have her husband paroled by giving up Bowie, although the authority's declaration that she is saving "a lot of people a lot of grief" by turning in a man who can only go on stealing to live draws her response, "I don't think that's gonna help me sleep nights."

Returning to the Justice of the Peace who had married them because Hawkins had suggested Mexico as their honeymoon destination, stressing that he had made "a lot of good friends" there when he lived there a few years, Bowie finds his request to help them get to Mexico spurned. "I won't sell you hope when there ain't any," Hawkins maintains, and Ray films a despondent Bowie walking out of the house to the tune of the "Wedding March" as another hopeful couple is married within. Realizing he must leave Keechie at this point for her safety, he gives Mattie money for a doctor to keep tending to her because she's been ill. Hatred and anguish alternate across Mattie's face as she convinces Bowie to look in on the sleeping Keechie one last time before he leaves; Mattie knows the police are waiting to ambush him. Bowie asks for paper to write Keechie a note, which Mattie reads over his shoulder, assessing, "That's fine. She'll like that," her face hard and upset at the same time.

While Bowie walks slowly and inexorably toward his cabin in the darkness, the camera shows viewers the barrels of police shotguns following his progress across the courtyard. A train whistles in the distance. As Bowie continues to pace onward, the train can be heard chugging more and more loudly, getting closer, moving faster, until the whistle is quite near. Bowie looks in the cabin door's window at his sleeping wife, the police order "Raise 'em boys" is heard from offscreen, a bright light illuminates Bowie against the door, and he is shot dead as Keechie screams out his name. She rushes out and touches his still back, takes the crumpled note out of his hand, and slowly rises, looking at the police in silence. Ray films her back as she walks toward the cabin, reading: "Hello girl. I'm going to miss you. I got to do it this way. I'll send for both of you when I can. I've got to see that kid. He's lucky, he'll have you to keep him square around," echoing Keechie's earlier observations that she and Bowie were lucky to have each other and that she was good for him. Ray has her look back at Bowie's body, silently mouth "I love you"—presumably Bowie's closing phrase on his note to her, tenderly blow him a silent kiss, and mouth "I love you" again to Bowie's body before Ray lets a dark shadow fall over her face.

The novel's end is far less poignant, and indeed, the book is far less poetic throughout than Ray's soundtrack and visual depiction portray the two lovers' time together. Bowie and Keechie, who do not marry in the novel, are holed up at Mattie's, their run to Mexico held up by Keechie's severe morning sickness and exhaustion. Mattie tells the two they'll have to move on, and although she does get a doctor to come, she reiterates that she doesn't want any trouble and she's done with them. Bowie springs Chicamaw from the Bingham Prison Camp because he's convinced Chicamaw's their only hope of getting to Mexico, but the two quarrel since Chicamaw is highly jealous of Bowie's newspaper notoriety, so Bowie leaves him by the side of the road. Back with Keechie, Bowie opens the door to leave to get her a strawberry soda when a voice commands him to stand still; Bowie draws his gun but is no match for the forces who have come for the fugitives. The novel closes with a newspaper story relating what happened:

> The crime-blazed trail of the Southwest's phantom desperado, Bowie Bowers, and his gun-packing girl companion, Keechie Mobley, was ended here early tonight in a battle with a sharp-shooting band of Rangers and peace officers who beat their covered quarry to the draw. The escaped convict, bank robber and quick-triggered killer, and his woman aide were

trapped in the cabin of a tourist camp, one mile east of this city, and killed instantly in one burst of machine and rifle fire.[30]

Medicine the doctor had left for Keechie is reported as an abundance of narcotics. Mattie had supplied the law with a tip as to Bowie and Keechie's hiding place in a deal to free her husband from prison, and the warden told reporters they used all their resources to bring down such a "ruthless, cunning criminal" as Bowers.[31] So closes Anderson's novel, with the newspapers publishing an overblown story of gun-toting, murderous thieves, while Anderson's interludes throughout the book had depicted a serial thief who naively hoped to hide out forever with his pregnant gal in Mexico.

Nicholas Ray's subsequent films include the films noir *In a Lonely Place* (1950) and *On Dangerous Ground* (1951), among others, but he is best remembered for the aforementioned drama *Rebel Without a Cause*. In that film he reprises the theme of the problems young people face, albeit in an upper-middle-class 1950s setting; the high school juvenile delinquents are far more privileged than Keechie and Bowie, but Ray still brings poignancy to the telling of their tragic stories.

Whit Masterson, Orson Welles and *Touch of Evil*

Orson Welles grasped tragedy in broad strokes, and throughout his career, from his Mercury Radio version of *Heart of Darkness* (1938) through *Citizen Kane* (1941) and *Macbeth* (1948), he delighted in playing powerful figures rotting themselves away from within. Ironically, *Touch of Evil*, a B-movie that was all Hollywood would offer him, afforded him the opportunity to make that rot palpable and almost horrifying in the character of Police Captain Hank Quinlin, a revered veteran cop and ex-drunk whose brilliant reputation springs from planted evidence and character assassination.

When asked whether he had read Whit Masterson's novel *Badge of Evil* (1956), Welles said not until after he made his film, declaring the novel to be "better than the script they gave me—it isn't that bad a book."[32] Yet Frank Brady observes, "The similarities between the Masterson novel, the original screenplay by Paul Monash, and Welles' final efforts on the screen are quite marked and prove that at least thematically, and in some cases structurally (to the point of using dialogue and action as it appears exactly in the novel or in the Monash script), Welles, despite his denials, used both forms freely."[33] This had, in fact, been sorted out a few years prior in John C. Stubbs's article, "The Evolution of Orson Welles's 'Touch of Evil' from Novel to Film." Stubbs closely examines the novel, Paul Monash's screenplay for Universal Studios (dated July 24, 1956), Welles' screenplay (dated February 5, 1957), and the final film. *Touch of Evil* contains dialogue and other material that appear in the novel but not in Monash's screenplay, as well as dialogue and material that appear in the screenplay but not in the novel, thus Welles undeniably used both sources for his own screenplay and final film.[34] Before noting the intriguing use Welles made of his source materials and his thoughtful innovations, it's useful to address the novel.

Whit Masterson was actually one of the pen names used by Robert Allison

Wade and Bill Miller as together they wrote over thirty novels. *Badge of Evil*'s investigative figure, Mitchell Holt, is an assistant district attorney, an American family man with a seven-year-old daughter, Nancy, and a Mexican wife, Connie (née Consuela Mayatorena), and it is the family vacation rather than the film's honeymoon that gets put on hold as Holt—a methodical, driven investigator—pursues the truth. Successful businessman Rudy Linneker's death by an exploding bomb in his home spurs the crime plot, and the suspect because of planted dynamite is his daughter Tara's fiancé, an American shoe clerk named Delmont Shayon. The roles of good and bad cop are reversed in the film: in the novel Captain Loren McCoy is the planter of evidence and Sergeant Hank Quinlan is his unwitting and honest partner who once took a bullet for him and now walks with a limp and the aid of a cane. After the work of these two convinces authorities that Shayon is guilty, Holt can't let go of the case because he had determined Shayon and Tara had an airtight alibi, so "His mind kept returning to the case, like a wistful vulture to a carcass whose bones had already been picked clean."[35] All of the action of the novel takes place in the Los Angeles area, save a comment about Connie's fleeing with Nancy to her father's ranch in Mexico for safety after the Holts' home is blasted by threatening shotgun fire.

Holt has gotten too close to the truth, and while he investigates to tie up all the loose ends, Connie returns to support him emotionally as well as intellectually, since Holt tends to bounce ideas off of her throughout the novel. But she disappears, turning up unconscious in a skid-row hotel, dressed only in her slip, surrounded by liquor bottles and reeking of marijuana. She's booked for possession and use of narcotics, and Holt leaves her in the protective confines of jail as he pursues McCoy, who had set up Connie to destroy Holt's reputation and taken Holt's gun from her should he need it to frame Holt.

After some persuading by Holt, Quinlan agrees to wear a wire to bring down his long-term partner, the confrontation occurring at McCoy's turkey ranch while Holt crouches in the backseat of Quinlan's car outside listening. To Quinlan's query of whether McCoy ever framed anyone he calmly replies, "Nobody who wasn't guilty," going on to state he was merely doing his job to make sure criminals didn't get away with murder.[36] Quinlan, shattered by McCoy's admission, mumbles, "But faking evidence, lying—" to be cut off: "'It wasn't lying,' snapped McCoy. 'It was aiding justice.'"[37] Quinlan says it was dirty to frame Connie and inadvertently reveals that Holt is the reason he's confronting McCoy by referring to McCoy's having Holt's pistol; when Quinlan tries to take McCoy into custody McCoy shoots him dead with that pistol. Discovering the wire, McCoy realizes Holt is listening, runs outside shouting that Holt killed Quinlan, and shoots at Holt as he drives away. Holt sustains a gunshot wound yet will be fine, whereas McCoy shoots himself in the head—news Holt hears while sitting in District Attorney Adair's offices that are decorated with Old West tin sheriff's badges and pistols, "left-over tokens from yesterday's dream of simple justice."[38]

Stubbs explains how in Monash's screenplay, the good and bad cop roles are exchanged, with Captain Thomas Quinlan being corrupt and Sergeant Jack Miller, his limping partner, having taken a bullet for Quinlan. Delmont Shayon remains the suspect, but Monash makes him guilty and an accomplice with Linneker's daughter, now named Marcia. In the novel, Holt has recently prosecuted a case against Emil Buccio, head of an Italian crime family. Monash changes the family name to Grandi, although they are still Italian, and makes them more active when the sons beat Mitch up after their father Vincent is convicted. Linneker is still blown up in his home, although now in the company of Gail Harte, an exotic dancer.[39]

Along with these character changes, Stubbs notes Monash's development of new scenes that Welles would use, albeit altered, in his film. The first involves police at the crime scene of the explosion, which includes "a mildly antagonistic exchange between Holt and Quinlan" that Welles would escalate into a "confrontation between Quinlan and Vargas [that would] bristle with racial hostility."[40] Another is Holt's rejected accusation to the D.A. and police chief of Quinlan planting the dynamite, when Quinlan "asserts himself as a maligned servant of the public," a scene Welles expands to afford "Quinlan a moment of victory in his sham of outraged innocence prior to his fall."[41] And a third is set in the Grandis' nightclub, with Holt attacking one of the sons in retaliation for his wife's arrest; Stubbs finds Welles using the scene to evidence Vargas' rage, which he "parallel[s] with Quinlan's sustained compulsion to avenge the murder of his wife."[42] In "The Justice of Jurisdiction: The Policing and Breaching of Boundaries in Orson Welles' *Touch of Evil*," Austin Sarat and Martha Merrill Umphrey observe, "When he finally sets aside his cosmopolitan detachment and commitment to procedure, Vargas seems to come alive, smashing tables and tossing gang members around the room."[43] They find that "The film's narrative movement is unidirectional: both Vargas and Quinlan move toward the use of greater and greater violence, shifting the line of its legitimate use…. Representatives of two distinct, territorial legal orders, they are moved to ignore jurisdictional impediments by the claims of justice."[44] Indeed, the two characters become unhinged in parallel form in Welles' film, culminating in Vargas' spectacular takedown of Quinlan in the seedy wasteland of the border.

The two most important changes Welles made when working up his screenplay were "open[ing] up narrative point of view" and adding American racism as a major theme.[45] Whereas the point of view in the novel and Monash's screenplay were close to Mitch Holt, Welles broadens it to scenes focusing on Quinlan or on Vargas' wife Susan, enriching both the narrative and characterization.[46] The novel and Monash's screenplay were set in and around Los Angeles, but Welles makes the U.S.-Mexican border town of Los Robles his venue and transforms the Holt character into Ramon Miguel Vargas, whom his American wife Susan calls Mike (he calls her Susie). Stubbs catalogs her unconscious racism—such as Americanizing his name.[47] More to the point is Quinlan's overt racism, which comes out in nearly every encounter he has with Vargas. Welles also made Marcia Linnekar's (for some reason changing the spelling of the family name from Linneker) boyfriend a Mexican, changed the gangster Grandi family from Italian to Mexican, and made Quinlan's wife's murderer half-Mexican.[48] This latter gave my recent film students an explanation to hang onto for Quinlan's in-your-face racism against Mexicans, but they still quite rightly found this aspect of his character extremely unpalatable. In that sense, one of Welles' messages in his film *Touch of Evil* succeeded nicely.

Welles had an unerring visual sense, and *Touch of Evil* seems to have inspired in him a prolonged fever dream that both magnifies the characters and renders them expendable. The famous opening scene, one long tracking shot of newlyweds Vargas (Charlton Heston) and Susie (Janet Leigh) at the U.S.-Mexican border, almost four minutes long, is followed by a barrage of cuts filmed at multiple angles. Welles explained that he did skip-framing, zooming in on the fire of the car explosion and later taking out "every other frame in the shot," "because a zoom is never fast enough for me."[49] In an interview with Peter Bogdanovich Welles pointed out there was, "technically, a much more difficult crane shot" in the film that "runs almost a reel"—the scene in the apartment of Mexican shoe clerk Manolo Sanchez (Victor Millan), whom Quinlin (Orson Welles) frames for the murder by planting dynamite—which "has inserts and long shots and medium shots and everything."[50] The set had breakaway walls, allowing the camera to follow the actors moving through three rooms without a cut, a long take that, as Bogdanovich observes, "gives a great feeling of claustrophobia."[51]

The cinematography is at its seediest and jumpiest when Susie Vargas gets abducted, threatened, and ultimately victimized by gangsters, thugs, and hopheads at the remote Mirador Motel. The editing grows erratic, whereas the scenes focusing on Mike Vargas tend to settle in for study—which is good since important things occur behind his back, over his shoulder, almost continually. At the Mirador, Dennis Weaver gives a frenetic performance as the night manager, a polar opposite character from the initially laid-back Norman Bates who would appear two years later in Alfred Hitchcock's masterpiece, *Psycho*, set in another remote motel and having Leigh again play a victimized guest. Welles claims to have written the part for him just to have Weaver in one of his movies; he admired him that much as an actor.[52] Vargas' interaction with the manager hints forward to that between Marion Crane's boyfriend and Norman Bates as the motel register is examined for each missing woman's name. Having their honeymoon interrupted by the Linnekar murder adds a layer of covert sexual tension to the scenes involving Susie, as when she is unwillingly photographed with one of the Grandi boys just prior to a meeting with "Uncle Joe" Grandi (Akim Tamiroff) she attends only because she was lured there with the promise of information for her husband, or when she is being watched undress in her and Mike's Mexican hotel room from someone across the way, presumably a Grandi male. But the menace follows her across the border to the American situated Mirador Motel. Quite horrifying is the scene with Susie in bustier night lingerie and the butch gang member (Mercedes McCambridge), whose slowly spoken "I wanna watch" must have inspired David Lynch in *Blue Velvet* (1986) and any number of his films. For this trauma Susie is injected with sodium pentothal, not heroin, although a heroin-tinged syringe and a marijuana cigarette are left in the motel room as evidence of her drug use.

Where many directors borrow his technique of low-angle photography to emphasize might and menace, Orson Welles typically uses it to suggest hubris and an imminent downfall, characters poised tottering above the viewer. This is especially effective with Welles as Quinlan, a shambling mass of nerves and impenetrability. After "Uncle Joe" Grandi gets Quinlan drinking again he's a shuffling husk, bloated and hollow at the same time. Grandi wants retaliation against Vargas for

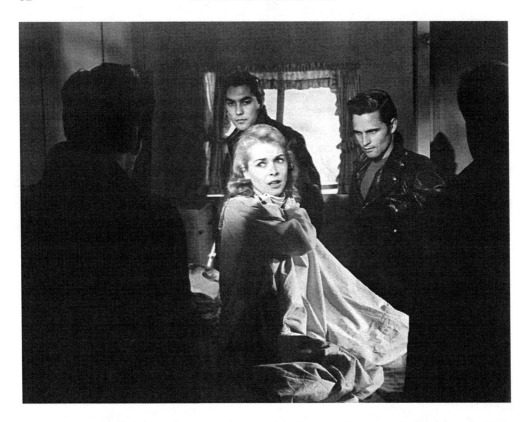

In *Touch of Evil* (1958), Susie (Janet Leigh, center) is threatened by Grandi thugs Pancho (Valentin de Vargas, left behind her) and Pretty Boy (Michael Sargent, right behind her) (Universal Studios/Photofest).

convicting his brother Vic and thus suggests the abduction and planting of narcotics on Susie, which will benefit Quinlan as well by tarnishing Vargas' reputation as a drug addict who got his wife hooked. Later, Quinlan realizes he's in a position where Grandi could blackmail him and needs to eliminate that threat. In the scene at the Hotel Ritz where Quinlan is about to strangle Grandi (the same method by which Quinlan's wife was murdered), a gently pulsing neon light brightens the otherwise completely dark room; street music plays in the distance. There's a shot from over Quinlan's shoulder looking down on Grandi, whom he forces to hold the candlestick phone so he can speak into it to his partner, Sergeant Pete Menzies (Joseph Calleia), and therefore keep his gun trained on Grandi while he holds only the receiver. Informing Menzies he received an anonymous tip that led him to finding Susie in room 18 at the Hotel Ritz, he also tells him to break Sanchez in interrogation. Moving in for the kill, Quinlan steadily walks toward Grandi, who backs away at the same pace, then desperately breaks a skylight to yell for help. The camera cuts to Susie, tossing her drug-fogged head back and forth as she lies on a bed in the same room. Quinlan twists a stocking, mutters "Resisting arrest," and garrots Grandi at the foot of the bed. Robert Miklitsch, in *I Died a Million Times: Gangster Noir in Midcentury America*, points out that Quinlan's strangling Grandi with Susie's stocking "suggests that the captain is simultaneously avenging his wife's death, fantasmatically murdering the 'half-breed' who murdered his wife, and figuratively doing what Vargas, despite the 'hot Latin lover' stereotype, never gets around to doing in the film: consummating his relationship with Susan."[53] Grandi pauses at the door to look back before exiting, and the scene ends with Susie looking up at Grandi's dead face, his eyes bugged out, hanging over the bedstead. As ironic comment on the cane Quinlan leaves behind that will convince his long-time partner Menzies to assist Vargas in bringing down Quinlan by wearing a wire, a posted notice by the hotel room door reads, "Stop. Forget anything? Leave key at desk."

When Menzies shows Vargas Quinlan's cane, which was indeed found in the hotel room with Grandi's body and Susie, he agrees to help Vargas clear his wife's name by wearing a wire, although he admits that Quinlan made him an honest cop: "I am what I am because of him." He and Vargas find Quinlan drinking at the brothel of former girlfriend and madam, Tanya (Marlene Dietrich), a Gypsy who tells Quinlan, in reply to his request that she read his fortune and tell him what his future is going to be, "Your future's all used up." Indeed it is, for when Quinlan catches a glimpse of Menzies outside and follows him, the two walk through a landscape of power lines, equipment, and an oil dredge that resembles a predatory praying mantis—yet another motif, this one industrial, that David Lynch would find inspiring. Menzies tries to steer their conversation toward Grandi as Vargas trails them, through water under a bridge that makes their words through the recording device echo until Quinlan hears them and accuses Menzies of carrying a bug for Vargas. Shooting Menzies, Quinlan sees blood on his hand and goes down to the river to wash it off, a possible allusion to *Macbeth*, a tear dropping from his eye. Vargas confronts him to say this is something Quinlan can't talk his way out of, yet Quinlan, not one to give up, retorts, "You want to bet? You killed him. The bullet is from your gun," shooting at Vargas as Vargas runs toward an approaching car to make him stop and turn around in order for Quinlan not to shoot him in the back. Menzies leans over the bridge and shoots Quinlan just before dying, and as the D.A.'s assistant Al Schwartz (Mort Mills), who had been driving the interruptive automobile carrying Susie to be reunited with her husband, replays the incriminating tape, Quinlan rouses himself to walk over to the bridge arch under Menzies, reaches out his arm only to have Menzies' blood drop upon it, staggers backward, and falls to his death in the trash- and sludge-ridden river shallows. Tanya runs up to have the film's last words, responding to Schwartz's observation that Quinlan had been a great detective with "And a lousy cop," yet allowing, "He was some kind of a man. What does it matter what you say about people?," walking away as the brothel's pianola music takes over the soundtrack.

Touch of Evil is Welles' tour-de-force study of the axis of power and corruption. The director's deft use of crane shots, skip-frame editing, and breaking up a line of dialogue with multiple cuts all contribute to this highly stylized study of criminal deviance occurring just south of the U.S. border. Earlier Welles had worked his stylistic talents on *The Stranger*, a film discussed in the next chapter within the context of its director's and the United States' focus on politics.

THREE

Commies, Nazis and Fascists

Politics in Film Noir

As James Naremore observes in *More Than Night: Film Noir in Its Contexts*, many American noir directors in the 1940s "were members of Hollywood's committed left-wing community," as were a number of writers and actors associated with the genre.[1] He argues that while the genre itself is not political, "it has formative roots in the left culture of the Roosevelt years—a culture that was repressed, marginalized, and virtually extinguished during the postwar decade, when noir took on increasingly cynical and even right-wing implications."[2] In his study *A Divided World: Hollywood Cinema and Émigré Directors in the Era of Roosevelt and Hitler, 1933–1948*, Nick Smedley explains that post–World War II "a fiercely conservative reaction set in" that led political leaders to view the New Deal "as a dangerous flirtation with left-wing philosophy."[3] Thus, "The celebratory liberalism and idealism of the 1930s was replaced by an anxious, defensive climate. American values were no longer proclaimed with confidence, but defined in opposition to communism."[4] Even during the war, in 1944 the Motion Picture Alliance for the Preservation of American Ideals was established to dispel any notion that the industry was controlled by Communists. Their Statement of Principles declared that "co-existence is a myth and neutrality is impossible … anyone who is not FIGHTING Communism is HELPING Communism."[5] Post-war, in 1947 the Alliance invited the House Un-American Activities Committee (HUAC) to Los Angeles, which effectively "conscripted" Hollywood into the Cold War.[6] The films dealt with in this chapter each, in their own way, evoke the horror of American democracy being invaded from without and eroded from within. That is, they are propaganda, a form at which Hollywood excels as much as it lacks courage. And given that these movies are film noir, logic is a fungible concept at best, like Fox News with better actors.

Graham Greene, Fritz Lang and *Ministry of Fear*

That Fritz Lang was a masterful director, even a genius as far as some of his early German films attest, is indisputable. Two of those silent films he made in Germany, *Metropolis* (1927) and *M* (1931), are staples in film studies courses, and any number of his American films—beyond the two discussed in depth in this book—are worthy of study, *Scarlet Street* (1945), *The Blue Gardenia* (1953), *The Big Heat* (1953), and *Beyond a Reasonable Doubt* (1956) being just a few of the fifteen films noir out of the over-all twenty-two films he made in the United States. With Walt Disney Studios being the exception, Lang made films for every major studio, directing "some of the most important crime films and films noir of the American Studio era."[7] His personal political associations, however, have raised some unclear issues. He was fond of telling, and many people of repeating in print, how a meeting with Joseph Goebbels precipitated his departure from Germany. In an autobiography published in *Fritz Lang*, by Lotte H. Eisner, a film historian and personal friend of Lang's, Lang writes that Goebbels told him that "Hitler had instructed him to offer me the leading post in the German film industry. 'The Fuhrer saw your film *Metropolis* and announced, 'That's the man to make national socialist film!' ... I left Germany the same evening," ostensibly taking a train to Paris and fleeing with a few personal belongings and whatever currency he could get his hands on.[8] However, Patrick McGilligan, author of the definitive biography *Fritz Lang: The Nature of the Beast*, examined Lang's passport for currency transactions and exit visas and found that he was "purchasing foreign currency repeatedly" between April and July 1933, and that "the final German exit stamp does not appear until July 31, 1933, roughly three months after Lang's supposed face-off with Goebbels, the Fuhrer-of-film proposition, and that 'overnight' train to Paris."[9]

Michael Tratner, in *Crowd Scenes: Movies and Mass Politics*, writes about how Lang tried unsuccessfully to counter those critics who claimed his early German films helped Nazism's rise because his wife and collaborator on those films, Thea Von Harbou, actively supported the Nazi Party and because a Nazi propaganda film used a clip from *M* out of context. Tratner explains that *The Eternal Jew* (1940) "uses the confession of the child-killer Hans Beckert in *M* as a representation of a Jew making fraudulent excuses for his evil acts. The 1940 propaganda film implies that *M* is not just the story of a strange maniacal killer but also a work revealing the diseased mentality of the Jews, and so a call for a group like the Nazis to come to power."[10] The last two films Lang made were done in Germany after his wife died, and they were remakes of the first and last film he and Von Harbou had worked on together. Tratner sees these remakes as Lang's attempt to "create what are essentially allegorical 'explanations' of how he could have been himself an anti–Nazi and yet have made films which ended up seeming to serve the Nazi cause."[11] The plot of each demonstrates how a man with no political goals himself becomes involved "in corrupt political plots" by using a "classic Hollywood formula: the heroes fall in love with women who are inextricably entwined with corrupt political systems, so that the heroes have to become involved with politics in order to save the woman."[12] According to Vincent Brook, whose study *Driven to Darkness: Jewish Émigré Directors and the Rise of Film Noir* specifically explores how émigré directors' ethno-religious identity affects their films, "Lang outdid all the German and Austrian refugees in his anti–Nazi stance and most of them in his left-leaning politics."[13] His 1944 *Ministry of Fear* is one of the films that demonstrates Lang's anti–Nazi stance. It is based on Graham Greene's 1943 novel *The Ministry of Fear*. Greene was leftist in politics, briefly a member of the Communist Party, and in the British Secret

Intelligence Service during World War II. He was also a movie critic for *Night and Day* and then *The Spectator* from 1930 to 1940, and said, "I hate the adaptations of my books, except when I do them myself, and then I don't always like them."[14] Lang admired Greene as a writer and had sought to obtain rights to the novel to film it, but Paramount outbid him—however, the studio gave him the opportunity to direct it. Lang repeatedly said in interviews that his agent did not get a clause in his contract allowing him to work on the script, which Seton I. Miller, also an associate producer on the film, wrote. Lang also said in an interview that he felt the script "had practically none of the quality of the Graham Greene book" and when he "wanted to have changes made in it, the writer resented it deeply."[15] Nonetheless, *Ministry of Fear* clearly displays Lang's stamp, and the director himself allowed, "While I don't care for *Ministry of Fear* as a whole, there are still some things in it that I like," citing the séance scene and performances by Hillary Brooke, Marjorie Reynolds, Percy Waram, and Dan Duryea.[16] Of Duryea, whom Lang used in several of his films, he says, "He was excellent, I thought, in the scissor-stabbing scene, which was my own invention and not in the book."[17] There *is* a scissors-stabbing scene in the book, but Lang did alter it, as will be seen.

As Richard Lingeman observes in *The Noir Forties: The American People from Victory to Cold War,* Lang and some of his fellow émigré directors "gravitated toward the themes of war, violence, psychosis, amnesia, alienation, fear and flight that recurred in the Weimar cinema. They favored stories about characters wrenched from their homes, as the émigrés had been, or loners bounced about by the blows of fate."[18] Indeed, Lotte H. Eisner points out that *Ministry of Fear* is "full of typical Langian concerns: the ambiguity of guilt, a breaking through a moral trap towards redemption and redefinition of identity, a realistic nightmare where seemingly secure certainties give way suddenly. It is also something more than this: Lang wanted to make another anti–Nazi statement; and his realist fantasy is used to good effect."[19] A close analysis of the film alongside references to Greene's novel will demonstrate these claims.

At the outset of both Greene's novel and Lang's film, the protagonist, Arthur Rowe in the first text and Stephen Neale in the second, has just been released after a lengthy stay in an asylum, over a year in the novel and two years in the film. Readers and viewers learn later that he was sentenced there for assisting his terminally ill wife's suicide. The guilt Arthur feels for this act is an essential part of his character—he thinks of himself as a murderer—whereas Stephen only bought the poison because his wife begged him day after day and when it came to it, he was unable to give it to her and hid it; she found it and took it herself. Book I of Greene's novel is titled "The Unhappy Man," and there is indeed a sadness about Arthur, who is drawn to attend a fete in London's Bloomsbury neighborhood because it "called him like innocence: it was entangled in childhood, with vicarage gardens, and girls in white summer frocks, and the smell of herbaceous borders, and security."[20] Arthur dwells upon his happier past to the point of dreaming about his deceased mother, arguing with her about how the world has changed from her day when people played croquet and had tea on the lawn; now life is like a thriller with "spies, and murders, and violence, and wild motorcar chases."[21] He approaches Bloomsbury Square feeling as if he's intruding or returning from exile. Arthur carries this outsider sense with him throughout the novel.

In his film, Lang imbues the opening scenes with visual elements that will recur throughout and bind his narrative together as poetically as Greene's beautiful prose had his novel. The pendulum of a wall clock swings behind the opening credits, which end to reveal Stephen (Ray Milland) sitting in his asylum room awaiting 6:00 p.m., his release time, watching the clock as the lighting emphasizes his hands gripping the ends of the chair's arms. (Lang effectively uses this spotlight effect throughout the film, often making Milland's face glow like the moon in close-ups.) As he leaves Lembridge Asylum, the gates have small windows barred by metal grates and topped by spikes; the walls surrounding the asylum grounds have spikes on their tops as well. These are both practically physical items for and symbolically images of barring things out to protect what lies within as much as of imprisoning what is inside. Stephen, having told his doctor about his eagerness to become immersed in the bustling life of London and be among people, is attracted by the sounds of a fete even as he is buying his train ticket from Lembridge to the capitol city. Milland's expression conveys a sort of boyish joy at the thought of attending, effectively translating the youthful enthusiasm Greene had given Arthur for fetes from words to the screen, but henceforth Stephen's character will differ, displaying none of Arthur's deeply conflicted, even tortured, elements.

In both narratives the linchpin is a cake—or more precisely, a tiny roll of film negative hidden within the cake. This film is being passed to Nazi spies, but readers, viewers, and the protagonist are unaware of this until late in the texts, which creates the intrigue as Arthur/Stephen becomes enmeshed in events and tries to sort out what is happening around and to him. It is mere chance that places the cake in his hands when he accidentally misidentifies himself as the intended spy recipient at the fete by speaking the spies' passphrase that triggers the fortune teller to tell him a specific weight to guess for the cake that will in turn trigger the cake booth attendant to hand it over. When the late-arriving target spy recipient of the cake says the pass phrase to the fortune teller just after Arthur's/Stephen's reading and she realizes her error in giving the specific weight to the wrong man, various volunteers running the fete try to get the cake back from Arthur/Stephen, unsuccessfully. At this juncture Lang's film departs further from Greene's novel than changes in characters' names, opening locales, and other minor elements. It is worth noting that Lang flanks the fortune telling tent entrance with placards of a large hand to indicate palm reading and the zodiac wheel; a cloth zodiac wheel is hanging inside the tent above the fortune teller's round table. These elements connect to Stephen's hands on the chair arms in his asylum room and the round clock face and pendulum of the film's opening image, and they will appear again in a later scene.

Greene's Arthur returns to his boarding house room in an area of London that had been bombed early in the blitz, the ruined neighborhood somehow fitting for the damaged man. The next day a new border, deformed by polio, joins Arthur to listen to the radio news, engages him in conversation about politics as they eat slices of the cake, then tells Arthur he wasn't meant to win it, cryptically saying he's been sent to retrieve it and "we'll" pay for it.[22] Remembering the concerted effort at the fete to get the cake from him, when Arthur's inquiries about what is going on and why they want the cake are met with silence, he changes the topic and fetches the kettle for more tea, during which time the border puts hyoscine in his teacup. Tasting the drug Arthur drops the cup just before a plane drops a bomb on the building, injuring the other border, who is taken to the hospital and disappears upon his release. At novel's end readers learn that the bomb destroyed the cake and film, yet Arthur's subsequent inquiries to try and find out why the cake was so sought after put him in various dangers from the Nazi spies, some of which Stephen undergoes as well.

Lang's film tightens up the action considerably, pulling viewers more swiftly into the thriller-intrigue aspect of the tale. Leaving the fete Stephen boards a train for London during a Red Alert and ominous sounds, possibly methodical footsteps, are heard approaching his compartment as he awaits departure. The sounds turn out to be the tapping of a blind man's cane. He joins Stephen in the car and the two discuss the dread sound bomber planes make. When Stephen offers the man cake and becomes intent upon slicing it, a quick close-up on the blind man (Eustace Wyatt) shows viewers he is feigning lack of sight. Oddly to Stephen, the man crumbles his slice before eating any morsels, then observes that he hears the Nazi bomber planes approaching and surmises their target is a munitions plant located a mile away. When Stephen peeps out of the blackout shades of the now stopped train, the man hits him with his cane, grabs the cake box, leaps out of the compartment, and runs frantically across the countryside. Stephen recovers from the attack and chases the man to the ruined shell of a farmhouse amidst firing from the planes above and then pistol shots from the man in the house. A bomb hits the ruin, its terrific explosion creating a crater in the dirt and causing the remaining framework of the house to burst into flames. Stephen retrieves the man's pistol from the crater—the camera shows viewers that a piece is missing from the grip—and walks away.

The scene cuts to London, where Stephen visits the Orthotex Private Inquiry Bureau. Attentive viewers will see graffiti on the building's exterior reading "Johnny Biggs is a fool," which the spies will try to play Stephen as; "Mary goes with Bert," an emphasis of Stephen's current singleness as well as a foreshadowing of his relationship state at the end of the film; a drawing of a train, where the cake was stolen; and a few games of tic-tac-toe, emblematic of Stephen's upcoming interactions with the spies. Entering the Orthotex offices he finds the bureau's proprietor, George Rennit (Erskin Sanford), drinking from a fifth of liquor. As the two men drink some more from teacups, Rennit giving himself a decidedly longer pour than that which he gives to Stephen, Stephen relays how his hotel room was ransacked while he was out at breakfast and how he'd been robbed on the train and shot at, which sort of trouble Rennit suggests should send him to the police, not to a private investigator. "I don't wish to be mixed up with the police," Stephen objects, reminding viewers that upon his departure from Lembridge Asylum Dr. Norton (Lester Matthews) had advised him, "Don't get involved with the police again in any way. A second charge wouldn't be easy," to which Stephen had replied, "A quiet life from here on." It has, of course, been anything but, and for 20 pounds he now hires Rennit to accompany him to the offices of the Mothers of the Free Nations to try to obtain the address of

Mrs. Bellane, the fortune teller at the fete benefiting that charity. As Rennit waits in the hallway in case there is trouble, Stephen meets Carla (Marjorie Reynolds) and Willi Hilfe (Carl Esmond), Austrian siblings who run the charity. Showing them the pistol with which he was shot at, Stephen asks, "Could any of your volunteers be using this organization as a shield?" "For what?" Willi wonders, Stephen rejoining, "Some kind of crime?" Thus, Willi volunteers to go with him to call upon Mrs. Bellane while Rennit trails behind, unseen by Willi.

In a twist absent from Greene's novel, the Mrs. Bellane (Hillary Brooke) they find at home is a much younger and more attractive woman than the fortune teller at the fete, thus Stephen thinks she is lying when she claims she did tell fortunes there, but in a later scene she will explain that a local woman had taken her place when she left. She asks Stephen whether he is one of their group, meaning had he planned in advance to join her séance, and Stephen's reply, "By adoption, yes," will have further implications than at first apparent when various members of the Nazi spy group take interest in Stephen as he continues his investigations. Lang visually emphasizes circles again when the séance participants sit about a round table placed within two circles on the carpet that contain astronomical symbols between them; on the table is a statue of a dragon grasping a glowing globe. In the séance circle Stephen is seated between a Mr. Newby (Byron Foulger) and Martha Penteel (Mary Field), an artist. Other participants include Dr. J.M. Forrester (Alan Napier) and the late-arriving Mr. Cost (Dan Duryea, who plays another disreputable character in Lang's 1944 film *The Woman in the Window*, released shortly after *Ministry of Fear* and to be discussed in Chapter Six). Recognizing Cost as the fete attendant whom he was told had guessed the cake's weight more accurately than he, Stephen greets him with "Seems we met before," but Cost says he doesn't recall it, leading Stephen to unobtrusively nod at Willi to indicate Cost is a person of interest. As lights dim when the séance begins, Lang overlays the swinging clock pendulum from the opening scene in front of Stephen, who blinks as if he's entering a suggestive state. A faint, indistinct, whispering voice is heard that gains increasing clarity and volume to say, "I had to find you. I watched it too, Stephen. Stephen! You sat there watching the clock. I know you waited for me to die. Was the poison strong enough? The clock stood still. You killed me. The poison! The clock stood still. You murdered!"—at which Stephen breaks the spell by demanding, "Who speaks? Who said that? Who told you that?" A shot rings out and when the lights come back on Cost is dead, Martha Penteel accuses Stephen of having broken the chain by letting go of her hand, and all participants save Willi are eager to leave the presence of the assumed murderer and wait for the police in another room. Stephen is panicky about being framed and Willi declares that as an alien he doesn't want to get into trouble with the police either, so he suggests Stephen knock him out to give him an alibi for Stephen's escape and then slip out the window before the police arrive, which Stephen does. When he opens the window Lang foregrounds the spike-topped iron fence surrounding Mrs. Bellane's yard, harkening back to the asylum. After jumping out of the window Stephen runs up to the fence to look across the street, placing the spikes in the extreme foreground of the next frame showing children playing on the sidewalk across the way—Rennit, who had been there when he and Willi entered the home, is gone. The spiked fence retreats to the back of the final shot in the sequence as Stephen runs away from it.

Heading to the Orthotex office for a haven, Stephen closes the front door to the building after entering and then looks out its window to see if anyone has seen him. The boarded-over broken window of the other double door recalls the pattern on the barred asylum gate windows as Stephen observes a man slowly walk out from behind the building across the way, along its side, casting his shadow on its wall, and then along its front as he proceeds down the street, the last glimpse of him being seen through the boarded-over broken window. Within the frame to the man's left this entire time is a "Danger" sign, ostensibly referring to the rubble of a bombed building, but given the man's ominous pace and the visual allusion to the asylum's gates, viewers are made tense about Stephen's predicament. Indeed, it turns out that the Orthotex office has been ransacked, files thrown all about, and Rennit is nowhere to be seen. Before leaving Stephen cautiously looks out the window and sees the same man he had seen when entering the building, buffing his fingernails on the lapel of his coat. Here, Lang has him standing by a broadsheet headlined "Warning" and reading, "Thousands of lives were lost in the last war because valuable information was given away to the enemy through careless talk," underscored

Inspector Prentice (Percy Waram) stalks Stephen in *Ministry of Fear* (1944) (Paramount Pictures/Photofest).

by "Be on your guard," making viewers wonder about this stalking figure's intent. Stephen prudently leaves by the building's back entrance and calls the Mothers of the Free Nations office looking for Willi but instead reaching Carla, who informs him Willi reported that none of the others at the séance were held and the police are searching for him. "Where will you hide?" she asks, to which Stephen replies, "I don't know yet. I thought I had a place, but it seems that my unknown friends got there first," so she gets his location and urges him to wait for her arrival. Once there Carla reveals that she knows a place he can hide, but an air raid has begun so they can't get there now.

Lang films the air raid sequence in a way that captures both the urgency and the routine nature of wartime London. Sirens wail as people head for shelter in the Underground: older couples in bathrobes, commuters off a bus, a young girl with a basket of kittens whose mother urges her along as she herself carries a baby, an old man with a bird cage—all stream into the tube station, some carrying bedding. Within the station people cram in wall to wall, lying down, sitting up, or reclining against the wall like Carla and Stephen. This situation affords Stephen the opportunity to tell Carla about his wife's death and being sent to the asylum for his part in what the courts called a mercy killing. Undaunted, Carla still wants to help him. At this point the stalking man comes down the stairs into the station, and the strategically placed "Way Out to street" sign with the arrow pointing directly at him because of the low camera angle Lang uses makes an ironic comment on Stephen's predicament, while the poster to the far right of the frame reads "Keep it under your hat! Careless talk costs lives" and comments upon Stephen's next action: he covers his face with the hat of a man sleeping next to him to avoid being seen. After paring his fingernails with his pocket knife the stalker casts a look behind him and boards a tube train, where Lang has him look out of the car window while standing next to a sign reading "Don't help the enemy! Careless talk may give away vital secrets," further association that he is a spy. Is the stalker looking at Carla? His vision seems intent on something, but viewers cannot be certain of what it is he sees, which adds to the tension.

When the all clear siren sounds very early the next morning, Carla takes Stephen to a bookstore run by her friend Mr. Newland (Thomas Louden), who had previously sheltered an Austrian émigré for her. A large display of the hefty book *The Psychoanalysis of Nazidom* by Dr. Forrester is in the front of the shop; big swastikas adorn its front and back covers and spine, and Newland says the volume is selling very well. He explains that Forrester is a psychiatrist and sort of an advisor to the Ministry of Home Security who writes propaganda; as the Ministry is the heart of Britain's defense system Stephen later wonders out loud to Carla about Forrester, since he was at the séance and there has been nothing in the newspaper about Cost's murder. He's curious too whether others from the séance are listed in the files of the Mothers of the Free Nations. Carla intends to search and see, while Stephen pays a visit to Martha Penteel.

Interestingly, Mrs. Bellane opens the door to Penteel's apartment, which is decorated with Picasso-like art work. She invites him to sit down and have a drink, which he does after making sure the other room is not concealing anyone. As they converse Stephen surreptitiously weighs her handbag behind her back to sense whether there is a gun in it, and indeed, after feeling inside the bag he extracts a tiny pistol, which she tells him he can unload if he wants, revealing she had been aware of his movements all the time. He wants to know how she knew about him to rig the séance with his wife's supposed voice from beyond. Her explanation that her assistants keep excellent files on people and his testimony had been in the newspapers so they merely looked him up when he appeared at the séance does not seem to satisfy him. She also readily admits that she knew about the cake because the woman who ran the cake booth had told her what weight to give the client who said the proper phrase, however she acts innocent about its purpose, asking, "Was there supposed to be something in the cake?" Throughout their conversation Mrs. Bellane flirts unsuccessfully with Stephen, until Martha Penteel comes home and sees him, screams "It's him!" and leaves, after which he does too, taking Mrs. Bellane's gun with him.

Meanwhile Carla shows Willi cards of all the volunteers recommended to the Mothers of the Free Nations by Dr. Forrester. "We've been patriotically slaving for three years to help a spy ring," she laments, and these spies were recommended by a man who assists the Ministry of Home Security. Ascertaining from their secretary that the cards were mailed to the office in the same fashion that Carla mails cards when on holiday or away at meetings, the siblings converse while Lang initially places them standing before and on either side of a closed oversized office door, subtly emphasizing their division. "They even know how we mail our cards," Carla declares. "They're Nazis, Willi. I know it. The same as they were in Austria. It's the way they work all around you. Knowing about everybody, everything. Where to find you—that night they hunted us—." Willi tries to calm her down with, "Carla, not the old fear again. We're not there now." "They are here, in London," Carla insists. "You are imagining too much," Willi soothes her, "Something is going on. But you can't charge people with being Nazis just because they belong to a charity. Especially an advisor to the Ministry. The police would laugh at us." This dialogue is as close as the film comes to its title, whereas in Greene's novel the Ministry of Fear is actually referred to when a character named Johns, an assistant of Dr. Forester's (whose name is spelled differently in the novel and film), explains that the Germans kept detailed cards on all sorts of people to have information to blackmail them and keep them in line. It's likely they are doing the same thing in England, Johns remarks. "They formed, you know, a kind of Ministry of Fear," he explains, and not just by having information about you: "It's the general atmosphere they spread, so that you feel you can't depend on a soul."[23] That atmosphere most certainly permeates Greene's novel from start to finish, and it is directly discussed in the final pages as Arthur Rowe walks to Anna (Carla in the film) Hilfe's apartment while recalling Johns' phrase "Ministry of Fear": "He felt now that he had joined its permanent staff. But it wasn't the small bureau to which Johns had referred, with limited aims like winning a war or changing a constitution. It was a ministry as large as life to which all who loved belonged. If one loved one feared."[24] This comes right before Arthur lies to Anna so that she doesn't realize he remembers having killed his wife. In the novel, an exploding suitcase gives Arthur amnesia and before he dies Willi Hilfe maliciously tells him Arthur had poisoned his wife. Anna only wants Arthur to remain happy without this memory, so Arthur lies that Willi had killed himself before he reached him. The elision of amnesia from Stephen's character in Lang's film disappointed Greene, who had no input on Seton I. Miller's screenplay. Admittedly, it simplifies the protagonist, who, as noted earlier, is deeply troubled in Greene's text.

Another significant element of the office scene between Carla and Willi is a small caged bird. Although it had never moved during a previous scene when Stephen first visited the siblings in search of Mrs. Bellane, now it is highly agitated and hops back and forth in its cage from Willi's side to Carla's side as the two argue about Stephen while standing on either side of the cage, which is slightly in the background. Willi is less than pleased that his sister is hiding Stephen from the authorities, having found out he had been sentenced for murder two years ago, while Carla maintains that his wife's death was a mercy killing. However, the siblings reconcile at the end of the scene when Carla admits she is falling in love with Stephen. There is a dissolve to the bookstore, where Carla has brought the volunteer cards to Stephen, proposing she go to the Ministry of Home Security and try to tell them what is going on. Stephen dissuades her, saying that as aliens, she and Willi would be suspected. Dr. Forrester phones Newland at this point, who proposes delivering the nineteen-volume set of *Oxford Medicine* the doctor purchased, and since Stephen and Carla are on their way out for dinner, they agree to take the books to Forrester's flat for him, although as it turns out, the flat belongs to a Mr. Travers, who left orders with the porter to let them in. The flat is oddly barren of personal markers—there's nothing on the bookshelves, in the cabinet or cigarette box, and little on the desk; even the phone line is not activated. When Stephen opens the suitcase to unload the books because Newland had emphasized that he not forget to bring back the valise as leather is hard to get, there is a bomb inside that leaves Stephen just enough time to run across the room and knock Carla protectively to the floor before it explodes.

Lang has viewers look through Stephen's blurry perspective as he opens his eyes in a hospital-type bed and sees the man who has been stalking him while practicing his habit of attending to his fingernails; now he's rocking back on a chair and paring them, patiently waiting for Stephen to wake up. He closes the pocket knife and rolls it between his hands as he asks Stephen who the girl was at Travers' flat with him. When Stephen denies anyone was with him the man opens the pocket knife and runs his finger along the blade, asking whether Stephen killed her too. Stephen accuses the man of being a Nazi and setting the bomb, which is a logical assumption for both Stephen and viewers to make, the former because so many people seem to be in the spy ring he's uncovered and the latter because of the visual clues via the war propaganda Lang included in previous scenes. As it turns out the man is Inspector Prentice (Percy Waram) and Stephen is in a bed at Scotland Yard. A stenographer enters to take Stephen's statement, but when he says he didn't kill Cost, that man's murder is news to the police, confirming Stephen's belief that everyone involved in the séance are enemy agents. Eager to turn over the volunteer cards from the Mothers of the Free Nations with information about the spies, Prentice informs him there were no cards in his coat pocket and accuses him of killing the private investigator Rennit, who was bludgeoned to death. Stephen tells Prentice how the Nazis wanted something hidden in the cake he won at the fete, which makes Prentice question his sanity. Even with his record of having been in the asylum, Stephen insists, "You can't take it upon yourself to say that German agents aren't working in London. You saw that bombed apartment. I tell you they did it." He begs Prentice to search the bomb crater outside Lembridge for what might be left of the cake, which Prentice orchestrates. They do find part of the blind man's coat, the missing piece from the gun butt, and part of the cake box, so Stephen starts digging desperately through the dirt for more evidence, crumbling the sand as the blind man had crumbled the cake before officers bring shovels and screens from the nearby factory for a more thorough sifting, but that turns up nothing, although elsewhere on the site the man's shoe is found, evoking the crack "He was bloody well scattered about" from one of the officers, who tosses it into the basket of findings. They are leaving when Stephen spots two birds fighting over something up on the rubble of the farmhouse, which turns out to be what's left of the cake in its box, the portion with a capsule containing a tiny roll of film. Observing that the film shows "drawings or something," Prentice says they'll ask the Ministry about it.

The film has photo negatives of the Ministry's new embarkation plans on their Channel mine fields; said plans have only been out of the vault twice, for a conference Saturday and again yesterday. Concerned that since the original film stock had not been recovered by the Nazi spies a new copy might have been made yesterday, it is ascertained that while Forrester had not been present, the tailor he recommended had been, measuring someone on staff for a suit. That this tailor was a Mr. Travers, bearing the same name as the man who had leased the flat where the bomb went off, is enough for Prentice to arrange being measured for a suit at Travers & Brathwaite, Ltd., under an assumed name. On the way there in the police car, Stephen gives Prentice (who is still fussing with his fingernails) the names of Mrs. Bellane, Martha Penteel, and Mr. Newland, whom Prentice orders to be brought in for questioning. (Viewers have to wonder just how wide this spy ring had been. Given that shortly they will learn that Willi is in charge of it, it will make sense, although it is saddening, that the kindly Mr. Newland, who seemed so avuncular toward Carla, is a member and took active participation in trying to kill her. Any number of people at the fete beyond the fortune teller and cake stand ladies could have been members, since the crowd had fallen silent instantly when Stephen proclaimed the cake's weight given to him by the fortune teller, and viewers will spot a clergyman among the bystanders, a figure in Greene's novel who actively tries to get the protagonist to put the cake back up for bidding once it is discovered the wrong man has gotten it. Such thoughts increase the viewers' sense of how overwhelming and inescapable the situation seems to be for Stephen, especially since he's about to encounter what he thinks will be yet another spy, Travers.) Prentice again pushes to learn the identity of the girl Stephen is protecting and the friend he mentioned, and Stephen loyally insists, "I've told you everything I know that can be of help. My friends have nothing to do with it. I don't want them involved," which surprisingly elicits "That's a fair answer" from Prentice.

At the tailor shop Prentice enters first and Stephen follows after five minutes as told to, asking to see Travers. The back wall of the establishment is covered with a mirror and Lang cleverly shows much of the action in its reflection, with the camera tight on Stephen sitting in a comfortable armchair before the mirrored wall. This lets the viewer share Stephen's visual perspective in a unique way until Travers comes out of the fitting room and the camera is on him directly for a moment, putting viewers in Stephen's perspective more directly. Then Lang uses a close-up to show viewers Stephen's surprise that Travers is actually Cost. The tailor pretends not to recognize Stephen, excuses himself to make a phone call, and dials the telephone on the table beside them with the scissors he's holding, scissors that are not in this scene in Greene's novel. These are no ordinary household scissors as would be used for the murder weapon in Lang's *The Woman in the Window*. These are oversized fabric sheers that scream out to the viewer they will be employed for violence, against whom one is uncertain unless one's read Greene's novel—and even then one can't be sure that the film will remain loyal. Given all that Stephen's been through, he certainly looks concerned as to whether they will be turned against him, what with Cost/Travers opening and closing them and looking at them after he finishes dialing and is speaking. Cost/Travers tells whoever answers that his suit has been dispatched, observing, "I think when you've worn it once you'll find that the shoulders will settle," a remark which captures Stephen's attention. Prentice steps out of the fitting room, which Cost/Travers sees in the mirror, and Stephen nods at the inspector and then at the tailor to indicate that Cost/Travers is the person they want, a motion Cost/Travers also sees in the mirror. Looking between his scissors and Prentice advancing toward him from across the room, which advance viewers see in the mirror, Cost/Travers says, "Personally I have no hope sir, no hope at all," on the surface in reference to obtaining more of the same fabric with which to make another pair of trousers, but in reality meaning of evading arrest. For when Prentice is unintentionally hindered in his advance by a cluster of male customers and an employee, Cost/Travers sprints to lock himself in a private room, an action Lang shows viewers reflected in the wall mirror rather than directly, and when the camera next shows Cost/Travers directly it is just after he has thrust the scissors into his chest in an act of suicide. The only mirror at the tailor establishment in Greene's novel is in the fitting room, where the character—known variously as Cost/Travers/Ford—commits suicide with a pair of scissors by holding them between his knees as he sits in a chair and bends over them to stab his throat. Greene's Prentice had hoped to catch this suspected spy in the fitting room because, as he put it, "I want to have him where I can watch him—in all the mirrors."[25] This becomes translated into a truly rich and nuanced scene of noir cinema with Lang's directorial interpretation.

Having carefully watched Cost/Travers dial the telephone and noted the number, Stephen redials it. A bronze statue on the table with the telephone depicts a man in athletic trunks running with uplifted and outstretched arms, a visual echo of Stephen's Herculean task to catch members of the Nazi spy ring. When he is rather shocked that Carla answers his call Stephen hangs up, decides to leave by the back entrance to avoid having the remaining police in front of the shop follow him, and obtains the address to which the suit was delivered from the returning delivery man. Viewers catch a glimpse of Dr. Forrester sitting in a car outside the Prince Consort Mansions, looking quite surprised to see Stephen arrive. Willi welcomes Stephen at the door of the flat and is donning the new suit's jacket when Carla enters the room and tells Stephen that it is Willi who gives the orders, not Forrester, and thus it was he who tried to kill them with the bomb. "It was too good a charity to lose," Willi says casually by way of explanation. "And you'd kill your sister to save it?" Stephen asks, evoking Willi's response, "You killed your wife. People do such things under the strain of necessity," creating an uncomfortable association for Stephen of his moral character with Willi's. When Willi orders Carla to get ready to leave with him she throws a candlestick at him, leading Willi and Stephen to scuffle until Stephen is able to make him drop the gun he's holding, which Carla obtains and points at her brother. Stephen demands the suit jacket and locates by feel where the film canister is hidden in the shoulder, but Willi punches him, grabs the coat, turns out the light, and states "You wouldn't shoot your brother, Carla" while exiting the flat into the lighted hallway, whereupon Carla does shoot through the closed door and kills him with one shot.

The couple are attempting to flee when they see the elevator light indicate someone is coming up, which shortly turns out to be Forrester, and his men are coming up the stairs also, forcing Stephen and Carla to take the stairs to the roof of the building. Lang uses an overhead shot down through a skylight onto the top landing of the stairwell right before the two exit to the roof. The skylight has muntins dividing the panes and the glass is inset with chicken wire, another visual reminiscent of previous images of entrapment. Indeed, Stephen and Carla are forced to the edge of the roof, cowering behind brick chimneys, from where Stephen exchanges shots with the men who came up the stairwell behind them. After Stephen hits one of the men the others turn out the lights in the stairwell to gain advantage as more shots are exchanged. Suddenly the lights come back on and the men within the stairwell are seen firing down the stairs until they are themselves gunned down. Viewers watch Prentice walking very slowly up the stairs and through the doorway towards Stephen and Carla, still an ominous figure since he is carrying a gun pointed toward them, although viewers know he is on the side of the law.

Lang makes an abrupt cut from this dark, rainy night scene to an almost blindingly sunny daylight scene in which Stephen is driving a convertible along the coast with Carla at his side. "I've always dreamed of having a church wedding," she exudes happily, "We'll have music, flowers, a big cake—" "CAKE!" Stephen yells, looking at her in horror. It's a decidedly humorous note on which to end the film, a very different note than that on which the novel concludes. While Book IV of *The Ministry of Fear* is titled "The Whole Man," and Arthur declares his love to Anna, who pledges hers back, as mentioned earlier he has lied to her about remaining ignorant of the haunting act of killing his wife. Henceforth Anna always will be watchful to protect him from his memory returning, and they both must "tread carefully for a lifetime, never speak without thinking twice."[26] Yet Arthur believes it might be possible to "atone even to the dead if one suffered for the living enough," and Greene's final line is, "It seemed to him that after all one could exaggerate the value of happiness..." (ellipses in original).[27] Arthur may be a whole man with Anna, but he still retains aspects of the unhappy man from Book I, and the price of atonement for ending his wife's life is a dear one.

Arch Oboler and *Strange Holiday*

A far less nuanced film than Lang's *Ministry of Fear* is Arch Oboler's anti-fascist *Strange Holiday* (1945), which exploits right wing paranoia to the point of endorsing it. It started as a short titled *This Precious Freedom*, the film version of Oboler's 1940 radio play of the same name. General Motors commissioned the film in response to the December 1941 attack on Pearl Harbor. As John T. Soister explains, "While still in the process of retooling for the war, General Motors was actively concerned about the perils of sloth and/or indifference in a populace accustomed to a liberty that seemed assured—at least in part—by the wide expanse of the Atlantic Ocean."[28] The short was intended as a warning against being inattentive and not taking action during wartime and was screened in those cities containing GM war plants, its target audience being the plant workers and their family members. Shortly after, it was obtained and shelved by MGM. Elite Pictures Corporation, which Oboler co-owned with A.W. Hackel, Edward Finney, and Max King, all B-movie producers, added scenes to make it feature length and put the film into general release in October 1945, but since Japan had surrendered on September 2 after the atomic strikes against Nagasaki and Hiroshima, this made the release untimely. Soister also observes that if the film had been made "by someone with more visual acumen than the radio-oriented Oboler," it might have been more successful at the box office.[29] The short and the feature both had low budgets, resulting in the use of stock footage of atomic explosions and marching Nazis and artificial-looking backlot streets. Soister even points out that "At one point, [Claude] Rains opens and enters the same room (from opposite ends) a half-dozen times. He's supposed to be wandering through his house, searching out his family members, but not even the repeated change of paintings on the wall behind him makes the illusion successful."[30] Another flaw for Soister is repeated dialogue that might work in radio but becomes "an irritant to the [viewing] audience."[31]

The film stars Claude Rains, who by this point in his film career had behind him much remarkable work. His first American film was a Universal sci-fi horror vehicle, James Whale's *The Invisible Man* (1933), in which Rains gives a stellar performance even though his face is not shown to viewers until the scene in which his character dies, at the end of the film. Other notable roles had included Senator Paine in *Mr. Smith Goes to Washington* (1939), Captain Louis Renault in *Casablanca* (1942), and the titular phantom in *Phantom of the Opera* (1943). In the feature-length version of *Strange Holiday*, which still only runs 61 minutes, Rains plays businessman John Stevenson. Before viewers meet his character, the film opens with various stock footage of actual or recreated battles throughout history and around the world, fought on foot and horseback, or using planes and ships. As a martial drumbeat plays in the background, a voice-over intones, "Ladies and gentleman, you are about to see amazing scenes of a great battle…. Men long since dead are fighting for what they believe is right…. Armies, long since dust, fight for what they believe are their rights as men…. Always standing up to fight for what he believes is his right as a man. Now has come the time to bring you a story about a man and his fight." As the footage ends and the camera moves in on Rains sitting on the floor of a jail cell, leaning against a bed with head despondently hanging down, the bars of the cell door are thrown in shadow upon the wall behind him. He lifts his head to haltingly speak, akin to a man having undergone torture trying to recall who he is, "My name is John Stevenson. I have a wife and three children. Three … children," before his head falls back down and music ushers in the opening credits. These are presented in an unusual fashion, with an arm reaching for the thickest book out of several book-ended on a tabletop, one whose spine reads *This Freedom: Story of a Strange Holiday.* The book is opened to present the credits on its printed pages, then the final credit, "Written and Directed by Arch Oboler," appears over a close-up of Stevenson in his cell, who says "My children" before a dissolve to a scene of his three children standing before a yet-to-be decorated Christmas tree having their picture taken by him. After he goes to bed the children start decorating the tree and talking, with the oldest boy, John Stevenson, Jr. (Bob Stebbins), saying he just wants to be like his pop, while the youngest child, Violet—also known as Peggy Lee (Barbara Bate)—says she wants to be a mother, a perpetuation of their parents' roles, right down to the son bearing the same name as his father. The middle child, Woodrow (Paul Hilton), is class valedictorian and in this role another scene shows him reciting a poem at school by William Ernest Henley, "Invictus," written in 1875 and published in Henley's *Book of Verses* in 1888. The poem underscores the film's theme that one must go on fighting to maintain control of your own destiny:

Out of the night that covers me,
Black as the Pit from pole to pole,
I thank whatever gods may be
For my unconquerable soul.

In the fell clutch of circumstance
I have not winced nor cried aloud.
Under the bludgeonings of chance
My head is bloody, but unbowed.

Beyond this place of wrath and tears
Looms but the Horror of the shade,
And yet the menace of the years
Finds, and shall find, me unafraid.

It matters not how strait the gate,
How charged with punishments the scroll,
I am the master of my fate:
I am the captain of my soul.

After this scene a dissolve to Stevenson in his cell shows him thinking of his wife, saying "My wife," nodding, then repeating "My wife" before a dissolve to his wife in their kitchen, wearing an apron and preparing a bowl of salad for a quiet dinner alone with her husband while their children are out at the movies. He speaks about their home as their castle; what with the world all mixed up like the salad she's making, there they are, safe, happy, content. She thinks they should plan for their children, their futures and responsibilities in the world, then decides they should just stay children for a while. He reiterates that he's happy, content, just before a dissolve back to him in his cell where he is trying to piece together what has happened: "My wife and my children. But this"—he glances at the cell—"how did it happen?

Where did it begin? The North woods, up in the North woods, with Sam. Sam Morgan." A dissolve takes viewers to the camp site, with Sam (Milton Kibbee) having a conversation with himself about how hot it is, how annoying the mosquitoes are, and how the fishing hasn't been great, thinking they should head home, apparently not happy that Stevenson talked him into coming on this trip just because he wanted to get away from the war news. Stevenson merely wants to lie there and nap, but when Sam's continued chatter leads him to say the date, Stevenson suddenly remembers it's his wedding anniversary and he has to get home for the party his wife has planned. As Sam pilots their small plane he says he felt wrong about taking a vacation "in times like these," meaning with the war going on, but Stevenson objects: "Does a man have to work himself to death? The government's running things. Why should I work so hard? What's in it for me?" "But the war," Sam protests, to which Stevenson rejoins, "The war, the war, the war. What difference does my vacation make to the war? We can lick them without me breaking my neck."

When they are forced to land their plane in a field because of engine trouble, no one is working on the farm, and viewers see a man cowering behind the drapes of his farmhouse watching them approach. The farmer (Walter White, Jr.) suspiciously wants to know who they are and won't let them in to use his phone. After they wait on the main road for an hour without seeing any vehicles, a produce truck finally comes along heading in the opposite direction from which they need to go, so Stevenson has to pay the driver an outrageous $20 for a ride back to town while Sam remains with the plane. The surly driver (Wally Maher) is taciturn, saying he doesn't know any answers to Stevenson's inquiries about what has been going on in the world during the few weeks he's been out in the woods, finishing by barking, "You'll find them out for yourself."

Like the road, the town's sidewalks are empty. Outside of the National Manufacturing Company, where Stevenson works, he runs into one of the secretaries, a Miss Sims (Helen Mack), who reluctantly lets him drag her into a shop—aptly named Pandora given what is about to happen to Stevenson—to help him pick out an 18th wedding anniversary present for his wife. Asking her what's wrong when she doesn't comment on any of his possible purchases, she responds "Don't you know?" and runs out of the shop. The saleswoman (uncredited) just sits there, and when he asks her to wait on him, she tells him "Nothing is for sale" and "We can't sell anything, you know that," then, when he asks why, she tells him to just go away. Back on the sidewalk he wants to buy a newspaper, but the newsboy Tommy (Tommy Cook) has no papers, and also asks him "Don't you know?" before running off. Going to his office because he promised to send someone from there to get Sam, he discovers there is no elevator attendant and the general offices are locked, so he lets himself in with his key to find a chaotic scene: a man's hat left on a desk, file cabinets rifled, a chair turned over, phones not working. The building manager, Regan (Griff Barnett), comes in and asks him if he's looking for someone, not recognizing him at first and then stating he thought he had died. Demanding to know what is going on, Stevenson gets the usual "You don't know?" sort of response from Regan, which angers him to the point of grabbing Regan's lapels, who calmly says, "You can't ask questions, Mr. Stevenson. Go home, please, go home quick."

Stevenson does so, and, in the sequence Soister objects to as noted previously, the camera keeps a medium close-up on him as he wanders through the rooms, ultimately to find his family is not there. But two men enter and try to frisk him, telling him to keep his mouth shut. "Get out of my house!" he warns, "You've got no right to come into my house without a warrant," whereupon he's hit with a blackjack and told, "There's your warrant, mister." The screen goes black to suggest Stevenson's unconscious state, and viewers next see his Black cellmate (Thaddeus Jones, whose character has no name in the film) leaning over him as he lies on a cell bed, then bringing him a dipper of water after making sure no one outside the cell is watching. "Are they police?" Stevenson asks him. "Yeah, in a way," his cellmate responds, and when Stevenson insists there must have been a terrible mistake, he says, "No mistake, Mr. Stevenson." After making sure no one outside the cell is listening, he explains that he knows him because he used to work for the same company, but when Stevenson wants to know where he is he says, "There's some things I can't tell ya." Stevenson wants to get in touch with the police chief because he is a friend of the family, but his cellmate tries to get him to quiet down and tells him that he doesn't understand, things are different. "Please sit down and listen to me," the cellmate goes on. "I've seen lots of things happen here in the last two weeks. But I didn't know any of them. But I know you, kinda. So I'll tell ya…. Maybe you're the only one in the whole country who don't know about it." He goes on to try to explain what has happened: "That part of the Constitution, they throw it out…. That part of the Constitution, you know, about rights. They throw it out. Well, there wasn't much we could do about it, was there?" When Stevenson first thinks the man is crazy, then drunk, he calls for someone to come to their cell, wanting to know what are the charges against him and repeatedly demanding a lawyer, but no one comes.

The next scene finds Stevenson hauled before The Examiner (Martin Kosleck), who has a vaguely German accent. The shadows of the barred office windows are cast symbolically on the surrounding walls behind Stevenson as he sits in a chair, declares he has rights and wants a lawyer, and maintains that he is not a criminal. Asking for the police chief, Stevenson learns that he is dead. The Examiner wants to know whom Stevenson met with while he was out of town, but Stevenson stays focused on wanting to know the charges against him, getting a lawyer, and letting his wife know where he is because she wasn't home when he was taken away. Asking Stephenson whether he knows where his wife is, The Examiner has her brought in by a guard. Jean cries and covers her face with her hands, but when Stevenson asks her to stop crying and talk to him, The Examiner states that she knows better. She's taken away, he's knocked out, strapped face down on an examining table, and beaten with a rubber hose by The Examiner as he proclaims, "Discipline!" Viewers get an under-the-table view of The Examiner's lower legs and Stevenson's arm in the foreground hanging down until it goes limp to indicate he has become unconscious; even after this, the blows continue.

After another black screen transition, the subsequent scene opens into a close-up of Stevenson's well-lit face and The Examiner indoctrinating him, first with a slap and then the discourse, "Discipline. That's the first lesson you must learn in this new state of ours. Discipline. Always discipline." He wonders why there is no fear on Stevenson's face, just astonished wonder. "Could you possibly be ignorant of the facts?" The Examiner asks, leaning in close to continue. "This glorious new state that we are planting here? This fulfillment of the dream some of us have had since the day we heard a voice telling us of our destiny? A dream that will come true. This will soon be our nation now, Mr. Stevenson. Ours, all of it. Your men are fighting, yes, but we will win." A spinning emblem comes to a halt and dominates the screen as in voice-over The Examiner informs him of "The Plan." The emblem contains two crossed bayonets overlaying what appear to be two crossed scrolls that each have a hatchet running along their side; these elements are framed by a square. "Surely you have heard of The Plan, Mr. Stevenson. The Great Plan that has won us victory," The Examiner asserts. At this point the screen becomes filled with talking mouths, whose words are as yet unclear because The Examiner's voice continues, "We used your own sentimental democratic weaknesses against you. We hid behind many faces as we spoke every whisper, and what did we say, Stevenson, remember?" The voices become clear and various male and female voices say, "Blame the Catholics for your trouble," "It's dog eat dog, get what you can get," "The churches are running the country," "Blame the Protestants for your trouble." "Confusion, Stevenson," The Examiner's returning voice-over points out, as a mock book of The Plan with the emblem on its cover is superimposed upon the talking mouths. "How we gave you confusion…. Yes, we waited, Stevenson, everywhere in the world, we who believed in our destiny hid and waited, and soon out of the mouths of you fools and self-seekers and power hungry came the words we had been waiting for." The voices from the mouths become clear once again: "There's no true democracy anymore," "There can be no real democracy in this government," "We have no statesmen, only politicians," "Smash it down and start all over," "Change comes only through revolution," "We need one strong party and one strong leader." "Their voices were our voices, and soon there was nothing but confusion!" The Examiner's voice-over triumphantly declares. The screen shows footage of riots, then an overhead shot of a huge gathering of people at a rally while The Examiner narrates, "Then a strong man rose among you, a great man of blood and fire. Now there is order, order, Stevenson, order, the New Order." Images of cartridges rolling off the assembly line in a factory appear and there are low camera angles on the legs of men marching as The Examiner punctuates these visuals with "Discipline, order, the New Order" before military tanks are shown rolling by. Bonfires and religious statues appear as The Examiner continues narrating: "Your freedom are bonfires around which to march now. Your churches of Christ and Moses, out of the flames that are burning them, a new America is rising. An America of order, and those who will not join will die. Men, women, and children." To emphasize this destruction, footage of an atomic blast and then burning buildings while people are heard screaming rolls. "Do you hear me Stevenson?" The Examiner asks, taunting him that he cannot help his own daughter because he has no rights; "No one has rights but we who are the leaders. Leaders of the blood. This is our America!" The camera shows The Examiner rising up, enthralled as he says this, then wiping his brow as if exhausted by his own rant, admitting he got carried away. The emblem becomes superimposed over his face as The Examiner tells Stevenson he wants to know which of their enemies are hiding out where he was in the woods. When Stevenson maintains he was only on a vacation, The Examiner begins beating him with the rubber hose again while asking repeatedly who are his friends, whom did he meet, where did he go.

As an unconscious Stevenson is dragged back to his cell a voice asks whether he's dead yet; at the response, "No sir, not yet," the voice states, "He will be." When Stevenson comes to on the floor in his cell, the voice of The Examiner interrogating him starts running through his head. He allows to himself that he is mixed up and needs to think things through from the start, so he backs up to when he was coming home from his vacation. A montage of the farmer, truck driver, newsboy, office manager, and cellmate are superimposed over Rains as he sits there, nodding as he recalls their warning phrases and how he didn't know what was going on. The Examiner's voice proclaims, "This will be our America now!" "No! No!" Stevenson cries out, crawling to the water bucket to dip his face into it. "It didn't happen," he maintains, "None of it happened. It's all in my mind. It's all in—Jean. Jean, where are you? Jean. Where are the children? Jean! Cry out, why should I cry out." Like a prisoner of war, he starts reciting facts about his life to try to keep a grip on reality: "I'm John Stevenson. I work for the National Manufacturing Company in the Central Building. I have a house on Arcade Street. I have a wife and three children, two boys and a girl. We have a good life, good life." Hearing "Dead ... not yet ... dead," the last word repeated multiple times, he wonders, "Why do I keep hearing that? Who said that to me?" Then he answers himself, "Oh yes, I remember. Um hmm. They're going to kill me. I'm an enemy of the state," as are his wife and children, but then he declares willfully that he can do what he wants, can get up and out of there. "You can't accuse me without giving me a fair trial. You can't come into my house. You can't take away my job. I'm a free man," he asserts, then, smiling at the recollection, states, "I'm an American." But the voice of The Examiner enters his mind again to contradict, "It will be our nation soon, ours," followed by his cellmate's remarks, "With the Japs giving the Nazis all the oil and rubber they wanted there wasn't much we could do about it, was there?" Then Stevenson remembers that he himself had said, apathetically, "The government's running things. Why should I work so hard? What's in it for me?" He looks over at the cell wall where, ominously, the shadow of a swastika appears, then that of a machine gun, while a voice with intonations that suggest Hitler's declares that man has no rights. "What's in it for me," he says, "What I had—"; a close-up on his hanging head dissolves to a picnic scene with family and friends as his mind flashes back in remembrance.

Two teenagers off by themselves echo his own attitude about war and complacency, Mary (listed in the credits as Betty, played by Priscilla Lyon) repeating to her boyfriend Joe (David Bradford) her father's belief that they are the lucky generation because they were too young for the last war and will be too old for the next one, and because of the peace plans, "everything's settled and wonderful, and we can have everything and anything we want," causing the imprisoned Stevenson to reflect that men had died on the battlefield so that others like himself might live, but out of their victory he had made nothing. Speaking directly to his wife out loud in his cell, he allows that he's not afraid to die, he's afraid to go on living if this isn't all a bad dream. To underscore the film's message at this point the shadows of the prison bars show prominently on the wall behind him as he realizes that wherever he would turn, those in charge would be there giving him orders such as "Shut your mouth," "Come with us," "You can't do that," "We accuse you of," and so forth. "I can't live with that!" he rebels. "All my life I've lived with freedom. Jean, we didn't know it was freedom, did we?," with his monologue going on to outline what American values need to be protected: "Living in our house, a good life, our neighbors, not hating anybody, feeling sure of the future for the kids because whatever was wrong here, we ourselves could fix with work, with our votes, with what we knew was right in our hearts." Holding onto the prison bars as he speaks, the camera looks at him from without the cell to give weight to his words as he launches into his final monologue:

> I never said this is freedom. But it was. It was! Whenever they talked to me about losing it I said, don't be fools. No one will take it from us. I thought freedom was like the air, always with me as long as I lived. I thought you didn't have to do anything about it. Jean, I was wrong. I've got the words to say it now. What I had wasn't a gift, it was a victory, and I can't live without it.

The Examiner's words interrupt to taunt him onward: "Some of your democracy lovers are out there fighting, but we will win, we will win." "No!" Stevenson yells, "You can't win! Do you hear me out there? You can't win! We're fighting, and we'll go on fighting." Music swells as he finishes up: "To say what we think is right. To do what we think is right. That's the only life we want. It is life. We'll live for it, we'll fight for it. This precious freedom." After this rousing speech, the film shifts back to the campsite where the napping Stevenson hears his friend Sam chattering away, mentioning the date, whereupon he wakes up fully and tells Sam they need to pack up and get back to town, while Sam, observing him frantically preparing to leave, comments, "Well how do you like that guy!" A fade to black precedes a shot of turbulent clouds over the moon in a dark sky and a voice-over hits home the moral of the film, intoning, "This is a story that must never happen, and will never happen as long as we remember that freedom is never a gift but a victory which each of us must guard with heart and mind." The opening credits technique is used to show "The End" on the page of a book, after which the rest of the credits are delivered via the usual screen shot.

Cinematically *Strange Holiday* is a happenstance collage. Clearly the scene change from Stevenson ranting patriotically in his prison cell to him complacently napping at the camp site are meant to indicate that his experience with a Fascist regime taking over America was merely a bad dream, so one wonders why Oboler didn't slip in just a little more propaganda and have Stevenson tell Sam about the warning nightmare he had received. Could it be that Stevenson just isn't that self-reflexive? If viewers carefully observe his interactions with others his character comes across as self-absorbed, entitled, and curt to the point of rudeness. Sam, ostensibly a very good friend, he orders about and does not converse pleasantly with, even telling him he's going to knock Sam's block off once they land because he wouldn't make their plane fly faster. Miss Sims, a secretary Stevenson works with on regular basis, is commandeered against her will to help him shop. Tim, the newsboy he gets his daily paper from, is told brusquely to give him a paper quickly because he's in a hurry. His wife Jean, patiently submitting to having her picture taken while she is making a salad for their dinner, has to listen to him complain about having to eat it. Transformed by the end of his nightmare into a mouthpiece for the need to actively protect American values and rights, when Stevenson awakes, he seems to be the very same self-absorbed personality. Viewers are left surmising that one doesn't have to be nice to be a patriot.

To look at other techniques Oboler employs, the use of repetition in dialogue is meant to emphasize Stevenson's disorientation while figuring out what is going on, similar to Kafka's technique in *The Trial*, and Stevenson's repeatedly entering the same room in his house conveys his sense of being lost in (or outside of) time. What some critics deem flaws can be taken as thematic elements, however unintentional they might have been on Oboler's part. Rains is the centrifugal force holding the film together, giving an admirable performance whatever one might think of the script and overall production, and the actor would happily go on to have a long career in film and television, including playing Alexander Sebastian in Alfred Hitchcock's *Notorious* (1946) and appearing in five episodes of the television show *Alfred Hitchcock Presents* (1956–1962). Oboler made cinematic history by directing the first 3D movie in color, the adventure film *Bwana Devil* (1952), and his handful of other films as director include another 3D film, the sci-fi *The Bubble* (1966).

Orson Welles and *The Stranger*

A subtler message about vigilance than Oboler's in *Strange Holiday* would appear the next year in Orson Welles' *The Stranger* (1946). Welles was not reticent about his liberal political views. One tangible example of his political involvement was his campaigning for Franklin Delano Roosevelt's re-election for a fourth term in the fall of 1944 when he ran against Thomas E. Dewey. As part of this Welles stood in for the candidate at the *Herald Tribune Forum* held in the Waldorf Astoria Hotel in New York City, which aired nationwide, and "on election eve, over four networks, at Roosevelt's personal request, he broadcast a speech for the Democratic National Committee."[32] He spent a good deal of time traveling with Roosevelt during the campaign, and unaware that Welles was himself thinking of entering politics, Roosevelt "suggested that he seek public office" and advised him "that if he ever wanted to make a bid for the White House, he should start by running for the Senate."[33] For his study *The Magic World of Orson Welles*, James Naremore mined Welles' editorial columns in the *New York Post*, which appeared from January 22, 1945, to June 1945, and notes that they are "especially valuable as a record of his preoccupation with world affairs—a preoccupation that bears upon some of the films he would make."[34] *The Stranger* is one of those films.

Victor Trivas received an Academy Award nomination for Best Writing, Original Story, and Anthony Veiller was credited on the film as its screenplay writer, although John Huston and Welles also contributed to the screenplay. Clinton Heylin examines in great detail the differences between the shooting scripts and the final product, basically between the film Welles wanted to make and the film that made it to the screen, in *Despite the System: Orson Welles Versus the Hollywood Studios*.

Producer Sam Spiegel essentially had the film "pre-edited" by hiring Ernest Nims to trim down the script, losing, among other things, a sequence in Latin America.[35] This analysis shall deal solely with the final film product.

Welles was left "uneasy" by Victory in Europe Day "because he felt that the spirit of Hitler was only dormant, surviving through the old device of the Red Scare."[36] The basic situation in *The Stranger* is that of Allied War Crimes Commission investigator Mr. Wilson pursuing a "mastermind" of the Holocaust, Franz Kindler, to the Harper, Connecticut, home where he lives under a new identity as Professor Charles Rankin at Harper School for Boys. This idyllic village (whose village green is first shown in a literal postcard image) and the school itself are modeled on Woodstock, Illinois, and the Todd School there, which Welles had attended and wanted to shoot at,[37] and Naremore points out that "the film contains several inside jokes about that school."[38] Welles' biographer Barbara Leaming identifies two of these as "the name of one of its beloved staff members, Coach Roskie, appearing on a sign in the gymnasium" and the similarity of Rankin's outfit while teaching to that worn by Roger "Skipper" Hill, the headmaster's son who served as gym teacher and basketball coach.[39]

Behind the opening credits the huge clock that will play such an integral part of the film is seen, its face and the statues that adorn it of an angel holding a sword extended horizontally before it and a demon being shown in various close-up shots. The clock was sourced from the Los Angeles County Museum, where it had been housed after being removed from the Los Angeles County Courthouse.[40] A 1928 photograph of the courthouse shows that the figures of the angel and demon are not part of the original clock; they were added for the film. When the tower was shortened the clock was removed, and a March 2, 1932, photograph shows officials presenting the clock face to representatives of the Los Angeles County Museum. Today the clock resides in the Natural History Museum's California History Room.[41]

The film's action kicks off when Wilson (Edward G. Robinson—Welles had wanted Agnes Moorehead for this role, but Spiegel nixed this[42]) argues that Konrad Meinike (Konstantin Shayne), a former concentration camp commander, should be allowed to "escape" from prison in order to lead him to Kindler, whom Wilson is so adamant be destroyed that he slams his pipe on a table during his rant and breaks its stem. The taped-together pipe appears with Wilson in subsequent scenes, most significantly when Meinike sees him smoking it aboard ship after his escape and then when it tumbles onto a seat of the bus Meinike has taken to Harper, letting him know he's being tailed when he deboards. Actually Wilson is not a subtle tail at all, virtually jogging after Meinike as he makes his way across the village green to the gymnasium of the Harper School for Boys, so it's really no surprise to viewers when Meinike throws an iron ring on a hanging rope down from an upper walkway, knocking out Wilson on the gym floor below. A sign on the door as Meinike exits makes ironic commentary on this event: "Anyone using apparatus in this room—does so at their own risk."

Meinike is thus free to go to Rankin's home unfollowed, to find his fiancée Mary Longstreet (Loretta Young) there hanging curtains on the afternoon before her 6:00 p.m. wedding ceremony. Rather than wait he decides to meet Rankin on his walk home from campus, whereupon a startled Rankin (Orson Welles) tells Meinike to wait behind the church as some of his students approach. They invite him to join their paper chase, a training exercise in which the lead runner drops pieces of paper to create a trail the others must follow, which he declines. As they walk toward and through the woods, Rankin tells Meinike that his upcoming marriage will be part of the perfect camouflage for his identity, as Mary is "a daughter of a Justice of the United States Supreme Court, a famous liberal…. Yes, the camouflage is perfect. Who would think to look for the notorious Franz Kindler in the sacred precincts of the Harper School, surrounded by the sons of America's first families? And I'll stay hidden until the day when we strike again." This declaration that there will be another war upsets Meinike, who has reformed because he has found religion. He feels his release from prison was a miracle orchestrated by God, whereas Rankin realizes he was set free so he would lead the authorities to him, so he's keen to find out whether Wilson—whom Meinike believed was the Devil—was the only man trailing Meinike. Assured that he was, when pressed by Meinike, Rankin consents to confess his sins in order to attain salvation, rotely repeating, "I despair of my sins. Oh God of all goodness—" cutting off his words as he strangles Meinike to death. He hastily throws leaves over the body when he hears the students on the paper chase approaching, picking up the papers the lead runner had dropped nearby and redistributing them so as to lead the chase away from the body.

The wedding ceremony occurs, and after Wilson comes to in the gym he goes to the town drugstore for aspirin, learning from soda counter patrons that the Judge's daughter has married "a stranger in town," one layer of meaning to the film's title, and also signifying how much of a stranger Mary's husband will become to her once she learns his true identity. Pretending to be an antiques buyer who has come to Harper for an upcoming special antiques sale and is nervous about the competition, he ascertains that another person also recently arrived and left his suitcase there at the drugstore, but he was "a missionary type" and not likely an antiques dealer. A scene change to the wedding reception reveals Kindler is missing, having returned to the woods to bury Meinike's body more thoroughly—although not thoroughly enough, as will be seen later.

As an antiques dealer, Wilson ingratiates himself into being invited to dinner at the home of Judge Adam Longstreet (Philip Merivale), an avid antiques collector, being joined by the returning newlyweds Mary and Charles Rankin. Wilson had heard of Rankin's interest in repairing the church clock when, while he was going through his list of new arrivals to Harper within the last twelve months, he noticed the hands on the church clock going backward and then forward, investigated, and met Mary's brother Noah (Richard Long; the biblical first names of the three Longstreets are hard to ignore), who was only cleaning it but explained that his brother-in-law would work on it when he got back from his honeymoon: "He's an expert, but it's more of a hobby for him." This interested Wilson, clocks being a hobby of Kindler's as well. Another dinner guest, town doctor Jeffrey Lawrence (Byron Keith), establishes through innocent conversation about having treated him for a bump on the head that Wilson had arrived in Harper on the day of Rankin's wedding, allowing Rankin to put it together that this was the man following Meinike. When Mary asks her father how his meeting with the Foreign Policy Association went, table talk turns to politics and the remote possibility that the Germans are having secret drills and otherwise preparing for another conflict. Wilson takes the opportunity to ask, "Do you know Germany, Mr. Rankin?" Rankin allows that his views are unpopular, explaining,

> The German sees himself as the innocent victim of world envy and hatred, conspired against, set upon, by inferior peoples, inferior nations. He cannot admit to error, much less to wrong-doing. Not the German. We chose to ignore Ethiopia and Spain, but we learned from our casualty lists the price of looking the other way. Men of truth everywhere have come to know for whom the bell tolled. But not the German. He still follows his warrior gods, marching to Wagnerian strains, his eyes still fixed upon the fiery sword of Siegfried. And in those subterranean meeting places that you don't believe in the German's dream world comes alive, and he takes his place in shining armor beneath the banners of the Teutonic Knights. Mankind is waiting for the Messiah, but for the German, the Messiah is not the Prince of Peace, he's another Barbarossa, another Hitler.

When Wilson asks whether he has faith in the reforms being effected in Germany, Rankin says he doesn't believe people can be reformed except from within, and that "the basic principles of equality and freedom never have, never will take root in Germany. The will to freedom has been voiced in every other tongue. 'All men are created equal.' 'Liberte, egalite, fraternite.' But in German—," Noah interrupts him to point out Marx's "Proletarians, unite. You have nothing to lose but your chains," yet Rankin notes, "But Marx wasn't a German. Marx was a Jew." He believes the only solution is to annihilate every German because they will never stop trying to conquer the world. Welles provides a close-up of Wilson looking meaningfully at Rankin while declining Mary's invitation to a faculty tea on Tuesday because his work in Harper is finished and he'll be leaving the next day. After dinner Wilson calls Washington, D.C., to declare Rankin "above suspicion" for being Kindler because of his views of Germans.

After Mary and Rankin go home Rankin takes her dog, an Irish Setter somewhat ironically named Red given the film's politics, for a walk, an excuse to check on Meinike's grave, which turns out to be fine until Red starts digging purposefully in it, leading Rankin to narrow his eyes and viciously kick the dog away, whereupon there is an abrupt cut to Wilson suddenly waking up in bed as if he'd been kicked and phoning Washington again, saying, "Who but a Nazi would deny that Karl Marx was a German because he was a Jew? I think I'll stick around for a while." Welles uses shadows brilliantly in the next scene to build menace. Returned from his walk, Rankin enters the bedroom as Mary sleeps, his dark shadow towering over her threateningly on the wall behind the head of the bed as he approaches. She wakes with a gasp of fear, telling him she was dreaming about "the little man," by which she means Meinike. "I've never had a dream like that before," she expounds. "It frightened me. The little man was walking all by himself, across a deserted city square. Wherever he moved, he threw a shadow. But when he moved away, Charles, the shadow stayed there behind him and spread out, just like a carpet." Her nightmare is emblematic of Rankin's situation in being unable to escape his past. As she relates this dream, the camera is filming from over Rankin's right shoulder and viewers see him from the back, all black as if he himself were a shadow, and the camera angles down on a well-lit Mary in a light-colored nightgown with white pillows behind her as she sits up in bed looking up at him. His physical power over her is compounded by his other rule over her when Red barks and Rankin explains that he locked him in the cellar for the night and from now on the dog will be kept on a leash during the day. When Mary objects to this treatment Rankin firmly says that he knows what's best. Welles ends the scene with a close-up on Mary's troubled face as she tries to fall asleep while Red whimpers offscreen.

Wilson reveals his true occupation to Noah in the next scene, when, having followed Red to the fishing dock, he accepts Noah's invitation to join him in a small boat named *Mary*. Telling him his sister may be in great trouble Wilson enlists Noah's help in tracking Rankin's movements on his wedding day in an attempt to link him to Meinike. Himself wanting to verify that the suitcase at the town drugstore belongs to Meinike, Wilson encourages the store's owner, Solomon Potter (Billy House), to look inside it. Wilson's able to recite a list of its contents while looking the other way as Potter roots through it. Rankin and Mary come into the drugstore for coffee and Rankin's supper-to-go for while he's working on the clock, and since Wilson and Potter are talking about the mysterious stranger, Mary asks whether he had an accent, whereupon Wilson observes Rankin grabbing her wrist hard to silence her. At that point Noah comes in to report that Red isn't coming home for his meals (Mary had sent him back to her father's so he could run free), and when Rankin and Mary leave for the church, Wilson tells Noah they need to arrange it so that Mary figures out Rankin's true nature by herself.

At the church, Rankin concocts the story that Meinike was the brother of a girl he knew back in Geneva when he was a student. She had drowned herself by jumping out of the boat they were in because he wouldn't agree to marry her, and even though the brother knew it had been an accident, he was blackmailing Rankin under threat that he would tell authorities it was murder. As he relates this fabrication, Welles repeats the blocking from the bedroom scene, with Rankin standing up beside the pew on which Mary is sitting; he is mostly offscreen and Welles focuses on Rankin's hands, which are fretful as they grasp upon the pew's arm and back. The selfless Mary says he should have told her and not borne this alone. He asks whether she wants him to walk her home, which she declares is unnecessary because "In Harper, there's nothing to be afraid of."

But of course, there is. Noah finds Red's dead body and brings it to the fishing dock, where Wilson suggests they take it to Dr. Lawrence, who diagnoses that Red was poisoned. Mud and leaves between the dog's front paws lead Wilson to surmise Red had been digging for Meinike's body, and Noah realizes that his brother-in-law is a murderer—of people and pets, the latter being as much a crime as the former to the youth. When Rankin comes into Potter's store for machine oil and learns the town is starting a search for the body of the mysterious stranger, his face expresses great concern and he dashes out, and in the next scene he is packing a suitcase and telling Mary that he's leaving her and she won't object once she knows what kind of man he is: he killed Red because he was digging at the grave, and he had killed Meinike because he was planning to extend his blackmail scheme to include Mary's father. Since he declares he should have run before but he loved her, was weak and had stayed, and since she's the only one who can connect him to Meinike, Mary declares she'll keep quiet about it. Meanwhile Meinike's body has been found and Wilson tells Noah it is time for Mary to hear the truth.

The next day when Rankin is trying to coach Mary on what she'll say if she's asked to identify Meinike's body, her father calls and wants her to come see him, alone and not with Charles. As they are speaking on the telephone Welles places Rankin in the foreground, adjusting the hands on a grandfather clock. He had previously stated that working on clocks calms him, and Welles uses this to good effect in scenes with the grandfather clock to indicate what upsets Rankin. He again films Rankin from the back and in shadow as he approaches Mary, who is wearing a white blouse and is very much in the light, as she's finishing the telephone call. Rankin intends to go work on the church clock, and Mary's expressed fear about the visit with her father causes his face, which Welles shows in close-up after Mary leaves the room, to reflect concern and possibly a bit of dismay that he might need to kill her too.

At her father's, Wilson reveals to Mary that it's his job to bring escaped Nazis to justice, which is why he came to Harper trailing Meinike, who had been a commander in charge of "one of the more efficient concentration camps." "I've never so much as even seen a Nazi," Mary declares, to which he responds, "Well, you might, without your realizing it. They look like other people and act like them, when it's to their benefit." To convince her of Rankin's genocidal past, he plays footage of concentration camps. *The Stranger* is the first post-war film to have done so. In his *New York Post* columns Welles said the actual footage "'must be seen' as an index of the 'putrefaction of the soul, a perfect spiritual garbage' associated with what 'we have been calling Fascism. The stench is unendurable.'"[43] As viewers and an appalled yet transfixed Mary look at a gas chamber, lime pit, and detainee on a stretcher, Wilson explains, "All this you're seeing, it's all the product of one mind. The mind of a man named Franz Kindler. He was the most brilliant of the younger minds of the Nazi party. It was Kindler who conceived the theory of genocide, mass depopulation of conquered countries, so that regardless of who won the war, Germany would emerge the strongest nation in Western Europe, biologically speaking." Then he makes Mary's role in all of this apparent: "Unlike Goebbels, Himmler, and the rest of them, Kindler had a passion for anonymity. The newspapers carried no picture of him. Oh no. And just before he disappeared, he destroyed every evidence that might link him to his past, down to the last fingerprint. There is no clue to the identity of Franz Kindler ... except one little thing. He has a hobby that almost amounts to a mania—clocks." He explains releasing Meinike in hopes he would lead him to Kindler, but that Kindler murdered Meinike and then Red when the dog found Meinike's grave, so that "Now, in all the world, there is only one person who can identify Franz Kindler. That person is the one who knows, knows definitely, who Meinike came to Harper to see." At this point the newsreel film comes to the end of the reel, and its flapping startles Mary into jumping up and insisting, "No, he's not a Nazi. My Charles is not a Nazi!" She runs out of the room but Wilson is relentless in his interrogation and follows, however Mary persists in denying Meinike came to

Rankin's house and further gives her husband an alibi in saying that he was with her that afternoon. "You're trying to use me to implicate him and you can't," she accuses, "You can't involve me in a lie. That's all it is, is a lie. It's a lie, you know. It's a lie. It's a lie!" She runs out of the house, so her father goes after her to calm her down with hugs, asking her to face things honestly and tell him the truth, and when she keeps defending her husband's goodness, he points out that he knows that Charles wasn't with her that afternoon because she had told him previously that he hadn't been. She runs off after saying that her father has never liked Charles and to leave them alone. Wilson reassures Judge Longstreet that Mary's subconscious is their ally and her will to truth will let her see.

The church clock is striking 11:00 p.m. as Mary climbs the tower to tell her husband about Wilson trying to convince her he is Franz Kindler but that she doesn't believe it. The townspeople come running because the clock is working again, and as she and Rankin exit the church, she assures him they will face the townspeople together. The opportunity arises when the Rankins host a faculty tea party in their home and guests are discussing the murder in the woods. Rankin arrives late because he stopped to get sleeping pills for his wife at the drugstore, where he also learned that Wilson had already picked up the ice cream his wife ordered for the party, and as he enters his home a guest is trying to remember a Ralph Waldo Emerson quotation about crime that begins, "Commit a crime, and the earth is made of glass." When asked if he knows it, Rankin says he doesn't, but Wilson chimes in:

> Commit a crime, and the earth is made of glass. Commit a crime, and it seems as if a coat of snow fell on the ground, such as reveals in the woods the track of every partridge and fox and squirrel and mole. You cannot recall the spoken word, you cannot wipe out the foot-track, you cannot draw up the ladder, so as to leave no inlet or clew. Some damning circumstance always transpires. The laws and substances of nature—water, snow, wind, gravitation—become penalties to the thief.

Because of Emerson's tendency to use repetition in his prose, these sound as if they might be lines of poetry, but they come from his essay "Compensation." Importantly, the lines Wilson recites are immediately preceded by, "The league between virtue and nature engages all things to assume a hostile front to vice. The beautiful laws and substances of the world persecute and whip the traitor. He finds that things are arranged for truth and benefit, but there is no den in the wide world to hide a rogue."[44] A little later in the essay Emerson, whose father had been a Unitarian minister and who himself was an ordained pastor until he resigned after questioning the validity of the Lord's Supper (although he never lost his belief in God), wrote, "We feel defrauded of the retribution due to evil acts, because the criminal adheres to his vice and contumacy and does not come to a crisis or judgment anywhere in visible nature. There is no stunning confutation of his nonsense before men and angels. Has he therefore outwitted the law? Inasmuch as he carries the malignity and the lie with him he so far decreases from nature. In some manner there will be a demonstration of the wrong to the understanding also; but, should we not see it, this deadly deduction makes square the eternal account."[45]

The lines recited by Wilson in the film should make Rankin fear being exposed for who he really is and thus brought to justice, and indeed, snow will fall rapidly in a subsequent scene when Wilson, Judge Longstreet, and Noah arrive to save Mary from immediate physical harm from Rankin; and the ladder to the clock tower will still admit Mary and Wilson up to it when Rankin is hiding there. The lines that appear in the essay right before the recited ones reinforce the same theme that the truth will out and a criminal has no place to hide. But the later lines expressing Emerson's belief that if a criminal is not punished in a way others can see he is still punished inside are less interesting than how the film overturns his phrase "There is no stunning confutation of his nonsense before men and angels," for Rankin's demise literally will be enacted by an angel before the townspeople. It can't be definitively proven that Welles was familiar with Emerson's essay in its entirety, nor even that it was he who substituted the Emerson lines for a passing reference made at that point in the shooting scrip to the 18th-century French author Claude Joseph Dorat, but the quotation and full essay certainly fit Welles' film beautifully. Not that the Dorat reference didn't bring its own set of allusions and meaning. No specific work by Dorat is named or quoted in the shooting script, a guest at the faculty tea party merely asks Rankin if he's familiar with the author, who, the guest deems, "Wrote some very amusing light verse. With nice Gallic cynicism."[46] A few of Dorat's works were *Abelard's Answer to Heloise*, *The Fatal Effects of Inconstancy*, and *The Sacrifices of Love*, the first alluding to an infamous relationship variously interpreted by scholars and the second two being collections of people's personal correspondence. Some other works translate as *The Kisses*, *Mystery Lover*, and *The Feigning Lover*. All of these titles comment upon the Rankins' relationship in one way or another, although what specific text by Dorat was in the mind of whichever author at work on the shooting script included the reference to him is now beyond anyone's ken.

While Wilson recites, Welles has Mary looking nervously at Rankin rather than at Wilson, then focuses the camera on her as she walks toward it, working her way through the party guests after a woman comes up to tell Wilson that he is the number one suspect in the murder. Rankin follows her into the kitchen and as he shuts the door behind them the voice of a woman is heard saying, "Mr. Rankin, I wish you'd left that clock alone. Harper was a nice quiet place until it started banging," an apt commentary on the chaos he has brought to this village where he sought haven. After they see out the last of their guests Mary desperately seems to need to loosen the clothing and jewelry around her neckline but has trouble getting the clasp of her necklace undone; when Rankin offers to assist, she overreacts by breaking the strands to get it off, then turning away from him. The expression on his face shows that he now knows for sure that she can't be trusted not to betray him, that she is likely starting to believe that he is Franz Kindler.

While Mary sleeps Rankin goes to the church to saw through and then glue together a rung on the ladder to the clock tower. The next afternoon he writes a list planning his upcoming crime while at his desk in front of his class that will start at 2:30:

3:25 Phone Mary
3:30 go to Potters Drug Store
ESTABLISH TIME (which he underscores after completing the list)

4:00 leave Potters
4:05 Home

Since he telephones Mary from Potter's store, this isn't quite accurate. Nonetheless, it's important to notice that while he is waiting for Mary to answer the telephone, he doodles a swastika on the wall message pad hanging by the phone, which he quickly obscures by overlaying additional lines. He asks Mary to come to the church tower but not to tell anyone she's going there. Mary's housekeeper Sara (Martha Wentworth) has been ordered not to let Mary out of her sight so that Rankin can't harm her, thus when Mary tries to leave her home Sara throws a fit about Mary's recent treatment of her to stall, and when that doesn't work she feigns heart pain to get Mary to stay with her. Mary calls Noah and asks him to go in her stead, but not to tell anyone. Of course, Noah dutifully calls Wilson, who accompanies him to the church while Rankin is playing checkers with Potter at the drugstore to establish his alibi. Rankin is so bent on nailing down the time of his being there with Potter that when two librarians come into the store, he remarks exactly upon what time it is; Welles uses a long shot to show Wilson and Noah entering the church out of his range of vision. Viewers see the two climbing the ladder and Wilson breaking the rung but not falling, then observe Rankin burning his written plan for homicide in the stove at the drugstore as the clock strikes 4:00 just before he leaves.

Welles casts a shadow silhouette of Mary on the living room wall as Rankin enters his home so that viewers know that she is in the dimmed room, but Rankin is shocked to find Mary alive—Welles moves in slowly on his face to show how unhinged he becomes, after which he winds the grandfather clock, adjusts its hands, and fusses with its works. Mary wants to know what was so important that he needed to see her, at which he says it was nothing, "It's my sense of proportion that's failing me these days," and when she touches him, causing the clock's chimes to clamor, he allows that he's begun to feel a strain and has his weak moments too. When she finds out he had not encountered Noah at the church Mary realizes he meant to kill her since he had not gone there to meet her as arranged during their phone call. Ranting that her meddling has caused all the problems, starting with being at his home when Meinike appeared, Rankin admits that Noah would have been killed if he went up the ladder. She calls him Franz Kindler and tells him to kill her as long as he doesn't put his hands on her because she can't face life knowing what she's been to him, meaning having shared his bed, and that she's ultimately responsible for Noah's death, but he throws down the poker she hands him and flees—all that Welles shows us of Rankin's departure is the swinging kitchen door—just before Wilson, Judge Longstreet, and Noah rush in, whereupon Mary faints at seeing her brother alive.

The camera shows viewers the angel statue crossing the face of the clock as it strikes 11:00 p.m., a foreshadowing of the path it will inexorably take in a scene to come shortly. Wilson orchestrates the search for Rankin, having roadblocks set up and the railroad watched, already having established that he's not hiding in the woods. Mary puts her coat on over her nightgown and takes a box akin to the one her husband's take-out meal had been in with her to the church; when Sara discovers she is gone, Wilson thinks Rankin could be hiding in the clock tower, but he stumbles and falls down the stairs as he and Noah start to go there, so he sends Noah on ahead to try to save his sister.

Welles provides a beautifully vertiginous shot from below of Mary climbing up the clock tower ladder using one hand, rung by rung, then a downward shot from her perspective to the floor far below when she reaches its top. A disheveled Rankin tells her to stop because he has a gun, but she assures him he doesn't need it because she's alone. She has to grasp his hand for him to pull her up into the tower since the final rungs are missing from his previous attempt to murder her, and Welles films her hanging there from Rankin's hand over a sheer drop to the floor that would obviously kill her while he asks her if she's telling the truth and she responds, "Why should I lie?" As it turns out, the box she brought is empty, her pretense of bringing food in order to get him to let her up. "I came to kill you," she announces, leading him to chuckle and respond, "No, no Mary, it's you that's going to die. You were meant to fall through that ladder. You're going to fall." "I don't mind, if I take you with me," she responds, eliciting "You are a fool" from her husband. He's confident he'll get away since they won't search the woods again and she has been on the verge of a breakdown, which they'll assume is why she came to the clock tower to kill herself. Enter Wilson, who tells Rankin he's finished, and indeed, the townspeople are swarming toward the church. The ordinary citizens of Harper whom Rankin had laughed at can no longer be fooled, will come after him. As Wilson continues his speech, Welles lets viewers see the backlit angel statue in the background behind him, to his right, advancing along its path: "Oh sure, you can kill me, Mary, half the people down there. But there's no escape. You had the world and it closed in on you till there was only Harper. That closed in on you and then there was only this room. And this room, too, is closing in on you." Welles has Wilson's character advance toward Rankin as he says this, a nice parallel to the advancing angel, while Rankin backs away. Sweating and panicked, Rankin tries to deny his actions, saying, "It's not true, the things they say I did. It was all their idea. I followed orders." "You gave the orders," Wilson corrects, whereupon Rankin reiterates, "I, I only did my duty. Don't send me back to them, I can't face them. I'm not a criminal." "You are," Mary states calmly, distracting him so that Wilson has the opportunity to strike the gun from his hand, which Mary picks up and commences firing, hitting the clock works and speeding them up. Rankin climbs higher up into the tower as Mary shoots at him, hitting him in the shoulder; Wilson wrests the gun from her but it is empty. Woozy from his wounds, Rankin falls out of the window onto the ledge beneath the clock's face on which the statues circle.

The clock is still running at an advanced pace and the statue of the demon passes by in its rotation, which Rankin manages to avoid, but the angel comes at him next, impaling him on its sword. The camera pulls back to show the angel crossing the face of the clock with Rankin stuck on the sword, the townspeople below screaming in horror at this sight. Rankin extracts himself from the sword, pushes the angel off the clock ledge, then, after teetering a moment, falls himself. Welles then gives a close-up of the clock's hands spinning around. There is a dissolve to Mary being helped safely off the bottom of the ladder and Potter asking what happened, to which Wilson replies, "V Day in Harper." Declaring he will wait for a new

Kindler/Rankin (Orson Welles) escapes the demon in *The Stranger* (1946) (RKO Radio Pictures, Inc./Photofest).

ladder to be brought for his own descent, the film rushes to an incongruous close with Wilson calling down from the tower, "Good night, Mary. Pleasant dreams," as he lights his pipe and "The End" fills the screen.

Welles' belief that Fascism would continue to exist in post-war Germany results in a fascinating double identity noir thriller. As Rankin had said to Meinike, "Who would think to look for the notorious Franz Kindler in the sacred precincts of the Harper School, surrounded by the sons of America's first families? And I'll stay hidden until the day when we strike again." Another noir drama is Welles' *The Lady from Shanghai* (1947), although he also worked in other genres, such as his versions of Shakespeare's *Othello* (1951) and his drama *The Magnificent Ambersons* (1942), along with films mentioned elsewhere in this study.

Gordon Douglas and *I Was a Communist for the F.B.I.*

Hearkening back to the crusade against Communism mentioned at the opening of this chapter, the FBI had long used undercover informants to garner information about Communist Party members and activities, and in the late 1940s and in the 1950s said informants testified to Congressional committees during the prosecution of Party leaders. Matt Cvetic testified before HUAC in 1950—"to the shock of both his comrades and non–Communist associates in western Pennsylvania, this minor CP functionary turned out to have been an FBI informant for nearly a decade."[47] Cvetic was based in Pittsburgh, which, "with its large Eastern European immigrant population, was a logical setting for Red-scare paranoia. However, Cvetic's testimony is indicative of the fear gripping the entire nation during the Cold War and, all over the country, other informants were identifying Communist leaders in their communities."[48] As such, his story would become ripe for use by the entertainment media as a means for spreading anti–Communist propaganda.

Cvetic gave a six-day testimony on "the Communist presence in western Pennsylvania," during which he named some 290 people as Party members and "describ[ed] in detail allegedly subversive activities of various Communist leaders."[49] As Dan Leab observes, "Cvetic's HUAC testimony fitted the mood of the day and garnered favourable attention across the country," leading to a series titled "I Posed as a Communist for the FBI" in the *Saturday Evening Post*,[50] written by Pete Martin from stories Cvetic told him, which was published on July 15, 22, and 29, 1950. This in turn was made into a radio show, *I Was a Communist for the FBI*, which aired over 70 episodes from 1952 to 1954 and starred Dana Andrews. Although movie studios were interested in Cvetic's story, it sold to Warner Brothers in August 1950 for a mere $12,500 (Leab notes that Twentieth Century–Fox had paid $75,000 for Soviet defector Igor Gouzenko's story in 1947[51]). The Warner Brothers film was intentionally low-budget to "cash in on the contemporary anti–Red hysteria," and indeed, Leab claims that "economics more than politics governed the production of anti–Communist films."[52]

Far from an accurate depiction of Cvetic's life and activities, *I Was a Communist for the F.B.I.* (1951), directed by Gordon Douglas from a screenplay by Crane Wilbur, "embellished Cvetic's story and caricatured the history of the Communist Party."[53] Whereas the real-life Cvetic was a divorced father of twins, a womanizer with a drinking problem, his celluloid version is stoically unattached, rebuffing his son's teacher when she shows up at his boarding house room and invitingly says, "I came here because I thought you were lonely. I'm lonely too." His only child, Dick, lives with Cvetic's mother; Dick's mother is never referred to. The film plays up the self-sacrificing nature of Cvetic's nine-year isolating undercover work. It's meant to be painful that the viewer knows Cvetic's beloved, wheelchair-bound mother dies without learning his true allegiance. One brother calls him a "slimy Red"; his son gets in fights at school defending his father's reputation, but when Dick learns his father really is a member of the Communist Party, he says, "Don't ever come near me again." This affords the opportunity for Cvetic to write a letter to be given Dick by the family priest in the case of his death that uses patriotic rhetoric such as "I am helping to fight a dark and dangerous force." Writing that he was proud of his son's stance against Communism, he pens, "That's one thing I always want you to remember: If your conscience tells you a thing is right, always stand up for it."

The film is overt in its anti–Soviet, pro–America message from the beginning. It opens by punching the title at viewers one word at a time over the background of a man in a dark hat and suit striding toward the camera through cavernous stone archways, simultaneously suggesting secrecy and evoking the halls of the government. Matt Cvetic (Frank Lovejoy) tells his story in voice-over through many scenes, with discussion among FBI agents or Communist Party members filling in the narrative in other scenes. The initial plot is kicked off when Communist agent Gerhardt Eisler (Konstantin Shayne) arrives in Pittsburgh as part of his rounds through the nation to mobilize and strengthen the Communist Party in America. When Cvetic goes to Eisler's hotel room to meet him for the first time, there is a lavish spread—including a full roasted turkey, caviar, and champagne—laid out on a silver service, and Cvetic is told, "Better get used to it. It's the way we're all gonna live when they take over." Eisler gives Cvetic the position of Chief Party Organizer for Pittsburgh and tells those gathered that in order to bring about the success of Communism in America they need to incite riots and cause discontent. The first step toward this will be a Communist Party meeting held at the ironically named Freedom Hall.

There, Jim Blandon (James Millican) gives a speech to a largely Black audience with the aim to cause unrest and confusion. As Cvetic's voice-over tells viewers, "There are more ways than one to sabotage the safety of a country. The one he used was as dangerous as blowing up defense plants. It was the old rule of divide and conquer." Later Blandon remarks to his white Party colleagues, "Those niggers ate it up, didn't they?" Cvetic corrects him with "negroes" (still offensive to viewers today, but a more acceptable term at the time), but Blandon says he only calls them that when he's trying to sell them the Party line. It comes out that Party leaders intend to use the Blacks to raise money for the Party—if a Black man hit a white man during a riot, perhaps killing him, and was convicted by an all-white jury, the Party could raise a lot of money from its members for a legal defense fund. A minimum would be used from that fund to provide incompetent legal defense that would leave the Black man convicted and the Party with the rest of the money. Further callousness is shown at the steel mill where Cvetic works in personnel: a worker has been deliberately hurt on the job and will lose his arm; his replacement carries a Party card.

Soviet Communism's atheism is slipped in at Cvetic's mother's funeral. Blandon and another Party member attend, even sent a rose wreath, but after the Catholic funeral mass Blandon says sarcastically to Cvetic, "That's quite a show they put on in there. I saw you kneeling with those other sheep…. Were you praying with the rest of them? … Be careful Matt, you're in danger of losing your soul." Cvetic's brother Joe

(Paul Picerni) hits him with the rose wreath and declares, "I've been waiting a long time for this. Put up your hands. I said put up your hands, you dirty Red!" Cvetic does not defend himself, but Joe still punches him in the gut, then strikes him on the head, knocking him to the sidewalk. Father Novac (Roy Roberts) breaks up the fight, but during the scuffle Cvetic drops the letter to Dick that the priest had just given him back due to being called to Rome. Dick's teacher, Eve Merrick (Dorothy Hart), swoops it up and places it in her purse. When Cvetic later misses it, still upset by his brother's attack he goes to his FBI contacts and tells them he wants to get out: "You've got to wipe this Red smear off of me. I can't take it any longer!" Told that he can quit but the FBI will publicly disown him and he'll need to clear his own name, Cvetic reconsiders and valiantly says, "I want to go on living in a country where you can walk around holding your head up. Where you can talk back to cops and you can yell out in print. Where the secret police won't be dragging you out of bed at 4:00 in the morning. Sound like corn?" His FBI handler, Ken Crowley (Richard Webb), replies, "Not to me," and Cvetic tells him he'll stay on the job. "He's quite a guy," Crowley remarks to a fellow agent after Cvetic leaves.

More duplicitous maneuvers by Communist Party infiltrators into the steel workers' union, such as filibustering at a union meeting so that tired workers will leave and the few remaining can be coerced to strike, leads to a strike at the North American Steel Company, Cvetic's place of employment. A newspaper fills the screen with the huge front-page headline, "Wildcat Strike Hits North American Steel," and a smaller article is titled, "Union Leaders Say Communist Inspired." The Party prepares to send women dressed as union wives to incite the crowd, picket signs read "We fight fascism at home and abroad" and "Capitalistic bosses hate good union people," and tough Party members from New York are imported to wield lead pipes. However, these pieces of pipe are to be wrapped in Jewish newspapers, laying any blame for strike violence upon this minority group.

At the strike, the crowd gets excited when union officers and others—including Cvetic's brother Joe—arrive to break up the picket line. The Party women yell "Kill those rotten scabs!" and Blandon orders the imported thugs to start breaking skulls; Joe is one of the casualties sent to the hospital. Eve, upset at the use of Jewish papers to conceal the lead pipes, now refuses to egg on the violence like the other Party women plants, saying, "I don't like any part of what happened here today. It's right to fight for what we believe in, but why can't we do it in the open, and why have we got to blame it on others?" Called out for treason by another woman, Cvetic has to protect Eve by lambasting her: "All that bothers you is that we've pinned it on the Jews? Sure, we pinned it on them. Jews, Catholics—till we get them all fighting with each other and tearing each other's throats out, how do we expect to feed them and establish a Soviet America?" He sends her home and in a later scene with several Party members tells Eve she should be dropped from the Party. At first upset by this announcement, Eve says she joined the Communist Party because she thought it was an intellectual movement, "A movement toward true freedom.... I've been completely disillusioned. I found out that its only object is to gain complete control of every human mind and body in the world. Communism is a mockery of freedom." Declaring she will tell the school board the names of every teacher who carries a

Party card, one member tries to stop her from leaving, but Blandon says to let her go, and Cvetic assures them he'll make sure she doesn't follow through on the threat.

Hastening after Eve, Cvetic is surprised when she gives him the letter he wrote to his son and reveals how reading it started to change her mind about the Party. He tells her she needs to pack a light bag, get out of town that night, and lay low, then he cases out a back alley exit from her apartment building because he suspects Party members will be coming for her—throughout the film Party members have been following other Party members to make sure they are loyal, so at the very least Eve will be watched closely from now on. And indeed, Blandon sends two men to "get up there and finish it" whenever they see that Eve has turned off the lights in her apartment for the night. They observe Cvetic driving away from the front of the building, but they don't see him drive around to the alley. Eve and Cvetic give the two men who enter the building the slip, but Blandon is outside and sees them drive out of the alley, so it's no surprise for viewers that at the train station after Eve boards, Cvetic spies two Party members heading to the platform. They try to throw Eve off the train, but Cvetic has boarded too and fights them after pulling the brake cord. All four exit the train to continue the pursuit into a train tunnel. Cvetic pushes Eve into a hiding spot and runs off to draw the men's gunfire. He manages to push one of them down stairs onto the tracks just as a train arrives to run over him. Retrieving the man's gun from the chain link stair railing, he exchanges fire with the remaining man until one of Cvetic's bullets hits him fatally in the head.

With Eve stashed safely in an out-of-town hotel, Cvetic attends a Party meeting at which a leader named Clyde Garson (Hugh Sanders) speaks:

> Comrades, I don't need to tell you that the Un-American Activities Committee is becoming a danger to us. The hearings it's conducting in Washington are bad counter-propaganda. Moscow has ordered a nationwide campaign…. All Communists are to spread the word that the Un-American Activities Committee is a group of fat-headed politicians whose only aim is to crash the headlines. We want them laughed at, ridiculed. If we start the ball rolling there are plenty of big-mouthed suckers in this country who will do the rest.

He goes on to note that North Koreans will invade South Korea any day, which will be the first step in the Communist march toward victory. Communists in America will then demoralize citizens so they are too weak to fight. At this point a man brings in a newspaper for Blandon containing an article about the two dead Communists found in the train tunnel; immediately he is suspicious of Cvetic's involvement in helping Eve get away. Cvetic is taken to Party headquarters and beaten up as a traitor, but the police come in and arrest him on suspicion of murdering an FBI agent who had been killed by the two thugs in Eve's apartment while trying to apprehend them. Although he's still suspicious, Blandon arranges to have Cvetic sprung as soon as possible.

Not long after, Blandon and other Pittsburgh Communist Party leaders, including Cvetic, are called before the Un-American Activities Committee in Washington. Crowley has arranged for Cvetic's brother Joe and son Dick (Ron Hagerthy) to be there. Whereas the other Party leaders have refused to answer the question of whether they are members of the Communist Party, when Cvetic takes the stand, he says he has been for nine years. "I joined it as an undercover agent for the Federal Bureau of Investigation," he says, explaining, "I was what is commonly known as a plant." Party members in the audience boo him, while his brother and son—the latter in his Navy Seabee woolens—display pride on their faces. Cvetic continues: "I learned chiefly that its political activities are nothing more than a front. It is actually a vast spy system founded in our country by the Soviet. It's composed of American traitors whose main purpose is to deliver the people of the United States into the hands of Russia as a slave colony." This testimony causes the audience to go wild, various members booing and cheering, while his relatives continue to look thrilled. "The idea of Communism as common ownership and control by the people has never been practiced in Russia and never will be," he concludes, exiting the room to boos and applause. Two Party thugs try to follow him but are arrested for the murder of the FBI agent in Eve's apartment; Blandon happens to be waiting in the room to which Cvetic exits and attacks him, but Cvetic punches him and, subdued, Blandon is taken away to testify.

The film moves towards its close as Joe and Dick come in, Dick asking for forgiveness. "I was proud to know that my boy was all the things that I wanted to be," Cvetic tells him, "That you had the brains to see this slimy thing for just what it is. That you had the guts to stand up against me and all the world and fight against it. Even when you hated me, I loved you for it." The music of "The Battle Hymn of the Republic" starts fading in as he speaks, then swells to high volume as Cvetic and Dick hug, and all three exit the chamber while the camera centers in on a bust of Abraham Lincoln.

John Sbardellati, in *J. Edgar Hoover Goes to the Movies: The FBI and the Origin of Hollywood's Cold War*, notes that *I Was a Communist for the F.B.I.* "irked the FBI director."[54] While Cvetic was a valuable source as an informant, "Hoover especially grew annoyed at Cvetic's grandiose definition of himself as an undercover FBI agent, when in fact he had been only a confidential informant" and anticipated that when the film was released viewers would take the "very bad title ... as official."[55] Reviews of the film were mixed. Louella Parsons, the gossip columnist for William Randolph Hearst's anti–Communist publications, deemed it "the strongest exposé of dread Communism to date," while *Time*, another anti–Communist publication, judged it "crude, over-amplified, mechanical."[56] Whatever the critical response, as Leab proposes, "That this meretricious, crude, fanciful, highly propagandistic film was nominated for an Oscar as the best full-length documentary of 1951 is some indication of the paranoid mood of the U.S. at that time."[57] Indeed.

Gordon Douglas had a lengthy career as a director, ranging in genre from the comedy horror film *Zombies on Broadway* (1945), to the musical romance *Young at Heart* (1954), the war drama *Bombers B-52* (1957), a remake of John Ford's 1939 *Stagecoach* (1966), the action adventure *In Like Flint* (1967), and the crime drama *They Call Me Mr. Tibbs!* (1970), just to note a few of his films.

Richard Condon, John Frankenheimer and *The Manchurian Candidate*

A more specific kind of Communist threat than that addressed in *I Was a Communist for the F.B.I.* would emerge in a film released just over ten years later. To say

John Frankenheimer's late noir, *The Manchurian Candidate* (1962), is a complex film is an understatement. To that point, the original movie poster included the declaration, "If you come in five minutes after this picture begins, you won't know what it's all about!" Based upon Richard Condon's best-seller 1959 novel of the same name (not incidentally, Condon had been a movie publicist before turning to novel writing), with a screenplay by George Axelrod, the shifting point of view from a cinematic perspective is achieved by very subjective camera work. Viewers are told at the film's opening that the scene they are watching occurred in Korea in 1952. Major Bennett Marco (Frank Sinatra) and Staff Sergeant Raymond Shaw (Laurence Harvey) gather their men from a local bar to have their Korean interpreter-guide lead them through dangerous terrain where they are then captured. The guide shakes hands with an American officer, then the men are taken away in helicopters and the opening credits are presented. After those, Raymond Shaw is feted as a hero when he returns to Washington, D.C., to receive the Medal of Honor for saving the lives of nine members of his patrol. As Raymond alights from his plane, his mother takes control of the scene as a publicity stunt for her husband's re-election. Eleanor Shaw Iselin (Angela Lansbury) is a Red-baiter who claims those disagreeing with her right-wing reactionary views are Communists. But as will be seen, actually she herself is a Communist agent implicated in brainwashing her son to make him a political assassin, part of a plan to gain Communist control of the United States by securing the presidency for Raymond's stepfather, Senator John Yerkes Iselin (James Gregory). By film's end viewers learn that Raymond's patrol was taken by a Russian airborne unit across the Manchurian border to the Pavlov Institute, where they were worked on for three days while considered "missing in action." Two surviving members of the patrol are plagued with reoccurring nightmares, which Frankenheimer depicts via disorienting and intriguing sets and camerawork.

The first nightmare is Marco's. He and the other soldiers from the patrol sit in boredom in the lobby of the Spring Lake Hotel in New Jersey, listening to Mrs. Henry Whittaker (Helen Kleeb), whom the event placard proclaims is the "foremost authority on hydrangeas," discourse on "Fun with Hydrangeas." Some of the garden club women in the audience look a bit bored as well, distracted by touching up their makeup or smoking a cigarette, although others seem intent and take notes. Suddenly the set becomes a lecture theater with large photographs of Stalin and Mao behind the speaker, and while the soldiers remain the same, the others present have changed: Mrs. Whittaker has become the Chinese Dr. Yen Lo (Khigh Dhiegh), and members of the audience are Chinese and Russian Comrades. Dr. Lo speaks of having "conditioned" the soldiers, "or brainwashed them, which I understand is the new American word," he qualifies. Frankenheimer cuts between Mrs. Whittaker and Dr. Lo, the garden club women and the Comrades, whereas continuity is present because whether a soldier is addressing Whittaker or Lo, he uses "ma'am" (in the novel he always uses "sir" and is always addressing Lo). By this Frankenheimer conveys that the men are hypnotized into thinking they see a woman even though they are being addressed by a man. Raymond will demonstrate his conditioning by strangling Private Ed Mavole (Richard LePore) with a weapon offered up by an audience member, a scarf; he does, and Marco wakes from his nightmare.

The second nightmare is experience by Corporal Allen Melvin (James Edwards). In his dream, all the women of the garden club are Black; since Melvin is Black, this shows the subjective point of view of the men's nightmares. This time, Private Bobby Lembeck (Tom Lowell) is the victim, shot through the forehead with the pistol Marco lends Raymond. After he wakes screaming, Melvin's wife urges him to write to Raymond Shaw, whom Melvin rapidly declares "is the bravest, kindest, warmest, most wonderful human being I've ever known in my life," which were the same adjectives Marco had used to describe Shaw when asked how he felt about the staff sergeant after revealing his nightmare to his army superiors. Much later in the film, Marco finds this rote response evidence that their minds had been altered since while he believes it as he is speaking it, it isn't true because Raymond is impossible to like.

The visual trigger for Raymond to act as he is ordered to is the playing card Queen of Diamonds, which the audial trigger "Why don't you pass the time by playing a little solitaire?" leads him to turn up. Raymond needs to be tested before his big assignment because two years have passed since his conditioning. A fake hit and run accident is staged so that this can happen, also affording a scene in which Dr. Lo can explain to a colleague that because Raymond has no memory of having killed, he has no guilt or fear. "His brain has not only been washed, it's been dry cleaned!" Lo remarks jovially. Raymond has been working as a journalist for Holborn Gaines (Lloyd Corrigan), Gaines is selected as the test victim, and Raymond kills him at 4:00 a.m. while Gaines is reading in bed (dressed, amusingly, in his late wife's fluffy-trimmed bed jacket).

A further way to check on Raymond is by having the interpreter-guide from the opening scene, Chunjin (Henry Silva), become his employee. Chunjin shows up at Raymond's apartment declaring that Senator Iselin has secured him a visa and now he needs a job; despite his dislike of his stepfather Raymond employs him as valet-cook. Marco, having been forced to take leave when his superiors think his eighteen months of active duty in Korea have caused him to suffer from combat fatigue, goes to New York to tell Raymond his suspicions that they've been manipulated in some way, and when Chunjin answers the apartment door, Marco has the shock of recognition—very nicely described by Condon as "To Marco he was a djinn who had stepped into flesh out of that torment which was giving him lyssophobia."[58] Marco hits him, whereupon a knock-down, drag-out fight ensues, during which Marco keeps asking Chunjin how the old lady turned into a Russian and what Raymond was doing with his hands (which Marco later realizes was playing solitaire). A neighbor calls the police and Marco is arrested, to be released into his soon-to-be new girlfriend's custody, Eugenie Rose Chaney (Janet Leigh), a woman he met on the train to New York. As they take a cab, viewers spot a theater marquis it drives by advertising Walt Disney's *Pinocchio*, Frankenheimer's suitable commentary on Marco's inability to get straight answers throughout his inquiry into just what had happened to the men in his patrol. Yet this soon changes when Marco finally gets to talk with Raymond, who describes the scene from Marco's nightmare and tells him about the letter from Corporal Melvin. Marco goes to Washington and identifies two of the men in his dream, whom Melvin had also identified, finally kicking off a joint CIA-FBI investigation. Bound by their shared mysterious experiences, Marco and Raymond drink champagne on Christmas Eve, which leads Raymond to start talking about how much he hates his mother, then protest that Marco doesn't want to hear it. Marco assures him, "It's fine. It's like listening to Orestes gripe about Clytemnestra." Later, he will remember what Dr. Lo said about Raymond associating the Queen of Diamonds with his mother, making it a powerful trigger.

Nora Sayre, in *Running Time: Films of the Cold War*, deems Eleanor Iselin the culmination of "the disemboweling, all-destructive mother" type in Cold War films.[59] It's also worth noting here that she completely controls her husband as well, telling him to let her do the thinking because while there are things he is good at, thinking is not one of them. At one point she dismisses him from their party by saying, "Run along, the grown-ups have to talk," and at the delegates' convention near the end of the film she leads him by the hand through the crowd, like a child in tow. Lansbury, who was nominated for Best Supporting Actress for her role as Eleanor, appeals to Raymond's patriotic side in trying to get him to break up with Jocelyn (Leslie Parrish), the daughter of Senator Thomas Jordan (John McGiver), whom she declares is a Communist. "I want to talk to you about that Communist tart," she announces, ordering him to sit down when Raymond objects and launching into a diatribe:

> If we were at war and you were suddenly to become infatuated with the daughter of a Russian agent, wouldn't you expect me to come to you and object, and beg you to stop the entire thing before it's too late? Well, we are at war. It's a Cold War. But it will get worse and worse until every man, woman, and child in this country will have to stand up and be counted, say whether they are on the side of right and freedom or on the side of the Thomas Jordans of this country. I will go to Washington with you, tomorrow if you like, and I will show you documented proof that this man stands for evil, that he is evil, and that his whole life is devoted to undermining everything that you and I and Johnny and every freedom of every American—

Then Frankenheimer cuts to a scene of Raymond telling Marco, "She won, of course. She always does. I could never beat her. I still can't." Indeed, after their one-way conversation, under his mother's direction, Raymond broke off the engagement with Jocelyn, and the next day he enlisted.

Opportunistic Eleanor later submerges her hatred of Senator Jordan and reunites Jocelyn and Raymond at a costume party held for the young woman's return from abroad only because she hopes the senator will not block her husband's party nomination for vice president. Jocelyn's costume has a Queen of Diamonds card as its front, which snaps Raymond out of the hypnotic state his mother had put him into before being called away to welcome Senator Jordan to her party and leads the two young people to embrace and kiss. Senator Jordan's declaration that he'll bring impeachment proceedings against Iselin if she tries to sway the delegates or get her husband's name on the ticket decides Eleanor's next course of action: Senator Iselin appears on television charging Jordan with high treason and intending to move for his impeachment when Senate reconvenes, plus a civil trial after that. This press conference is referred to in the novel after it happens and is described in summaries of two newspaper articles. Frankenheimer makes the television set an important element of the press conference, as he had in an earlier scene when

Senator Iselin declared at another press conference that he held a list of the names of 207 persons that the Secretary of Defense knows are members of the Communist Party yet who are helping to shape the policy of the Defense Department. Eleanor had watched her husband on a television monitor in the room rather than looked at him directly, by which Frankenheimer underscores the spectacle the media creates. Lights placed around the room by press staff shine toward the movie's viewers, making the audience part of the media circus as viewers take in live action and monitor at the same time. Frankenheimer creates yet another scene to make commentary on the media when Jocelyn and Raymond, who had left the costume party to get married, are on their honeymoon and she turns on the television set in their hotel room. Raymond observes that there are two kinds of people, those who come into a room and turn on a television and those who come into a room and turn it off. One gets the sense that Raymond is the kind who would turn it off since he is more interested in Jocelyn than in what is being broadcast—until he realizes what his stepfather is announcing about persecuting Senator Jordan, whereupon he tells his new wife to return to her father's home since he is going to Washington to beat up his stepfather. But it is his mother who greets him when he arrives there. Frankenheimer ends that scene ominously by having Eleanor take out a deck of cards, then cuts to Senator Jordan at home late at night, surprised that Raymond has turned up at his door, yet welcoming Raymond into the family. Frankenheimer frames a shot so that an American eagle ornamental plaque on the wall over a doorway behind Raymond is prominent when he takes out a gun and shoots Jordan while they are in the kitchen. Jocelyn runs down from upstairs to witness Raymond finishing off her father with a shot to his head, then he shoots her dead. Tears run down Raymond's face as he walks away from their house.

When he sees the headline that the senator and his daughter were slain, Raymond calls Marco from a hotel room across from Madison Square Garden, where the delegates' convention is being held and the presidential and vice-presidential party nominees will be accepted. Marco has figured out that the Queen of Diamonds is Raymond's trigger and has acquired a trick deck consisting of all Queen of Diamonds cards. Asking, "How about passing the time by playing a little solitaire?" he gives Raymond the deck. The first card Raymond turns over leads to the revelation that the patrol was taken by a Russian airborne unit and flown to the Pavlov Institute where team specialists worked on them for three days; Raymond remembers strangling Mavole and shooting Lembeck. The second card causes him to remember killing Gaines as a test before being turned over to his American operator, and that a bartender's overheard remark led him to jump into the lake at Central Park— Frankenheimer used a rolling drum military soundtrack in that scene as Raymond resolutely followed these "orders." The third card makes Raymond remember killing Senator Jordan, but Marco stops him before he remembers killing Jocelyn and tells him to forget everything that happened at the senator's home. Raymond can't answer Marco's question of what they "built" him to do, but he knows it will happen at the convention. When Raymond despairs, "They can make me do anything, Ben, can't they? Anything," Marco reassures, "We'll see, kid. We'll see what they can do and we'll see what we can do," and shows him the deck of 52 Queen of

Diamonds, which causes Raymond to snap to in a hypnotically attentive state. Marco continues:

> Take a good look at 'em Raymond, look at 'em, and while you're looking listen. This is me, Marco, talking. 52 red Queens and me are telling you, you know what we're telling you? It's over. The links, the beautifully conditioned links, are smashed. They're smashed as of now because we say so. Because we say they ought to be smashed. We're busting up the joint, we're tearing out all the wires, we're busting it up so good all the queen's horses and all the queen's men will never put old Raymond back together again. You don't work anymore, that's an order. Anybody invites you to a game of solitaire you tell 'em "Sorry buster, the ball game is over."

As soon as this rant concludes Frankenheimer punctuates the scene with a ringing telephone, which Marco nods his okay for Raymond to answer. Holding his hand over the mouthpiece, Raymond tells Marco that it is time for his American operative to give him his plan, then he resumes speaking on the phone and identifies the caller—his American operative—as his mother. After Raymond hangs up, Marco tells him to call investigation headquarters by 8:30 p.m. before the convention reconvenes at 9:00 p.m. so Marco and the authorities know what Raymond will be ordered to do. He reminds Raymond that the wires have been pulled, they can't touch him anymore, he's free. This "freeing" of Raymond from control does not appear in Condon's novel. Instead, after listening to Raymond's explanation of how he is to kill the presidential candidate and shoot his stepfather in the shoulder to make it appear he is wounded because he'll be bullet proofed and wearing a crystal compound that will look like blood when it's hit, Marco instead orders Raymond to kill his stepfather and mother. After he does so at the convention, Marco enters the spotlight booth where Raymond shot from, gives him the loaded deck of Queen of Diamonds cards, and leaves the booth. A gunshot is heard within the booth, and Marco says to the government agents who had lagged behind him, "No electric chair for a Medal of Honor man."[60] Frankenheimer's movie departs from this in a way that strengthens the emotion of the film's denouement.

Lansbury as Eleanor Iselin is chilling as she gives Raymond his orders. He'll have a two-piece Soviet Army sniper's rifle and is to "shoot the presidential nominee through the head," after which her husband will "rise gallantly" to take up the bloody body of the nominee and make a speech. "The speech is short, but it's the most rousing speech I've ever read. It's been worked on here and in Russia on and off for over eight years," and with it Johnny will rally "a nation of television viewers into hysteria, to sweep us up into the White House with powers that will make martial law seem like anarchy." She further instructs Raymond, "You are to hit him right at the point that he finishes the phrase, 'Nor would I ask of any fellow American in defense of his freedom that which I would not gladly give myself. My life before my liberty!' Is that absolutely clear?" Raymond confirms that it is, then Eleanor, still chilling in tone but with the coldness seemingly directed at those who orchestrated brainwashing her son, comes close to Raymond's face and says,

> I know you will never entirely comprehend this, Raymond. But you must believe I did not know it would be you. I served them. I fought for them. I'm on the point of winning for them the greatest foothold they will ever have in this country. And they paid me back by taking

Eleanor Iselin (Angela Lansbury) displays unmotherly love toward her son Raymond (Laurence Harvey) in *The Manchurian Candidate* **(1962) (M.C. Prods/UA/Photofest).**

your soul away from you. I told them to build me an assassin. I wanted a killer from a world filled with killers, and they chose you. Because they thought it would bind me closer to them. But now we have come almost to the end. One last step. And then when I take power they will be pulled down and ground into dirt for what they did to you. And what they did in so contemptuously underestimating me.

Eleanor then kisses her son on the forehead and cheek, finishing with a long, lover-like kiss full on his lips—a quite disturbing display of rather un-maternal love. Some of the dialogue quoted above from the film comes directly from Condon's novel, with a few edits to trim it down, an important one being Eleanor's statement that "just as I am a mother before everything else I am an American second to that" before her declaration that they will be pulled down and ground into the dirt for what they did to Raymond.[61] This patriotism is absent in the film's Eleanor, as are her heroin addiction and incestuous lust for Raymond. During Condon's scene Eleanor is wearing a Chinese dressing gown and when she holds Raymond's face in her hands, she expounds upon the way he looks like her father, especially when he smiles. Directing him to smile for her, she gushes that when he smiles, "for that instant I am a little girl again and the miracle of love begins all over again. How right that seems to me. Smile for me again, sweetheart. Yes. Yes. Now kiss me. Really, really kiss me."[62] Condon ends the scene with Eleanor pulling her son to her on the chaise upon which she lies and opening her dressing gown; she remembers her father "and the sound of rain high in the attic when she had been a little girl, and she found again the ecstatic peace she had lost so long, long before."[63] These bizarre facets of Eleanor's character in the novel thankfully are left out of Frankenheimer's film, which is complex enough without them.

A nervous Marco paces in headquarters as time for the convention draws near and Raymond does not call; deciding "Raymond was theirs, he is theirs, and he'll always be theirs," meaning the Communists', he rushes to Madison Square Garden. As "The Star-Spangled Banner" is sung Marco looks nervously about for signs of Raymond's intervention in the proceedings. Spying a light on in an unused spotlight booth he races up to it, but arrives just after Raymond has shot not the presidential nominee, but his stepfather and his mother, fatally in the forehead. When Raymond sees he has killed his mother he puts his Medal of Valor around his neck. Telling Marco, "You couldn't have stopped them. The Army couldn't have stopped them. That's why I didn't call," he then groans, "Oh God, Ben," and shoots himself in the forehead. Frankenheimer melts the sound of that shot into the sound of a clap of thunder in a storm in the final scene of the film where Marco is telling his now-fiancée Eugenie Rose about Raymond's heroism. He is reading citations aloud from *The Compact History of the United States Army*, then shuts the book and says, "He was wearing his medal when he died.... Made to commit acts too unspeakable to be cited here by an enemy who had captured his mind and soul. He freed himself at last, and in the end, heroically and unhesitatingly, gave his life to save his country. Raymond Shaw. Hell, hell."

The other declaration on the movie poster for *The Manchurian Candidate* is "When you've seen it all, you'll swear there's never been anything like it!" That's somewhat of an understatement. In a 2015 interview with Angela Lansbury made for The Criterion Collection's 2016 DVD release of the film, she observes that *The Manchurian Candidate* "occupies a very rare and wonderful niche." Filmmaker Errol Morris, interviewed for the same DVD release, offers the context of the "extreme paranoia" of American culture in the post–World War II era as the United States developed the atomic bomb, followed by the Soviet Union and China acquiring the same. This threat of nuclear destruction by enemy powers was added to with the possibility of different kinds of weapons, those that could control people's thoughts and actions and thus "subvert us from within" because it is an unseen enemy; "It's a really dark and in so many ways quintessentially fifties idea in America," Morris observes. The anti–Communist American journalist Edward Hunter is generally credited with coining the term "brainwashing," although scholars have disputed this. Hunter had served two years in the Morale Operations section of the Office of Strategic Services (forerunner of the CIA) during World War II and published his book, *Brainwashing in Red China: The Calculated Destruction of Men's Minds*, in 1951. There was great concern during this period about the indoctrination of American soldiers when they served abroad in Communist countries. Condon's novel and Frankenheimer's film concretize these fears so effectively.

The history of Frankenheimer's film is quite curious. It was released on October 24, 1962. As part of what came to be known as the Cuban Missile Crisis, President John F. Kennedy had gone on national television on October 22 to announce the discovery of Soviet missiles in Cuba. Kennedy was assassinated on November 22,

1963, and United Artists pulled *The Manchurian Candidate* from theaters in 1964, ostensibly out of respect (the pulling has been attributed to Sinatra, who had been friends with Kennedy, but this has been debunked). While the film was televised in 1965 and 1974, it was not seen on the big screen again until 1987, when the New York Film Festival celebrated its 25th anniversary. It received theatrical re-release in 1988 and has been available in video and subsequent formats since then. Frankenheimer's biographical drama *Birdman of Alcatraz* (1962) had been released on July 4, slightly before *The Manchurian Candidate*, and the director would go on to make many films in various genres, including an adaptation of Eugene O'Neill's play *The Iceman Cometh* (1973), the action crime *French Connection II* (1975), and the sci-fi *The Island of Dr. Moreau* (1996), from H.G. Wells' novel of the same name.

Jonathan Demme's 2004 remake, also titled *The Manchurian Candidate*, substitutes the Gulf War for the Korean War, contains some major plot changes, and has a cast of stars that earned the film its own well-deserved positive reviews. Tina Sinatra was involved as a producer, along with Scott Rudin; Daniel Pyne and Dean Georgaris wrote the screenplay, but due credit is given to Axelrod's screenplay and Condon's novel. Denzel Washington plays Ben Marco, Liev Schreiber is Raymond Shaw, and Meryl Streep is cast as Eleanor Shaw. The opening scenes are set in Kuwait in 1991, after which it shifts to "Washington, D.C, today." Instead of hypnotic suggestion, implanted microchips control both Raymond and Marco. A few major changes include Eleanor Shaw having assumed her husband's Senate seat twenty years prior when he died; her manipulations gain the vice-presidential nomination for Raymond, pushing Senator Thomas Jordan (Jon Voight) out of the running. Rather than a Communist threat, the War on Terror is the specter used to rally the American people behind war hero Raymond, and the Chinese and Russian Communists are replaced by Manchurian Global, a private equity fund that backs the experimental technology—implant behavior modification—used on Raymond and Marco. Marco becomes the assassin in this remake (he, as well as Raymond, had killed someone during their conditioning), with the aim of killing the president right after the election victory is declared so that Raymond can assume leadership. But Raymond, quite aware of Marco's intent, deliberately misses the marker on the stage where he is supposed to stand alone, invites his mother to join him for a victory dance, then nods to Marco his permission to shoot him, which shot goes through him to kill his mother as well. Rosie (Kimberly Elise), a character who stands in for some of Bennett Marco's functions in the original, shoots Marco in the shoulder before he can commit suicide, and Marco lives to work on recovering from the whole experience. Demme's remake contains enough allusions to the original to satisfy viewers familiar with it (one being that Raymond wades out into a lake to meet and kill Senator Jordan when he returns from his early morning kayaking excursion, a clever reference to the original scene where Raymond wades into the lake in Central Park), and its updated politics and mind-control technology keep it fresh and relevant for all viewers.

In his cultural study *The Noir Forties: The American People from Victory to Cold War*, Richard Lingeman notes that "the number of anti–Communist movies warning about the danger of internal subversion grew from 10 percent of all films made during World War II to 25 percent of all made between 1945 and 1955."[64] The films discussed in this chapter are a palatable sample of nationalist paranoia dressed up as patriotism, the menace lurking in Wonder Bread. Given the country we live in now, the choice between being "brainwashed" or wiretapped, they offer a sort of Cold War comfort. The next chapter examines a different kind of threat to one's way of life: con artists and their scams.

Four

"Something Further May Follow..."

Con Artists and Scams in Film Noir

It is not surprising that con artists working their scams drive the narratives of a number of films noir, given that the genre overall presents such a bleak view of human nature. A look into the features of con artistry in America as presented in its fiction and non-fiction affords a useful lens for examining the classic noirs *Detour* (1945) and *Nightmare Alley* (1947), as well as the neo-noirs *The Usual Suspects* (1995) and *The Spanish Prisoner* (1997).

Herman Melville was almost pathologically honest, yet he wrote *The Confidence-Man: His Masquerade* in 1857, one of the most penetrating, if not easily accessible, depictions of grifters and suckers and their need for each other. The novel is set on April Fools' Day aboard the ironically named steamer *Fidele*, French for faithful, which is running from St. Louis, Missouri, to New Orleans, Louisiana, on the Mississippi River. A placard near the captain's office announces a reward "for the capture of a mysterious imposter, supposed to have recently arrived from the East; quite an original genius in his vocation, as would appear, though wherein his originality consisted was not clearly given; but what purported to be a careful description of his person followed."[1] The ambiguities in that portion of Melville's sentence alone are indicative of his usual tendency to obfuscate so that the reader must sort out what meaning to take away from his words (one of his other novels is even titled *Pierre; or, the Ambiguities*), but the ambiguity is especially apt in regard to his character of the Confidence-Man, whose outward appearance changes and whose motives are unclear.

The titular character is not the only con artist aboard, however, and as R.W.B. Lewis points out regarding the book's characters, "Most of these are types one could find on a Mississippi steamer something over a century ago, products and representatives of the bustling, greedy, inventive American Middle West."[2] Since Melville is most often termed a Dark Romantic, along with Nathaniel Hawthorne, Edgar Allan Poe, and, sometimes, Emily Dickinson, the topic of con artists and their prey is a suitable one of exploration for this writer looking at humanity's darker tendencies. To speak broadly, the Romantic period of literature saw a growing focus on the individual, on nature, and on the divinity in nature and in the individual. There is great optimism in the work of American Romantic writers such as Ralph Waldo Emerson, Henry David Thoreau, and Walt Whitman. On the converse, Dark Romantics do not believe that humans are inherently good. At best, they are a mix of positive and negative impulses, but more often these writers' works reveal that evil is the greater part of human nature. The cruelty of the human soul is a dominant trait in their work. Melville's novel ends with the line, "Something further may follow of this Masquerade."[3] One could interpret this to mean that such masquerades and scams as those depicted in Melville's novel will occur again, if in different iterations. R.W.B. Lewis notes that Melville's Confidence-Man "is not the bringer of darkness; he is the one who reveals the darkness in ourselves. Whether this is the act of a devil or an angel may not, when all is said and done, really matter."[4] And film noir most definitely shares Melville's post–Calvinist view that everyone is potentially corruptible and most are already corrupt.

There is an earlier Dark Romantic than Melville who wrote about con artists, albeit in a much more playful, humorous, and entertaining manner. Edgar Allan Poe's essay, "Diddling Considered as One of the Exact Sciences," appeared in the *Broadway Journal* on September 13, 1845. Like Melville, Poe seems doubtful of humanity's ability to be good always, and he uses the verb "diddle" to mean "to swindle." "A crow thieves; a fox cheats; a weasel outwits; a man diddles," he writes; "To diddle is his destiny," thereby indicating that all humans are swindlers.[5] And have been for a very long time: Poe traces diddling back to humanity's infancy, even suggesting that Adam was the first diddler. Calling Adam a diddler is bold commentary on the legacy of the human race, but then Poe was always bold in print. His essay lists the especial attributes of the diddler, which are "minuteness, interest, perseverance, ingenuity, audacity, *nonchalance*, originality, impertinence, and *grin*," upon which he elaborates.[6]

By "minuteness" Poe means the diddler operates on a small scale, usually for cash, because "Should he ever be tempted into magnificent speculation, he … becomes what we term 'financier.' This latter word conveys the diddling idea in every respect except that of magnitude."[7] This is a typically Poesque snide remark about the American financial system to which the frequently impoverished writer had outsider status. "Interest" means self-interest, as in the diddler getting money for himself, and "perseverance" means that the diddler doesn't easily get discouraged. The diddler's "ingenuity" is that "He has constructiveness large. He understands plot. He invents and circumvents," which feeds nicely into the portrait of Melville's ever-evolving Confidence-Man.[8] Also like the Confidence-Man, Poe outlines that a diddler is bold, or has "audacity," and must have an attitude of "nonchalance," never displaying nervousness.

In what will be seen shortly in this chapter, Poe's next attribute of a diddler is not necessarily accurate in totality. Poe writes that a diddler conscientiously demonstrates "originality," would never use another diddler's tricks. In real life, of course, many scams and cons have been recycled over the centuries. The next attribute will be manifested in various degrees and ways in the texts under analysis in this chapter: "impertinence." As Poe describes the diddler, "He swaggers. He sets his arms a-kimbo. He thrusts his hands in his trousers' pockets. He sneers in your face. He treads on your corns. He eats your dinner, he drinks your wine, he borrows your money, he pulls your nose, he kicks your poodle, and he kisses your wife."[9] This is, of course, Poe wandering into excess to be entertaining, but the description will be worth keeping in mind during subsequent analysis of the characters Roger "Verbal" Kint in *The Usual Suspects* and Jimmy Dell in *The Spanish Prisoner*.

The final attribute, the "grin," is unsurprisingly absent from most film noir incarnations of "diddlers." While Poe writes, "Your true diddler winds up all with a grin," not all of the con artist characters in film noir get away with their cons, Verbal being an exception, as most are eventually found out and become broken, jailed, or dead.[10] For Poe though, the diddler grins at the end of his workday, even if it is just to himself.

In his personal memoir of working for carnivals in the 1960s before heading off to college, *Eying the Flash: The Education of a Carnival Con Artist*, Peter Fenton says he appreciated listening to experienced carnies tell their tales "based on the theory that absorbing their bull would help me become equally adept at shooting the shit. Because I was discovering that on the midway, career success was a function not of the veracity of what I said, but how believable I made it sound."[11] Fenton also makes an observation that carries over from the world of carnivals into the general society that con artists work within: "Carnies were nearly always 'on,' as ready to nick or ding their coworkers, pals, or even loved ones as they were midway marks."[12] It will be useful to bear this in mind during discussion of Stanton the Great in *Nightmare Alley*.

To back up a bit on the terminology that has been used in this chapter, as T.D. Thornton explains in his biography of a fascinating American con artist, *My Adventures with Your Money: George Graham Rice and the Golden Age of the Con Artist*, "The term 'con artist' would sweep into vogue around 1915, with Jacob [Jacob Simon Herzig, who later assumed the name George Graham Rice] at the vanguard of get-rich-quick profiteering, feasting on a nation of gullible prey."[13] Rice published his "half memoir, half exposé of Wall Street" titled *My Adventures with Your Money* in 1913; it went into ten printings and made swindling a hot news item: "A few months after *My Adventures* was released, the term 'con artist' first appeared in *The New York Times* to describe a highly specialized grifter."[14] Earlier, "cheats who fostered trust for the sole purpose of exploiting it got their own specific term in the American vernacular, when the actions of one Samuel (William) Thompson were reported in the July 8, 1849, *New York Herald* under the headline 'Arrest of the Confidence Man'...."[15] Thompson inspired the term because he would ask his marks whether they had enough confidence in him to lend him their expensive pocket watch until the next day—which of course he absconded with, never intending to return it to the lender. Thornton notes too that a survey of police officers in New York City taken in 1860 "estimated one out of every ten city criminals was a confidence man."[16]

In *The Confidence Game: Why We Fall for It ... Every Time*, Maria Konnikova delves into the psychology of confidence games. "We've done most of the work for them; we want to believe in what they're telling us," she explains about victims. "Their genius lies in figuring out what, precisely, it is we want, and how they can present themselves as the perfect vehicle for delivering on that desire."[17] Indeed, linguistics professor David W. Maurer, in his classic 1940 study, *The Big Con: The Story of the Confidence Man and the Confidence Game*, claims the confidence man "is really not a thief at all because he does no actual stealing. The trusting victim literally thrusts a fat bank roll into his hands. It is a point of pride with him that he does not have to steal."[18] This helps explain why many con artists get away with their cons: victims don't want to admit their own criminal intent in those situations where they hope to gain large sums of money by dishonest means. Both Konnikova and Maurer note how cons flourished during the Gold Rush and westward expansion. People in boom-towns "had money and were speculation-bound. The feverish atmosphere west of the Mississippi River was a healthy one in which con-games could flourish and grow."[19] So con artists and scams found fertile soil in America and have maintained a robust existence in its society. As Maurer observes, "Confidence men trade upon certain weaknesses in human nature. Hence until human nature changes perceptibly there is little possibility that there will be a shortage of marks for con games."[20]

Martin M. Goldsmith, Edgar G. Ulmer and *Detour*

One hapless character who didn't intend to con anyone but who drifted into a position of dishonest deception is Al Roberts in Edgar G. Ulmer's *Detour*. Ulmer was a Jewish émigré director who made five films noir in America (some say six by including the horror film *Bluebeard* [1944]): *Detour, Strange Illusion* (1945), *The Strange Woman* (1946), *Ruthless* (1948), and *Murder Is My Beat* (1955). *Detour* was made at what is known as a mini-studio, Producers Releasing Corporation (PRC), considered also to be a Poverty Row studio, and Vincent Brook notes that Ulmer "continued to work outside the classical studio system—despite the lower budgets, tighter shooting schedules, and lesser talent—because of the greater autonomy that such relative independence afforded."[21] Along with Edmund Goulding's *Nightmare Alley* and Billy Wilder's *Sunset Boulevard*, the latter of which was analyzed in Chapter One, *Detour* was influenced by the kinds of films made in Weimar Germany, especially Kammerspiel film and street films, which Brook declares, because of "their dark look, claustrophobic feel, and everyman antihero caught in a web of urban angst and transgressive sexuality, must be regarded as clear precursors of film noir."[22] Brook assigns Ulmer, along with directors considered in Chapter One (Wilder and Otto Preminger), to the first wave of Jewish émigré directors, who came to Hollywood as the Nazis gained power in the 1920s and 1930s.[23]

Noah Isenberg's book, *Edgar G. Ulmer: A Filmmaker at the Margins*, is the most comprehensive study of the man and his work to date. While facts about Ulmer's education and early theater work are somewhat hard to verify, it is known that Ulmer went to New York in 1924 to work on Max Reinhardt's Century Theatre production of *Das Mirakel (The Miracle)*.[24] Universal Studios head Carl Laemmle hired Ulmer that same year, and he worked in the Art Department "from roughly the end of 1924 to the middle of 1928," meeting "future collaborators such as the cinematographer Benjamin Kline, cameraman of *Detour* and a regular during Ulmer's PRC years two decades later."[25] Ulmer began assistant directing Westerns, then co-directed *The Border Sheriff* (1926) with Robert N. Bradbury, albeit uncredited. He worked with F.W. Murnau on *Sunrise* (1927), the German Expressionist director's first film in Hollywood, made for Fox Studios. As Isenberg observes, "The lessons that Ulmer learned while working with Murnau—the obsessive emphasis, for example, on the aesthetic over mere commercial considerations—would stick."[26] Early 1928 found Ulmer in Berlin working on the set design of *Die Verbrecher* (*The Criminals*) for Max Reinhardt's staging and picking up work on some "minor German film productions for Ideal-Film and Merkur-Film, ancillary companies connected to Heinrich Nebenzahl's more prestigious Nero-Film."[27] When director Rochus Gliese quit *Menschen am Sonntag* (*People on Sunday* [1930]) after a few days, Ulmer took over directing the feature film with Robert Siodmak. Isenberg explains how city locations were used instead of studio sets, and that overall this project had a significant influence on Ulmer's subsequent work: "Not merely the improvisational quality of the film, and the need to work on the fly, but also its extreme minimalism (that enduring principle of less is more) and lack of a sizable budget, the tight shooting ratio (in this case, roughly five to one), and the nonexistence of studio enhancement—all of these would become recurrent facets of Ulmer's cinema."[28] And they would indeed serve him well during the Great Depression as through the 1930s and early 1940s, back in the United States, he made health films, musical shorts, ethnic films, and race films for various production companies, in between which he made *The Black Cat* (1934) for Universal, featuring Boris Karloff and Bela Lugosi. Regarding budgetary constraints, the budget for *Detour*, long misreported as about $30,000, was $87,579.75, although it actually ended up costing $117,226.80 to make.[29]

Detour is based on Martin M. Goldsmith's 1939 novel of the same name; however, much from the novel is altered for the film, some things censored because of the Hays Code, some things changed due to Ulmer's or Martin Mooney's alterations of Goldsmith's screenplay (Mooney was also an associate producer on the film). One aspect of the novel that needed to be changed to translate it to a relatively brief film of 68 minutes is that the chapters alternate being told in the first person by Alexander Roth (Al Roberts in the film), who had potential to become a concert violinist but plays in a jazz joint, and his girlfriend Sue Harvey, a chorus girl in the same club. Goldsmith's novel opens with Alex getting picked up by Charles J. Haskell, Jr., in New Mexico while he's hitchhiking to Los Angeles to reunite with Sue, who had gone to Hollywood right before they were going to get married. Later readers learn that Alex's real name is Aaron Rothenberg, which he had changed ten years prior at his musical instructor's advice. But Alex's deceptive ways go beyond taking a stage name. He flatters Haskell for being shrewd enough to ascertain he wasn't a robber and thus stopping to give him a ride, telling the reader, "I thought I'd make him feel good. They tell me that is the secret of success—you know, winning friends and influencing people. From the looks of the buggy, I figured this guy should be good for a hamburger."[30] With no need to do so, he lies that he is from Detroit, admitting, "I don't know why I said that; there really was no call to lie. Maybe I was so accustomed to lying it had become a habit, I don't know. But that's me all over. For the life of me, I can't figure myself out."[31] That he doesn't really try to figure himself out or own up to his actions sets off alarms in the reader, such as when it's revealed that he was jailed in Dallas for stealing fruit and he rationalizes, "I'm no thief, but, boy, three days of penny candy can make a great difference in a fellow's scruples."[32] Now when Haskell stops to eat Alex tells him he'll wait in the car, "trying to look as forlorn as possible—without hamming it," so that Haskell offers to buy him dinner.[33] Readers quickly learn that Alex's scruples when it comes to his girlfriend aren't quite what they should be either. He notes that since Sue left he'd "been living the life of a monk.... Well, practically the life of a monk."[34] He allows that Sue told him she didn't expect him to be faithful, but hadn't liked that: "I wanted her to want me to be faithful—even if I wasn't."[35]

Sue Harvey in the film appears to be a virtuous, if self-seeking woman, whereas Sue in Goldsmith's novel invites herself to stay at Alex's apartment when she's had too much to drink, and they sleep together. When Sue's mother learns this, she throws her out, whereupon they begin living together and while Alex keeps asking her to marry him, she puts him off for three months before agreeing to—then, as noted previously, runs off to Hollywood right before the wedding to advance her career. There she finds work as a car hop and has sex with the small-part actor Raoul Kildare even though she doesn't want to. "Ye gods, what was this town doing to me?" she thinks. "With my looks I should have been working in the studios, not hopping cars in a Melrose Avenue hot-dog stand; going around with directors and producers and even stars, not with nobodies like Mr. Kildare."[36] She feels swindled by the movie magazines that lured her to Hollywood with promises of fame: "I soon saw that there were only two classes of society: the suckers, like myself, who had come to take the town; and the slickers who had come to take the suckers. Both groups were plotters and schemers and both on the verge of starvation."[37] And Sue continues revealing herself as a plotter and schemer when the chapter containing that philosophy ends with her practicing a scene in the mirror telling Alex she'll always love him and always be waiting for him, then thinking, "It was great, a natural. Who said I couldn't act? Of course it wasn't all acting. I repeated the scene two or three times more, experimenting with tone, quality and diction. Then I ran hot water and looked around for the douche," this last since she had slept with Raoul.[38] Near the end of the novel when she believes Alex is dead, she rationalizes, "He had been very sweet and considerate; but people die every day and, no matter how much they may have meant, life, like the show, must go on."[39] She schemes to get Raoul to marry her, then decides to forget him too when she learns he's still married to the woman he's separated from, and plans to sleep with her agent to get a screen test at Selznick's.

Sue Harvey all but disappears from Ulmer's film after she goes to Hollywood. The story is firmly Al's from start to finish; even the opening shot of a desert road unwinding behind the camera underscores Al's journey. Viewers first see him walking along such a road at night, then about to get dropped off near the end of a hitched ride, and next, drinking coffee in the Nevada Diner, where the jukebox record another patron plays angers him. Viewers soon learn why as the camera moves in for a tight close-up of Al (Tom Neal), the diner goes dim around him, and a bar of light highlights his eyes as his voice-over begins his story. Ulmer offers an extreme close-up of Al's coffee mug so that it looms large on the screen before the camera turns to the jukebox and its spinning record, which becomes covered by a close-up of a bass drum as a transition to begin a flashback set in the Break O'

Dawn nightclub. Here Al plays piano with a small band while Sue (Claudia Drake) sings "I Can't Believe That You're in Love with Me," the same song that had played on the jukebox. That happy scene may just about be the last one in which viewers see Al smile in a genuine manner. For after the club closes one night and he's playing classical music on the piano before he and Sue leave, Sue observes that he'll be playing Carnegie Hall someday, at which he says yeah, if he doesn't get arthritis first. As they walk along heavily fogged streets to their respective abodes (Ulmer's brilliance in using the fog machine and a couple of street signs to mimic on-scene filming in New York City has been observed by many), Sue reveals her tiredness at being pawed by a drunk customer, rebuffs Al's proposal that they get married next week, and announces she's leaving Sunday for Hollywood. He tells her that's the most stupid thing he's ever heard of and what about him, why is she busting up their plans and separating them for possibly years? "I thought you loved me," he says bitterly, which she asserts she does, but that he needs to see her side of it, and he might come join her later on, which merely evokes "So long" from Al. When she asks him for a kiss good night he rotely says, "Sure, why not," gives her a perfunctory kiss, wishes her good night, then walks away morosely.

With Sue on the West coast, Al plays solo at the club, until a $10 tip for playing a request that the waiter who brings it to him calls hitting the jackpot leads him to call Sue from the club's phone booth. When he learns she's slinging hash to survive he urges her to keep going to the casting offices, he'll be on his way out to her, and they can get married as soon as he arrives, which she seems to assent to. After hocking everything he owns he barely has enough money to feed himself on the journey, so he has to hitchhike. Portentously, in a voice-over he allows, "Thumbing rides may save you bus fare, but it's dangerous. You never know what's in store for you when you hear the squeal of brakes. If only I'd known what I was getting into that day in Arizona." Al placates the driver who picks him up a bit, Charles Haskell (Edmund MacDonald), such as affirming "That's the stuff" when Haskell brags about throwing a woman hitchhiker out of his car after she scratched him for his advances and about having put a kid's eye out dueling with his father's Franco-Prussian sabers, which led him to run away fifteen or sixteen years prior, but he's not the streetwise Alex from Goldsmith's novel. When Haskell suggests they stop for a bite to eat Ulmer uses a camera shot from behind the two men in the front seat of the car, showing viewers just Al's eyes in the rearview mirror as he admits his hunger in a voice-over but worries that he'll lose his ride to the coast; he's not scheming how to score a meal from Haskell, he just wants the man to know he can't afford to eat in the place they are stopping at. The munificent Haskell sports him a meal during which he explains how he's a bookie, got rooked in Miami for $38,000, and intends to go back there flush next season. After the meal Haskell sleeps and Al drives all night, happy because he'll be with Sue again. He begins thinking of their future, "which couldn't have been brighter if I'd embroidered it with neon lights," his voice-over says, again accompanied by viewers seeing Al's eyes in the rearview mirror. While this use of the mirror brings viewers closer to Al as a character, as had the close-ups in the diner near the beginning of the film, it also suggests that Al's best times are behind him, like that unwinding empty road in the rear shot that opened the film.

But for now, Al is thinking how nice it is to imagine Sue shooting it to the top. Ulmer uses an interesting rectangular iris shot that opens to supply the embodiment of Al's vision of Sue singing "I Can't Believe That You're in Love with Me" in an evening gown while a three-piece wind ensemble of clarinet, saxophone, and trumpet are shown as silhouetted shadows behind her. The rectangular iris shot closes in, boxlike, on Al's eyes in the rearview mirror after this interlude, commenting on his impending entrapment.

For it starts to rain and Al needs to put the convertible's top up, has great difficulty doing so, but can't seem to wake up Haskell for assistance. Al's retrospective voice-over explains, "Until then I'd done things my way, but from then on something else stepped in, and shunted me off to a different destination than the one I had picked for myself. For when I pulled open that door—," Haskell falls out and hits his head on a rock. Ulmer provides another cut to Al in the Nevada Diner, eyes again highlighted, as he runs over his options. Flee and be recognized as having been with Haskell when they had dinner, tell the truth and likely be hanged for a crime he didn't commit, or hide the body in a gully and take the car. He chooses the last, his initial intent just to cover the body with brush, not rob Haskell, but then he realizes he'll need gas money and Haskell's driver's license, not to mention his clothes, in order to look like someone who could afford to drive such a nice car. Ulmer provides a tight close-up on Al's face as he thinks through these things and decides his destiny.

It's important here to note again differences between Ulmer's Al and Goldsmith's Alex. Alex is well aware of Haskell's rich father, and driving at night while Haskell sleeps, he admits,

> I would be handing you a lot of Abe Lincoln baloney if I said I wasn't tempted once or twice during the night to slug Mr. Haskell over the head and roll him for his cash. So I won't say it. The guy was treating me right and I couldn't bring myself to the point of hurting him. It took plenty of self-control, though. Remember, I was desperately in need of money; and in the glove-compartment of the car was a small Stillson wrench and a pair of heavy driving gloves I could have used for padding. It was a cinch set-up if ever there was one.
>
> I realize all this sounds bad. But try to get me straight. I'm a musician, not a thug. The few dishonest things I did I didn't want to do—I had to do. Anyway, this is one of the things I passed up—and I'm not asking you to pin a merit-badge on me, either. The only Boy Scout rule I ever followed was: "Be Prepared."[40]

Something elided from the film is that Alex helps himself to Haskell's cigarettes while he's sleeping, only to discover they are marijuana, so he slams on the breaks and the car starts to slide down a slope. After putting on the emergency brake and throwing up, he tries to put up the car top, but, needing to open Haskell's door to do so, Haskell falls out and hits his head on the running board. The basic situation is the same, although the use of the rock in the film underscores the strong possibility that Al would be taken for an active murderer. The voice-over on Fate in the film is very close to what Goldsmith wrote in the novel and, presumably, his screenplay: "Up to then I did things my way; but from then on something else stepped in and shunted me off to a different destination than the one I had planned for myself," although Alex's resignation to this is missing from the film: "And there was nothing in the world I could do to prevent it. The things I did were the only things left open for me to do. I had to take and like whatever came along."[41]

What comes along for Al in the film is a motorcycle cop just as he is finishing getting the top up on the car. He's admonished for leaving the wheels so far on the road as to possibly cause another car to hit his; Al's admission that he didn't think elicits "Next time, do so" from the officer, advice the viewer could suggest that Al apply to his actions at this seminal point in the plot. A nicely crafted line from Goldsmith's novel is retained in the film as Al drives away from the scene: "It was still raining, and the drops streaked down the windshield like tears."[42] Yet all is sunny when Al reaches the California border and makes it through the inspection station masquerading as Haskell. Exhausted, he stops at a motel for much needed sleep. Ulmer hovers the camera over him as he sleeps in Haskell's striped pajamas, somewhat suggestive of jail inmate garb, while superimposing images from Haskell's demise over him as Al fitfully calls out during a nightmare, "You can't die, they'll think I did it. No, Mr. Haskell!" The room's Venetian blinds also suggest prison, especially since Al has put Haskell's suit jacket on a hanger that he hooks over the curtain rod so that in the morning, sunlight coming through the window casts partial horizontal stripes on the jacket as it shines through blinds and then through the material. Aware that every minute he has to pose as Charles Haskell is dangerous, Al is eager to get to a city where he can leave the car and "be swallowed up." He goes through Haskell's things to learn what he can about the man, finding an unmailed letter to his father in which Haskell says he sells hymnals—as Al observes, Haskell was a chiseler who was going to rook his old man.

Back on the road he needs to stop to put water in the radiator, and as he pulls up to a gas station the camera peers from the rear of the car to show Al driving and, through the windshield, a woman standing by the side of the road with her suitcase. A few notes in the same key as "I Can't Believe That You're in Love with Me" intersperse with the musical soundtrack as he alights to pop the car's hood. "Hey you, come on if you want a ride," Al calls out to the woman as he's pouring the water in. She stands straight and pulls the bottom of her button-front cardigan down over her pencil skirt as she appraises him, then picks up her suitcase and, with clutch purse in hand, strides purposefully toward his car as the camera moves in to show her upper torso and head.

Not twenty minutes after he picks her up the woman, who says he can call her Vera (Ann Savage—the perfectly apt stage name taken by Bernice Maxine Lyon), falls asleep with her head on the car door, which makes Al uncomfortably remember Haskell's deep sleep. "With her eyes closed and the tenseness gone out of her," he observes, "she seemed honest enough. Instead of disliking her, I began to feel sorry for her. The poor kid probably had had a rough time of it," an attitude that reveals Al's generally empathetic nature and, as it will turn out, incessantly poor judgment of character. He thinks that in a few hours he'd be in Hollywood, would park the car somewhere, look up Sue, and "This nightmare of being a dead man would be over. Who this dame was, well, it was no business of mine." At that precise moment Vera wakes up and demands to know where he left the body of the car's owner because he's not fooling anyone, the car belongs to Haskell. "There was nothing I could say,"

Al's voice-over intones; "It was her move." Viewers are taken to the close-up on Al's eyes in the Nevada Diner as he ruminates, while the melody from "I Can't Believe That You're in Love with Me" plays, that it was just his luck to pick up Vera, the very last person he should have met: "That's life. Whichever way you turn, Fate sticks out a foot to trip you." A lap dissolve back to the two in the car shows that Vera is making her next move by declaring that she doesn't believe his story about Haskell's death being an accident, but since there is no reward, she won't turn him in because the cops are no friends of hers. "Thanks," Al says lamely, eliciting her retort, "Don't thank me yet. I'm not through with you by a long shot. Let's see that roll," this last a demand for Haskell's money. Her avarice becomes apparent when she thinks there is more money than Al hands her because Haskell said he was going to bet $3,000 on a horse. When Al declares Haskell was just stringing her along, was a blowhard, Vera replies, "Why should I believe you? You've got all the earmarks of a cheap crook," which Al truly takes offense at. "Just remember who's boss around here," she goes on, in a pithy exchange by which she establishes her control. When Al reveals his plan to abandon the car, not sell it as she suggests, this sets Vera off: "Not only don't you have any scruples, you don't have any brains…. Maybe it's a good thing you met me. You'd have got yourself caught for sure. Why you dope, don't you know an abandoned automobile always rates an investigation?" Unworldly Al did not.

Far from it being a good thing that Al met Vera, the trap she sets becomes more restricting when they rent an apartment posing as husband and wife. As they explore the small space, Vera asserts, "In case there is any doubt in your mind, I'll take the bedroom." They have a telling faceoff when she seeks out the revolving Murphy bed the landlady said was behind a wall panel. Vera flips it open, flirtingly asking, "You know how to work it?" as she ever-so-slightly undulates her body toward Al. "I invented it," Al snaps as he flips the bed back into the wall. A memo from Joseph I. Breen on behalf of the Production Code Administration had wanted Al and Vera to rent different apartments and stated, "There should be, of course, no suggestion of a sex affair between them."[43] But Ulmer sneaks suggestions in, primarily issuing from Vera's character, as when, just after the folding bed exchange, Vera pulls downward on her cardigan and softly says, "I'm first in the bathtub." After her bath she wears fishnet stockings, lounges on the sofa in her bathrobe, offers Al her liquor, reaches out for his hand twice when they are talking, and, later, puts her hand on his shoulder when she softly says she's going to bed—but as in her earlier attempts to touch him, she is rebuffed when he looks down at her hand, at her, then moves his shoulder away. It's quite different in Goldsmith's novel. In the film Al telephones Sue after Vera goes to bed, the soundtrack plays "I Can't Believe That You're in Love with Me," yet Al can't bring himself to speak and thinks, "No, not yet darling. Tomorrow, maybe—" as he looks at the bedroom door. Viewers could surmise he is thinking of the trap Vera is holding him in until they sell the car. Readers of Goldsmith's novel have no such ambiguity because Alex's commentary is, "I wanted Sue so much that night, I went into the bedroom and had Vera. There's reality for you. Go out and roll in it."[44] Both novel and film are self-reflexive about themselves as texts, the novel more so in terms of Hollywood. After the previously quoted line Alex goes on, "If this were a movie, I would fall in love with Vera, marry her and make a decent woman of her. Or else she'd make some supreme Class A sacrifice for me and die, leaving me free to marry Sue. She would experience a complete and totally unwarranted change of heart, wipe out her sins by a dramatic death, pleasing me, the Hays office and the morons in the mezzanine."[45] Ulmer's film substitutes "novel" for "movie" and says close to the same thing, albeit skipping the sentence about the Hays office. Goldsmith subsequently spends three paragraphs on how things come out for the best for the characters in Hollywood movies, starting with, "You know, it would be a great thing if our lives could be arranged like a movie plot. M.G.M. does a much better job of running humanity than God."[46] But for both Alex and Al, Vera is her usual nasty self the next morning when they set off to sell the car, and things will continue to get worse.

After Al makes a deal to sell the car for $1,850 and Vera is left to empty the glove compartment while he signs the papers, she mutters "that dirty crook" about the car dealer even as she herself finds Haskell's fancy cigarette case in the compartment and slips it into her purse. While Al is faltering because the dealer asked him who his insurance company is, Vera bursts into the office and stops the sale. They go to a drive-in to talk, where his hopelessness at being under Vera's control comes out even in his lunch order: Vera had ordered coffee and a ham sandwich, and when the car hop asks what he'll have he says, "Oh, I don't care, the same." It turns out that Vera had bought a newspaper while waiting for the car sale to be completed and learned that Haskell's father, president of an exporting company, is dying of bronchial pneumonia and a search is underway for his son. Vera's scheme is to wait until the father dies and then have Al show up claiming to be his son and thus gaining the personal fortune assessed at over 15 million. Al wants no part of this, worried that he'll be found out for murdering Haskell Jr., and he and Vera argue about this for hours back in their apartment. She's gotten rather drunk and threatens to call the cops and turn him in, he finally telling her to go ahead because "At least they'll give me a square deal," unlike her manipulation of him. Al's time with Vera has changed him, for he goes on, "But I'm warning you. If I'm pinched, I'll swear you were in on it. I'll say that you helped me. If I fry, I'll get even with you." Ulmer keeps the camera in a tight close-up of each of them in turn as they threaten each other, then the camera pulls back to view them voyeuristically through the window from outside the apartment as Al's voice-over conveys that they argued over her plan to have him pose as Haskell; viewers watch Al grabbing Vera by the shoulders and then her pushing him away. Al walks offscreen to return with a liquor bottle and glass, pouring her a drink while the camera moves back inside the room. Vera continues to threaten to call the police while Al refuses to pose as Haskell, leading him to grab her wrist forcefully to prevent her from picking up the telephone. Vera protests that he is hurting her, so he says he'll let go if she promises to leave the phone alone; she does, but when trusting Al goes to open the window at her request, she makes a dash for the phone and runs into the bedroom with it, locking the door behind her.

Ulmer's film makes an important departure from Goldsmith's novel regarding Vera's death. Alex and she argue over his pretending to be Haskell to get the father's money and she threatens to call the police, and when she does dial them, he tries to get the phone receiver out of her hand. "Somehow, as we struggled for the thing, her

Al (Tom Neal) realizes the result of his anger at Vera (Ann Savage) in *Detour* (1945) (PRC/ Photofest).

throat got in the way," Goldsmith writes. "I grabbed on to it and squeezed. It was soft, much softer than I'd dreamed; because when she let the phone fall and slumped against me, I noticed the marks of fingers, blue and deep. I let go of her then and she dropped to the floor. God, it's easy to kill a person."[47] Ulmer's innovation is much more in line with his overall characterization of Al as an unwitting pawn in Fate's game with humans—although admittedly a not-so-bright pawn who needs to control his temper. In the bedroom, Vera drunkenly wraps the telephone cord around her neck and then passes out on the bed. Al has been pounding on the door for her to open it, now calls out that he'll break the phone, and pulls harder and harder on the telephone cord coming out from under the door. Then he breaks the bedroom door open and stands there; the camera is on him, showing viewers he looks surprised and distraught at finding Vera dead, strangled by the telephone cord he had forcefully drawn taught. The camera moves behind him so that viewers see the mirror on the dressing table and thus view Vera's body as a reflection in it.

While Al's voice-over panics about how he wouldn't be believed that this was not premeditated, the camera goes out of focus first while on a close-up of his face, then moves onto various items around the room, coming into sharp focus on each and going out of focus to move to the next: Vera's face; the phone with the receiver not in the cradle; her lipstick, hairbrush, perfume and other toiletry items on the dressing table; her shoes; an empty dress box; clothes on a chair; and lastly, the phone cord coming out of the wall, which the camera then pans along as it leads to the bed. This visual technique demonstrates Al's fears over having killed Vera and how many people could connect him to her since they had gone shopping together. His voice-over continues, "While once I'd remained beside a dead body planning carefully how to avoid being accused of killing him, this time I couldn't. This time I was guilty, and knew it, felt it." As he walks slowly into the living room Al thinks that the saxophone player, whose music has been invading the apartment to taunt Al because it was a love song, is no longer playing a love song, but a dirge. His knees seem to grow weak for a moment until he steadies himself by putting his hand on the back of an armchair, then, having retrieved the apartment key Vera had kept in her purse because she was locking him in the apartment at night, he keys himself out, puts on his hat and coat, lays the key on the bureau by the door, and leaves in darkness.

A dissolve takes viewers to the Nevada Diner and another close-up on Al's eyes in an equally dark scene. His voice-over observes that he has to stay away from New York because Al Roberts is supposedly dead, he can't go back to Hollywood because someone might recognize him as Haskell, and as the lights come up in the diner, he thinks of Sue and glances at the jukebox. "I could never go to her with a thing like this hanging over my head," he mulls, "All I could do was pray she'd be happy." Walking out of the diner into the night, viewers might think he will go on wandering forever because he observes, "I was in Bakersfield before I read that Vera's body was discovered and that the police were looking for Haskell in connection with his wife's murder." Stopping to light a cigarette under a street lamp he goes on, "Isn't that a laugh? Haskell got me into this mess, and Haskell was getting me out of it. The police were searching for a dead man." Walking along the road, just as Al's voice-over says, "I keep trying to forget what happened," he walks past a large sign across the road reading "DANGER, Slow Down, See the Curves," a wonderful commentary on hindsight meant only for viewers because Al does not see it; he's walking in the opposite direction. He wonders what his life might have been if Haskell's car hadn't stopped. "But one thing I don't have to wonder about, I know. Someday a car will stop to pick me up that I never thumbed," his voice-over says as a highway patrol car pulls up beside him and stops, an officer gets out, takes an unprotesting Al by the arm and ushers him into the back seat, shutting the door for a second time to make sure it's secure, as Al's voice-over continues, "Yes, Fate, or some mysterious force, can put the finger on you or me, for no good reason at all." The car drives off and "The End" appears on screen. Ulmer added this apprehension scene to satisfy Breen, whose memo insisted that Al "be in the hands of the police" by the end of the film.[48] In Goldsmith's novel, Alex makes it to Seattle before reading in the newspaper that Haskell is wanted for Vera's murder. His shot at a classical music career is gone and he'll drift from town to town playing in "cheesy bands."[49] He's had to give up Sue too, which hurts even more, yet, he observes, "there was a certain satisfaction in what I was doing. I was aware that giving up the only girl I ever loved, and the only one who'd ever loved me, was maybe the first decent thing I'd ever done. If I sent word to her, and she came running to me to be my wife, it would be hell on her the rest of her days. Thank God I loved her enough to make this sacrifice."[50] Readers can only hope he continues to take consolation from this, knowing as they do that Sue is completely unworthy of his love. Alex says when he thinks of what his life might have been if Haskell hadn't picked him up, he wants to curse or cry. "Dramatics, buddy?" he asks. "No, sir. No dramatics. God or Fate or some mysterious force can put the finger on you or on me for no good reason at all," which resonates with gloom as the final line of Goldsmith's novel and suitably closes the film noir Ulmer made from the book.[51]

The 1992 remake of *Detour* by Wade Williams, a man devoted to the preservation of Hollywood film and early television, gets panned more than it gets praised, but it is worth watching. An independent film shot in Arizona and Missouri and produced at Film Works Studio in Kansas City, it was shown at film festivals but had limited VHS release. Williams and Roger C. Hull worked on the screenplay, which lifts large portions of voice-over and dialogue from Ulmer's film and Goldsmith's novel, but with the longer running time of 91 minutes it restores Sue Harvey's perspective and thus the two-narrator structure of the original text. It also imports the callous attitude of Goldsmith's characters. While a number of camera shots and angles and some blocking are faithful to Ulmer's film, there are a few significant changes worth noting. Color permits an effective use of neon lights, and the musical soundtrack by Bill R. Crane is like that heard in documentaries about film noir. Sue's song has significantly been changed from "I Can't Believe That You're in Love with Me" to "Careless," which would suit this Sue (Erin McGrane) perfectly if she were singing about herself because the lyrics chastise a lover for being careless toward the supposed beloved.

The film stars Tom Neal, Jr., as Al in his only acting role, showing mostly what a strong gene pool he comes from since he looks and sounds remarkably like his father had in the original. The best performance in the film is given by Lea Lavish as Vera. It was her only film, although she did go on to do a lot of theater through the 1990s. Sue's roommate, another struggling working girl in Goldsmith's novel, here becomes an older woman she rents a room from, a Hollywood has-been who is bitter about her life. Evie is played by Susanna Foster, who hadn't made a film since 1945 and whose most well-known one was *Phantom of the Opera* (1943). A significant change is that the end of the film suggests that Al wanders rather than being apprehended by the police, but what really must have Joseph I. Breen rolling in his grave are Vera in her negligee trying to seduce Al, their steamy make-out scene, and Sue telling an actor she just slept with, "You're not very good in bed."

William Lindsay Gresham, Edmund Goulding and *Nightmare Alley*

In contrast to the unplanned deception that is suggested even by the title *Detour*, deliberate and scripted cons are played in *Nightmare Alley*. The film's director, Edmund Goulding, grew up in London and acted in West End theater until he served in World War I. Honorably discharged after being wounded in France, he had small roles in two silent films and continued stage acting. While Goulding sailed to New York in May 1915, he returned to London almost immediately, apparently due to a family crisis related to his father, but by July he was back in New York looking for work as a singer.[52] Goulding sang and acted in the United States and London, worked briefly as an apprentice film cutter, then wrote screenplays until he again served in World War I. Resuming screenplay writing after the war, he turned one of them into the novel *Fury* (1922), and then was scenarist when Henry King directed its silent film incarnation by the same title (1923).[53] Goulding made his directorial debut with *Sun-Up* (1925) and directed numerous silent films until transitioning to sound and directing through the late 1950s. He worked in many genres and is best remembered for *Grand Hotel* (1932), *The Dawn Patrol* (1938), *The Razor's Edge* (1946), and *Nightmare Alley*.

Maurer's aforementioned study of con artists and games reports, "The American circus was a grifter's paradise on wheels. Until very recently, most circuses carried grifters and confidence men as a matter of course, for the grift was a source of great profit…."[54] *Nightmare Alley* plunges viewers into that carnival world at the outset by announcing the Geek that fascinates Stan Carlisle (Tyrone Power) via a banner in the background behind a barker that reads, "Body of a Man, Soul of a Beast." "How do you get a guy to be a Geek?" Stan muses. "Is that the only one? I mean, is a guy born that way? … I can't understand how anybody can get so low," and the balance of the film is a lesson in just how. As a barker for Zeena (Joan Blondell) and her husband Pete's (Ian Keith) mind-reading act, Stan feels contempt for the "yokels" in the crowd, stating, "It gives you a sort of a superior feeling, as if you were in the know and they were on the outside looking in." The word code Zeena and Pete developed for their vaudeville act is their nest egg, but Stan sees an opportunity to use Pete's drunkenness as reason for Zeena to teach him the code so he could work from the audience if Pete can't perform his usual role of feeding Zeena information from under the stage. He comes on to her and suggests they build up a new act together, but Zeena won't go against her Tarot cards, which show the Wheel of Fortune and predict money, happiness, and great success for her and Stan, yet she sees no sign about Pete in the fortune since his card, the Hanged Man, is in the undealt portion of the deck—until Stan says, "Maybe this is Pete," and picks up the Death card from the floor. It had been face down, which means Pete will die soon. The film is based on William Lindsay Gresham's novel *Nightmare Alley* (1946) and Gresham, who was fascinated with Tarot, uses the deck's trump cards for the titles of the chapters.

One night, Stan buys a quart of grain alcohol off the carnival provider and, hearing Pete coming, stashes the bottle in Zeena's prop trunk. The Geek (George Beranger) runs amok in the background as the two men converse, observing that he probably got the heebie-jeebies because he didn't get his daily bottle of booze; once caught and given his bottle, the Geek sings with joie de vivre. Pete starts to sag and Stan reaches in the trunk to give him his bottle to drink from, but unwittingly grabs the bottle of wood alcohol Zeena uses in her act. Pete drinks the whole bottle that night and is found dead in the morning. Stan is truly remorseful, but keeps silent about his role in the accidental death because, as Zeena observes once she teaches him the word code to become her new partner in the act, "He's a quick study." One

Stan (Tyrone Power) finds the Death card from Zeena's (Joan Blondell) Tarot deck in *Nightmare Alley* (1947) (20th Century–Fox/Photofest).

night when Stan and Zeena are working the crowd, the Rural Marshal (James Burke) arrives to shut down the carnival because of cruelty to the Geek and Molly's (Coleen Gray) scant costume she wears in her Electra act. Stan convinces the marshal that regular clothing would burst into flames by having Molly demonstrate her act, in which electricity passes from the fingertips of one of her hands to the other. Then Stan pretends to have second sight, telling the marshal that someone near to him is jealous of him and his ability as a peace officer, but there's also trouble connected to the love of a good woman and his spiritual life. "I see a Sunday morning in a beautiful, peaceful little church…. Love your neighbor, do not hate your enemies," Stan advises him. Molly, impressed with Stan's con of the police chief, lets him kiss her, and Stan assures her that he had only been kidding Zeena along because he wanted the code. That night while celebrating that the marshal did not shut them down at a local restaurant, Stan tells his carnival coworkers that he was raised in a county orphanage, which is where he learned the gospel because they give it to you on Sunday after beating you black and blue all week. When he ran away, he got put in reform school; "That's where I got wise to myself," Stan brags, saying he let the chaplain "save" him and got a parole in no time, observing that salvation comes in handy when you're in a jam. As he progresses up the con food chain, Stan will increasingly manipulate his marks with Christianity.

Because both Stan and Molly had gone missing after the marshal left, Molly's self-appointed protector Bruno the Strongman (Mike Mazurki) and Zeena figure out they've slept together and force Stan to agree to marry Molly. This occurs in Gresham's novel too, although he also includes a scene where Stan loses his virginity to Zeena before Pete dies, it's only Bruno who pushes for Molly and Stan to marry, and they never do get married. In the film, the newlyweds leave the carnival to begin a nightclub act using the code, Molly assisting "The Great Stanton." Religion creeps into the act when Stanton assures a woman curious about her daughter's suitor, "He not only attends church on Sunday, but he practices his religion seven days a week." A psychologist, Lilith Ritter (Helen Walker), is also in the audience that night, and she knows Stanton is a fake. She asks whether her mother will recover from her present illness; Stan intuits he's being tested and says the mother has been dead for some time. Taking off his blindfold, he and the most appropriately named Lilith look at each other as if they have each met their match. Stan responds to a note she sends him and goes to her office, where they have a tête-à-tête about his having a feeling her question at the nightclub wasn't on the level, a feeling he has again about her. "What's on your mind, lady? What are you up to?" he inquires. "Don't worry, Carlisle," she responds, "I never make the same mistake twice." "Me neither," he flings back. Their discourse is interrupted when a patient arrives for an emergency session, but she says he can call her at her apartment when she's not working on Wednesday or Saturday. The patient is Mrs. Peabody (Julia Dean), who is distraught over her dead daughter Carol. Viewers observe that Lilith records her patients' sessions on vinyl records. Stan has snuck back into Lilith's office, having fixed the latch when he went out, because he wanted to get a line on her. "Maybe we can do a little business after all," he suggests. "You don't realize what you've got here. We could set this town on its ear. Or is that what you wanted to talk to me about?" Lilith protests that anything her patients tell her is confidential. Figuring out Stan is thinking of using her patients' information to swindle those who want to communicate with the dead since he alluded to their affluence and mentioned that a couple of big spook people had sent him letters, she directs, "Will you get out of here? I should have known you were one of those—," but Stan cuts her off with, "Ah, ah, takes one to catch one."

Zeena and Bruno show up at Stan and Molly's hotel room because their carnival got rained out, and Zeena does a Tarot reading, warning Stan, "You're making a mistake ... if you make the change in the work you're thinking of.... It doesn't say what this new stunt is, but you're going to the top like a skyrocket." Dealing a card, she directs, "Stan, turn that card over and we'll see how it'll end up." Stan turns over the Hanged Man card. Molly asks if it's bad and Zeena says not if he doesn't go against it. "Wasn't that Pete's card?" Stan asks. "Sure, now it's yours," Zeena levels back. Stan angrily throws the two out, declaring, "Get out! I know what I'm doing. I don't need any help from a couple of cheap carnival freaks!" Zeena returns in a moment for her cards, finding the Hanged Man face down on the floor. As she leaves, Stan imagines he hears the faint maniacal cry of the Geek. When he has a massage that night to relax, the smell of the rubbing alcohol disturbs him so much that he hears the scream of the Geek again and looks up Lilith in the phone book, going to her home to confess his implication in Pete's death. Feeling better, Stan declares he was a chump to fall for Zeena's card reading and intends to go ahead as planned, announcing, "The spook racket—I was made for it." Lilith doesn't charge him for the session, calling it a "professional courtesy," and Stan says that maybe he can return the favor someday. "Maybe you can," she says. "What do you mean by that?" he asks. "Remember, takes one to catch one," she replies. He is the most hapless of grifters, believing he has the upper hand even as Lilith all but tells him that she intends to exploit him.

Lilith's patient Mrs. Peabody comes to the nightclub and Stan tells her he can see someone between them—ostensibly the dead daughter—and that she wants to speak to her mother, then he faints. Mrs. Peabody tells her friend Ezra Grendell (Taylor Holmes), "This young man has brought me the greatest spiritual comfort I've ever known," and says she'll go on at any cost to help him bring others the same spiritual comfort. "If I had my way, I'd build him the finest tabernacle in the world," she asserts. (In the novel, Mrs. Peabody gives Stan her house to make into the Church of the Heavenly Message, and earlier Stan had become a mail-order ordained spiritualist minister.) Having been at the nightclub with Lilith—he's also her patient— Grendell knows Stan's an "uncommonly shrewd young trickster," and saying to a friend he'd like to get a crack at him, the friend arranges a meeting between the two. After their meeting, Stan schemes with Lilith in her motorboat. He reports that at first Grendell threatened to have him investigated, but when Stan started slipping him information about his past that Lilith had given Stan, especially about a woman he loved who has been dead thirty-five years, Dorrie, that floored him. Grendell wants to communicate with Dorrie, but Stan told him he needed to prepare with prayer and good works, and two hours later, Stan says, patting his suit jacket breast pocket, he came back with a whole lot of good works. Grendell gave Stan enough money to start building the finest tabernacle in the whole country and will give him his own radio station. The catch is that he wants to "see" Dorrie. Stan gives Lilith the $150,000 cash to put in her jewel safe, telling her, "I'm not going to start building anything until we have Grendell really in the bag. This is only peanuts!" The only hint of a romantic relationship between Stan and Lilith in the film is when, at the end of this scene, she asks him to go have a drink with her, which he refuses because they shouldn't be seen in public together. In Gresham's novel they have a sexual relationship and in one bizarre scene, Stan gives Lilith a pedicure while she looks at her collection of gemstones.

Manifesting Dorrie puts Stan in a predicament, both moral and practical; of course, he disregards questions of right and wrong. Still, the practical aspect of how to pull off the scam requires an apostolic degree of rationalization. When Molly comes out of their hotel bedroom, he cradles his forehead in his hand and pours it on thickly. "It's that new convert of mine," he tells her, explaining how Grendell wants him to materialize his dead sweetheart. "But you can't do that," Molly points out. "That's right, but we've got to look at it this way, darling," Stan croons. "A man's faith is trembling in the balance. A man who was a confirmed skeptic about anything relating to religion now stands on the threshold. The door is open. One more step will bring him inside the fold. What should I do? Should I let the man's soul be lost forever? Or should I stake my own to save it? Or yours?" Conning Molly into helping him, he goes on, "Of course, I realize it's in the nature of a subterfuge, but our motives are so pure, so unselfish." "Wait a minute Stan," Molly objects. "I knew it! I knew it!" "You knew what?" Stan asks. "You never were on the level! You lied to me.

Zeena was right," Molly retorts, closing her trunk in preparation to leave. Stan tries to make her feel guilty for leaving him, then switches gears: "Honey, look, it's not me that I'm thinking about, but what about this poor guy Grendell? What's going to happen to him? Mrs. Peabody? All those other people that I've helped?" Molly tells him he needs to stop it or she'll walk out on him, saying she's scared because he's going against God: "You make it sound so sacred and holy, when all the time it's just a gag with you. You're just laughing your head off at those chumps. You think God's going to stand for that? You want Him to strike you dead?" Stan assures her he's met a lot of spook workers and they're all hustlers just like he is, and none of them are wearing a lightning rod. Molly says other spook workers don't talk like ministers. "There's no difference between this and mentalism. It's just another angle of show business," Stan argues, causing Molly to point out, "You're not talking to one of your chumps, you're talking to your wife!" She says the only way to stop him is to leave him. Stan's never told Molly that he loves her, so he pulls out all the stops and, with a Shakespearean dramatic stance, declares, "I'm no good. I never pretended to be. But I love you. I'm a hustler. I've always been one. But I love you. I may be the thief of the world, but with you I've always been on the level." He kisses her, and sweet Molly actually falls for this bravado and agrees to dress like Dorrie and manifest at Grendell's home. In the novel Stan tries to get Molly to agree to manifest as a naked Dorrie and have sex with Grendell—which she does and they do.

On the grounds of Grendell's estate Stan remarks to him, "Those great trees and moonlight, they give the whole place a cathedral-like atmosphere." Grendell admits this is his secluded retreat for praying, at which Stan observes, "I see you've been reading the Bible.... We know that it tells us that prayer, like good works, should be done in secret." "Dorrie" appears in the distance and Grendell tries to go toward her, but Stan orders, "That means we're on hallowed ground. Kneel! Kneel!," which Grendell joins him to do. When a weeping Grendell begs Dorrie's forgiveness and for her to ask God to forgive him and give him one more chance, Molly can't deceive him any longer and reveals herself. Stan and Grendell struggle, Grendell accusing, "You crook! You dirty sacrilegious thief!," so Stan pushes him down and flees. Why Dorrie died and why Grendell needs to beg her and God's forgiveness isn't explained in the film, but Gresham's novel clears up the mystery: Dorrie got pregnant with Grendell's child out of wedlock when he was in college; he arranged for her to get an abortion, after which she was "shaky and depressed"; then, when she was hospitalized, she refused to speak to him.[55]

Extremely angry with Molly, Stan nonetheless tells her to change clothes and meet him at Englewood Station. He goes to Lilith's and tells her he thinks he accidentally hurt Grendell. She gets the $150,000 from her jewel safe since he's leaving town; when he tries to leave some of the money with her so he'll have fall money, she stops him from opening the envelope by saying she doesn't want him to lead anyone back to her. In a taxi to the train station Stan discovers the envelope she gave him has only $150 in dollar bills. He heads back to Lilith's, climbs through her bedroom window, and grabs her in her bed, saying, "You're good. You're awful good, just about the best I ever saw ... a gypsy switch." Pretending not to know what he's talking about, when her maid, Jane (Florence Auer), comes in with a gun, Lilith tells her it's all right because he's a patient. Lilith plays Stan well: "Please, Mr. Carlisle, these delusions of yours in regard to me are a part of your mental condition. When I first examined you, you were being tortured by guilt reactions connected with the death of that drunken mentalist during your carnival days.... All these things that you think you have done lately or that have been done to you are merely the fancy guilt of your past life projected on the present. Do I make myself clear? You must regard it all as a nightmare." She informs him that she recorded the session in which he confessed to Pete's accidental death. When he says he can prove she's been in on it with him she says part of his malady is that he sees her as a co-conspirator. Police sirens are heard approaching and growing louder. "Please Mr. Carlisle, put yourself in my hands. You can trust me absolutely," Lilith says, having pretended not to hear the sirens, and Stan exits by the fire escape he came in on.

Molly finds him hours later in the train station waiting room; he's seen a newspaper with the headline "Police Looking for Miracle Worker" and sends her back to the carnival, giving her the $150 and telling her to keep out of sight as much as possible. Hiding from the police in a hotel room, Stan doesn't eat for three days, refuses a doctor, and buys a pint of gin from the bellboy. As he drinks, he imagines he hears the Geek howling, the portentous sound of a state he wants to avoid even as he slides inexorably downward toward it. After hoboing it for a while, entertaining his compatriots with a stock mind-reading exactly like one Pete had given him, a very ragged Stan approaches a carnival owner with his attraction, Sheik Abracadabra, but McGraw (Roy Roberts) says he doesn't hire boozers—Stan smells like beer. Desperate, he says he'll do anything, at which McGraw produces a bottle and offers him a shot, then another. When Stan's about to leave after having been turned down for offering to do palmistry or magic, McGraw says, "Wait, I just happened to think of something. I might have a job you can take a crack at. Of course, it isn't much and I'm not begging you to take it, but it's a job.... We'll keep you in coffee and cakes, a bottle every day, place to sleep it off in. What do you say?" Pouring Stan a third shot, he continues, "Anyway, it's only temporary, just until we can get a real Geek." "Geek!" Stan snaps to with horror. "You know what a Geek is, don't you?" McGraw inquires. "Yeah," Stan says despondently, "Sure, I know what a Geek is." "You think you can handle it?" McGraw asks. "Mister, I was made for it," Stan replies, downing the shot, a lame echo of his enthusiastic response to Zeena at the film's opening when she asked him about the carnival, "You like this racket, don't you?": "Oh lady, I was made for it!"

After his first day on the job, Stan runs amok at night, raving and brandishing a club. Power really transforms himself to embody this role. Coincidentally, Molly has joined this same carnival, recognizes him, follows the workers pursuing him, and calls out, "Stan! It's me, Molly!" She tells him she's been looking everywhere for him. "I've been waiting for you. Don't you know me, honey?" she asks. "It's me, Molly. Everything's going to be all right now. I'll look after ya." Looking at her as if he's never seen her before, Stan finally inquires, "Molly?," and desperately hugs her to him. The carnival owner McGraw is amazed that this man was Stanton the Great. "How can a guy get so low?" one worker asks him, echoing Stan's observation about the Geek at the start of the film. "He reached too high," McGraw replies. And so the film comes to one of the most bizarrely lame morals in the history of fables: No matter how big a jerk you are, there's always someone smarter and more ruthless to put you back down where you belong. Fate lies in acuity.

In Jules Furthman's first draft of the screenplay, Molly divorces Stan to marry Bruno and Stan becomes a Geek, but the Production Code Administration "insisted this resolution be softened."[56] It was worse for Stan in Gresham's novel. Molly has two children with a gambler named Cincinnati Burns and seems relatively happy—whether they are married is unclear. Stan tries pitching horoscopes on the street, and grotesque descriptions of his view of passersby convey his declining mental state: "Their faces suddenly became distorted, like caricatures of human faces. They seemed to be pushed out of shape. Some of them looked like animals, some like embryo chicks when you break an egg that is half incubated. Their heads bobbed on necks like stalks and he waited for their eyes to drop out and bounce on the sidewalk."[57] A police officer who told Stan to get out of town previously drags him into an alley and beats him with his nightstick until Stan is able to use a chokehold a fellow carny had taught him and kills him, so he goes on the lam. The book is similar to the film in the scene where Stan approaches the carnival owner with his unwanted act, but the novel ends with the owner's offer of the Geek job, suggesting a bleak future for Stan. Gresham's own life was nightmarish, his struggle with alcoholism just one facet of it. Married three times, his second wife, Joy Davidson, left him for C.S. Lewis. He committed suicide in 1962 just after turning 53. Found with him were business cards that had "Retired" in their center and "No address," "No phone," "No business," and "No money" in the four corners.[58]

Guillermo del Toro has been working on a remake of *Nightmare Alley*, retaining the title of the novel and first film, which is slated for release in December 2021. Stan will be played by Bradley Cooper, Rooney Mara assumes the role of Molly, and Lilith will be portrayed by Cate Blanchett. Viewers can anticipate a very dark noir from this master of horror. Del Toro has indicated the film contains no supernatural elements and will focus on the underbelly of society.

Bryan Singer and *The Usual Suspects*

Leaping forward almost fifty years, a manipulative con on a grand scale with devastating results is at the heart of Bryan Singer's *The Usual Suspects*, and just what is truth and what is fabrication is part of the game for the law enforcement involved and the film's viewers alike. Singer has named several directors as being influential on him, including David Cronenberg, Martin Scorsese, Steven Spielberg, and Peter Weir, and artistry from all of them can be seen in his second feature film.[59] His first was the thriller *Public Access* (1993), and he's gone on to direct superhero films, some television, and, most recently, the Freddie Mercury biopic *Bohemian Rhapsody* (2018). The title *The Usual Suspects* alludes to the order Captain Louis Renault gives near the end of *Casablanca*, but Singer says it came to him through the title of an article he saw in a magazine; he thought it would make a good film title. His long-time collaborator Christopher McQuarrie wrote the screenplay, with Kevin

Spacey in mind for the character of Verbal; Spacey had seen Singer and McQuarrie's first feature and wanted to work with them. It was a winning combination in that McQuarrie received an Academy Award for his screenplay and Spacey won one for Best Actor in a Supporting Role. This neo-noir engrosses viewers because of its intricate plot, clever employment of voice-over, and effective visuals. The lynchpin that holds everything together at the same time it ruptures them apart is Keyser Soze, a mythical figure who nonetheless may actually exist to wreak havoc and mayhem on those who cross him—and anyone related tangentially to those who cross him.

In their commentary that accompanies the MGM Home Entertainment DVD version released in 2002, Singer and McQuarrie supply useful information about the film, one such piece being that the intertitles of location and time were given to help orient viewers as the film got underway: "San Pedro, California—last night," "New York City—6 weeks ago," "San Pedro, California—present day." The basic arc of the opening sequences is that aboard a ship, a wounded man is shot to death and the ship is set on fire by the killer; five men are rounded up as suspects in a crime where a truck bearing guns was hijacked, each is interrogated separately, then they are put in the same jail holding room; and an investigation gets underway into the fire on the ship that ultimately contained twenty-seven dead men. Two men survived, one of them, Arkosh Kovash (Morgan Hunter), badly burned and in a coma in the hospital; the other, Roger "Verbal" Kint (Kevin Spacey), who has cerebral palsy, is in police custody. The three investigators into the case are FBI agent Jack Baer (Giancarlo Esposito), Sergeant Jeffrey Rabin (Dan Hedaya), and Customs agent Dave Kujan (Chazz Palminteri). The bulk of the film involves Kujan's conversations with Verbal as he tries to find out why so many men died for drugs that were supposed to be on board but were not.

After Kovash comes to and mentions the name Keyser Soze, there is a cut to Verbal taking in the contents of Rabin's office, in which he will be questioned by Kujan. It's a cluttered and claustrophobic space, and Singer notes that keeping the Venetian blinds open on the windows that look out to the outer office area helps relieves that feeling. This is true, but they also nod to noir décor. Repeat viewers—and at least one repeat viewing is required—will observe Spacey's eyes moving rapidly across the large bulletin board that dominates the wall opposite him. Kujan notes to Verbal, "According to your statement you're a short-con operator, run-of-the-mill scams." What will become clear at film's end is that Verbal is anything but; he is a criminal mastermind who manipulates people to do his will and who spins elaborate tales to obfuscate those around him. Kujan's assumed superiority to Verbal will be his downfall. "Let me get right to the point," he tells him, leaning in so that they are face to face. "I'm smarter than you. And I'm going to find out what I want to know. And I'm going to get it from you whether you like it or not." Those are challenging words to the aptly named Verbal, and the two lock eyes in a test of will, the camera giving a close-up of each in turn to underscore this. At this point Rabin returns with two mugs of coffee, one for each of them, and an extreme high-angle shot shows Verbal looking at the bottom of Kujan's mug.

Just how much any of the tales Verbal tells Kujan is true is up for viewers to decide. He claims that after the five suspects were released, they decided to work together to pull off a jewel heist that would not only score them big money, but would expose "New York's finest taxi service," a corrupt police escort service for smugglers and drug dealers that had shut down but would be coming out for one more job: escorting a jewel smuggler with emeralds. Internal Affairs has been waiting to catch corrupt officers in the act, so this is the suspects' way of sticking it back to the police who had rounded them up for no good reason. After the heist the gang—Fenster (Benicio del Toro), Hockney (Kevin Pollak), Keaton (Gabriel Byrne), McManus (Stephen Baldwin), and Verbal—heads to the West coast to sell the gems to a fence named Redfoot (Peter Greene). In one of numerous noir-ish shots, Keaton goes to take leave of his girlfriend, lawyer Edie Finneran (Suzy Amis), but she's in consultation, so he looks down on her from a balconied doorway set high in the room above her. There is a low-angle shot on him, then a high-angle shot from his perspective on her, emphasizing their separation. Verbal comes to tell him they have to go or they'll miss their plane, and a low-angle shot holds Edie's profile up close in focus with Keaton out of focus in the background; she goes out of focus and he comes into focus, then steps out of the doorway; she comes back into focus and looks up at the now out-of-focus doorway, sensing someone had been there. It's a touching commentary on their connectedness yet inability to stay together.

Kovash regains consciousness and tells Baer the harbor shootout was not about dope but about people, begging for protection from the Devil because his life is in danger. Asked who the Devil is, he replies "Keyser Soze," so a sketch artist (Michelle Clunie) works with him to capture Soze's likeness. Verbal tells Kujan that a lawyer named Kobayashi (Pete Postlethwaite) informed the five suspects they had all done jobs that Soze would have profited from, hence they unwittingly stole from him; the lineup was designed to bring them together. Now Soze wants them to thwart an upcoming sale of $91 million in cocaine the Argentinians are trying to negotiate to strengthen their organization; if the five destroy the cocaine they can keep any money that changes hands and will be free of their obligation to Soze.

In telling Kujan about Soze, Verbal observes, "The greatest trick the Devil ever pulled was convincing the world he didn't exist." He repeats a story he'd been told that involved a gang of Hungarians coming into power and going after Soze in Turkey. The screen goes to sepia and illustrates the scene as Verbal narrates how members of the gang went to Soze's home, raped his wife, slit the throat of one of his children, and when Soze came home, told him they wanted his territory and all his drug business. "Soze looks over the faces of his family," Verbal narrates, "then he showed these men of will what will really was" by shooting his wife, children, and two of the thugs and telling the surviving thug that he would rather see his family dead than live another day after this. After his wife and children were buried he went after the rest of the mob, killing them, their children, and basically anyone who knew them, burning their properties as well. (Singer explains that the sepia scene depicting events at Soze's home was shot with a six-frame, step-printing process: six frames per second are shot, then in post-production each frame is printed four times and one gets the effect that is seen onscreen.) Then Soze goes underground, Verbal continues, and "Nobody's ever seen him since. He's become a myth, a spook story that criminals tell their kids at night: Rat on your Pop, and Keyser Soze will get you."

Kujan says if Verbal turns state's evidence they can get Soze, causing Verbal to lean forward toward him and say, "You think you can catch Keyser Soze? You think a guy like that comes this close to getting caught and sticks his head out? [a quite ironic line for repeat viewers since Verbal/Soze is literally doing this as he speaks it] If he comes up for anything it'll be to get rid of me. After that, my guess is you'll never hear from him again."

A jump cut shows the sketch artist finishing her work at the hospital, then it cuts back to Verbal as he continues the story with Fenster turning up dead on the beach. A night shot of the beach has the actors in dark clothing against a black sky background so that, as Singer notes on the DVD commentary, they virtually become silhouettes, a nice noir touch; Singer credits his cinematographer Newton Thomas Sigel for shooting this effectively with virtually no light. As two of the survivors bury Fenster's body while being framed by the mouth of the coastal cave they are in, the shot dissolves to an overhead shot of Verbal's coffee mug, the two circular images matching up beautifully. The remaining four suspects are bent on finding Kobayashi since he informed them where they could find Fenster. They track him to an office building and, after a vertiginous shot into a glass elevator shaft, the two men accompanying Kobayashi are executed on the elevator by McManus; when Kobayashi is about to be killed, he tells them Edie is upstairs, having flown in yesterday for an extradition case. Kobayashi warns if he sees any of them before Friday, when the ship will be ready for them to attack, Keaton and Edie will both die. This affords another opportunity for visual underscoring of the couple's separation from each other: Keaton's face, lit from below, is seen reflected in the outer window of the office Edie sits in with another person, not aware he is, again, watching her.

Verbal narrates the events at the dock and on ship the night of the attack, with McManus sharp shooting some men on the dock and everyone but Verbal going aboard, only to discover there are no drugs on the ship. The camera shows a man wearing a bathrobe cowering in his cabin, convinced and fearful that Soze has come aboard ship. Viewers see Verbal limping along the dock to an entrance to the ship, then the camera gives the perspective from whoever is walking on the ship approaching the man's cabin. The interior door handle of the cabin turns and the door opens to reveal the man's bodyguard (Peter Rocca), now dead. A very bright light is cast on the cowering man and then the shadow of whoever has entered the cabin looms over him as he swears he told them nothing. An abrupt cut has the camera outside the cabin showing its porthole being splattered with blood as two shots are fired and the camera tracks back, away from the porthole.

McManus comes up to Keaton saying "The strangest thing," then pitches forward onto his face to reveal a pipe protruding from the back of his neck. A man in a coat—the same figure from the opening scene—shoots Keaton in the spine and the ship explodes. Kujan asks Verbal if he knows about Arturro Marquez (Castulo Guerra), a stool pigeon for the Justice Department who had sworn a statement to federal marshals that he could positively identify Soze and had intimate knowledge of his businesses, including drug trafficking and murder; this was the man in the bathrobe who had been cowering in the ship cabin. Marquez's own people were selling him to a gang of Hungarians, and Edie had been his extradition advisor; she knew who he was and what he knew. So the four suspects were tricked into attacking the ship for the drugs/money, whereas it was really a hit, a suicide mission to take out the one guy who could identify Keyser Soze. As Kujan lays out the possibility that Keaton is Soze, clips of Keaton from earlier in the film are shown; his expressions and the looks he casts become sinister in this new context. Kujan keeps pushing Verbal as to why Keaton would have let him live; Keaton is the kind of man who could have killed, and Edie's been found in Pennsylvania shot twice in the head. Kujan explains that Keaton chose Verbal to tell the story: "He programmed you to tell us just what he wanted you to." Why him and not the others, Verbal wonders, crying over Edie's death. "Because you're a cripple, because you're stupid, because you're weaker than them," Kujan asserts. It was Keaton's idea to hit the taxi service, wasn't it, he asks Verbal, who appears to cave in and admit, "It was all Keaton. We followed him from the beginning." Kujan wants Verbal to turn state's evidence and they'll protect him, but he says he's not a rat and will take his chances.

There are several jump cuts that heighten the tension as the film moves toward its close. One shot shows the hospital faxing the artist's sketch, another shows Verbal getting his personal belongings back, another shows Kujan and Rabin discussing that Keaton is alive, whether he is Keyser Soze or not. "A rumor is not a rumor that doesn't die," Kujan's voice-over says cryptically as Verbal is walking through the police station on his way out. "Man, you're a slob," Kujan says about Rabin's desk. "It all makes sense when you look at it right," Rabin responds. "You gotta, like, stand back from it, you know?" Kujan does just that, looking over the bulletin board. He drops his coffee mug and the camera moves in on various elements of the board as voice-overs from Verbal's previous narratives play. The blackboard brand, Quartet, made in Skokie IL (Verbal had recalled he was in a barbershop quartet in Skokie); an alias someone uses of Redfoot; a picture of an overweight woman (the baritone in the quartet was a "big fat guy"); Guatemala on a flyer ("Back when I was picking beans in Guatemala," Verbal had said); Kobayashi is the brand name written on the bottom of Kujan's broken mug on the floor. He runs out of the office as a fax comes in and Baer approaches the machine. Verbal walks along the sidewalk while Kujan's voice-over says, "I'm smarter than you and I'm going to find it out whether you like it or not"; select passages from Verbal's narratives also play in voice-over, revealing to viewers the grand deception that has been played on Kujan. Verbal stops dragging his foot and lights a cigarette with his previously unusable hand. There's a cut to Baer looking at the sketch from the fax machine, which matches Verbal. "After that, my guess is you'll never hear from him again," Verbal's voice-over notes, and a car stops at the curb that he gets into; Kobayashi is the driver. After pulling away the car makes a right turn and is seen gliding along the street behind Kujan, who stands on the sidewalk in the foreground looking around for Verbal. Verbal's voice-over states, "The greatest trick the Devil ever pulled was convincing the world he didn't exist," while Kujan continues to look. "And like that"—as Verbal's voice-over goes on, the screen shows an earlier clip of him in close-up going "puff," then goes black for him to say, "he's gone."

Likely it's impossible for first-time viewers to anticipate that Verbal is the heinous Keyser Soze since he's so self-deprecating and self-effacing throughout the film, off in the background during the holding cell scene, calling himself stupid and a cripple when talking with Kujan. Kujan's superior attitude doesn't help him get to the truth, yet he's not stupid. McQuarrie says he likes police characters to be smart too, otherwise it takes away from the victory of the criminal, and Kujan does piece it all together quickly at the end. Plus, as Singer points out, each of the three investigators working on the case have a piece of the puzzle, but none of them have the whole picture. As for viewers trying to puzzle it together, McQuarrie notes that a challenge for him in writing the screenplay was showing something happen in the opening scene and then convincing viewers they hadn't seen it, only to overturn that again to convince them they had indeed seen it. For his part, Singer says it was an exciting opportunity to present images and sounds to convince the audience of something, then later bring out new elements shown in a different light to convince them of something quite different. Why is Kobayashi driving the car that picks up Verbal? According to McQuarrie and Singer, to convey that under every lie there is some truth. Indeed, in the great American tradition, that is the secret to a successful con.

David Mamet and *The Spanish Prisoner*

Whereas Keyser Soze's scheming was outré in its uniqueness, some cons are repeated over time and across the globe. The con of the Spanish Prisoner seems to have arisen in England in the late 16th century, making it one of the oldest known long cons. Marks are told that a wealthy compatriot is being held prisoner in Spain and the grifter has been contracted to raise money to secure their release, for which the mark will be rewarded. All sorts of difficulties arise of course, requiring more money, until the mark is given the brush-off. The con reached the height of its notoriety in the United States in the 1920s, and in 1940 Maurer recorded in his study of con artists and cons, "Just as this is being written, a pair of con men in Mexico City are trying to revive the old *Spanish prisoner* con game on a wholesale basis, using *Who's Who* as their sucker list" (315). And of course this con still exists; desperate pleas on the Internet to save Nigerian orphans or Indian sex slaves are its more recent variations.

The Spanish Prisoner, written and directed by David Mamet, bears nothing in common with Mamet's 1973 minimalist play of the same name beyond an allusion to the titular con game. The film twists and turns the mark Joe Ross (Campbell Scott) and the viewer numerous times. The camera shows a warning for both after the opening credits: an airport sign asking, "Did you pack your own bag? Are you carrying gifts or packages for anyone you don't know? Has your bag been out of your sight since you packed it?" A reference associated with Joe throughout the film begins when he offers to help Susan Ricci (Rebecca Pidgeon, whom Mamet had married in 1991)—the "new girl" in his office, as she calls herself—with her luggage, eliciting her thanks, "Do you know, you are a real Boy Scout." Joe and his colleagues are heading to a corporate retreat on a Caribbean island, part of which involves discussing with investors something he developed called "the Process" that can control the global market—it's all left rather vague, as is the windfall the Process could garner

In *The Spanish Prisoner* (1997), the mark Joe Ross (Campbell Scott) is roped in by Susan Ricci (Rebecca Pidgeon) when she tells him the company is high on him because they told her to put his local calls on their expense tab (Sony Pictures Classics/Photofest).

since the figure is written on a blackboard viewers aren't shown, one of many tricks Mamet plays on viewers. Joe tries to get his boss, Mr. Klein (Ben Gazzara), to tell him how much his bonus will be for his work on the Process, but Klein won't discuss it. The hapless aspect of Joe's character that will get him into so much trouble comes out when he's told by a hotel employee that he can get a better currency exchange rate at a bank and he replies, "Oh, well, I suppose I should have done it that way, but that's all right." When he and Susan are taking photographs on the beach a man who was in the background of one of the snapshots approaches and says he'll give $1,000 for Joe's disposable camera; Joe hands it over, saying it's his gift to him. That evening he runs into the man again on the tennis courts and Julian "Jimmy" Dell (Steve Martin) says he's in Joe's debt and asks him if he wants to get a drink. Dell explains that the woman Joe had inadvertently photographed Dell with is a princess, married to a friend of his, noting that it was "a lovely gesture" for Ross to have given him the camera. He asks if Joe would drop off a package for his sister in New York, saying he would be in town Friday and they could meet for dinner.

On the plane ride home, Susan deems it an "extraordinary gesture" for Joe to have upgraded her to first class with his friend George Lang's (Ricky Jay, "the most recognized conjurer and sleight-of-hand artist of the 80s," whom Mamet used in several films[60]) casino winnings; George insisted Joe take half of them. The flight attendant asks to see Susan's ticket, leading her to remark, "Shows to go you, you never know who anybody is," telling Joe a woman she met in the hotel bar the previous night is an FBI agent, producing the business card of Pat McEwen (Felicity

Huffman). Later she repeats, "You never know who anybody is, with the exception of me. I am what I look like." "No," she points out, "anybody could be anybody, mysterious or—take that guy who got off that seaplane, take him," planting a suspicion about Dell in Joe's mind by saying Dell had just come in a boat from the direction of the seaplane; no one actually saw him get off the plane. "Who in this world is what they seem?" she asks. This spurs Joe to retreat to the lavatory to open the brown-paper package he is transporting for Dell, reassured to discover it is a book, *Budge on Tennis*, but he has accidentally torn the binding by opening the package. Inside the front cover he finds a stationery card with the initials JWD reading, "I thought you'd enjoy this. Also think you will enjoy the bearer, whom I recommend as a good fellow. How about seeing someone I approve of for a change? Let's have Din. Friday? Love J." Not only is Joe relieved he's not smuggling something illegal, he sees Dell as a nice guy who likes him well enough to set him up with his sister. In the limousine from the airport his friend George tells him his problem is he's too nice, "Everything for everybody else, nothing for yourself," and indeed, Joe gets out when he sees a used bookstore to buy a replacement copy of the Budge book for Dell's sister, a Mrs. DaSilva.

At work George mentions he thinks he's coming down with the flu, leading Susan to speak another line that's repeated in the film, "A lot of it going around." Joe wants recognition for his work on the Process, but Klein keeps putting him off, saying he'll receive it at the next stockholders' meeting. "Let's all just do our jobs and, uh, we'll be rewarded according to our just desserts," Klein says, his hesitation mid-sentence a tell for repeat viewers. He walks off and the camera shows Joe looking after him, sharing half the screen with a framed poster bearing the title "Someone talked" and picturing a man in the water pointing a finger toward the viewer. Previously Joe had asked Susan, "What do loose lips sink?" after locking the Process in a safe behind a painting; Joe wears the key to the safe around his neck; his boss, Klein, has the only other key.

Some misunderstandings and apologies occur between Joe and Dell, all of them Dell's manipulations to lure Joe into a fast friendship. One gesture is Dell's opening a Swiss bank account for him when Joe said he wouldn't even know how to do that. Another is taking Joe to his club, but it's members-only night, so he gets Joe a membership. "It's my nature. I'm a problem solver and I have a heart of gold," he says genially, having Joe sign a certificate that he can't fully see. In their dinner conversation, Dell observes, "People aren't that complicated, Joe. Good people, bad people. They generally look like what they are." Yannis Tzioumakis' book-length study of this film includes screen shots of the certificate Joe signs and the one presented to him later by authorities accusing him of planning to go to Venezuela, revealing another of Mamet's tricks on viewers. Of the one he signs at the club, viewers can read CLU BER IP DECREE; of the later certificate they can read the entire title, CONSULDO DE VENEZUELA.[61] Obviously, they are two different certificates.

After playing tennis with Dell the next afternoon—a game that was supposed to include Dell's sister, but she has the flu—Dell advises Joe that if a company is morally but not legally indebted to you, they'll screw you over. Thus Joe becomes concerned that his boss Klein might be trying to take advantage of him when he's asked to sign a revalidation of his agreement with the company. He wants his law-yer to review it and calls Dell about this while standing in front of that "Someone talked" poster. Twice Susan thwarts Joe's attempts to send Mrs. DaSilva flowers, so he returns to the used bookstore to purchase a signed photograph of Budge, takes it to her apartment building, and discovers that Emma DaSilva is an elderly woman. He also discovers from looking at Susan's trip scrapbook at the office that the "prin-cess" in a photograph with Dell that Susan had taken at the resort is a worker from the airport concession stand. "So you never know who anybody is, and it would pay to be a little careful," Susan warns him. At that point Dell telephones and tells him to bring his contract and a copy of whatever he's done for the company for a lunchtime meeting and his lawyer will get Joe straightened out. Suspicious, Joe takes the FBI agent's business card from Susan's trip scrapbook and calls her; when they meet, Pat McEwan says Dell will change their upcoming lunch meeting, which he does, to a 10:00 a.m. meeting at the carousel in Central Park. Joe had been playing with his Boy Scout knife while talking on the phone with Dell, and right after he hangs up he gets a call from the FBI, as if they had tapped his line and knew the details of his conversation with Dell, instructing him to be at the Navy Fountain in Central Park at 9:30.

FBI "agents" are planted around the park as workers and tourists who guide Joe, with his Process notebook, into the men's room, where a male agent informs him that the Spanish Prisoner con is being played on him, so he'll wear a wire and refuse to do what Dell asks in order to get him on record offering money or threat-ening Joe. On his way to the carousel Joe is bumped into by a skater, then directed by a sweeping park worker via pointed finger to get on the carousel. Mamet gives a visually striking homage to the carousel scene in Hitchcock's *Strangers on a Train* (1951) with disconcerting camera angles and ominous shots of the carved horses. Alighting, Joe sits on a bench and finishes eating the popcorn he bought from a ven-dor. He notices that the park worker sweeping is a different man. He calls the num-ber on McEwan's business card and gets a non-working number. Looking up the FBI in the phone book, when connected to Pat McEwan he gets a male voice. Open-ing the Process notebook, he discovers all of the pages are blank. At some point— when he was being wired, when the skater bumped into him—the real Process was stolen.

Joe and the police discover Dell's apartment is completely empty and devoid of fingerprints, the "office" of the club a waiter had disappeared into to get the mem-bership certificate is a coat-check room, and the "club" is a restaurant. Questioned by the police, Susan says she joked about the seaplane and Dell as an excuse to talk with Joe. The police are suspicious because Joe bought her first-class plane ticket and some new clothes during the trip with cash. "Do you have any undisclosed bank accounts?" he's asked. Thanks to Dell, he has that Swiss bank account, and the club membership form was a request for political asylum in Venezuela, which has no extradition policy. He is arrested but bailed out by Klein, who drops the charges and begs Joe to bring the Process back to him, not to let it go to the Japanese.

Joe calls his friend George for help and advice, is told to come over, and lets himself in the apartment with a key kept on the door's head jamb because George is down with the flu. He touches various objects around the apartment before discovering his friend has been stabbed fatally in the chest with Joe's Boy Scout knife, which he also touches. Hearing sirens approaching he flees using the fire escape, leaving his bloody eyeglasses behind. In a nearly-empty subway car a woman notices his bloody hands while the camera also takes in a sign saying "Everybody's business" to the right of the windowed door to the next car; a police officer can be seen through the window approaching the car. The officer enters, there is a stop so Joe gets off, yet the woman doesn't alert the officer to follow him. Unlike Joe, she seems to be someone who can intuit a person's real character by their face. Or maybe, this being New York City, she just figured it wasn't her business.

Riding another subway car Joe notices an ad for Horizons Technical Institute (which ironically includes the wording "Your Career Now!" and "Have a Bright N—") bearing a logo similar to the one on the bag Susan had brought him from the Sunshine Bakery she lives over, so he goes to her for assistance. Even though Susan declares, "Someone has singled you out to take advantage of you," he thinks he's in some way responsible, fretting over his greed for being paid for the Process. She calls in sick with the flu to help him, reassuring, "You're the innocent, the victim," and he allows, "I'm the Boy Scout." Her apartment security monitor prompts Joe to realize the cameras at the resort would have captured Dell's image, so Susan drives him to the airport, giving him cash and her unused air ticket because he had bought her the first-class one. It is St. Patrick's Day (Dell had made Joe's passcode for the Swiss account "Paddy") and the police are stopping cars; to get out of the road check Susan yells at Joe for being drunk, which does cause them to be waved through, and she drives him to Boston airport.

In line at the airport a mother rebukes her child for getting fingerprints all over his book, which triggers Joe to remember he has the Budge book with Dell's prints on it, so he rushes out of the terminal—narrowly escaping arrest, because viewers see the bag Susan had given him with a camera in it go through the screening machine to reveal it contains a gun, not a camera. As Joe leaves the terminal viewers also see the airline ticket Susan had given him is for Caracas, Venezuela. He spots Susan talking to a woman; viewers see it is the fake FBI agent McCune, but Joe isn't wearing his glasses, so when Susan runs to him they get onto an airport shuttle that takes them to a ferry boat. Susan goes off at his bidding to call Klein and have him take the Budge book to the police. When the ferry captain asks him for his ticket, Joe absentmindedly gives him the airline ticket and so learns it's for Venezuela. This time he can see Susan talking with the fake McCune, as well as with other people, so, having noticed where the captain had put the key to the box containing the ferry signal horn, he unlocks it and gives the signal for the ferry to depart. Susan makes it aboard with him but the others are thwarted.

"Now why would someone do that?" Joe muses aloud to Susan on board the ferry; "Why would somebody go into a life of crime?" "I don't know," she replies; "I think there are people we can't understand." Joe continues, "To steal what others worked for. To kill." "We can't know, Joe. Golly Joe, I—," Susan halts because Joe is looking at her and she realizes he's figured it out. "Why?" he wants to know. "Why? For the money," she responds, walking off the deck to sit inside the boat's enclosure.

Joe follows, to discover Dell is there. "And we come to the end of a perfect day," Dell says, Susan chiming in, "Clang, clang, end of the line," an allusion to *Double Indemnity*'s recurring use of "straight down the line," where the final stop is the cemetery. The idea is for the authorities to think that Joe has stolen the Process, killed George, and kidnapped Susan, all for the money; overcome with remorse he will now take his own life. Trying to escape onto the captain's level, Joe approaches a Japanese tourist (Takeo Matsushita) for help, who inquires, "Didn't your mother have a dog named Paddy?" "What?" Joe asks, confused. "Didn't she have a dog named Paddy?" he repeats. "This must be a big day for you," the man says, turning over the St. Patrick's Day boutonniere Susan had him buy at the airport to reveal a microphone. "See if you can get them to tell you where the Process is. We need to know where the Process is. You're doing fine," the man says before walking off, leaving an astonished Joe in his wake.

Dell comes on deck with a gun and Joe dutifully asks him what he did with the Process. "That's you're last request?" Dell queries. "Yes, could you grant me that?" Joe replies. "We took the report and we sold it to Switzerland," Dell starts, but the rest of what he says is blotted out by a tugboat horn. A Japanese woman (Seiko Yoshida) suddenly pulls a gun out of a poster tube and shoots Dell with a tranquilizer dart. "And now I suppose you'll take the Process to Japan," Joe says to the Japanese man he'd been talking with before, who responds, "U.S. Marshal Service, actually." It turns out Klein had set the whole con up. There are only two keys to the safe in which the Process was kept, and Klein obviously couldn't purloin it himself, so Joe had to take the fall. As Susan is being led off in handcuffs she asks Joe, "Can you help me? You're the Boy Scout. Can I be your good deed for today? Can't you help me, Joe?" She doesn't really sound like she thinks he will, and indeed, he shakes his head no and responds, "I'm afraid you're going to have to spend some time in your room," at which she smiles. Joe is left alone on the pier as sirens sound when the marshals' van departs, then he walks forward out of the frame and the screen goes to black before the credits roll.

In a curiously optimistic conclusion for Mamet, Joe escapes wiser but more or less untainted. Granted, he's lost his best friend George and been betrayed on a dizzying number of levels, but he is resilient. After all, his friend's killer used Joe's Boy Scout knife to frame him. He can always buy another. With *The Spanish Prisoner* Mamet has developed as a filmmaker to the level of textual nuance that he brings to his plays. He has become a nimble enough director to allude to Hitchcock or Wilder without being obvious, but the heart of his story, as always and as it should be, lies in the language he deploys, from naming the McGuffin "the Process" in an echo of Kafka's *Der Prozess*, known in English as *The Trial*, to the signature use of cliché and repetition elaborated into verbal theme and variation. As more than one character in *The Spanish Prisoner* mentions, "There's a lot of it going around." Likewise, as Maurer points out, "Confidence games are cyclic phenomena."[62] Individual ones may "drop into obscurity," but "Sooner or later they are revived, refurbished to fit the times, and used to trim some sucker who has never heard of them."[63] As for future con artists and scams? "No one can say with any accuracy what will happen in the days to come; we can only speculate on the basis of past events," Maurer writes;

"Many different forces, some of them perhaps entirely new, will probably leave their mark on the big-time confidence games."[64] Thus we can be assured that in film noir as in life, "Something further may follow...." It had for Mamet, whose 1994 *Oleanna* had also concerned con artists and their prey, and the director's other thrillers have included *House of Games* (1987) and *Heist* (2001).

FIVE

Double Crosses

Religious Delusion in Film Noir

Given the post–Calvinist view of the last chapter on con artists and scams, that everyone is potentially corruptible and most are already corrupt, one could wonder what role religion might play thematically in a genre so generally cynical about spiritual values and convictions. A distorted one, to be sure. Remnants of the Great Awakening, that last gasp of Puritanism, appear in the pathological, messianic figures that manipulate the lives of innocent and criminal alike in noir films from the classic period through the late 1990s. Harry Powell in *The Night of the Hunter* (1955) justifies his murderous greed through undigested scripture. In *Mean Streets* (1973), Charlie staggers into mayhem trying to negotiate between his Catholic fervor and life on the street. Another incarnation is "John Doe" in *Se7en* (1995), who believes he is saving humanity by killing embodiments of the Seven Deadly Sins. The makers of these films show that skepticism does not preclude vision.

The Great Awakening

Historians vary as to the dates they assign to the spiritual revivals in America, with 1740 coming up most often as the inception of the First Great Awakening. Eugene Taylor's *Shadow Culture: Psychology and Spirituality in America* assigns the broad period of 1720 to 1750 to the Great Awakening.[1] J.M. Bumsted prefaces his edited collection of primary documents related to the Great Awakening, *The Great Awakening: The Beginnings of Evangelical Pietism in America*, by noting that it "did not really begin in America until after the arrival of George Whitefield in the colonies in 1739."[2] Thomas S. Kidd, in *The Great Awakening: The Roots of Evangelical Christianity in Colonial America*, muddies the waters by saying that calling the revivals that happened "from about 1740 to 1743" the Great Awakening presents "historical problems" because "important, widespread revivals" occurred before and after this period.[3] From his perspective, "The long First Great Awakening started before Jonathan Edwards's 1734–35 Northampton revival and lasted roughly through the end of the American Revolution, when disestablishment, theological change, and a new round of growth started the (even more imprecise) 'Second' Great Awakening."[4] However one dates and labels the religious revivals of colonial and early national America, their impact on the culture of their times and after is inarguable.

As Bumsted observes, "Colonial America was always a crazy-quilt of religious sects, but the revivals ensured that denominational fragmentation dominated by strong overtones of Protestant pietism would prevail in what would become the United States and Canada."[5] In *Inventing the "Great Awakening,"* Frank Lambert explains how the evangelicals involved in the Great Awakening "viewed themselves as, first, discoverers of a 'Work of God' and, second, instruments in promoting that work. They preached with fervor and prayed with expectation for an effusion of God's Spirit."[6] Believing "that extraordinary dispensations called for extraordinary measures, ... the awakeners employed a cluster of methods, some old, some new, designed to arouse men and women to a sense of the deplorable state of their religious lives and the necessity of the 'one thing needful,' a spiritual New Birth."[7] Thus their sermons were "aimed at getting people to acknowledge their sinful condition and turn to God, whose grace alone could save them from eternal damnation."[8] Eugene Taylor notes that people in the audiences listening to the sermons responded in various ways: "Trance states, ecstatic whirling, automatic utterances, falling down in the spirit, joyful exuberance, and spiritual happiness were all common occurrences, and all were fully sanctioned by the very governing church bodies that had forbade such behavior in public in the past."[9] While there were numerous preachers during the Great Awakening, two figures in particular stand out: Jonathan Edwards and George Whitefield.

Jonathan Edwards' (1703–1758) father and maternal grandfather were both reverends, and the latter, Solomon Stoddard, was an important figure in New England Puritanism. Edwards was home schooled and entered Yale College at age 13, going on to study divinity after graduating in 1720 and earning his M.A. in 1723. When his grandfather died after having served as pastor of the Congregationalist Church in Northampton, Massachusetts, from 1669 to 1729, Edwards was appointed to the position and served until he was dismissed in 1750 for overturning his grandfather's requirements for receiving the Lord's Supper, once again instituting that only those who were converted could take the Eucharist. By "converted" Edwards, and other Puritans, meant people who had more than doctrinal knowledge; they experienced and were moved by their religion. Having lost his pulpit, Edwards became a missionary in Stockbridge, Massachusetts, serving the Housatonnuck Indians, and was pastor of the frontier church there. He left these endeavors to become—reluctantly—president of the College of New Jersey (now Princeton), but died three months after assuming that office from taking the new smallpox vaccination.

From the mid–1730s through the 1740s, Edwards preached in the spirit of the Great Awakening that was occurring throughout the colonies, but especially close to him in the Connecticut River Valley. "Sinners in the Hands of an Angry God," a sermon he delivered on Sunday, July 8, 1741, in Enfield, Connecticut, contains imagery, language, and tactics typical of revival preaching that aimed to gain new converts in the church. The controlling image of the sermon is that "natural men are held in the hand of God, over the pit of hell; they have deserved the fiery pit, and are already sentenced to it; and God is dreadfully provoked."[10] God's power to condemn the unconverted to Hell is repeated through a variety of vivid images: "the pit is prepared, the fire is made ready, the furnace is now hot, ready to receive them; the flames do now rage and glow. The glittering sword is whet, and held over them, and the pit hath opened its mouth under them."[11] If the unconverted cry out to God for pity, He will be so far from pitying them that "He will crush you under His feet without mercy; He will crush out your blood, and make it fly and it shall be sprinkled on His garments, so as to stain all His raiment."[12] How many will remember this sermon in Hell, Edwards asked his congregation. Bringing the sermon to its close, Edwards advised his unconverted listeners, "Therefore, let everyone that is out of Christ, now awake and fly from the wrath to come. The wrath of Almighty God is now undoubtedly hanging over a great part of this congregation."[13]

George Whitefield (1714–1770) was a Church of England evangelical preacher who preached in the United Kingdom and the American colonies. His studies at Pembroke College, Oxford, led to a friendship with John and Charles Wesley, Methodist missionaries. Whitefield's performance method of delivering sermons— dancing, crying, yelling—was not acceptable in London churches, so he became an open-air preacher and in 1739 headed for the American colonies with the intent of touring. There Whitefield's preaching drew huge audiences—and great pushback from some established churches and clergy. Eugene Taylor reports how 50,000 gatherers on Boston Common gave their rapt attention to Whitefield as he spoke of the coming millennium, for which "he was censored by the Anglicans in Boston, the conservatives in Philadelphia, and, in 1744, denounced by the faculty at Harvard as an 'enthusiast,' meaning pejoratively one who mistakes some mechanical or psychological disturbance for the Word of God."[14] These denigrations of Whitefield's preaching get at important distinctions of the time that will help further delineate the aspects of religion to be discussed in relation to the fiction and films analyzed in this chapter.

As Thomas S. Kidd explains the spectrum of religious experiences available during the Great Awakening, "On one end were the *anti-revivalists*, who dismissed the revivals as religious frenzy or 'enthusiasm.' In the middle were the *moderate evangelicals*, who supported the revivals at their outset but became concerned about the chaotic, leveling extremes that the awakenings produced. Finally, on the other end were the *radical evangelicals*, who eagerly embraced the Spirit's movements, even if social conventions had to be sacrificed."[15] To break it down even more simplistically, as David Harlan does in *The Clergy and the Great Awakening in New England*, whether one's name was found on the subscription lists for Jonathan Edwards' publications or for Boston minister Charles Chauncey's was telling: "If a minister subscribed to Edwards' *Some Thoughts Concerning the Revival*, he is taken for a friend of the Awakening—and, *ipso facto*, a friend to revelation, mystery, theism, emotion, conservatism, supernaturalism, and medievalism; conversely, if a minister's name is found on the subscription list for Chauncy's *Seasonable Thoughts*, he is assumed to have been a critic of the revivals and committed to reason, clarity, liberalism, and the rest."[16] Both Chauncy and the Blandford, Massachusetts, Presbyterian minister John Caldwell were critical of revival preachers to the point of almost calling them frauds. Frank Lambert explains that Chauncy felt that "the events some considered to be of divine origin were human contrivances" and that George Whitefield, whom he referred to as the "Grand Itinerant," had basically invented an Awakening "as a product of slick publicity and promotion."[17] Likewise, Caldwell "questioned the motives of the evangelists, wondering if their efforts were not intended more to raise a following and fill their coffers than to save souls… [,] whether evangelistic cries for piety did not mask their quest for profits."[18] Some two centuries later, one religious figure who definitely wanted to fleece the pious would appear on the big screen.

Davis Grubb, Charles Laughton and *The Night of the Hunter*

In *The Night of the Hunter*, the only film Charles Laughton directed, the mad preacher Harry Powell (Robert Mitchum) latches onto and marries a widow, Willa Harper (Shelley Winters), whose children know where their bank-robber father hid $10,000—a nice sum even if the film weren't set during the Great Depression. Preacher, whose crude knuckle tattoos of LOVE and HATE speak volumes about the deranged simplicity of his evangelism, was arrested for stealing a car and had done time with Ben Harper (Peter Graves) while Harper awaited execution for two deaths that occurred during the robbery. "I come not with peace, but with a sword," Powell declares, referencing the switchblade that figures prominently in defining his character. "What religion you profess, Preacher?" Ben asks, earning Powell's retort, "The religion The Almighty and me worked out betwixt us." Then follows a shot of him through the prison window, the bars acting as a cross, with his hands held in a position of prayer, the blade of his knife coming out of his fingertips. Religious symbolism infuses the film to a feverish degree characteristic of James Agee's writing. Agee adapted the screenplay from Davis Grubb's first novel, *The Night of the Hunter* (1953), which in turn was based on the real-life figure of serial killer Harry F. Powers.

Powers was born in The Netherlands as Harm Drenth in the late 19th century; birth dates vary from source to source, but it was likely in 1892 or 1893. His first name would almost seem contrived, but it is the short form of Harmen and would be Americanized as Herman. Drenth's parents and he immigrated to Iowa. As an adult, although he was already married to Luella "Lulu" Strother, he placed Lonely Hearts ads to attract widows with money, using various aliases like Powers and Cornelius O. Pierson. It's known that he killed Asta Eicher and her three children, Annabel (age 9), Hart (age 12), and Grethe (age 14), and Dorothy Lemke—their bodies were recovered on his property. Authorities found a trunk full of correspondence from women all over the United States in his house in the Blue Ridge Mountains of West Virginia. He was known as West Virginia's Bluebeard, and his trial was held in Moore's Opera House because so many spectators wanted to attend. It took the jury less than two hours to convict him. In addition to Harm's own given name, other remarkable names were his ironically named defense attorney, J.E. Law, and the appropriately named Sheriff W.B. Grimm. Officials were never able to prove Powers killed more than five people, although it was suspected he killed at least two more, and some speculate he killed fifty or so people, mostly women. Powers does not seem to have assumed the guise of prison chaplain that Grubb assigns to the character based upon him. The real man lingers on in the American imagination and inspired Jayne Anne

Phillips' 2013 novel *Quiet Dell*, an eloquently written, sensitive, imagined exploration into the lives of Powers' victims, their circle of friends, and the journalists and law authorities involved in the case that folds historical documents such as newspaper articles, trial testimony, and photographs into its narrative.

In *The Night of the Hunter*'s opening sequence, in which the upper bodies and faces of children and Rachel Cooper (Lillian Gish), a widow who takes in homeless children, are superimposed over a star-filled night sky, she warns her charges, "Beware of false prophets which come to you in sheep's clothing but inwardly they are ravening wolves. You shall know them by their fruits." Then children playing hide-and-seek find a dead woman in a storm cellar and viewers see Preacher driving along talking to God about His not minding the killings Preacher's done but instead minding the "perfumed-smelling things." After these thoughts of Preacher's in the novel, Grubb writes about how he would grasp his knife's handle with the hand tattooed LOVE as "his soul rose up in flaming glorious fury. He was the dark angel with the sword of a Vengeful God. Paul is choking misogynistic wrath upon Damascus Road."[19] It's emphasized in the film that Preacher is a misogynist when, watching a burlesque show, he puts his HATE hand into his coat pocket to activate the switchblade, which rips through the cloth phallically. Grubb expounds upon this scene to convey Preacher's extreme revulsion against women, noting how his sweaty fingers rubbed his knife as he seethed "in a quiet convulsion of outrage and nausea at all that ocean of undulating womanhood beyond the lights."[20] The smell of the men and women, the scent of cheap perfume, cigar smoke, and corn liquor that soured the air sends him stumbling out from the burlesque show, "his whole spirit luminous with an enraptured and blessed fury at the world these whores had made."[21] After Ben's execution, the film intercuts between a scene of Willa and her ice cream parlor employers, the Spoons, talking and the train bearing Preacher speeding toward town, another phallic image, all the more ironic because Preacher turns out to have a misogynistic revulsion toward conjugal relations.

The casting of Robert Mitchum as Preacher contributes to the film's sense of corruption and disorientation; as sexy as a real evangelist, he plays the anti–Mitchum. At the Spoons' ice cream parlor, Preacher tells the story of "right hand and left hand" with all the wit and aplomb of a hung-over vacuum-cleaner salesman. The left hand, HATE, represents Cain, while the right hand is the hand of LOVE. His two hands wrestle until Preacher yells, "Hotdog! Love's a winning!" Naively impressed with this performance, Icey Spoon (Evelyn Varden) tells her friends that Willa ought to snap him up because "She's not the only fish in the river," a horribly prescient comment given that Willa's corpse will indeed wind up at the bottom of the river. Willa seems to undergo a sort of religious purification as she falls for Preacher, declaring, "I feel clean now. My whole body is just quivering with cleanness." But she is plainly an innocent imposter, her human need transplanted to holy passion. On their wedding night she comes bashfully into the bedroom, where Preacher harshly informs her there will be no begetting of more children. Willa prays, "Help me to get clean, so I can be what Harry wants me to be." She so becomes what he wants her to be that she accompanies him to do some campfire revival preaching. The camera shows Willa framed by torches blazing on either side of her in the foreground; Preacher is behind her to the left, looking appropriately pious as she delivers her story with great emotion and using the repetition common to evangelical preaching:

> You have all sinned! But which one of you can say, as I can say, that you drove a good man to murder because I kept a-hounding him for perfume, and clothes, and face paint? And he slew two human beings, and he come to me and he said, take this money and buy yourself the clothes and the paint. But brethren, brethren, oh, that's where the Lord stepped in! That's where the Lord stepped in! He said, the Lord to that man, you take the money, and you throw it in the river!

"In the river!" Preacher echoes in his deep bass voice, the crowd joining in with enthusiasm. Willa's preaching and the crowd's interaction with it go on longer in Grubb's novel, after which he takes note of Preacher's real aim with these revivals: counting the money they've collected from the crowd, which amounts to thirty-five dollars, along with a jug of maple syrup and two bushels of apples.

One night while Walt Spoon (Don Beddoe) worries out loud to Icey about Willa and that there's something wrong with Preacher, there is a cut to Willa's bedroom, which looks rather like a chapel with its vaulted, angled ceiling; its structure and the lighting hearken back to German Expressionist films. Willa is lying on the bed with her arms folded across her chest, like a body at rest in its coffin. "Are you through praying?" Preacher asks dully. Willa ruminates out loud that Ben had not told him

Willa (Shelley Winters) awaits her fate at Preacher's (Robert Mitchum) hand in *The Night of the Hunter* (1955) (Paul Gregory Prods/UA/Photofest).

the stolen money was in the river, whereupon Preacher backhands her face hard, yet Willa simply smiles up at the ceiling. As she speculates that John must know where the money is, that "it's still here amongst us, tainting us," Mitchum gives quite a performance in the background. "You must have known about it all along, Harry," Willa says calmly, "But that ain't the reason you married me. I know that much. Because the Lord just wouldn't let it be. He made you marry me so you could show me the way, the life, and the salvation of my soul." As she intones this Preacher reaches his arm, fingers splayed, up to the light coming through the bedroom's high window (an unnatural light that the bedside lamp would not be casting, plus when he pulls down the shade it is still there, so it's not coming from the gas light outside the house), head cocked as if he's listening to his God whisper instructions in his ear. The expression in his eyes and the slightest suggestion of a smirk on his mouth indicate he can't quite believe Willa has bought his righteousness so easily, become such a willing and passive convert. He abruptly puts his arm down and with a calm, almost blank expression on his face pulls down the window shade, gets his knife out of his coat's pocket, opens the blade, walks over to the bed, leans over Willa, and slowly arcs his arm up and over to plunge the knife down into her. Willa simply closes her eyes and waits for the blade to descend.

Preacher sinks her body and Ben's old car into the river, then weeps false tears at the Spoons', declaring, "A strange woman is a narrow pit. She lieth in wait as for prey and increases the transgressors among men," so that now, "It's my shame, it's my crown of thorns, I must wear it bravely." He lies that Willa had turned him out of the bed on their wedding night, has been drinking dandelion wine, and has run off. When the Spoons applaud him for assuming the role of single parent, he says with false modesty, "Oh, I reckon it was just ordained that way, Brother Spoon," and when they reassure him Willa will return he rejoins, "She won't be back. I reckon I'm safe in telling you that," and with his HATE knuckles prominently in view to underscore his murder of her, he looks meaningfully at Walt. "I tried to save her," he states, "But the Devil wins sometimes. Can't nobody say I didn't do my best to save her," whereupon he looks heavenward as a dissolve shot brings the river weeds into view that join Willa's hair flowing in the current. This horrifically beautiful image was achieved by cinematographer Stanley Cortez using wind machines and a wax dummy of Winters.

After their mother's disappearance, Preacher, outside the house, is calling for Willa's children, and an iris shot transition is used to show Pearl (Sally Jane Bruce) and John (Billy Chapin) peering through the basement window, emphasizing their entrapment. John doesn't like Preacher, but Pearl does, so Preacher has been working on getting her to reveal where the $10,000 is. With Willa gone he can do this more openly. "Want to see something cute?" he asks Pearl one day, holding up and opening his switchblade. When Pearl reaches for the knife, he pulls it back, saying, "No, little lamb, don't touch it. Don't touch my knife. That makes me mad. That makes me very, very mad," sounding like a psychosexually demented Abraham. Pressing her to tell him where the money is, Preacher nearly breaks her down, but seeing this is about to happen, John lies that the money is in the basement. When it isn't, Preacher holds John's head on an apple barrel akin to Abraham preparing to sacrifice Isaac. "The Lord's a talkin' to me now," he says, taking out his knife and threatening, "Speak or I'll cut your throat and leave you to drip like a hog hung up at butchering time." Pearl reveals that the money is in her doll to save her brother, and while Preacher is laughing over how the money basically has been in front of him the whole time, John extinguishes the candle and pulls out a board so that a shelf of jarred goods falls on him, actually causing Preacher to whimper. The children lock him in the basement and, while Preacher roars like a monster and yells, "Open that door, you spawn of the Devil's own strumpet," they run to their drunken but kindly riverboat "uncle" figure for refuge, a Noah of sorts. Uncle Birdie Steptoe (James Gleason) is beyond helping them as he has had too much to drink that night because he saw Willa's body while fishing, so the children take their father's skiff and float down river like Moses, which is underscored once they find safety with Rachel and she tells them the story. For now, though, as John struggles to get Pearl into the boat, the silhouette of Preacher rises up against the glow of the night sky in a low-angle shot of the steep riverbank. As John pushes off from the bank Preacher thrashes through the underbrush toward them, falls in the mud, and howls in primal rage while holding his knife as they drift out of his reach. In the novel Grubb describes the sound as "a steady, rhythmical, animal scream of outrage and loss" that the people on nearby houseboats hear as "something as old and dark as the things on the river's bed, old as evil itself, a pulsing, ragged bawling that came down the water to them in hideous rhythm," emphasizing Preacher's psychotic madness at the children's escape.[22]

But Preacher will not remain far behind them. He knifes a farmer and steals his horse, appearing as a plodding yet unstoppable silhouette while the children sleep in a hay loft one night, singing as he rides: "Leaning, leaning, safe and secure from all alarms; leaning, leaning, leaning on the everlasting arms." When they had been drifting down river the camera had focused one shot on two trembling rabbits on the bank, emblematic of John and Pearl's scared condition, and when they are adrift again the camera reveals a fox, suggesting Preacher's hunting of them, but the children at last find refuge with Rachel Cooper. Preacher tries to get information about Pearl and John from one of the older girls staying at Rachel's, Ruby (Gloria Castillo), when she is in town. Ruby is a flirt, and Preacher approaches her akin to a suitor, addressing her by name and saying, "I'd like to talk to you, my dear," at which she asks, "Can I have this?" about the *Modern Movie Magazine* she's been browsing and, "Will you buy me an ice cream?" Once they're seated in a drugstore Ruby asks, "Ain't I pretty?," and Preacher amiably responds, "Why, you're the prettiest thing I've ever seen in all my wandering. Ain't nobody ever tell you that before?" Done with the small talk, Preacher confirms that John, Pearl, and the doll are all at Rachel's, stands up abruptly, and rushes out of the drugstore. Ruby is just as fast running after him, grabbing his arm as if to speak, so he leans in to hear her ask, "Did you ever see such pretty eyes in all your born days?" Preacher straightens stiffly, simultaneously giving her a hard look and thrusting the open switchblade downward in his pocket, then saunters off. Grubb's Ruby is not the innocent flirt of her onscreen incarnation; she has "done it with men."[23] In her parting scene with Preacher she offers herself to him, leading him to yell "Get away from me!," push her away, and walk swiftly away from her, "striding furiously through the dust toward his horse, choking and cursing, his mouth gaping with nausea."[24] Grubb does not include the switchblade in this passage, but Agee and Laughton use it to visually echo Preacher's previous misogynistic violence toward women.

The next morning Preacher appears outside Rachel's house claiming to be John and Pearl's father and starts to tell the story of his knuckle tattoos, but shrewd Rachel cuts him short with questions about the children's mother. She's already seen through his act when John arrives to confirm her suspicions by denying he is their father, leading her to say, "No, and he ain't no preacher either," get her shotgun and force him off the property. "All right," he says as he goes, "but you haven't heard the last of Harry Powell yet. The Lord God Jehovah will guide my hand in vengeance. You Devil. You whores of Babylon. I'll be back when it's dark," he threatens. He does indeed return, whereupon he and Rachel have a call-and-response round of "Leaning on the Everlasting Arms" as the focus moves from Preacher in the background outside to Rachel in the foreground on the porch—until Ruby enters with a candle that Rachel blows out, revealing to them and the viewer that Preacher has disappeared. Quickly Rachel marshals her charges into the kitchen and tells them the story of the infant Jesus being saved from Herod's Massacre of the Innocents. Preacher's voice at the kitchen door demands for John and Pearl to be given to him. Rachel levels her shotgun at him and warns, "I'm giving you to the count of three to get outta here, then I'm coming across the kitchen shooting." A cat startles Preacher and Rachel fires, sending him howling like a wounded ape across the yard to the barn. When the police arrive in the morning, Preacher staggers out of the barn, weakened by his shoulder wound yet still able to raise his switchblade, although the police easily subdue him. When Preacher is handcuffed, John flashes back to his real father's arrest, screams "don't" repeatedly, and shakes the money out of the doll, saying, "I don't want it, Dad! It's too much! Here! Here!" until he faints in Rachel's arms.

A rather bizarre lynch-mob scene containing the Spoons, Icey wielding an axe, comes after Preacher's trial, so the police remove the prisoner via the back door of the police station for safe keeping before his execution. In the novel, the trial comes from John's perspective, and he reports that Icey yelled, "Lynch him! Lynch him! This court won't never see justice done to that Bluebird monster! [John mishears "Bluebeard" as "Bluebird."] For he lied and he taken the Lord's name in vain and trampled on His Holy Book!"[25] The judge orders her to be silent, and Icey protests that Powell sullied Jesus' name. When the judge reminds her the trial is for murder, not heresy, she comes back with it being worse than murder that Powell took God's name in vain and lied about being a man of the cloth. After one day's proceedings are done, Rachel, Pearl, and John are walking in the street and Icey points at the children while Grubb has her holler about Powell having sinned against those poor little lambs and dragged God's name "through the evil mud of his soul!"[26] She claims Christianity won't be safe unless Powell is hung and reiterates how they were lied to and tricked by his false sermonizing. After the trial is over Walt is part of the lynch mob, yelling about how Powell tricked them and is really "Satan hiding behind the cross!"[27] It's interesting that the Spoons seem to be more outraged at having fallen for Preacher's pretense to be a religious man than at his having murdered Willa.

Grubb doesn't come out and directly state that the lynch mob was successful, he only has Rachel remembering how she fled "the scene of Preacher's last, terrible night on earth," so readers assume he was strung up by the mob.[28]

Laughton's film closes with Rachel and her charges celebrating Christmas at home, she marveling how resilient children are: "They abide and they endure." Grubb's Rachel too thinks children abide, but shortly before this she had asked the Lord to save the little ones because each child has "a time of running through a shadowed place, an alley with no doors, and a hunter whose footsteps ring brightly along the bricks behind him."[29] Yet the novel closes with an image of true, not deranged, religion: John sleeps underneath a gospel quilt decorated with Biblical kings and shepherds, the latter having "guarded their small lambs against the night."[30]

Martin Scorsese and *Mean Streets*

Some twenty years later, a more complex world in which humans grapple with sin and God is depicted by Martin Scorsese in *Mean Streets*, which the director confesses is his most autobiographical movie. By that one assumes he is referring to the provincial New York milieu he grew up in and to the central themes, rather than the actual story. Certainly the film contains the most overt eschatological symbolism he has ever employed, even more so than *The Last Temptation of Christ* (1988), showing a rift between the sublime and the profane that magnifies the connection of the two. Scorsese was an altar boy and considered the priesthood in his youth, attending the junior seminary Cathedral College when he was 14. But he fell in love and wasn't concentrating on his schoolwork, so after a year he was expelled.[31] He finished high school at Cardinal Hays, and when his grades didn't get him into the Jesuit University at Fordham, he went to New York University, where he majored in film and minored in English.[32]

The film begins with a black screen and voice-over by Scorsese: "You don't make up for your sins in church. You do it in the streets. You do it at home. The rest is bullshit and you know it." Because Scorsese sees the main character Charlie (Harvey Keitel) as one incarnation of himself, in the voice-overs his voice and Keitel's are intercut, which Scorsese explains "was a way of trying to come to terms with myself, trying to redeem myself."[33] The camera shows Charlie in medium close-up waking up in his bedroom, going to look at himself in the wall mirror while sirens sound outside, then lying back down. "Be My Baby" booms over the opening credits that intermix with grainy home-movie footage of baptisms, family gatherings, and Charlie shaking hands with a priest on the steps of a church, glimpses of this close-knit community braced by Catholic ritual and structure. An overhead shot of the crowded Feast of San Gennaro shows its enormity; shots of this Italian-American festival punctuate the film and serve as a reminder of the Catholic presence Charlie must literally weave through on his daily business, as does a large statue of Christ with outstretched arms atop the corner of a building.

Charlie is a middling numbers runner who wants to make it big, but environment circumscribes his ambitions. Like many a native New Yorker, his world consists of his neighborhood; even a few blocks outside of it leaves him uncertain. His home turf is strange enough. Charlie's main hangout is the bar Volpe's that Scorsese shows in a perpetual lurid-red half-light—a Little Italy Hades, where violence erupts unpredictably, almost as punctuation marks to the central story. In one scene the bar's owner, Tony (David Proval), roughs up and kicks out a junkie; in another a drunk gets shot repeatedly by a kid looking to make a rep, prompting Charlie to comment that "the guy would keep coming at him, like Rasputin." (In a delightfully perverse touch of casting, David Carradine plays the drunk murdered by his real-life younger brother, Robert.) The only direct reference to contemporary events in the film is a welcome-home party at Volpe's for Jerry (Harry Northup), a soldier returned from Vietnam, which ends with the vet destroying his sheet cake and breaking apart a couple who is slow dancing to throw the girl (Juli Andelman) roughly to the floor. One pal tries to calm him by saying, "Jesus, take it easy, you're in America, Jerry." Yes, where could he feel safer?

Yet the bar's infernal quality reflects the depths of Charlie's internal conflicts, especially between loyalty and his Catholic faith. To say his friend Johnny Boy (Robert De Niro) is a loose cannon is to put it mildly. Perhaps the least of his offenses is to bring two Jewish women as dates to Volpe's. Johnny Boy owes money to several people, the most important one in Charlie's view being their friend Michael (Richard Romanus). Charlie is the peacemaker between Johnny Boy and Michael, and also literally puts himself between Johnny Boy and Tony to stop a fight when the latter gets angry over the former wanting to join a poker game when he owes money.

While Johnny Boy is his burden, Tony is Charlie's passive-aggressive enabler. At one point Tony derides Charlie for his gullibility in believing a made-up anecdote a priest related to him at a retreat, but he lends Charlie his car when he wants it, and in one scene Tony takes the boys into the back room to show off his new prized possessions, a pair of tiger cubs. Climbing into the cage, stroking one of the cats, he says, "I always wanted a tiger, Charlie. Y'know, William Blake and all that." The allusion to Blake's poem works very well for Scorsese's purposes, as "The Tyger" is in the poet's collection *Songs of Experience* and sits in opposition to the poem "The Lamb" in Blake's *Songs of Innocence*. The main question of "The Tyger" is "Did he who made the Lamb make thee?" The answer is, of course, yes, which raises issues of good and evil coexisting in the world and Charlie having to struggle with all that that means as he navigates the realms of church and street.

Charlie has a secret relationship with Johnny Boy's cousin Teresa (Amy Robinson), an epileptic. Epilepsy, of course, is associated with mystical visions, yet Teresa is one of the most rational characters in the film. Her patron saint, St. Teresa of Avila (1515–1582), entered a Carmelite Convent, fell ill, and after recovering from a three-year illness, ceased praying and lived her next fifteen years torn between a worldly life and a divine one. After a religious awakening she returned to the Carmelites and promoted complete withdrawal and an ascetic way of life. This allusional background to the film's Teresa makes her a suitable partner for the conflicted Charlie. She hates her cousin and wants to move uptown and make a life with Charlie. In a scene on the beach when she's complaining about Johnny Boy, Charlie asks her, "Who's going to help him if I don't?," going on, "That's what's the matter. Nobody,

Charlie's (Harvey Keitel) Catholic faith sometimes is at odds with his life outside church in *Mean Streets* (1973) (Warner Bros. Pictures/Photofest).

nobody tries anymore." "Tries what?" Teresa inquires. "Tries to, to help, that's all, to help people," Charlie replies. Teresa maintains the view that you need to help yourself first, leading Charlie to retort, "Bullshit, Terese. That's where you're all wrong. Francis of Assisi had it all down. He knew." "What are you talking about?" she mocks, "Francis of Assisi didn't run numbers." Charlie replies evenly, "Me neither, I don't run numbers." Charlie's admiration of St. Francis of Assisi (1181/82–1226) is yet another layer of complexity in his character. While St. Francis' acts of charity, sense of brotherhood, personal charisma, and evangelical zeal can easily be associated with Charlie, the last item especially in relation to his talks to Johnny Boy about paying his debts, Francis' insistence on poverty and denial of self don't seem to have an appeal for Charlie.

The scene cuts to Volpe's, where Charlie, both reacting to his argument with Terese and acting on an attraction he has been feeling, talks with one of the strippers, Diane (Jeannie Bell), about his upcoming opportunity to open his own restaurant. She could be hostess, he suggests, and they make a date for Chinese food to talk about it. At the last minute he chickens out and stands her up, thinking to himself that he was crazy to have even entertained the idea of being caught on a date with a Black woman. Once again, the strictures of Little Italy guide his actions.

Charlie's Uncle Giovanni (Cesare Danova) is the one who is arranging for Charlie to take over a restaurant, but for this to happen his uncle says he needs to stay away from Johnny Boy, who is "half crazy," and Terese, who is "sick in the head." "I understand you try to help him out because of our family and his family, that's nice, I understand, but watch yourself. Don't spoil anything. Honorable men go with honorable men," Giovanni lays out. On top of this order, Michael approaches Charlie to complain that he's given Johnny Boy all the breaks he can but since he isn't going to work, Johnny Boy won't have a paycheck for Michael. "Oh," Charlie laments in disappointment, "I talk to him and I talk to him." Giving a big sigh, Charlie asks "What more can I do?" as if he's truly trying to think of what he could try next, then proposes, "Tonight, Michael, at the party, the three of us get together and we knock some sense into his head, okay?" Michael grudgingly assents. But Johnny Boy doesn't show, and while Charlie works hard to successfully negotiate down the amount he owes Michael, if Johnny Boy doesn't pay up next pay day, Michael's going to find him and break his legs. A little later Terese comes into Volpe's to tell Charlie that Johnny Boy is on the roof of a building shooting at the Empire State Building. Dutifully, Charlie gets the gun from him but is unable to stop him from throwing a small bomb off the roof. Back on the street he pulls his friend into a church graveyard to hide from the cops and to give him a lecture about not going to work and owing money.

The next day Johnny Boy discovers Charlie and Terese are sleeping together and the two men get into a fight in front of her because Johnny Boy wants to know whether Terese has an epileptic fit when she has an orgasm, which actually causes Terese to have one then. Charlie has to leave her in the care of a woman (the director's mother, Catherine Scorsese) who has come into the hallway to see what is going on because Charlie needs to run after Johnny Boy to try to get it into his head that he must show up that night and give Michael money; he even lends his friend some for this purpose. But predictably, after Johnny Boy offers Michael the insultingly low amount of $30, he continues insulting him by saying Michael's the only idiot who will lend him money without getting paid back, then he sets a $10 bill on fire, causing Michael to try to leap across the bar at him, but Johnny Boy pulls a gun on him so he leaves. Charlie asks to borrow Tony's car because they shouldn't stay around there and Tony advises they go to a movie rather than drive around, gesturing from Johnny Boy to Charlie and saying, "This is no good," but giving him the car keys. In a pointed visual commentary on the Hell Johnny Boy has put Charlie in, Charlie's wish to avoid Hell in the afterlife, and previous scenes in which Charlie had held his hand to an open flame, the film they go see is Roger Corman's *The Tomb of Ligeia* (1964) and the scene on screen is of Verden Fell (Vincent Price) being engulfed in flames.

Charlie calls Terese from the theater lobby to borrow money to go to Brooklyn, telling her Johnny Boy is in trouble and he needs to get him money; she insists on coming along. In the car Charlie says, "I guess you could safely say that things haven't gone so well tonight, but I'm trying Lord, I'm trying." A car pulls alongside theirs. Michael is driving and says, "Now's the time," whereupon a gunman (Martin Scorsese) shoots six times into their car, hitting Johnny Boy in the neck and Charlie in the right hand. The attack causes Charlie to run over a fire hydrant, which sprays an ironic fountain of redemption into the air. After watching to make sure no one gets out of the car, Michael drives off, and Terese's bloody hand reaches through the shattered windshield. A long series of cuts brings the film to its close.

There is a quick cut from the accident to older couples dancing at the San Gennaro festival, then a cut back to Charlie getting out of the car and Johnny Boy limping along the street. A cut to more dancing at the festival, then a cut to Tony washing his hands in the restroom of his bar, which symbolically shows he will not be helping Charlie and Johnny Boy anymore. There is a cut to Uncle Giovanni having a drink and smoking at home; that path to the restaurant for Charlie is gone, and the next cut shows Charlie falling to his knees in the street, his hand bloody—when St. Francis had his vision, he became marked with stigmata. A cut back to Giovanni shows he is watching Fritz Lang's *The Big Heat* (1953), the scene where Dave Bannion's (Glenn Ford) dead wife Katie (Jocelyn Brando) falls into his arms when he opens the door after his car is blown up. To correlate with this the next cut shows a bloody Charlie, then there is a cut to a police car pulling into the alley where Johnny Boy is crouching on his knees. A close-up on Charlie indicates he seems to be thinking of Diane because there's a cut to her lighting a cigarette. The next cut shows Charlie being helped into an ambulance; he glances over to see rescue workers helping Terese out of the car. A cut to an overhead shot of the San Gennaro festival shows the crowd has thinned as it's coming to a close. A brisk rendition of "Home Sweet Home" plays while the camera shows the lighted skyscrapers of the city. Then Michael is shown smoking leisurely in his car, accompanied by the gunman. The final shot is of an apartment building where people are pulling their window blinds down for the night, while the soundtrack says, "Good night, good luck, and God bless ya," the closing benediction of the festival.

Scorsese has noted that the scene where Michael's gunman shoots into the car bearing Charlie, Johnny Boy, and Teresa was based on an experience he had while attending NYU, which actually was a near-miss of the experience. He and a friend had been in the car of a third friend; Scorsese and friend got out of the car not long before another car pulled up and fired a gun into the friend's car, shooting a passenger in the eye. Realizing he could have been killed, Scorsese worked backwards from the shooting to ponder how a situation like that could happen; this became the impetus for *Mean Streets*.[34] He's explained too that the theme of the film is how one leads "a good, moral, ethical life, when everything around you works the absolutely opposite way."[35] That's really what the opening voice-over lines are about. How can Charlie, concerned with his own salvation, do right by his fellow humans on the mean streets of the city? Compounding this challenge is that the one person he tries to help so much, Johnny Boy, does everything possible to thwart that help. Scorsese has said that all three of the characters survive the shooting and crash. But what and where does that leave them? The intercut scenes that move the film to its close suggest they will have no help from their community in Little Italy, the home sweet home they can't really expect to return to. In the end the three main characters, Charlie, Johnny Boy, and Teresa, battered and bloodied, reel under the pressure of undecided fate.

Scorsese's body of work is substantial and ranges through genres such as crime bio-drama: *Goodfellas* (1990) and *The Wolf of Wall Street* (2013); historical drama: *The Age of Innocence* (1993), from Edith Wharton's novel, and *Gangs of New York* (2002); and mystery thriller: *Shutter Island* (2010), from Dennis Lehane's novel. As deranged as some of his characters can be—Tommy DeVito in *Goodfellas* springs to mind—none seem to have religion as their impetus for violence, unlike the figure in the next film to be analyzed.

David Fincher and *Se7en*

Jumping forward twenty-two years from *Mean Streets*, the Seven Deadly Sins send a deranged killer on a mission to do what he believes is God's work in David Fincher's *Se7en*. Fincher shot commercials and music videos before making the bridge to feature films. "As luck would have it," he has said, George Lukas moved in on the same street as his family when he was a child.[36] He'd been taking filmmaking classes since elementary school, and by high school knew he wanted to be a director. After graduation Fincher worked for Korty Films as a production assistant and at Industrial Light and Magic "on various camera tech support" for, among other films, *Star Wars: Episode VI—Return of the Jedi* (1983) and *Indiana Jones and the Temple of Doom* (1984).[37] His first feature as director was *Alien 3* (1992); *Se7en* is his second; and he's continued to direct numerous well-respected features, including *Fight Club* (1999), *Zodiac* (2007), *The Girl with the Dragon Tattoo* (2011), *Gone Girl* (2014), and *Mank* (2020). This last is a bio-drama about Herman J. Mankiewicz's work on the screenplay for Orson Welles' *Citizen Kane*. Fincher's late father, Jack Fincher, is credited with writing the screenplay, and the film earned David a nomination for Best Director—indeed, the film received ten Academy Award nominations with two wins for Best Production Design (Donald Graham Burt and Jan Pascale) and Best Cinematography (Erik Messerschmidt). *Mank* was shot in black-and-white, and its use of light and shadow plus its camera angles are worthy of *Citizen Kane*.

Fincher has famously said, "I don't know how much movies should entertain. To me I'm always interested in movies that scar."[38] *Se7en*, a disturbing film that is far more artful than the initial clichéd situation of a cop one week from retirement encountering the most treacherous murderer of his career would suggest, certainly scars. Morgan Freeman as the older, wiser Black cop William Somerset and Brad Pitt as the younger, pugnacious white cop David Mills give incisive performances, an emotional nexus fractured by the serial killer John Doe, played by Kevin Spacey with a sick gravitas worthy of Claude Rains. Doe is killing off what he sees as embodiments of the Seven Deadly Sins one a day, first force-feeding a glutton, bound at ankles and wrists with barbed cord akin to Jesus' crown of thorns, until he dies, then making a greedy lawyer cut off a pound of his flesh, the crimes looking like some kind of enforced contrition. Somerset is the first to catch on, noting that the killer is preaching to them, explaining to Mills that there were Seven Cardinal Virtues and Seven Deadly Sins that were used as teaching tools in medieval sermons. Things turn even more unsettling when the two detectives learn the killer has planned his crimes for quite some time: one year to the day the killer leads them to an apartment where he had drugged, medicated, and starved a man for a year. "Sloth" was still alive, although he looked cadaverous and reeked. The doctor (Richard Portnow) at the hospital they take him to observes that his brain is mush and he had chewed off his own tongue long ago, commenting, "He's experienced about as much pain as anyone I've encountered, give or take. And he still has Hell to look forward to."

The film shows a distinctly noir touch with the detectives' shabby office and its paint-chipped radiator, battered file cabinets, and old lamps and typewriter, while the noise of the city drifts up from the streets. In one scene between Mills' wife

Tracy (Gwyneth Paltrow) and Somerset, apocalyptic urban noise sounds outside the restaurant as Tracy seeks advice on her pregnancy, unknown of by her husband. Somerset relates how a long time ago in a relationship he had that was very much like a marriage, the woman became pregnant, and he remembered thinking, "How can I bring a child into a world like this? How can a person grow up with all this around them?" But Tracy, the one bright spot in this film, wants to have children.

When Mills labels the killer a lunatic, Somerset counters, "It's dismissive to call him a lunatic." A note found hidden at the first murder, reading "Long is the way and hard that out of Hell leads up to light" from Milton's *Paradise Lost*, seems to have percolated in Somerset's mind, and he decides to make a list of what one would study related to the Seven Deadly Sins because the FBI monitors library reading habits and they might be able to track down the killer that way. *The Divine Comedy, History of Catholicism, Murder of the Madmen, Modern Homicide Investigation, In Cold Blood, Of Human Bondage, The Marquis de Sade, The Writings of St. Thomas Aquinas* (who wrote about the Seven Deadly Sins), these books were being checked out by Jonathan Doe. While the two detectives are waiting outside Doe's apartment for him to respond to their knock, a man appears at the end of the corridor carrying a grocery bag. He shoots at them and leads Mills on an elaborate chase through the building and onto the street, where Mills nearly catches him at a parked garbage truck, but Doe strikes him with a crowbar, causing him to drop his gun in a puddle. Reflected in the puddle, Doe is an ominous black figure in coat and hat, the style of which make him look like Preacher from *The Night of the Hunter*. When Mill gets up almost on his knees Doe holds a gun to his temple—the weapon fills most of the left half of the frame in the foreground while Doe's blurry silhouette, backlit, fills the right in the background. Somerset, who has revealed to Mills in a previous scene that he's never killed a man, comes running toward them, gun drawn; Mills says "No," and Doe swiftly removes the gun and leaves.

Inside Doe's apartment the detectives find display cabinets highlighting items related to his victims, an oversized red cross looming over Doe's spartan twin bed, and a bathroom turned darkroom. In the latter, Mills finds a photograph of himself taken when he had chased a photographer away from one of their crime scenes, making Mills upset that they had had Doe within their grasp but he got away. He got away because of Mills' temper; when he had raged at the reporter, Somerset had calmly observed, "It's impressive to see a man feeding off his emotions." Throughout the film viewers have seen that Mills has a short fuse.

While there are no fingerprints at all to be found in Doe's apartment, there are some 2,000 black and white marble composition notebooks, undated and randomly placed on shelves, of which Somerset observes, "Just his mind, poured out on paper." Mills tracks down a ringing phone amidst the apartment's clutter, and Doe's voice informs him, "I'll be readjusting my schedule in light of today's little setback. I just had to call and express my admiration. Sorry I had to hurt one of you, but I didn't really have a choice, did I? You will accept my apology, won't you? I feel like saying more, but I don't want to ruin the surprise." After hanging up Mills admits, "You were right, he's a preacher," to which Somerset responds, "Yeah, these murders are his sermons to us."

The "preacher" changes his pattern by making a john kill a prostitute in a luridly lit, red, Hellish sex club to punish Lust, then Pride dies from her nose being cut off. Inexplicably to the detectives, John Doe walks into their police station, covered in blood, and says, "You're looking for me." After arresting him, they find out he has been cutting the skin off the tips of his fingers so he would leave no prints. John Doe is independently wealthy, well-educated, and totally insane. He was two murders away from completing the seven, and he tells them he has indeed murdered two more victims. He will take only Mills and Somerset to the bodies, or they'll never be found; he will take the insanity plea unless they accompany him. If they accept his conditions, he'll sign a full confession and plead guilty.

In the police car as they are driving to the scene, Doe remarks, "Wanting people to listen, you can't just tap them on the shoulder anymore. You have to hit them with a sledgehammer, and then you'll notice you've got their strict attention." Mills asks, "The question is, what makes you so special that people should listen?" "I'm not exceptional, I've never been exceptional," Doe admits. "This is, though, what I'm doing here, my work." As they drive by powerlines that slightly resemble crosses, Doe speaks of being chosen. "I don't doubt that you believe that, John," Somerset remarks. "But seems to me that you're overlooking a glaring contradiction…. If you were chosen, that is, by a Higher Power, if your hand was forced, seems strange to me that you would get such enjoyment out of it. You enjoyed torturing those people. Just doesn't seem in keeping with martyrdom, does it?" Asking Mills how happy would he be to hurt him with impunity, Doe observes, "Nothing wrong with a man taking pleasure in his work. I won't deny my own personal desire to turn each sin against the sinner." Mills interjects, "Wait a minute, I thought all you did was kill innocent people." "Innocent?" Doe responds. "Is that supposed to be funny? An obese man? A disgusting man who could barely stand up?," going on to list the sins of those he's killed. "Only in a world this shitty could you even try to say these were innocent people and keep a straight face. But that's the point," he says, launching into his sermon: "We see a deadly sin on every street corner, in every home, and we tolerate it. We tolerate it because it's common, it's trivial. We tolerate it morning, noon, and night. Well, not anymore. I'm setting the example. And what I've done is going to be puzzled over and studied and followed, forever." Mills accuses Doe of delusions of grandeur, and, Christ-like, Doe replies, "You should be thanking me…. Because you're going to be remembered after this. Realize, detective, the only reason that I'm here now is that I wanted to be." After some heated exchanges between Doe and Mills, irate, Mills retorts, "You're no messiah, you're a movie of the week, you're a fuckin' T-shirt—at best." "Don't ask me to pity those people," Doe says. "I don't mourn them any more than I do the thousands that died at Sodom and Gomorrah." "Is that to say, John, that what you were doing is God's good work?" Somerset inquires. "The Lord works in mysterious ways" is Doe's calm reply.

They reach their destination, a desert-like space occupied by high-tension wires that somewhat resemble a series of crucifixes. According to Doe's arrangement, a delivery van arrives. Spying it, Somerset alerts Mills, who orders Doe to kneel at gunpoint, like a supplicant, while Somerset meets the van and accepts the square

Director David Fincher on the set of *Se7en* (1995) near the symbolic high-tension wires (New Line Cinema/Photofest).

box addressed to Detective David Mills. The logo on the van is a box with angelic wings, commentary on the deceased inside the delivered box, and ironically, given that Tracy's severed head is in the box, the package is labeled "Please, handle with care—fragile." While Doe tells Mills, "You've made quite a life for yourself, detective. You should be very proud," Somerset opens and becomes aghast at the box's contents, ordering the hovering SWAT helicopter to stay away no matter what they hear over the wires because "John Doe has the upper hand." Doe informs Mills he had visited his home that morning after Mills left. "I tried to play husband," he says, suggesting that he tried to rape Tracy. "I tried to taste the life of a simple man. It didn't work out. Oh, I took a souvenir. Her pretty head."

At this juncture Somerset runs up and asks Mills to give him his gun. "What's going on over there?" Mills wants to know, "What was in the box?" "Because I envy your normal life, it seems that Envy is my sin," Doe points out. "Become vengeance David, become Wrath," Doe directs, telling Mills that his wife begged for her life and the life of the baby inside her. Somerset backhands him and tells him to shut up. "Oh," Doe says, looking at Mills, then, turning to Somerset, he finishes, "he didn't know." Somerset orders Mills to give him his gun because if he kills Doe, Doe will win. A flash cut has Mills seeing Tracy's face, then Mills executes Doe, firing multiple shots into him after. Viewers' last glimpse of the shattered detective is as he is driven away in the back of a police car. While the police captain (R. Lee Ermey) assures Somerset they'll take care of Mills and Somerset supportively offers whatever Mills needs, the viewer knows that this is a completely destroyed human being. As Somerset and the captain walk away from the scene, Somerset's voice-over says,

"Ernest Hemingway once wrote, 'The world is a fine place, and worth fighting for.' I agree with the second part." The screen goes black and the SWAT helicopter is heard before the credits begin.

In some ways, *Se7en* is a diabolical celebration of far-right extremism, as John Doe pursues his holy mission with the single-mindedness of a sex addict. Equally narcissist and voyeur, he makes for a perfect saint. The logorrheic outpour of his journals echoes the incoherence of the Unabomber's manifesto—insanity trying to explain itself. John Doe is one of those "enthusiasts" denounced during the Great Awakening for mistaking his psychological disturbance for God's Word. *Se7en*'s screenplay writer Andrew Kevin Walker says he named Somerset after Somerset Maugham, his favorite author,[39] but the name also fits this weary detective near-ing the end of his career who no longer finds the world to be a fine place; his sum-mer days have set. "Mills" is suitable for the energetic character with turbulent emotions who, at the outset, was eager to take over the case from Somerset because he was "all over it." And John Doe, well, he's everyman, right? That is a very scary proposition.

Religious figures–gone-bad reach back far in literature, but if one goes back just to the Gothic period readers have the English novel *The Monk* (1796), by Mat-thew Gregory Lewis. Monk Ambrosio is renowned for his ascetic saintliness, but a fiend in human form named Matilda disguises herself as a boy novitiate to join the monastery, then seduces Ambrosio and drives him from crime to crime: Ambro-sio seduces a penitent, Antonia, kills her mother, and then kills Antonia. It turns out he was Antonia's long-lost brother, adding incest to his sins. When his crimes are discovered, he is tortured by the Inquisition and sentenced to death, but bar-gains with the Devil to avoid being burned to death—only for the Devil to hurl him to destruction and damnation in Hell. Jumping a few decades and an ocean, there is Nathaniel Hawthorne's 1836 short story, "The Minister's Black Veil," where the Puritan Reverend Hooper appears in church one Sunday with his face covered by a black veil that he refuses to explain to his terrified congregation or fiancée. He loses his fiancée and wears the veil the rest of his life, saying only that the veil is a symbol of the curtain that hides every man's heart and makes him a stranger to friends, lover, and God. He doesn't technically sin, unless estrangement and eva-sion are sins, but he's certainly an odd religious figure. Hawthorne's *The Scarlet Let-ter* (1850) is about the tragic consequences of concealed guilt in mid–1600s Puritan Boston. Hester Prynne has an illegitimate child and refuses to name her lover, ulti-mately discovered to be the Rev. Arthur Dimmesdale, a revered, seemingly saintly young minister. Dimmesdale struggles under the burden of his hidden guilt and does secret penance, but pride prevents him from publicly confessing. Finally, he does confess, and dies. Then there is Catharine Williams' *Fall River: An Authentic Narrative* (1833), based on the real trial of a Methodist minister for the murder of a pregnant mill worker in Fall River, Massachusetts, that he had seduced. As the back cover of its paperback edition notes, "While based in fact, the book raises themes of sexual and religious hypocrisy and exploitation that may be compared with those of novels like *The Coquette*, *Uncle Tom's Cabin*, and *The Scarlet Letter*."[40] There is no lack of corrupt and delusional religious figures in fiction and film, leading one only to hope that resolute humanism ultimately triumphs over a strangely nihilistic passion.

Several neo-noirs will be explored in the next chapter, although the focus of analysis shifts from maniacal religious figures to a different kind of identification, that of the continuity of the self.

Six

Highways, By-ways and Dislocations

The Self in Neo-Noir

Neo-noir movies of the early 2000s frame questions about the continuity of the self in ways wildly divergent from their classic film noir predecessors, both narrowing and expanding the inherent potential of the theme in the original genre. In Hitchcock films like *Shadow of a Doubt* (1943) and *Vertigo* (1958), for instance, the protagonist's reality (and identity) suffers jarring dislocations when the idealized loved one turns out to be someone utterly different than they believed. The niece Charlie (Teresa Wright) realizes her beloved Uncle Charlie (Joseph Cotten) has murdered a series of wealthy widows in *Shadow of a Doubt* and that he is trying to kill her for her discovery. Scottie Ferguson (James Stewart) in *Vertigo* falls in love with a woman named Madeleine (Kim Novak) whom he believes is his friend's wife, thinks she falls to her death in an act of suicide, meets a woman named Judy Barton (Kim Novak) who looks like Madeleine, and finally works out that his friend had an affair with Judy, got her to pose as his wife, and that the woman who had fallen was the already-dead, murdered real wife. By now in love with her, Scottie watches as Judy accidentally plummets to her death from the same mission bell tower Madeleine's body had been tossed off. Films of the early 2000s cage the psyche while broadening the playing—or killing—field. The self might become buried or disintegrate, as it does for the main characters in *Memento* (2000) and *A History of Violence* (2005), who have canceled out their previous identities all too successfully. Or the self might never have been integrated to begin with; in this vein *Identity* (2003) is a motel funhouse of fragmentation. Just as these narratives provide a guide (or psychopomp) akin to Virgil in Dante's *Inferno* (played by imposing yet endearing character actors), the cinematic techniques draw the viewer into a subjective relationship with the psychosis of the central figure, creating a sense of freefalling claustrophobia. Viewers are cast adrift in a stranger's head.

J.H. Wallis, Fritz Lang and *The Woman in the Window*

Before turning to neo-noir films, it is useful to note a classic film noir that takes a step toward the contemporary depictions of self, Fritz Lang's *The Woman in the*

Window (1944). Nunnally Johnson's screenplay is based on the 1942 J.H. Wallis best-selling novel *Once Off Guard*, republished in 1944 as *The Woman in the Window (Once Off Guard)*, but there are some important differences between the novel and film that a discussion of each will highlight. The original title refers to a remark made by lawyer Duras Lalor to his friends Moberley Barkstane, a physician, and Richard Wanley, a professor of English Literature, while the three relax at their Burghers' Club. Lalor warns that one needs perpetually to be on guard against one's natural inclinations, including the sex drive, for even in one's old age women are dangerous. Wanley thinks Lalor is exaggerating the need to be on guard because men like them who have made it to middle age (Wanley is 56 years old) without getting into trouble have good customs to keep them safe, plus little opportunity to stray. A "summer bachelor" because his wife and children have left New York City for the season,[1] Wanley remains in the club library after dinner to drink brandy and read *The Love Poems of the Greek Anthology*, ruminating that for the Greeks sex was a natural, enjoyable activity not necessarily connected to marriage. When he leaves the club at 10:00 p.m. feeling the brandy in his head and legs, Wanley walks down Park Avenue thinking of the poem "The Jewel of Asia," which concerns a woman knowledgeable about sexual relations, and reflects that his only sexual experience has been with his wife of thirty years, although he believes women have found him attractive and if he had lived in ancient Greece he most likely would have had sex with many women. He stops to look at a portrait of a beautiful and enticing young woman in the Durand-Ruel Gallery window and becomes aware of a woman standing near him who strongly resembles the one in the painting. Immediately he senses she has "the air of the illicit. She hinted of harlotry," but being well dressed and wearing a gold necklace, he thinks she is the mistress of a wealthy man, not a streetwalker.[2] She exists to fulfill men's desires, he reflects, finding it stimulating and dangerous to be near her. Their conversation leads to the revelation that her man is out of town for two weeks and, looking "invitingly" at Wanley, she asks him if he wants to find out what could happen in one night.[3] They give each other false names as they take a cab to her apartment, she sitting on his lap with her arms around him.

The name on her apartment reveals she is Alice Rete, while Wanley remains Reuben Westmore to her. The scene jumps to just after midnight when Wanley is once again clothed as Alice puts on a negligee and arranges herself on a chaise lounge, inviting him to see her again before her man returns. He says he will, although he has no intention of ever touching her again because "He felt soiled, filthy, ashamed" at having had sex with her.[4] Suddenly a man appears in the bedroom door and rushes toward Wanley, punches him on the jaw and nose, then backs up and rushes at him again, driving him against the side of the bed and then onto the bed, where the man starts choking him. All Wanley is able to do is beat his fists on the man's back until Alice puts scissors into his hand and he repeatedly drives their point into the man's back until he's dead. Wanley recognizes the man as Claude Mazard, a wealthy businessman, although Alice thinks his name is Elwin Howden. Not enlightening her as to Mazard's true identity, Wanley works out that even if the police accept that the killing was done in self-defense, his reputation and marriage would be ruined, so he plans to dump the body outside the city. He retrieves his car to do so, but gets pulled over on the way back to Alice's apartment for running a red light because he was preoccupied with having killed a man and didn't notice it. Observing that Wanley appears to be a decent guy, the policeman lets him off without a ticket. "You didn't do any damage. But see that you don't do it again," the officer warns, words that resonate beyond the traffic violation to include adultery and murder, and which rereaders of the novel will recognize as foreshadowing.[5] Throughout the novel Wanley will harp upon how ruinous his dalliance with an attractive "harlot" had been, and he will contemplate committing two additional murders.

On his voyage to dispose of Mazard's corpse, Wanley's actions reveal how inept he is initially at being a criminal. Nervous about paying the 10-cent toll for the Henry Hudson Bridge because the collectors are police, he drops the dime onto the road, offers another coin that turns out to be a penny, then hands over two nickels, telling the officer to keep the extra dime if he finds it—all incidents that would stick in the officer's mind because they are unusual, especially at 3:00 a.m. when hardly any cars are passing through the toll. At a red light Wanley jams his foot on the brake at the last minute, his car slightly into the intersection, and notices a motorcycle policeman, who would have pursued him had he run the light, observing him. His view of police has been altered by events; they are enemies, and while he is a reputable college professor, he now has the outlook of a criminal. Once at his destination, as he attempts to toss the body into the woods, he scratches his hand on a barbed wire fence, then tears his coat sleeve on it. He also contracts poison ivy from the underbrush when he dumps the body.

Catching a nap before heading to summer school for the first of his two lectures that upcoming day, the initial of several dreams Wanley will have occurs. His dream of armed policemen coming for him on a clanging fire truck coincides with his alarm clock waking him, and, thinking that he will always have to be on guard, he has his first thought of whether life will be worth living. After his second lecture he buys and wears a straw hat just like the one Mazard had been wearing that Wanley had burned to destroy evidence, and he shaves off the heavy mustache he has worn for years in an attempt to make it harder for Alice Rete to identify him should he run into her—her apartment is a mere six blocks from his club. The straw hat suggests his identification with the man he killed, who also was Alice's lover, while shaving off the mustache so that Alice will not recognize him is an attempt to estrange himself from her. This dual connection-rejection is peculiar and indicates both his sexual desire and his disgust at having committed adultery with a woman he constantly thinks of as a "harlot." After writing a poem, "The Penitent's Prayer," which conveys his wish that time could be turned back to before he met Alice, he falls asleep and dreams the exact same experience of meeting her while looking at the portrait. More guilt at his infidelity and thoughts of ending his life come to him that afternoon, and so as not to disgrace his wife Adele with a suicide note explaining the murder or to frighten her with a lack of explanation for his suicide, he wonders if he could kill himself in a way that the death appears to be natural. This too is a significant motif in Wallis' novel.

A recurring chant begins to haunt him every time he drives his car. To the hum of the motor the phrase "I have killed a man" floats through his head, later altering to "I have murdered Mazard."[6] He almost hits an old woman crossing the street while driving to his club, and for the first time feels chest pains. His friend and physician, Barkstane, reassures him he's fine physically, he shouldn't be distressed about growing older, and that his best work is to come because with his experience and research, he has things to say to people. Wryly, Wanley thinks that what he has to say is that he's murdered Mazard, that his experience is "harlotry, murder, concealment of crime, flight from justice."[7] He agrees with Barkstane that he needs rest, thinking that if he keeps on as he is going his mind will be a blend of reality and dreams, a significant thought that possibly influenced the screenwriter and Lang when they transformed the novel into film. Wanley's sleeping dreams and reveries while awake permeate the novel, as do his thoughts of suicide and about how his life has changed: "What a situation for a cultured, enlightened man, a man of position! How unreal! Was it real or just a long, frightful dream?"[8]

It most certainly is not a dream when Wanley returns to his apartment building and the night attendant informs him there is a woman, ostensibly a friend of his wife's, waiting for him upstairs. Alice Rete has come to let him know Mazard's bodyguard, an ex-policeman named Heinrich Feist, is blackmailing her for $5,000 because he knows she was Mazard's mistress and suspects she is responsible for his murder, either directly or with an accomplice. From her apartment Feist took Wanley's initialed pencil that was in the vest Wanley left as insurance he would return when he went for his car to transport the body, a flask Wanley and Alice had drunk whiskey out of, the scissors, and black and brown short hairs found on the floor near the head of her bed, one color of which matches Mazard and the other Wanley. This knowledge of solid evidence that could convict him enrages Wanley, transforms his character further to make him think why should a blackmailer like Feist be allowed to wreck his life? If it comes down to Feist's life or his, it's going to be Feist's because a blackmailer is "lower than a louse," more like "the bacteria of syphilis and pneumonia and rabies," and killing him would be a service to society.[9] Wanley explains to Alice that they could slip the thyroid medicine Wanley takes into Feist's drink; too large an amount will simulate a heart attack and be indetectable in an autopsy. When Alice laughingly suggests he should have been a murderer, he evenly replies that he's planning to become one. Wanley continues to rationalize that Feist deserves to die not only because he is a blackmailer, but because he betrayed his employer, and thus he is "the foulest kind of a germ—Syphilis Feist, Rabies Feist, Bubonic Feist" and should be killed.[10] Given the novel's publication during World War II—it even would be reprinted in a paperback Armed Forces Edition in 1945— giving a blackmailing character a Germanic name and equating him with pestilence is not surprising. Wallis' 1943 legal thriller, *The Niece of Abraham Pein*, concerns Jewish refugees who suffered persecution under the Nazi regime and face anti–Semitism in the United States, providing a more overt revelation of the author's political stance.

Soon Wanley's twisted logic transfers to his friend Lalor. Wanley asks to go with him to the crime scene where Mazard's body was found, ostensibly out of idle curiosity, but really to see whether he can remove any incriminating evidence, and during the car ride Wanley becomes convinced Lalor knows Wanley is the murderer and is just biding his time before arresting him. He also starts suspecting that Alice will blackmail him and contemplates her murder. At the crime scene he thinks Police Inspector Jacks and Lalor are playing a game with him, trying to get him to trip himself up in conversation about the murder. Indeed, when an officer asks Lalor if he wants to see where they found the body, Wanley is the only one who starts walking toward the exact place. But he catches himself, and when he turns back toward Lalor and the officer, they are facing away from him, looking up at the sky to survey an approaching storm, so he simply walks back to them. When they draw near to the dump site where Jacks is, Lalor points out poison ivy; Wanley is hyper-conscious of the rash on the back of his hand as he shakes hands with Jacks. Wanley finds a bit of thread from his suit on the barbed wire fence and tries surreptitiously to remove it, but Jacks notices, so he must turn it over, which leads him to think they deliberately left it for him to find. Wanley's paranoia has led him to create an elaborate narrative of the cat and mouse game he believes Lalor and Jacks are playing with him.

A fierce rainstorm strikes as Lalor and Wanley are driving back to the city, and the professor-poet indulges himself in a pathetic fallacy. To Wanley it seems "the storm was part of his state of fear and chaos. Rain—wind—lightning—thunder—battering in mad confusion outside in a rending world and for him a madder, more hopeless, irreparable destruction."[11] Although he believes Jacks and Lalor have plenty of evidence to convict him, he still thinks Feist should be killed on the slim chance that they don't, plus, he rationalizes, the blackmailer deserved to die. Further evidence that his moral compass has gone askew comes when he questions whether his thinking has become muddled or incorrect, then quickly sweeps this aside. He forays ahead with his murder plan by putting up his securities for the $5,000 Feist demanded and making a bundle of the cash and thyroxin crystals that he will pass to Alice in Grand Central Station. After giving a lecture at school, he again feels chest pains. The transfer to Alice accomplished, he tries to distract himself in a movie theater while Alice is meeting with Feist in her apartment. A slight believer in telepathy, Wanley imagines that he can "see" the events of that meeting. He leaves the movie—an understandably unsettling, for him, gangster film in which a couple of businessmen are knocked off—and heads home feeling weak and still having chest pains. The next day he reads in the newspaper that three blocks from Alice's apartment Feist had died of a heart attack and mulls over his situation: Alice could blackmail him; if Lalor and Jacks don't have enough evidence on him, they'll continue to suspect him for years and keep him under surveillance; and he has to face his wife. Suicide made to look like a natural death it must be.

He writes a farewell poem but burns it because it would be construed as a confession. Thinking of the happier phases of life he had written about in the poem, the chapter ends with Wanley's thought that life was valuable and maybe he could find a way out of his situation. The next chapter opens with Wanley calling the lobby attendant to inform him he's having a very bad heart attack. Indeed, he dies. Was this truly a natural death from heart attack, the culmination of the chest pains he has been walking around with for a couple of days? It would seem so, although a reader could also construe that he deliberately overdosed on thyroxin. Barkstane is called to Wanley's apartment by the lobby attendant, and while he's there Alice Rete phones to find out why Wanley didn't respond to the note she sent requesting he see her so she could tell him about the meeting with Feist. She would have told him Feist refused to drink with her and that she only gave him three thousand dollars. She was expecting him to return Saturday for the balance, unaware that Feist died of a natural heart attack. Wanley, of course, having read the newspaper article, believed that Alice, and he as accomplice, had murdered him.

For the novel's denouement, Barkstane and Lalor meet at the Burghers' Club, Lalor revealing that the police have absolutely no suspects in the Mazard case. Barkstane leaves the club, strolling and looking into the same galleries Wanley had four fateful days earlier, stopping to gaze at the portrait of the woman in the Durand-Ruel window. He realizes an alluring woman with an illicit expression is standing beside him. Conversing with her, Barkstane says that while she looks like the woman in the painting, *that* woman is innocent, implying the real-life woman is not. Moving close, she asks him if he's happy she's different, but he assures her that feminine wiles won't work on him and bids her good evening, after which he tips his hat and walks back to the club. This is quite the different ending from Lang's film.

In Lang's film, which the director repeatedly cited in interviews as one of his films that he likes because it critiques society, Richard Wanley (Edward G. Robinson), a staid professor at Gotham College in New York City, is delivering the lecture "Some Psychological Aspects of Homicide" at the film's opening in which he says, "The Biblical injunction 'Thou shalt not kill' is one that requires qualification in view of our broader knowledge of impulses behind homicide…. The man who kills in self-defense, for instance, must not be judged by the same standards applied to the man who kills for gain." "SIGMUND FREUD" is writ large on the blackboard behind him, under which "Divisional constitution of mental life" preheads the lists "Unconscious, Pre-conscious, Conscious" and "Id, Ego, Super-ego." This serves as a template for interpreting the psychology of the film, although the viewer won't realize it until the very end. While the Wanley in the novel actually commits adultery, kills a man, and dies, the Wanley in the film merely dreams of meeting a beautiful woman whom he spends an evening conversing with (nothing happens between them physically) dreams of killing a man, and dreams of committing suicide.

Wanley's loving wife (Dorothy Peterson) and two children (Robert Blake and Carol Cameron) are leaving New York for Maine for the summer, the wife urging him not to stay cooped up every night working. On the way to his men's club that night he notices the portrait of a striking woman in a storefront window, a woman his friends at the club deem a "dream girl." The two friends joke about his not going to a burlesque show on his "first night of summer bachelorhood," causing Wanley to gripe about the solidity and stodginess he feels in his middle age: "To me it's the end of the brightness of life, the end of spirit and adventure." His District Attorney friend Frank Lalor (Raymond Massey) notes that men their age "shouldn't play around with any adventure they can avoid," expounding, "I've seen genuine, actual tragedy issuing directly out of pure carelessness, out of the merest trifles. A casual impulse, an idle flirtation, one drink too many…. Trouble starts too from little things. Often from some forgotten, natural tendency." Wanley jokes that even if the spirit of adventure should beckon, and even in the form of the alluring woman in the painting, he'd likely mumble something idiotic and head the other way. While the D.A. and Wanley's friend and personal physician, Michael Barkstane (Edmund Breon), head off to see the newest Lana Turner movie, their idea of adventure, Wanley pulls a copy of *The Song of Songs Which is Solomon's* off the club's library bookshelves and settles in for an evening of reading with his third drink beside him—Barkstane had earlier noted Wanley was strictly a two-drink man. When club employee Collins (Frank Dawson) wakes him at 10:30 p.m. as previously requested, Wanley leaves the club and is gazing at the portrait of the woman when the reflection of its subject appears in the window because she is standing beside him on the sidewalk. Alice Reed (Joan Bennett) suggests they have a drink in a nearby cocktail lounge, after which she invites him to her apartment to see sketches of herself by the same artist who painted her portrait. Although Wanley says he doesn't think he should, having been warned by his friends against the siren call of adventure, he can't resist.

At the apartment, when Alice leaves the room for champagne, Wanley eyeballs a nude torso on the mantle, looking at it and then after Alice, clearly making an appreciative connection between the statue and its model. The two are looking at sketches and about to open a second bottle of champagne when the pull tab breaks, Alice leaves the room for a pair of scissors to cut the wire, and a man enters the apartment demanding to know who Wanley is. Alice returns, leading the man to yell, "I told you if you ever—," and strike her to the floor; outraged at Wanley's presence, he begins strangling him. Wanley gestures for and receives the scissors from Alice, stabbing his attacker to death. It turns out that Alice is the man's mistress; she knows him as Frank Howard (Arthur Loft) and saw him a few times each week, the two always staying in the apartment. "I'm ruined—my whole life," Wanley declares, going so far as to dial the operator to tell the police about the self-defense killing, but hanging up to muse that since no one knows about Alice's relationship with Frank, they could cover up the murder.

He refuses to tell Alice his name or what he does (remarkably, he hadn't told her in the several hours they socialized) and dumps the body miles away. In the process, he leaves an amateur's trail of circumstantial but incriminating evidence. The garage attendant marvels at his taking his car out in the wee hours of the morning; a policeman pulls him over for driving without his lights on and demands a second form of identification beyond his driver's license, whereupon Wanley gives him a letter from the Board of Education identifying him as an assistant professor; another tenant notices Alice peering out of her apartment prior to Wanley carrying the dead body out to his car, which is parked directly in front of the building; Wanley tosses a dime to the Henry Hudson Parkway toll booth attendant, it falls on the roadway, he backs up when the attendant yells at him to return, and gives him another dime, saying he can keep the first if he finds it (a memorable gesture, especially since the second coin handed over was initially a penny); he slightly overruns a stop light (the garage attendant had mentioned that his brakes are loose), then exchanges glances with the motorcycle cop on the side of the road. At the wooded location where he dumps the body Wanley catches his suit fabric on a barbed wire fence, cutting his arm as well, and the camera zooms in to show that he leaves a long and clear tire track in the

In a shot visually reminiscent of their first meeting, Alice Reed (Joan Bennett) and Richard Wanley (Edward G. Robinson) take their leave after the murder of Mazard in *The Woman in the Window* (1944) (RKO Radio Pictures Inc./Photofest).

mud when he pulls away. Wanley's self continues to alter. He stays up later, trying to write a letter to his wife at midnight. After an advertisement for heartburn and acid stomach medicine comes on the radio, which Wanley could use a dose of right about then, a news story about prominent Wall Street financier Claude Mazard being missing causes Wanley to recognize him as the man he killed. The next evening at his club Wanley is visibly discomforted as D.A. Lalor discusses the evidence in the case. Feeling he'll be found out anyway since shoe prints, the tire track, and fabric and blood on the fence will incriminate him, he pulls up his suit sleeve and displays the cut, asking, "Does this suggest anything to you?" "Yes," Lalor replies, "it suggests very strongly that you're eaten up with envy. You see my name on the front page of every paper, so you make a desperate effort to elbow your way into my case by insinuating that you're the guilty man. But it's no use, my boy. You scratched yourself for nothing." Wanley can hardly believe his luck, until they head for after-dinner coffee and cigars in the lounge and Lalor lets drop the information that "they got a line on a woman this afternoon" before being called aside by a colleague. Wanley admits to his doctor that he hasn't been sleeping well, whereupon Barkstane prescribes some sleeping pills, warning him that too many will mimic heart disease and kill him.

Lalor returns and pretty much lays out just how the murder went down, and also plants in Wanley's mind a suspicion that Alice might turn him in. Lalor invites both Barkstane and Wanley to visit the site where the body was dumped the next morning; Barkstane declines since he has surgery to perform, but as a doctor he "orders" his patient Wanley to go—"It'll give you something to think about," he cheerfully declares. Wanley has enough to think about, including being identified by the toll booth attendant when they stop there to pick up Inspector Jackson (Thomas E. Jackson) on their way to the site and whether Alice will be the woman the police picked up that morning and are bringing to the site. At the scene Wanley all but says out loud that he is the murderer by walking ahead of the police to the dump site, remarking it must have been difficult to carry the body through the woods at night, revealing he has poison ivy on his arm by the cut when poison ivy is there on the scene, and returning to the car feigning illness when the woman is about to be brought over. Wanley and the viewer never see the woman, but Lalor later calls her a "dingy type" and answers Wanley's query as to whether she was "cheap looking" with "bottom of the barrel." This at least comforts him that it was not Alice.

Things become more complicated when Alice tracks down Wanley because his picture was in the newspaper to announce his promotion at Gotham College and she tells him the man Mazard's business associates hired to tail him everywhere due to his temper, Heidt (Dan Duryea), showed up to blackmail her. Wanley's personality has so changed that when he meets with a panicky Alice because she doesn't know how to deal with Heidt, he calmly notes that there are three ways to deal with a blackmailer: keep paying, call the police, or kill him. He walks away from Alice ominously and steadfastly at the end of this scene, having decided that she will be the one to slip his sleeping powder into Heidt's drink. In an ironic comment on Wanley's entire predicament in this film, in the lobby scene where Wanley passes Alice the powder, a woman tugging her son onto an elevator is saying, "If you want to play, you must do your homework first. If you do your homework first, then you can go—" "Ma!" the boy interrupts in frustration. Of course, the attempt to slip Heidt the Mickey doesn't work, he takes the $5,000 from Alice and says he'll be back for $5,000 more the next night, and Alice calls Wanley to ask what they can do. "I don't know. I'm not sure. I haven't much more collateral," a defeated Wanley tells her, a photograph of his wife and two children on the table beside him. "I'm afraid I'm too tired to think about it anymore tonight. Too tired," he says in despair. After hanging up he walks despondently into the bathroom, fills a glass with water from the tap, and puts multiple packets of the sleeping powder into the glass. The scene cuts to Alice in her apartment, hearkening to gun shots outside. The police have killed Heidt, whom they recognized as Mazard's tail. He had an item monogramed CM on him, which he had taken from Alice, which she in turn had gotten off of "Frank's" dead body. Observing all this in the street she runs back to her apartment to phone the professor that they are both free from the blackmailer and beyond any suspicion in the murder, but there is no answer. The viewer sees Wanley nodding off and then slumping down in his bedroom chair, having drunk the powder that will kill him.

The scene changes to Wanley being awakened in his chair at the men's club. Lang did not make a cut here—Robinson was wearing break-away clothes that were pulled off to reveal the attire he had on at the club and the props were changed during a close-up of him slumped in the chair. It is 10:30 p.m., and Wanley is visibly shaken by what was only a nightmare prompted by his friends' appellation of "dream girl" to the woman in the portrait and his reading of *The Song of Songs*, not to mention his lecture on Freud. As he leaves the club, viewers see that the coat room attendant Charlie is Frank/Mazard and the doorman Tim is the blackmailer. Director Lang defended this hoariest of twist endings by claiming that he felt it was truer to life. He told interviewer Gene D. Phillips, "I personally felt that an audience wouldn't think a movie worthwhile in which a man kills two people and himself just because he had made a mistake by going home with a girl. That's when I thought of having him wake up after he had poisoned himself to discover that he had fallen asleep in a chair at his club."[12] Regardless of how well that parses aesthetically or logically, this is not *The Wizard of Oz*: when Wanley leaves the club this time, the world has turned seedier, almost sinister. The portrait of the striking woman is indeed still in the window, but when he turns to find a real woman (Iris Adrian) standing on the sidewalk beside him, she's a coarse peroxide job of questionable repute in a cheap foxtail stole, asking him for a light. As Tom Gunning puts it, "Instead of a morality tale of the most patriarchal sort, Lang devises a nightmare in which the stir of sexual desire opens up a world of fatality and the gradual destruction of the self. That this vision is self-inflicted, that it wells within Wanley's psyche, hardly makes it easier to sleep at night" (293). As well, the diagrammatic quality of its psychology belies the film's real strength as a character study emphasizing the permeability of the self, whether between layers of the mind or the interstices of society. In this way, *The Woman in the Window* is a precursor to neo-noir films in which reintegration of a fragmented self and consciousness serves as a framework for a largely subjective— yes, even permeable—approach to cinematic narrative.

Christopher Nolan and *Memento*

Nonlinear narratives are a specialty of the director Christopher Nolan, who based the screenplay for his second feature film, *Memento*, on the concept his brother Jonathan Nolan had for the short story "Memento Mori," which Jonathan would go on to publish in the March 2001 issue of *Esquire*. The situation in both texts is that the protagonist has anterograde amnesia because of a head injury inflicted by the man who raped and killed his wife, so he uses notes and tattoos to remember new things. The basic conceit Christopher Nolan uses for his screenplay owes a certain debt to progressive theater of the sixties, seventies, and eighties—for instance, Harold Pinter's *Betrayal* (1978), in which time runs backward from present to past, and Sam Shephard's *Fool for Love* (1983), in which former lovers work through their identities as half-siblings while their father makes comments in each of their minds—but grows more entangled through abrupt editing and the use of the camera as an unreliable, or complicit, narrator, leading to dislocations within dislocations. *Memento* progresses in reverse through discrete yet overlapping segments. These episodes are intercut with black-and-white scenes that at first seem to be stop-gaps, pauses for the viewer to get oriented. They even offer the reassuring lull of a dulcet voice-over from the protagonist. But gradually the interludes work into the main narrative, complicating the flow of events. The film's opening shot of a hand we come to know as Leonard's shaking a Polaroid photograph dry suggests the overall course of the film: the photograph gradually goes from a sharp image in vivid color to the indistinct, faded image one sees when a Polaroid first emerges from the camera.

Leonard Shelby's (Guy Pearce) recurring memory loss becomes the only stable element in the story. His inability to make new memories is ostensibly the result of a head wound received from the man who raped and killed his wife. Since that traumatic event, he has been searching for the murderer, a process severely hindered by his inability to remember what he discovers. One application of the film's title is Leonard's various compensations for his disability: making notations on his body, a kind of self-tattooing with indelible ink and needles, although he gets at least one professional tattoo; using a Polaroid to record clues and information visually and annotating them as well; and attaching Post-it notes to those photos he's mapping on the wall of his motel room. These mementos appear in various scenes as the viewer struggles to trace the narrative threads.

Leonard's disability has set him up to be used by those he encounters in various ways. The most benign is the motel desk clerk (Mark Boone Junior) at the Discount Inn who charges Leonard for two rooms. More exploitative is a woman named Natalie (Carrie-Anne Moss) who professes to be a friend, but who orchestrates her release from a man pursuing her for her drug-dealing boyfriend's money by angering Leonard to the point that he hits her; she leaves her house, a frantic Leonard can't find a pen to note their conflict, so when she reenters the house and says a man named Dodd (Callum Keith Rennie) beat her up, he believes her. To extract revenge for her beating, Leonard punches Dodd, hits him over the head with a bottle, ties him up, tapes his mouth shut, and puts him in the closet of Dodd's own motel room.

Leonard was warned not to trust Natalie by a character named John Edward Gannell (Joe Pantoliano), who goes by the nickname "Teddy." But can Leonard trust Teddy? Leonard has tattooed the sentence "John G. raped and murdered my wife" in reverse around his upper chest like a necklace, so he's reminded of his quest every time he looks in a mirror. He's told that Teddy is a snitch, a bad cop. Viewers see Leonard talking on the phone in his motel room in the black-and-white scenes, one time asking, "You know the truth about my condition, officer?"—is Teddy the listener viewers never see?

More disorientation for the viewer arises from the other black-and-white scenes unfolding the story of Sammy Jankis (Stephen Tobolowsky), evoked whenever Leonard notices his tattoo prompting him to "Remember Sammy Jankis." Leonard met Sammy while investigating his insurance claim. Like Leonard, Sammy had no memory after an accident, but he could perform acts that he had done prior to the accident, such as giving his wife (Harriet Sansom Harris) her insulin shots. Leonard thinks he sees recognition in Sammy's eyes when he pays another call on the Jankises in their home, suspecting that Sammy might be faking his condition, although he never tells Mrs. Jankis this suspicion when she comes to Leonard's office. Leonard tells her that Sammy's problem is mental, not physical, and that he should be physically capable of making new memories. This plants a seed of doubt in Mrs. Jankis' mind. Sammy's story ends horrifically when his wife, both testing him and desperately hoping he will start forming very short-term memories, keeps turning her watch back ten minutes and asking him to administer her insulin. She dies of insulin shock.

Leonard notes about his insurance investigative work, "It was useful experience because now it's my life," and indeed, Sammy turns out probably to be a fabrication, for viewers learn that Leonard's wife had diabetes. Teddy calls Leonard out on the Sammy Jankis story: "So you lie to yourself to be happy. There's nothing wrong with that. We all do it. Who cares if there's a few little details you'd rather not remember?" The few little details he forgot turn out to be that his wife survived the assault, but he killed her by over injecting her with insulin. Two quickly intercut images punctuate Leonard and Teddy's conversation, one in which Leonard injects his wife's thigh with a hypodermic needle and one in which he pinches her thigh with his fingers. Leonard—and viewers—struggle to determine which is the accurate memory. "I guess I can only make you remember the things you want to be true," Teddy observes shortly before he delivers the big reveal to Leonard: Leonard killed his wife's assailant John G. over a year ago—Teddy shows Leonard a photograph of himself grinning after the killing—but because he can't retain that memory, Teddy decided to take advantage of Leonard's "romantic quest" for revenge to make a little money, in this instance by having Leonard kill a drug dealer who Teddy misleads Leonard into thinking was his wife's murderer. "I gave you a reason to live, and you were more than happy to help," Teddy shouts at him. "You don't want the truth. You make up your own truth. Like your police file. It was complete when I gave it to you. Who took out the twelve pages?" Leonard did, Teddy says, to create a puzzle he could never solve. "A dead wife to pine for. A sense of purpose to your life. A romantic quest that you wouldn't end even if I wasn't in the picture," Teddy explains. Leonard realizes Teddy set him up to kill James F. Grant (Larry Holden), Natalie's drug-dealing boyfriend who, she had told Leonard, had taken $200,000 with him to meet someone named Teddy and never returned. "Cheer up," Teddy tells Leonard, "There's plenty of John G.s for us to find."

Viewers know from the opening of the film that Leonard kills Teddy. In a voice-over Leonard reflects, "I'm not a killer. I'm just someone who wanted to make things right. Can I just let myself forget what you've told me?" He writes "Don't believe his lies" on a photograph of Teddy and burns the photograph he took of the dead Jimmy Grant and the photograph of himself Teddy took after he killed his wife's assailant. "Can I just let myself forget what you've made me do?" Leonard speculates in voice-over. "You think I just want another puzzle to solve, another John G. to look for? You're a John G.," he thinks, writing Teddy's license plate number down as Fact 6 he will get tattooed on himself, "So you can be my John G. Do I lie to myself to be happy? In your case Teddy, yes, I will." So here Leonard is remembering. He remembers that he has already killed John G., his wife's attacker, and will deliberately kill Teddy to break free from being his hit man. He drives off in Jimmy Grant's Jaguar wearing the drug dealer's suit, both of which he has just acquired but that viewers have seen Leonard with since early on in the film. "I have to believe in a world outside my own mind," Leonard thinks. "I have to believe that my actions still have meaning, even if I can't remember them. I have to believe that when my eyes are closed, the world's still here. Do I believe the world's still here?" He closes his eyes and a scene is shown of Leonard and his wife (Jorja Fox) lying in bed; his necklace tattoo is in place, and in the space over his heart, where no tattoo had been throughout the film but where he told Natalie he would get a tattoo once he killed his wife's murderer, a tattoo reads "I've done it." "Is it still out there? Yeah," he reassures himself by looking at the street scene going by as he drives. "We all need mirrors to remind ourselves who we are. I'm no different," he thinks, stopping in front of the tattoo shop to get Fact 6 inked onto himself. "Now, where was I?" Thus ends the film.

There is a cerebral poignancy in thinking back to the beginning scene: viewers are left to wonder what became of Leonard after he killed Teddy. It's unlikely his condition would improve, and people happy to prey on the helpless are abundant in this ethos. Will the "I've done it" tattoo reassure Leonard that he killed his wife's murderer? Does that tattoo also reveal his acknowledgment of his own implication in his wife's death? He seems to have created a false memory of lying in bed with her bearing that tattoo. Is he, as Teddy claimed earlier, still lying to himself to be happy? Throwing additional layers of complication over this all is Leonard's insistence on not being called Lennie because his wife called him Lennie and he hated it. There also is a flashback scene in which his wife is reading a coverless, tattered novel and the two dicker slightly over her rereading it yet again. Leonard believes one reason to read a novel is because you don't know what's going to happen, whereas his wife declares that she rereads it because she enjoys it. In another scene Leonard burns the novel, a clock, his wife's hairbrush, and a *Teddy* bear, musing over how he can't remember to forget her. "That's who you were, not who you are," Teddy says to Leonard at one point. Just who Lennie and/or Leonard Shelby were or are is never resolved to some viewers' satisfaction, but if viewers remain puzzled, that may be exactly the point of the film.

Nolan followed *Memento* with the psychological thriller *Insomnia* (2002) and continues to make engaging films in several genres, including a war film, *Dunkirk* (2017). Sci-fi is a vein he works in often, *Inception* (2010), *Interstellar* (2014), and *Tenet* (2020) being some examples. He also created the successful Batman superhero trilogy, *Batman Begins* (2005), *The Dark Knight* (2008), and *The Dark Knight Rises* (2012). Regardless of the genre, Nolan's films deal often with protagonists grappling with trauma, which becomes a key element of their identity.

John Wagner and Vince Locke, David Cronenberg and *A History of Violence*

A willful suppression of the past occurs in David Cronenberg's *A History of Violence*, based on the 1997 graphic novel of the same name by John Wagner and Vince Locke, and adapted into a screenplay by Josh Olson. There are some fundamental differences of great importance between the film and the graphic novel, perhaps the most significant of which is that the Joey character in the graphic novel became a killer reluctantly, participating in the robbery of the mob's weekly "take," which his friend planned, only in order to finance his grandmother's heart operation, whereas the Joey in the film comes from a mob family and killed both for money and because he enjoyed it. The film is more of a domestic drama that brings the characters' psychology to the forefront, creating more complex characters. It also portrays the quintessential Cronenborgian theme of a potentially beneficial combination of desire and violence.

The film version of *A History of Violence* depicts a case of willful identity cancellation when a Philadelphia mob family member named Joey Cusack disappears into the Midwest and recreates himself as Tom Stall (Viggo Mortensen), owner of Stall's Diner in Millbrook, Indiana. His wife and two children have no inkling that their kind, loving father was once a gangster. Cronenberg establishes the Stall family closeness in the first scene in which they appear. The young daughter Sarah (Heidi Hayes) wakes up screaming from a nightmare and her father arrives first to comfort her that there is no such thing as monsters, followed by her older brother, Jack (Ashton Holmes), and the mother, Edie (Maria Bello). (That there is indeed such a thing as monsters is apparent to the viewer in the film's opening sequence, in which two drifting thugs kill a motel desk clerk, maid, and toddler; these two will soon turn up in Millbrook.) The next morning while Edie gathers files for her day's law work the other three eat breakfast together, talking about Jack's trepidation over his performance playing baseball that day in his high school gym class. At Tom's diner his cook (Gerry Quigley) converses with one of the regular customers about a girlfriend he had who dreamed he was "some kind of demented killer" instead of her boyfriend and stabbed him in the shoulder with a fork. When Tom assumes he broke up with her the cook declares he married her and it lasted six years, observing, "Nobody's perfect, Tom," to which Tom agrees, "I guess not"—all commentary on Tom's upcoming exposure as, to put it mildly, an imperfect person who indeed once was a demented killer.

A parallel narrative on violence emerges in Jack's experiences at school. To his surprise he catches a ball in the outfield to strike out one of the school's bullies (Kyle Schmid), who tries to get him to fight later in the locker room. Jack refuses to be egged into it, admitting that he is both little and a faggot as the bully had claimed. "What would be the point?" he asks when provoked to fight. "Doing violence to me just seems pointless and cruel, don't you think?" Frustrated, the bully leaves him alone—this time.

After work, Edie picks up Tom and tells him the kids are with friends and she intends to rectify the fact that they never got to be teenagers together. At home, Tom removes stuffed animals from their bed and Edie then emerges from the bathroom dressed in a high school cheerleading outfit. Eyes widening, he asks, "What have you done with my wife?" Here, *she's* role playing. Post-coital Tom reminisces, "I remember the moment I knew you were in love with me. I saw it in your eyes. I can still see it." "Of course you can," Edie responds, "I still love you." The scene's final exchange sets up the impending scrutiny of Tom's identity: "I'm the luckiest son of a bitch alive," he says, to which she rejoins, "You're the best man I've ever known. There's no luck involved."

The pastoral ideal explodes when the two killers (Stephen McHattie and Greg Bryk) from the opening sequence come into Stall's Diner. With the backdrop of a teenage couple sharing a sundae in a booth, one of the men points a gun at Tom and orders his accomplice to "do her," meaning the waitress (Deborah Drakeford) Tom had told to go home. In a matter of seconds Tom smashes a coffee pot against the head of the gun bearer, leaps over the counter to grab said weapon, fires four rounds into the would-be assaulter, sending him backward through the door's window, then, after being stabbed in the foot by the other killer, fatally shoots him in the head. The cook looks on in amazement, while Tom looks at the gun in his hand with a sigh, feeling the weight of his past.

Tom becomes a local hero, but the news coverage alerts the Philadelphia mobsters from his past to his current whereabouts, and soon one of them, Carl Fogarty (Ed Harris), turns up in the diner and keeps calling him "Joey" despite his protests that he doesn't know Fogarty and has never been to Philadelphia. Fogarty begins stalking the family, leading to one scene in the mall where he says to Edie, "Ask him why he's so good at killing." At dawn the next day Tom walks into town and is sitting in the diner when he sees Fogarty's car, first parked outside, then driving off in the direction of his home. Calling Edie to tell her to get the shotgun, he limps home as quickly as he can, only to find Fogarty did not go there. He explains to a wondering Jack that some men think he is somebody else that they don't like and he feared they would come after his family. Jack asks what if he's right about that, and Tom replies, "Then we deal with it," while clicking the shotgun closed for emphasis.

The title of the film relates not only to Tom's past but to the way violence becomes family history in a new way. In another encounter with the bully at school, Jack responds to the taunt that his tough dad would be ashamed of him by beating the kid so harshly that he lands in the hospital. Tom lectures his son, "You stand up to him, you don't put him in the hospital. In this family we don't solve our problem by hitting people," at which Jack tosses off, "No, in this family we shoot them."

Fogarty kidnaps Jack to force Tom into a confrontation with his past, right in his own front yard. He wants Tom to come back to Philadelphia. "You almost believe your own crap, don't you?" Fogarty asks. "You're trying so hard to be this other guy, it's painful to watch." Another of the men pulls Jack from the back seat of their car. "Don't make us hurt the kid, Joey," Fogarty says. "We just want you to come for a little trip with us down memory lane. Put the pop gun down and come over and talk with us." Tom sends Edie upstairs to stay with Sarah, puts the gun down and walks toward the men, telling Jack to go back to the house. Viewers—as well as Jack—see "Joey" coming out in the hardness on Tom's face.

After warning Fogarty, "It would be better if you just leave now," Tom kills one of Fogarty's henchmen brutally with his bare hands, then shoots the other with the gun he got off the first man. Fogarty shoots Joey in the shoulder and intends to blow his brains out, but Jack kills Fogarty with his father's shotgun—the history of violence is lengthening. Tom takes the shotgun forcefully from the boy's hands, then hugs him, gently resting the barrel of the gun on his son's shoulder, akin to a benediction of violence.

The conversation Edie and Tom have when she visits him in the hospital is crucial for developing the film's themes. Edie asks Tom to tell her the truth. "I saw you turn into Joey right before my eyes," she says. "I saw a killer, the one Fogarty warned me about." As Tom slowly shakes his head no, Edie asks, "You did kill men back in Philly, didn't you? Did you do it for money or did you do it because you enjoyed it?" "Joey did ... both. I didn't, Tom Stall didn't," which confession leads Edie to throw up.

Tom Stall (Viggo Mortensen) must become Joey again to fully erase his past in *A History of Violence* (2005) (New Line Cinema/Photofest).

Recomposed, she asks, "What are you, like some multiple personality schizoid? It's like flipping a switch back and forth for you?" "I never expected to see Joey again," Tom explains, his Philadelphia accent taking over as he speaks. "Oh yeah," Edie replies wryly, "Joey, what, was he in hiding, was he dead?" "I thought he was," Tom argues. "I thought I killed Joey Cusack. I went out to the desert and I killed him.... I spent three years becoming Tom Stall. Edie, you have to know this: I wasn't really born again until I met you. I was nothing." "I don't believe you," Edie snaps back, railing about how he didn't grow up in Portland like he claimed and he had no adoptive parents. She starts questioning her own identity: "And our name. Jesus Christ, my name. Jack's name, Sarah's name. Stall. Tom Stall. Did you just make that up? Where did that name come from?" "It was available," he calmly shrugs in response. "Yeah," Edie says. "I guess I was available too." She leaves in tears, and he cries as well after she's gone.

Once released from the hospital, a cab drops Tom at home to find his son sitting on the front porch at the step. His "Hey, Jack," elicits, "What am I supposed to call you now?" "You're supposed to call me Dad. That's what I am, your dad," he replies, somewhat puzzled at the question. "Are you really?" Jack tosses out. "So, you're some kind of closet mobster, Dad? I mean, if I go rob Millikin's Drugstore are you going to ground me if I don't give you a piece of the action?" "Please son," Tom protests, "don't." "If I talk to Sarah about you, will you have me whacked?" Jack challenges as he starts walking away, brushing off the hand Tom lays on his arm when he passes.

Sheriff Sam Carney (Peter MacNeill) stops by the Stalls' home for a visit one afternoon, wanting an explanation for events he just can't make sense of, the men from Philadelphia who were so serious about tracking Tom down. "Tom is who he says he is," Edie maintains. "That's all that really matters. Sam, hasn't this family suffered enough?" she asks, starting to cry on Tom's shoulder. "Thanks," Tom says to her after the sheriff leaves. Edie pushes away from him and starts to head upstairs. Violence and desire mix disturbingly in the scene that follows. "Get off of me!" Edie yells, slapping Tom, who grabs her by the throat. "Fuck you, Joey!" she yells, trying to run upstairs. He grabs her ankle, pulling her down; she kicks at him. He grabs at her neck, then is about to turn away when she pulls him back to her. They have violent sex on the stairs. After, both seem to have been gratified and they do kiss, but she pushes him off of her and walks upstairs, escaping his grasp on her ankle. When she emerges from the bathroom in an open robe after having showered, Tom is sitting on the bed. She looks at him angrily, walks out of the room, and slams the door behind her. Mortensen's facial expression and slight tip of his head conveys "Oh well, what did I expect?" as clearly as if he had said it.

Tom is sleeping on the couch when he gets a phone call from his brother Richie (William Hurt), who observes, "You're still pretty good with the killing. That's exciting. Are you going to come see me? Or do I have to come see you?" Not wanting any more violence to visit his Indiana town, he drives nonstop to Philadelphia to finish cutting the strings to his past. As the two brothers converse Joey's accent has again returned. Richie points out that Joey caused him a lot of problems before he disappeared by disfiguring Fogarty—a made man—and killing some of his henchmen. "Jesus, Joey," Richie observes, "you took his eye. Barbed wire, wasn't it? That's disgusting. You always were the crazy one." "Not anymore," Joey replies. "Yeah, I heard you're living the American Dream," Richie says in disdain. "You bought into it, didn't you? You've been this other guy almost as long as you've been yourself. Hey, when you dream, are you still Joey?" "Joey's been dead a long time," Joey says. "And yet here you sit, big as life," Richie notes. He rails about how much Joey cost him in time and money, loss of respect and trust with the mob. "You always were a problem for me," Richie observes. "When Mom brought you home from the hospital, I tried to strangle you in your crib." In a half-second of self-reflection he adds, "I guess all kids try to do that." Joey maintains that he's there to make peace and asks what he can do to make things right. "You could die, Joey," Richie says, turning his back literally and metaphorically on Joey as a cue for one of his men to garrote Joey with a wire. Reacting with lethal swiftness, Joey kills three of Richie's henchmen with his bare hands and escapes the room as Richie shoots at him. A fourth henchman joins Richie to look for Joey in the house, and when they separate as Richie steps outside the front door, Joey kills the assistant, takes his gun, opens the front door and points the gun at Richie's head. "Jesus, Joey," Richie says. Joey shoots him, then sadly remarks, "Jesus, Richie."

The next morning, Joey throws the gun into a pond on Richie's estate, takes off his shirt and washes the blood off his face, a ritualistic purification that, after sighing, allows Tom to drive home to Indiana. His family is eating dinner when he arrives. A plate and silverware are ready on the counter. Not a word is said. Edie bows her head over folded hands. Slowly, Tom rejoins the family when his daughter puts his plate on the table, his son passes the meatloaf, and his wife looks up with tears running down her face. Tom's eyes show a slight glistening as he and his wife look at each other, tentative yet hopeful. Joey has erased his past once and for all, and his family accepts him back as Tom Stall. Joey Cusack has become, hopefully, an aberrant memory, collectively suppressed.

Some comparative discussion of the film and the graphic novel brings out the strengths in each text. As noted earlier, an important distinction is that Joey Muni in the graphic novel was an unwilling killer during one heist pulled off while he was a high school student in Brooklyn, whereas Joey Cusack seems to have reveled in the occupation for some time as an adult member of a Philadelphia mob family. (Perhaps the saddest aspect of the graphic novel is that Joey/Tom later finds out his grandmother saved the $8,000 he gave her for her operation and died of a heart attack a few years after he left Brooklyn. The crime that forever altered his life was all for nought.) Richie Benedetto in the novel is Joey's friend, not brother, and much of his motivation for the heist is to kill mobster Lou Manzi, who had killed Richie's punk brother. This revenge motif evolves as the graphic novel continues, until ultimately it is revealed that Richie was abducted not long after the heist and tortured by Lou Manzi's son for the twenty years that Joey, reborn as Tom McKenna, was running McKenna's Soda Shop in Raven's Bend, Michigan. Indeed, in the graphic novel's denouement, Richie is a severely disfigured torso with radically stumped limbs and an unrecognizable face whom Tom mercy kills at Richie's request by placing his hands over his nose and mouth. Aside from the two killers who come into Stall's Diner, the psychopath in Cronenberg's film is Tom/Joey himself, not a crazed mobster's son bent on avenging his father's murder. As just noted, killing Richie in the graphic novel is an act of mercy, whereas in Cronenberg's film it is fratricide committed to enable Tom's life to return to some semblance of a fabricated normal. Another distinction between the texts is that Tom McKenna is missing the last joint of a little finger, a disfiguration he received in turn from having taken out the eye of John Torrino while trying to flee shortly after the heist; the barbed wire used on the eye defensively just happened to be on hand in the alley, not a cruelty deliberately inflicted, as it had been by Joey Cusack on Carl Fogarty. While film and graphic novel both have their share of violent scenes, the graphic novel's violence is more disgustingly perverse with the twenty-year torturing of Richie. There are also spectacular scenes, such as when McKenna shoots a propane tank on his front lawn that embeds shards of metal in the back of one of the three men who have come to threaten him; John Torrino is impaled by a long knife thrust into his mouth; and a henchman loses his caught hand when a cage elevator in a factory descends.

Perhaps the greatest disparity between film and graphic novel is the reaction of the wife to the revelation of her husband's violent history. Edie McKenna, not a lawyer but a co-worker with her husband in the soda shop, is taken aback at first, remarking, "So you're not Tom McKenna—you're this … Joey. Joey Muni. All these years we've been living a lie.… My God, Tom—What do I call you now—Tom? Joey?," to which Tom responds, "I'm Tom. Tom! Joey Muni died a long time ago. This is my life, Edie. You, Buzz—Ellie—you're all that matter to me."[13] After he explains why he fled New York and how he disappeared to escape the mob, he asks whether she forgives him. Her response is, "Of course I do, Tom. It's all been a … a bit of a shock, that's all. You're still the man I married—the man I love."[14] As discussed earlier, Edie Stall's reaction to her husband's history is not so forgiving—but then, he was more willfully and violently engaged with that past.

Cronenberg's earlier work includes some intriguing sci-fi horror films— *The Brood* (1979), *Videodrome* (1983), *The Fly* (1986), and *eXistenZ* (1999), among others—and his next feature after *A History of Violence* is *Eastern Promises* (2007), a complicated thriller involving the Russian mafia and again starring Viggo Mortensen. Other films include *A Dangerous Method* (2011), a bio-drama exploring the relationship between Sigmund Freud (Mortensen once more) and Carl Jung (Michael Fassbender), and the dramas *Cosmopolis* (2012) and *Maps to the Stars* (2014). Overall Cronenberg's body of work demonstrates his rise to a place of prominence among directors of the late twentieth and early twenty-first centuries.

James Mangold and *Identity*

James Mangold also has made notable films in a variety of genres—the crime thriller *Cop Land* (1997), the romantic comedy *Kate & Leopold* (2001), the Johnny Cash bio-drama *Walk the Line* (2005), the action remake of *3:10 to Yuma* (2007), the sci-fi action *The Wolverine* (2013)—but his psychological mystery neo-noir *Identity* may be his most cerebral. In this film, from an original screenplay by Michael Cooney, nobody turns out to be who they are because all of the characters are projections of a man named Malcolm Rivers (Pruitt Taylor Vince), whose mother abandoned him at a motel when he was a child, locked in a bathroom. But before viewers are astonished with that revelation near the end of the film, they are led through an intricately woven web of interrelationships and overturned identities. Viewers learn what little they know about Rivers at the opening of the film from the newspaper clippings and tape recordings in his case file that his doctor is reviewing. His mother, Callie Rivers, was a prostitute ("I remember my mother was a whore" is the way Malcolm bluntly puts it); he became a ward of the state; on May 10, 1998, the grown Malcolm Rivers committed mass murder. "Mountain Nightmare: Brutal Slayings in Lakeworth Apartments" reads the headline about "one of the most gruesome crimes in Nevada." Rivers, a local casino janitor, stabbed five women and one man to death, decapitating two of them with a large, machete-style knife. Police found him in a bathroom when they arrested him—the bathroom becomes a recurring important element of the film, as do the motel, prostitutes, and states—and when the doctor's voice asks Rivers if he remembers the murders, he replies, "I remember Columbia is the capital of South Carolina." What is very hard for first-time viewers to catch are other aspects of the newspaper articles and Rivers' notebook diaries because they go by so quickly onscreen. Careful replaying lets one see that when the murders are first discovered, one article notes, "Police refused to speculate on the identity of the perpetrator," and another article that takes up four columns of the newspaper has partial repetitions in columns two, three, and four—a few complete sentences are repeated, with a slight change in paragraphing, and new material added. This is quite a subtle clue to the separate, yet connected, identities that Rivers creates. The notebook diaries contain a drawing of six stick figures plus a stick figure with a triangular skirt holding hands with a small stick figure; red is colored on the heads of the six large stick figures. These images would seem to connect Rivers' boyhood maternal experience with his adult homicides. Elsewhere in the notebook diaries "Malcolm Rivers" is written backwards in childish printing; near the end of the film "Timothy York" and "Timmy" will be seen in them, also in childish printing.

These notebook diaries and tapes have opened the way for an insanity hearing for Rivers, who was about to be executed. But before that side story begins, the scene cuts to a motel on a rainy night, and adding further to the confusion as the film gets underway, there are time shifts. A man holding a woman and saying, "She won't stop bleeding," appears in the doorway of the motel's office; then there is a flashback to the man, the woman, and a child driving in a minivan whose tire becomes punctured by a spiked-heeled shoe; this cuts to a woman driving a convertible at sunset reaching for a lighter in her suitcase and involuntarily spilling clothes and that same shoe onto the road top. A return cut takes viewers to the York family with the flat tire: the mother waves happily at her young son, who is inside the vehicle, steps back from their minivan, and gets struck by a car. There is another jump back in time to reveal the chauffer of this car fumbling for batteries for his passenger-employer's cell phone, looking up at the road just as he hits the mother. Right from the start Mangold and Cooney have viewers jolting in their seats, which establishes the tense tone for the rest of the film.

There is a definite debt to Hitchcock's *Psycho* in the rainy night, off-the-beaten-track, run-down motel setting, with no guests staying there until the ten travelers arrive. The isolation is incredibly symbolic, perhaps the first clue that viewers are watching the psychological allegory of a mind closing in upon itself. The dead cell phone batteries of the passenger, Caroline Suzanne (Rebecca De Mornay), a has-been actress; the flooded-out road and empty gas tank that land Paris (Amanda Peet), a hooker trying to change her lifestyle, at the motel; the police officer Rhodes (Ray Liotta) telling the chauffer Ed (John Cusack) that he'll control car radio contact for help—all of these contribute symbolically to the insularity of a psyche whose various selves are bent on destroying one other.

As it turns out, for Malcolm Rivers to avoid execution, his killer identity must be destroyed. So his mind retreats into the motel scenario where all his identities meet and are reduced via creatively violent murders. First to be eliminated is Caroline, who, using a shower curtain (another homage to *Psycho*) as a raincoat while trying to get a cell phone signal, is decapitated and her head put in a clothes dryer; with it is the motel key to room 10. The multiple-homicide prisoner Robert Maine (Jake Busey) whom Rhodes is transporting somehow got free from being chained to a toilet—the first Rivers alternate identity to be re-imprisoned in Rivers' boyhood "prison"—and gets a baseball bat shoved down his throat, but not before a long pursuit that works important motifs into the film. Tracking Maine, Ed fails to spot what the viewer sees when lightning illuminates an old wooden sign for Tribal Tombs in storage, a local attraction another guest had been looking at a tourist brochure for when she checked in. When Timmy York (Bret Loehr) goes in to use the bathroom, his stepfather reassures him it will be okay, saying, "I'm going to be right here; I'm not going anywhere," which of course Rivers' mother had not been. In motel room six, newlyweds Ginny (Clea DuVall) and Lou (William Lee Scott) have a fight that causes her to lock herself in the bathroom to escape Lou's yelling; clearly she is traumatized when he tries to break in.

The slightly psychic Ginny had taken it as a good omen that she and Lou, who have been married for nine hours, were given room six, but when they first enter it and the door bangs shut, the number six swings down to become a nine. Nine is a big clue in the plot, for nine personalities have to be destroyed for the tenth to survive. Malcolm Rivers was nine years old when his mother abandoned him; Timmy York is nine years old. Officer Rhodes has a 9 mm pistol. As these instances of nine become implanted in viewers' minds, Ed continues his pursuit of Maine, going through a room containing girly magazines whose cover pictures of women have been disfigured, "SLUT" written in red on one of them. Tentatively coming out of the bathroom, Ginny sees a *Psycho*-like shadow of someone with a large knife drawn over their head, relocks herself in the bathroom and climbs out the window, only to shortly discover that Lou has been stabbed to death. Maine is shown running across the landscape with the motel shrinking in the background, making viewers think he is the killer, yet when he breaks into a diner, he's suddenly right back next to the motel. Rhodes appears and a fight ensues, which Ed soon joins. Subdued and tied up, Maine, left to be guarded by the motel manager, Larry (John Hawkes), tells him, "I'm good at keeping secrets. I got a whopper myself," which on rewatching should amuse viewers. As should their insider knowledge that Rhodes isn't really a police officer: he and Maine are *both* escaped convicts.

Things start to get pulled together for viewers—or at least, viewers are given more pieces of a puzzle to work over. A conversation between Paris and Ed causes her to ask him his birth sign, and they discover they share the same birthday, May 10, which viewers might recall was the date of Rivers' massacre. Ed explains he took medical leave from being a police officer because he started getting headaches and blacking out; appropriately enough, on this trip with his employer, he's brought along a copy of Sartre's *Being and Nothingness*. Lou's body, it is discovered, has the key to room nine on it. When Larry stops guarding Maine to get something from his office Maine is killed; subsequently the key to room eight is found by his body. Accused of being Maine's murderer, Larry (after all, he'd been carrying the bat around in previous scenes) tries to leave in his pickup truck, but fatally pins the stepfather to a building.

The film makes its second return from the motel scenes to Rivers' hearing, where it is revealed that the notebook diary entries were made just before the murders four years ago. Changes in handwriting style, tone, and point of view indicate that several people made them. Rivers' doctor, Dr. Malick (Alfred Molina), argues that he suffers from dissociative identity disorder and that "in theory, one must try to move the patient toward integration, a folding of their fractured psyche" back into one. After this tidbit viewers are sent back to the motel, where they hear Larry's backstory of having lost everything in Vegas and pulling up to the motel's gas station because he was running on empty. It turns out the motel manager—ostensibly also named Larry—seems to have died of a heart attack, so Larry put his body in the freezer and stepped into his role. With the remaining guests now holed up in one room as the storm causes the lights to wane and return, Ginny remembers a movie where all the characters had a connection they weren't aware of, so they start talking about where they were born and where they were going when they landed at the motel. Mrs. York dies, apparently from her injuries, and they find the key to room six under her body. Curious, they back up Larry's truck and discover the key to room seven is in the father's pocket. Panicky, Ed insists Ginny and Paris leave with Timmy, telling them to just go anywhere so long as they get away from the motel. When their car bursts into fire yet there are absolutely no bodily remains left, Ed starts to wonder. Checking around the motel, he and the others find all the dead bodies have disappeared. When the surviving guests discover they all share the same birthday of May 10, checking too the xeroxes Larry had made of the dead guests' drivers licenses, the motel's disintegration speeds up, with the lobby roof leaking and electrical wires coming loose and sparking. Looking at a map of the United States on the office wall, Ed puts it together that they all have states' names: Larry Washington, the (New) York family, Caroline Suzanne (Carolina), Ed Dakota, Paris Nevada, Ginny (Virginia), Lou Isiana, Robert Maine, Officer Rhodes (Rhode Island). Viewers become acutely aware that Malcolm Rivers' last name is itself a geographical feature and recall his line from the film's opening sequence, "I remember that Columbia is the capital of South Carolina."

The various personalities of Malcolm Rivers (Pruitt Taylor Vince) are destroyed in *Identity* (2003) (Columbia Pictures/ Photofest).

Yet another homage to *Psycho* is the use of a psychiatrist to put all the pieces together for viewers at the end of the film. However, Cooney and Mangold make greater use of this figure, having Dr. Malick, as noted, appear also at the opening of the film and in scenes interspliced throughout. He serves as a Virgil figure, leading Malcolm Rivers on his journey with a series of questions. When Ed spies the map he gets a headache and starts to hear Dr. Malick's voice asking, "Who am I speaking with right now?" Ascertaining it is the Ed personality, Dr.

Malick says, "Edward, you missed your last appointment. Where have you been?" Pulled into conversation with the doctor, Ed tells the story of driving to the motel and how they all couldn't get out because there was a storm, eliciting Dr. Malick's, "What happened at the motel?" Ed notes that people started dying and their bodies disappeared, whereupon Dr. Malick shows him a photograph of Malcolm Rivers and notes that he had a troubled life. "When faced with an intense trauma, a child's mind may fracture, creating disassociated identities. That's exactly what happened to Malcolm Rivers. He developed a condition that is commonly known as multiple personality syndrome." "Why are you telling me this?" Ed asks, naturally enough. "Because you, Edward, are one of his personalities," Dr. Malick replies, handing him a mirror in which Ed sees Rivers' face.

Shocked, Ed sees Rivers' face also reflected when he looks toward the room's darkened windows. Dr. Malick explains that he is undergoing a medical treatment that is forcing his various identities to confront each other for the first time and reduce in number. "One of the personalities you met tonight, Edward," Dr. Malick expands, "committed those murders four years ago. He took control of Malcolm's body as you have now, and released an unspeakable rage, and in 19 hours Malcolm Rivers will be put to death because of those actions unless I can convince that man [he gestures to indicate someone on the review board] that the killer is gone." Dr. Malick can see that Ed is starting to slip away, so he emphasizes, "Edward, I need you to understand, the killer cannot survive."

Ed is pulled back in his mind to the motel, where Paris finds the real police officer dead in the trunk of Rhodes' car and looks for Ed and Larry. Rhodes appears and demands the keys to Larry's truck, whereupon Larry hits him with a fire extinguisher, but Rhodes recovers and shoots both Larry and Ed, the latter of whom shoots Rhodes to death. "Where did you go?" Paris asks Ed, "What did you see?" "I saw you in an orange grove," Ed replies before dying, a line recited onscreen to viewers as coming from Rivers, who sheds a tear. The film goes to split screen, showing Rivers on one side and Paris driving away from the motel in the truck on the other. Paris had been on her way to Florida to take over running her family's orange grove when she was forced to stop at the motel, and now she departs for the Sunshine State.

Dr. Malick has convinced the review board that the killer personality is gone. One of them declares, "We witnessed the destruction of ten identities tonight. Nine were innocent, one was guilty. The violence that existed in him has been executed." Riding the next day in a prison van to the mental hospital in which he will be incarcerated now that he has been spared from execution, Rivers retreats happily in his mind to the orange grove, existing as Paris, who is tilling the earth with a three-prong hand cultivator at the base of an orange tree. She uncovers a motel key to room one in the soil, and suddenly the boy Timmy is standing beside her, having picked up the cultivator she had dropped. Flashbacks to the motel show Timmy holding his mother's nostrils shut so she suffocates, stabbing Lou, and leading his stepfather into the path of Larry's oncoming truck. "Whores don't get a second chance," Timmy and Rivers simultaneously declare, Timmy smashing the tool down upon Paris' head and Rivers choking Dr. Malick with the chains binding his hands together.

If the viewer does the math, they'll work out that there were actually eleven people at the motel, ten guests plus Larry, so if ten of Rivers' multiple personalities were destroyed, an eleventh still existed, which turned out to be the killer identity, Timmy. This is fitting since the initial trauma was undergone when Rivers was a boy himself. It is also fitting that the final personality killed is Paris, the stand-in mother/whore personality who has always been the real target of Rivers' rage. That she is killed in an orange grove, symbolizing Mother Nature, adds resonance.

All of this, of course, is absurd in terms of actual psychology and mental conditions, but the movie makes no claim to accuracy, or even verisimilitude, any more than does the Edgar Allan Poe doubling story "William Wilson." Somewhere between fever dream and allegory, *Identity* nurtures its own fractures. Its loose threads are its binding. Indeed, a pervasive thematic clue is a nursery rhyme that hinges on conundrums: "As I was going up the stair / I met a man who wasn't there / He wasn't there again today / I wish, I wish he'd go away." The film opens with Malcolm Rivers saying this in voice-over; Ed says it after looking at a map of the United States shortly before manifesting before Dr. Malick and the review board, altering the opening line to "When I was going up the stairs"; and Timmy's voice recites it as the transport police van containing Rivers and the dead Dr. Malick rolls off the road and halts just before the closing credits. The rhyme wasn't made up by Cooney or Mangold, it's an actual nursery rhyme, but the way they employ it is brilliant.

The Virgil figures in these films—Teddy in *Memento*, Fogarty in *A History of Violence*, and Dr. Malick in *Identity*—guides through the underworld, whether deceitful or benign, all come to a violent end, while the protagonists live on with a tenterhook hope of possibility. Hints of their futures lie in their surnames. Malcolm Rivers might continue his deranged plunge through alternate personalities and mis-remembered murders. Tom Stall will return to his bucolic life, ostensibly rid of past history. The name Leonard Shelby is more opaque, until one considers the wordplay of "shall be." That linguistic twist marks the polarities of the character: devastated as to who he is, he longs to be revealed or released. Amnesia, suppressed identity, multiple personalities killed by one of their own, these serve as metaphors for post-postmodern questions about continuity of the self in neo-noir.

Chapter Notes

Chapter One

1. Nino Frank, "A New Kind of Police Drama: The Criminal Adventure," translated by Alain Silver, *Film Noir Reader 2*, edited by Alain Silver and James Ursini (Limelight Editions, 1999), 15.
2. Frank, 16.
3. Frank, 17.
4. Frank, 17–18.
5. Frank, 18.
6. Jean-Pierre Chartier, "Americans Also Make Noir Films," translated by Alain Silver, *Film Noir Reader 2*, edited by Alain Silver and James Ursini (Limelight Editions, 1999), 21.
7. Chartier, 23.
8. Chartier, 23.
9. Nick Smedley, *A Divided World: Hollywood Cinema and Émigré Directors in the Era of Roosevelt and Hitler, 1933–1948* (Intellect, 2011), 121.
10. Smedley, 122.
11. Robert Horton, Introduction, *Billy Wilder: Interviews*, edited by Robert Horton (University Press of Mississippi, 2001), ix.
12. Qtd. in Ed Sikov, *On Sunset Boulevard: The Life and Times of Billy Wilder* (University Press of Mississippi, 2017), 198.
13. Qtd. in Ella Smith, *Starring Miss Barbara Stanwyck* (Crown, 1974), 170.
14. Foster Hirsch, *The Dark Side of the Screen: Film Noir* (Barnes and Company, 1981), 4.
15. Smith, 170.
16. James M. Cain, *Double Indemnity* (Vintage Crime/Black Lizard, 1992), 112.
17. Cain, 3.
18. John Kobler, "A Study of the Snyder-Gray Case," *The Trial of Ruth Snyder and Judd Gray*, edited by John Kobler (Doubleday, Doran and Company, 1938), 21.
19. Kobler, 22.
20. Kobler, 50.
21. Qtd. in Cameron Crowe, *Conversations with Wilder* (Knopf, 2001), 53.
22. Cain, 51.
23. Cain, 52, 53.
24. Cain, 53.
25. Qtd. in Crowe, 54.
26. Cain, 105.
27. Cain, 18.
28. Cain, 109.
29. Cain, 114.
30. Cain, 115.
31. Hirsch, *The Dark Side of the Screen*, 119.
32. Qtd. in Gene D. Phillips, *Out of the Shadows: Expanding the Canon of Classic Film Noir* (Scarecrow Press, 2012), 124.
33. Qtd. in Phillips, *Out of the Shadows*, 124.
34. Qtd. in Sikov, 298.
35. Sikov, 298.
36. Sikov, 299.
37. Vera Caspary, "My 'Laura' and Otto's," *The Saturday Review* (26 June 1971), 36.
38. Gene D. Phillips, *Exiles in Hollywood: Major European Film Directors in America* (Lehigh University Press, 1998), 102.
39. Otto Preminger, *Preminger: An Autobiography* (Doubleday, 1977), 71.
40. Foster Hirsch, *Otto Preminger: The Man Who Would Be King* (Knopf, 2007), 98.
41. Preminger, 75.
42. Caspary, "My Laura," 36.
43. Caspary, "My Laura," 37.
44. Caspary, "My Laura," 37.
45. Preminger, 72.
46. Caspary, "My Laura," 37.
47. Caspary, "My Laura," 37.
48. Vera Caspary, *Laura* (The Feminist Press, 2005), 160.
49. Qtd. in Hirsch, *Otto Preminger*, 107.
50. Caspary, *Laura*, 64.
51. Caspary, *Laura*, 65.
52. Caspary, "My Laura," 37.
53. Caspary, "My Laura," 37.
54. Edward Dimendberg, *Film Noir and the Spaces of Modernity* (Harvard University Press, 2004), 258.
55. Roman Polanski, *Roman by Polanski* (William Morrow, 1984), 349.
56. Polanski, 346.
57. Polanski, 354.
58. Polanski, 355.
59. Polanski, 348.
60. Ronald Schwartz, *Film Noir, Now and Then: Film Noir Originals and Remakes (1944–1999)* (Greenwood, 2001), 6.
61. Qtd. in Al Hinson, "Bloodlines," *The Coen Brothers: Interviews*, edited by William Rodney Allen (University Press of Mississippi, 2006), 13.
62. Qtd. in Hinson, 14.

63. William Rodney Allen, Introduction, *The Coen Brothers: Interviews*, edited by William Rodney Allen (University Press of Mississippi, 2006), xii.

64. Qtd. in Hinson, 14.

65. Hinson, 7.

66. Jeffrey Adams, *The Cinema of the Coen Brothers: Hard-boiled Entertainments* (Wallflower, 2015), 24.

67. Adams, 24.

68. Adams, 24.

69. Dashiell Hammett, *Red Harvest, Dashiell Hammett: Five Complete Novels* (Avenel Books, 1980), 102.

70. Hammett, 102.

71. Ethan Coen and Joel Coen, "Blood Simple," *Collected Screenplays Volume 1* (Faber and Faber, 2002), 57.

72. Hammett, 44.

Chapter Two

1. Raymond Chandler, "The Simple Art of Murder," *The Simple Art of Murder* (Houghton Mifflin, 1950), 527.

2. Chandler, "The Simple Art of Murder," 530.

3. Chandler, "The Simple Art of Murder," 533.

4. Stephen Knight, "'A Hard Cheerfulness': An Introduction to Raymond Chandler," *American Crime Fiction*, edited by Brian Docherty (St. Martins, 1988), 82–83.

5. Knight, 85.

6. Knight, 71.

7. Raymond Chandler, *The Big Sleep* (Vintage Crime/Black Lizard, 1992), 19.

8. Chandler, *The Big Sleep*, 36.

9. Fredric Jameson, *Raymond Chandler: The Detections of Totality* (Verso, 2016), 62–63.

10. Tom Williams, *A Mysterious Something in the Light: The Life of Raymond Chandler* (Aurum, 2012), xii.

11. Chandler, *The Big Sleep*, 51.

12. Chandler, *The Big Sleep*, 64, 99, 100, 100.

13. Chandler, *The Big Sleep*, 106.

14. Chandler, *The Big Sleep*, 168.

15. Chandler, *The Big Sleep*, 178.

16. Knight, 78.

17. Chandler, *The Big Sleep*, 23.

18. Todd McCarthy, *Howard Hawks: The Grey Fox of Hollywood* (Grove, 1997), 384.

19. Chandler, *The Big Sleep*, 192.

20. Chandler, *The Big Sleep*, 195.

21. Chandler, *The Big Sleep*, 230.

22. Gerald Mast, *Howard Hawks, Storyteller* (Oxford University Press, 1982), 16.

23. Martin Scorsese, Foreword, *A Third Face: My Tale of Writing, Fighting, and Filmmaking* by Samuel Fuller (Knopf, 2002), ix.

24. Samuel Fuller, *A Third Face: My Tale of Writing, Fighting, and Filmmaking* (Knopf, 2002), 291.

25. Fuller, 298.

26. Geoff Andrew, *The Films of Nicholas Ray:*

The Poet of Nightfall, 2nd ed. (British Film Institute Publishing, 2004), 23–24.

27. Edward Anderson, *Thieves Like Us* (Black Curtain, 2013), 18, 23, 147.

28. Anderson, 87.

29. Anderson, 86, 144.

30. Anderson, 168–69.

31. Anderson, 170.

32. Qtd. in Jonathan Rosenbaum, ed., *This is Orson Welles: Orson Welles and Peter Bogdanovich* (HarperCollins, 1992), 297.

33. Frank Brady, *Citizen Welles: A Biography of Orson Welles* (Charles Scribner's Sons, 1989), 498.

34. John C. Stubbs, "The Evolution of Orson Welles's 'Touch of Evil' from Novel to Film," *Cinema Journal*, vol. 24, no. 2 (1985), 20.

35. Whit Masterson, *Badge of Evil* (Prologue Books, 2013), 65.

36. Masterson, 191.

37. Masterson, 192.

38. Masterson, 202.

39. Stubbs, 25.

40. Stubbs, 25.

41. Stubbs, 25.

42. Stubbs, 26.

43. Austin Sarat and Martha Merrill Umphrey, "The Justice of Jurisdiction: The Policing and Breaching of Boundaries in Orson Welles' *Touch of Evil*," *English Language Notes*, vol. 48, no. 2 (2010), 121.

44. Sarat and Umphrey, 121.

45. Stubbs, 27.

46. Stubbs, 29–30.

47. Stubbs, 28.

48. Stubbs, 29.

49. Qtd. in Rosenbaum, 309.

50. Qtd. in Rosenbaum, 309.

51. Qtd. in Rosenbaum, 309.

52. Rosenbaum, 314.

53. Robert Miklitsch, *I Died a Million Times: Gangster Noir in Midcentury America* (University of Illinois Press, 2021), 159.

Chapter Three

1. James Naremore, *More Than Night: Film Noir in its Contexts* (University of California Press, 2008), 104.

2. Naremore, *More Than Night*, 104.

3. Smedley, 10.

4. Smedley, 10.

5. Qtd. in Nora Sayer, *Running Time: Films of the Cold War* (Dial, 1982), 18.

6. Stephen J. Whitfield, *The Culture of the Cold War*, 2nd ed. (The Johns Hopkins University Press, 1996), 127.

7. Barry Keith Grant, Introduction, *Fritz Lang: Interviews*, edited by Barry Keith Grant (University Press of Mississippi, 2003), vii.

8. Fritz Lang, "Fritz Lang: Autobiography," *Fritz Lang* by Lotte H. Eisner (Secker and Warburg, 1976) 14–15.

9. Patrick McGilligan, *Fritz Lang: The Nature of the Beast* (St. Martin's, 1997), 179.

10. Michael Tratner, *Crowd Scenes: Movies and Mass Politics* (Fordham University Press, 2008), 138.

11. Tratner, 139.

12. Tratner, 139.

13. Vincent Brook, *Driven to Darkness: Jewish Émigré Directors and the Rise of Film Noir* (Rutgers University Press, 2009), 64.

14. Qtd. in "Graham Green, 86, Dies; Novelist of the Soul," *The New York Times* (4 April 1991), A 1.

15. Qtd. in Charles Higham and Joel Greenberg, "Interview with Fritz Lang," *Fritz Lang: Interviews*, edited by Barry Keith Grant (University Press of Mississippi, 2003), 110.

16. Qtd. in Higham and Greenberg, 110.

17. Qtd. in Higham and Greenberg, 110–11.

18. Richard Lingeman, *The Noir Forties: The American People from Victory to Cold War* (Nation Books, 2012), 195.

19. Lotte H. Eisner, *Fritz Lang* (Secker and Warburg, 1976), 239.

20. Graham Greene, *The Ministry of Fear, 3 By Graham Greene* (Viking, 1943), 3.

21. Greene, 48.

22. Greene, 17.

23. Greene, 93.

24. Greene, 174.

25. Greene, 131.

26. Greene, 175.

27. Greene, 175.

28. John T. Soister, *Claude Rains: A Comprehensive Illustrated Reference to His Work in Film, Stage, Radio, Television and Recordings* (McFarland, 1999), 139.

29. Soister, 139.

30. Soister, 139.

31. Soister, 139.

32. Barbara Leaming, *Orson Welles: A Biography* (Viking, 1985), 294.

33. Leaming, 293.

34. James Naremore, *The Magic World of Orson Welles*, Centennial Anniversary Edition (University of Illinois Press, 2019), 125.

35. Clinton Heylin, *Despite the System: Orson Welles Versus the Hollywood Studios* (Chicago Review Press, 2005), 176.

36. Naremore, *The Magic World of Orson Welles*, 126.

37. Leaming, 315.

38. Naremore, *The Magic World of Orson Welles*, 136.

39. Leaming, 315.

40. Heylin, 181.

41. "Early Los Angeles Historical Buildings (1925+_," *Water and Power Associates*, Water and Power Associates (n.d.), https://waterandpower.org/museum/Early_LA_Buildings(1925+)_4_of_8.html.

42. Heylin, 176.

43. Heylin, 163.

44. Ralph Waldo Emerson, "Compensation," *Essays: First Series, The Complete Essays and Other Writings of Ralph Waldo Emerson* (Random House, 1950), 182–83.

45. Emerson, 186.

46. Victor Trivas, *The Stranger (1946): Shooting Script* (Alexander Street Press, 2003), 122.

47. Dan Leab, "I Was a Communist for the FBI," *The Movies as History: Visions of the Twentieth Century*, edited by David Ellwood (Sutton, 2000), 86.

48. Zach Brodt, "Record #17—Matt Cvetic HUAC Testimony," *ULS Archives and Manuscripts@Pitt*, University of Pittsburgh.

49. Leab, "I Was a Communist for the FBI," 87.

50. Leab, "I Was a Communist for the FBI," 87.

51. Leab, "I Was a Communist for the FBI," 87.

52. Leab, "I Was a Communist for the FBI," 88, 89.

53. Leab, "I Was a Communist for the FBI," 92.

54. John Sbardellati, *J. Edgar Hoover Goes to the Movies: The FBI and the Origins of Hollywood's Cold War* (Cornell University Press, 2012), 170.

55. Sbardellati, 170.

56. Qtd. in Leab, "I Was a Communist for the FBI," 93.

57. Leab, "I Was a Communist for the FBI," 94.

58. Richard Condon, *The Manchurian Candidate* (Simon & Schuster, 2004), 194.

59. Sayre, 96.

60. Condon, 358.

61. Condon, 332.

62. Condon, 332.

63. Condon, 332.

64. Lingeman, 183.

Chapter Four

1. Herman Melville, *The Confidence-Man: His Masquerade* (Signet, 1964), 9.

2. R. W. B. Lewis, Afterword, *The Confidence-Man: His Masquerade* by Herman Melville (Signet, 1964), 267.

3. Melville, 260.

4. Lewis, 276.

5. Edgar Allan Poe, "Diddling Considered as One of the Exact Sciences," *Edgar Allan Poe: Poetry and Tales* (Viking, 1984), 607.

6. Poe, 607.

7. Poe, 608.

8. Poe, 608.

9. Poe, 609.

10. Poe, 609.

11. Peter Fenton, *Eying the Flash: The Education of a Carnival Con Artist* (Simon & Schuster, 2005), 120.

12. Fenton, 121.

13. T. D. Thornton, *My Adventures with Your Money: George Graham Rice and the Golden Age of the Con Artist* (St. Martin's, 2015), 17.

14. Thornton, 196.

15. Thornton, 18.

16. Thornton, 20.
17. Maria Konnikova, *The Confidence Game: Why We Fall for It ... Every Time* (Viking, 2016), 5.
18. David W. Maurer, *The Big Con: The Story of the Confidence Man and the Confidence Game* (Pocket Books, 1949), 1.
19. Maurer, 8.
20. Maurer, 316.
21. Brook, 16.
22. Brook, 18.
23. Brook, 79.
24. Noah Isenberg, *Edgar G. Ulmer: A Filmmaker at the Margins* (University of California Press, 2014), 19.
25. Isenberg, 27.
26. Isenberg, 33.
27. Isenberg, 34.
28. Isenberg, 42.
29. Isenberg, 177.
30. Martin M. Goldsmith, *Detour* (Black Curtain, 2013), 7.
31. Goldsmith, 7.
32. Goldsmith, 22.
33. Goldsmith, 12.
34. Goldsmith, 14.
35. Goldsmith, 14.
36. Goldsmith, 45.
37. Goldsmith, 46.
38. Goldsmith, 56.
39. Goldsmith, 134.
40. Goldsmith, 29.
41. Goldsmith, 33.
42. Goldsmith, 40.
43. Qtd. in Isenberg, 183.
44. Goldsmith, 115.
45. Goldsmith, 115.
46. Goldsmith, 115.
47. Goldsmith, 128.
48. Qtd. in Isenberg, 184.
49. Goldsmith, 144.
50. Goldsmith, 144.
51. Goldsmith, 145.
52. Matthew Kennedy, *Edmund Goulding's Dark Victory: Hollywood's Genius Bad Boy* (The University of Wisconsin Press, 2004), 16–17.
53. Kennedy, 32–35.
54. Maurer, 175.
55. William Lindsay Gresham, *Nightmare Alley* (New York Review of Books, 2010), 221.
56. Kennedy, 249.
57. Gresham, 258.
58. Nick Tosches, Introduction, *Nightmare Alley* by William Lindsay Gresham (New York Review of Books), xiii.
59. Stephen Littger, *The Director's Cut: Picturing Hollywood in the 21st Century* (Continuum, 2006), 159.
60. Ira Nadel, *David Mamet: A Life in the Theatre* (Palgrave Macmillan, 2008), 153.
61. Yannis Tzioumakis, *The Spanish Prisoner* (Edinburgh University Press, 2009), 119–20.
62. Maurer, 315.
63. Maurer, 315.
64. Maurer, 313.

Chapter Five

1. Eugene Taylor, *Shadow Culture: Psychology and Spirituality in America* (Counterpoint, 1999), 17.
2. J. M. Bumsted, ed., *The Great Awakening: The Beginnings of Evangelical Pietism in America* (Blaisdell Publishing, 1970), 1.
3. Thomas S. Kidd, *The Great Awakening: The Roots of Evangelical Christianity in Colonial America* (Yale University Press, 2007), xix.
4. Kidd, xix.
5. Bumsted, 130.
6. Frank Lambert, *Inventing the "Great Awakening"* (Princeton University Press, 1999), 6.
7. Lambert, 8.
8. Lambert, 9.
9. Taylor, 18.
10. Jonathan Edwards, "Sinners in the Hands of an Angry God," *The Norton Anthology of American Literature*, vol. 1, 4th ed., edited by Nina Baym (Norton, 1994), 417.
11. Edwards, 414.
12. Edwards, 420.
13. Edwards, 423.
14. Taylor, 31.
15. Kidd, xiv.
16. David Harlan, *The Clergy and the Great Awakening in New England* (UMI Research, 1980), 3.
17. Lambert, 190, 191.
18. Lambert, 192.
19. Davis Grubb, *The Night of the Hunter* (Vintage Books, 2015), 30.
20. Grubb, 27.
21. Grubb, 27.
22. Grubb, 176.
23. Grubb, 211.
24. Grubb, 209.
25. Grubb, 233.
26. Grubb, 236.
27. Grubb, 241.
28. Grubb, 242.
29. Grubb, 244.
30. Grubb, 250.
31. David Thompson and Ian Christie, eds., *Scorsese on Scorsese* (Faber and Faber, 1996), 12.
32. Thompson and Christie, 13.
33. Qtd. in Thompson and Christie, 48.
34. Richard Schickel, *Conversations with Scorsese* (Knopf, 2011), 105.
35. Qtd. in Peter Occhiogrosso, *Once a Catholic: Prominent Catholics and Ex-Catholics Discuss the Influence of the Church on Their Lives and Work* (Houghton Mifflin, 1987), 92.
36. Qtd. in Littger, 167.
37. Lawrence F. Knapp, ed., *David Fincher: Interviews* (University Press of Mississippi, 2014), xxiii.

38. Qtd. in Mark Salisbury, "Seventh Hell," *Empire* (Feb. 1996), 83.

39. Mark Browning, *David Fincher: Films That Scar* (Praeger, 2010), 60.

40. Catharine Williams, *Fall River: An Authentic Narrative*, edited by Patricia Caldwell (Oxford University Press, 1993), back cover.

Chapter Six

1. J. H. Wallis, *The Woman in the Window (Once Off Guard)* (World Publishing Company, 1945), 9.

2. Wallis, 17.

3. Wallis, 18.

4. Wallis, 20.

5. Wallis, 38.

6. Wallis, 121.

7. Wallis, 124.

8. Wallis, 136.

9. Wallis, 162.

10. Wallis, 166.

11. Wallis, 198.

12. Gene D. Phillips, "Fritz Lang Remembers," *Fritz Lang: Interviews*, edited by Barry Keith Grant (University Press of Mississippi, 2003), 185.

13. John Wagner and Vince Locke, *A History of Violence* (Vertigo, 1997), 172.

14. Wagner and Locke, 187.

Filmography

Note: If what seem to be some odd choices appear on this filmography, it is because this study mentions additional films made by the directors and films that appear within the films analyzed, which are not necessarily films noir or neo-noirs. Actors are listed alphabetically, thus not necessarily in order of top billing. Producing companies are listed rather than distributors, and first billed producing companies only.

Alien 3. Directed by David Fincher, performances by Charles Dance, Charles S. Dutton, Paul McGann, and Sigourney Weaver, Twentieth Century Fox, 1992.

American Beauty. Directed by Sam Mendes, performances by Annette Bening, Wes Bentley, Thora Birch, and Kevin Spacey, Dreamworks Pictures, 1999.

Anatomy of a Murder. Directed by Otto Preminger, performances by Ben Gazzara, Arthur O'Connell, Lee Remick, and James Stewart, Otto Preminger Films, 1959.

Angel Face. Directed by Otto Preminger, performances by Mona Freeman, Herbert Marshall, Robert Mitchum, and Jean Simmons, RKO Radio Pictures, 1953.

Barbary Coast. Directed by Howard Hawks, performances by Walter Brennan, Miriam Hopkins, Joel McCrea, and Edward G. Robinson, The Samuel Goldwyn Company, 1935.

Barton Fink. Directed by Joel Coen and Ethan Coen, performances by Judy Davis, John Goodman, Michael Lerner, and John Turturro, Circle Films, 1991.

Batman Begins. Directed by Christopher Nolan, performances by Christian Bale, Michael Caine, Katie Holmes, and Liam Neeson, Warner Bros., 2005.

Beyond a Reasonable Doubt. Directed by Fritz Lang, performances by Dana Andrews, Sidney Blackmer, Joan Fontaine, and Arthur Franz, Bert E. Friedlob Productions, 1956.

The Big Chill. Directed by Lawrence Kasdan, performances by Tom Berenger, Glenn Close, Jeff Goldblum, and William Hurt, Columbia Pictures, 1983.

The Big Heat. Directed by Fritz Lang, performances by Jocelyn Brando, Glenn Ford, Gloria Grahame, and Alexander Scourby, Columbia Pictures, 1953.

The Big Lebowski. Directed by Joel Coen and Ethan Coen, performances by Jeff Bridges, Steve Buscemi, John Goodman, and Julianne Moore, Polygram Filmed Entertainment, 1998.

The Big Sleep. Directed by Howard Hawks, performances by Lauren Bacall, Humphrey Bogart, John Ridgely, and Martha Vickers, Warner Bros., 1946.

Birdman of Alcatraz. Directed by John Frankenheimer, performances by Neville Brand, Burt Lancaster, Karl Malden, and Thelma Ritter, Norma Productions, 1962.

The Black Cat. Directed by Edgar G. Ulmer, performances by Julie Bishop, Boris Karloff, Bela Lugosi, David Manners, Universal Pictures, 1934.

Blood Simple. Directed by Joel Coen and Ethan Coen, performances by John Getz, Dan Hedaya, Frances McDormand, and M. Emmet Walsh, River Road Productions, 1984.

The Blue Gardenia. Directed by Fritz Lang, performances by Anne Baxter, Raymond Burr, Richard Conte, and Ann Sothern, Alex Gottlieb Productions, 1953.

Blue Velvet. Directed by David Lynch, performances by Laura Dern, Dennis Hopper, Kyle MacLachlan, and Isabella Rossellini, De Laurentiis Entertainment Group, 1986.

Bluebeard. Directed by Edgar G. Ulmer, performances by Nils Asther, John Carradine, Jean Parker, and Ludwig Stossel, Producers Releasing Corporation, 1944.

Bluebeard's Eighth Wife. Directed by Ernst Lubitsch, performances by Claudette Colbert, Gary Cooper, Edward Everett Horton, and David Niven, Paramount Pictures, 1938.

Body Heat. Directed by Lawrence Kasdan, performances by Richard Crenna, Ted Danson, William Hurt, and Kathleen Turner, The Ladd Company, 1981.

Bohemian Rhapsody. Directed by Bryan Singer, performances by Lucy Boynton, Ben Hardy,

Gwilym Lee, and Rami Malek, Twentieth Century Fox, 2018.

Bombers B-52. Directed by Gordon Douglas, performances by Marsha Hunt, Karl Malden, Natalie Wood, and Efrem Zimbalist, Jr., Warner Bros., 1957.

The Border Sheriff. Directed by Robert N. Bradbury and Edgar G. Ulmer, performances by Olive Hasbrouck, Gilbert Holmes, Jack Hoxie, and S. E. Jennings, Universal Pictures, 1926.

Bringing Up Baby. Directed by Howard Hawks, performances by Walter Catlett, Cary Grant, Katharine Hepburn, and Charles Ruggles, RKO Radio Pictures, 1938.

The Brood. Directed by David Cronenberg, performances by Henry Beckman, Samantha Eggar, Art Hindle, and Oliver Reed, Canadian Film Development Corporation, 1979.

The Bubble. Directed by Arch Oboler, performances by Michael Cole, Johnny Desmond, Kassie McMahon and Deborah Walley, Arch Oboler Productions, 1966.

Bwana Devil. Directed by Arch Oboler, performances by Barbara Britton, Nigel Bruce, Ramsay Hill, and Robert Stack, Arch Oboler Productions, 1952.

The Cardinal. Directed by Otto Preminger, performances by Dorothy Gish, Carol Lynley, Maggie McNamara, and Tom Tryon, Otto Preminger Films, 1963.

Carmen Jones. Directed by Otto Preminger, performances by Pearl Bailey, Harry Belafonte, Dorothy Dandridge, and Olga James, Otto Preminger Films, 1954.

Casablanca. Directed by Michael Curtiz, performances by Ingrid Bergman, Humphrey Bogart, Paul Henreid, and Claude Rains, Warner Bros., 1942.

Chinatown. Directed by Roman Polanski, performances by Faye Dunaway, John Huston, Perry Lopez, and Jack Nicholson, Paramount Pictures, 1974.

Citizen Kane. Directed by Orson Welles, performances by Dorothy Comingore, Joseph Cotten, Agnes Moorehead, and Orson Welles, RKO Radio Pictures, 1941.

Cop Land. Directed by James Mangold, performances by Robert De Niro, Harvey Keitel, Ray Liotta, and Sylvester Stallone, Miramax, 1997.

Cosmopolis. Directed by David Cronenberg, performances by Kevin Durand, Sarah Gadon, Paul Giamatti, and Robert Pattinson, Alfama Films, 2012.

Cul-de-sac. Directed by Roman Polanski, performances by Francoise Dorleac, Jack MacGowran, Donald Pleasence, and Lionel Stander, Compton Films, 1966.

A Dangerous Method. Directed by David Cronenberg, performances by Vincent Cassel, Michael Fassbender, Keira Knightley, and Viggo Mortensen, Recorded Picture Company, 2011.

The Dark Knight. Directed by Christopher Nolan, performances by Christian Bale, Michael Caine, Aaron Eckhart, and Heath Ledger, Warner Bros., 2008.

The Dark Knight Rises. Directed by Christopher Nolan, performances by Christian Bale, Joseph Gordon-Levitt, Tom Hardy, and Gary Oldman, Warner Bros., 2012.

The Dawn Patrol. Directed by Edmund Goulding, performances by Donald Crisp, Errol Flynn, David Niven, and Basil Rathbone, Warner Bros., 1938.

Death and the Maiden. Directed by Roman Polanski, performances by Ben Kingsley, Krystia Mova, Sigourney Weaver, and Stuart Wilson, Fine Line Features, 1994.

Detour. Directed by Edgar G. Ulmer, performances by Claudia Drake, Edmund MacDonald, Tom Neal, and Ann Savage, Producers Releasing Corporation, 1945.

Detour. Directed by Wade Williams, performances by Susanna Foster, Lea Lavish, Erin McGrane, and Tom Neal, Jr., Mossman-Williams Productions, 1992.

Double Indemnity. Directed by Billy Wilder, performances by Jean Heather, Fred MacMurray, Edward G. Robinson, and Barbara Stanwyck, Paramount Pictures, 1944.

Dunkirk. Directed by Christopher Nolan, performances by Lee Armstrong, Aneurin Barnard, Damien Bonnard, and Fionn Whitehead, Warner Bros., 2017.

Eastern Promises. Directed by David Cronenberg, performances by Joseph Altin, Mina E. Mina, Viggo Mortensen, and Naomi Watts, Kudos Film and Television, 2007.

The Eternal Jew. Directed by Fritz Hippler, performances by Curt Bois, Charles Chaplin, Albert Einstein, and Adolf Hitler, Deutsche Filmherstellungs-und-Verwertungs-GmbH, Berlin, 1940.

eXistenZ. Directed by David Cronenberg, performances by Willem Dafoe, Ian Holm, Jude Law, and Jennifer Jason Leigh, Dimension Films, 1999.

Fallen Angel. Directed by Otto Preminger, performances by Dana Andrews, Charles Bickford, Linda Darnell, and Alice Faye, Twentieth Century Fox, 1945.

Fargo. Directed by Joel Coen and Ethan Coen, performances by Steve Buscemi, William H. Macy, Kristin Rudrud, and Peter Stormare, PolyGram Filmed Entertainment, 1996.

Fight Club. Directed by David Fincher, performances by Zach Grenier, Meat Loaf, Edward Norton, and Brad Pitt, Fox 2000 Pictures, 1999.

The Fly. Directed by David Cronenberg, performances by Joy Boushel, Geena Davis, John Getz, and Jeff Goldblum, SLM Production Group, 1986.

French Connection II. Directed by John Frankenheimer, performances by Bernard Fresson, Gene Hackman, Philippe Leotard, and Fernando Rey, Twentieth Century Fox, 1975.

French Kiss. Directed by Lawrence Kasdan, performances by Timothy Hutton, Kevin Kline, Jean Reno, and Meg Ryan, Polygram Filmed Entertainment, 1995.

Fury. Directed by Henry King, performances by Richard Barthelmess, Pat Hartigan, Barry Macollum, and Tyrone Power, Sr., Inspiration Pictures, 1923.

Gentlemen Prefer Blondes. Directed by Howard Hawks, performances by Charles Coburn, Marilyn Monroe, Elliott Reid, and Jane Russell, Twentieth Century Fox, 1953.

The Girl with the Dragon Tattoo. Directed by David Fincher, performances by Daniel Craig, Rooney Mara, Christopher Plummer, and Stellan Skarsgard, Columbia Pictures, 2011.

Gone Girl. Directed by David Fincher, performances by Ben Affleck, Neil Patrick Harris, Tyler Perry, and Rosamund Pike, Twentieth Century Fox, 2014.

Grand Canyon. Directed by Lawrence Kasdan, performances by Danny Glover, Kevin Kline, Steve Martin, and Mary McDonnell, Twentieth Century Fox, 1991.

Grand Hotel. Directed by Edmund Goulding, performances by John Barrymore, Wallace Beery, Joan Crawford, and Greta Garbo, Metro-Goldwyn-Mayer, 1932.

Heist. Directed by David Mamet, performances by Danny DeVito, Delroy Lindo, Gene Hackman, and Sam Rockwell, Morgan Creek Entertainment, 2001.

A History of Violence. Directed by David Cronenberg, performances by Maria Bello, Ed Harris, William Hurt, and Viggo Mortensen, New Line Cinema, 2005.

House of Games. Directed by David Mamet, performances by Lindsay Crouse, Joe Mantegna, Mike Nussbaum, and Lilia Skala, Filmhaus, 1987.

I Was a Communist for the F.B.I. Directed by Gordon Douglas, performances by Philip Carey, Dorothy Hart, Frank Lovejoy, and James Millican, Warner Bros., 1951.

The Iceman Cometh. Directed by John Frankenheimer, performances by Jeff Bridges, Fredric March, Lee Marvin, and Robert Ryan, Cinevision Ltee, 1973.

Identity. Directed by James Mangold, performances by John Cusack, John Hawkes, Ray Liotta, and Amanda Peet, Columbia Pictures, 2003.

In a Lonely Place. Directed by Nicholas Ray, performances by Humphrey Bogart, Gloria Grahame, Frank Lovejoy, and Carl Benton Reid, Santana Pictures Corporation, 1950.

In Like Flint. Directed by Gordon Douglas, performances by Lee J. Cobb, James Coburn, Andrew Duggan, and Jean Hale, Twentieth Century Fox, 1967.

In the Meantime, Darling. Directed by Otto Preminger, performances by Jeanne Crain, Frank Latimore, Mary Nash, and Eugene Pallette, Twentieth Century Fox, 1944.

Inception. Directed by Christopher Nolan, performances by Leonardo DiCaprio, Joseph Gordon-Levitt, Tom Hardy, and Elliot Page, Warner Bros., 2010.

Indiana Jones and the Temple of Doom. Directed by Steven Spielberg, performances by Kate Capshaw, Harrison Ford, Amrish Puri, and Ke Huy Quan, Paramount Pictures, 1984.

Insomnia. Directed by Christopher Nolan, performances by Martin Donovan, Al Pacino, Hilary Swank, and Oliver 'Ole' Zemen, Alcon Entertainment, 2002.

Interstellar. Directed by Christopher Nolan, performances by Ellen Burstyn, Mackenzie Foy, John Lithgow, and Matthew McConaughey, Paramount Pictures, 2014.

The Island of Dr. Moreau. Directed by John Frankenheimer, performances by Fairuza Balk, Marlon Brando, Val Kilmer, and David Thewlis, New Line Cinema, 1996.

Kate & Leopold. Directed by James Mangold, performances by Hugh Jackman, Breckin Meyer, Meg Ryan, and Liev Schreiber, Konrad Pictures, 2001.

Kidnapped. Directed by Alfred L. Werker and Otto Preminger, performances by Freddie Bartholomew, Warner Baxter, C. Aubrey Smith, and Arleen Whelan, Twentieth Century Fox, 1938.

Knife in the Water. Directed by Roman Polanski, performances by Zygmunt Malanowicz, Leon Niemczyk, and Jolanta Umecka, Zespol Filmowy "Kamera," 1962.

The Lady from Shanghai. Directed by Orson Welles, performances by Glenn Anders, Rita Hayworth, Everett Sloane, and Orson Welles, Mercury Productions, 1947.

The Last Temptation of Christ. Directed by Martin Scorsese, performances by Willem Dafoe, Harvey Keitel, Barbara Hershey, and Steve Shill, Universal Pictures, 1988.

Laura. Directed by Otto Preminger, performances by Dana Andrews, Vincent Price, Gene Tierney, and Clifton Webb, Twentieth Century Fox, 1944.

Le Roman d'un Tricheur (The Story of a Cheat). Directed by Sacha Guitry, performances by Sacha Guitry, Adolphe Borchard, Marcel Lucien, and Raymond Clunie, Cineas, 1936.

The Lost Weekend. Directed by Billy Wilder, performances by Howard Da Silva, Ray Milland, Phillip Terry, and Jane Wyman, Paramount Pictures, 1945.

M. Directed by Fritz Lang, performances by Inge Landgut, Peter Lorre, Otto Wernicke, and Ellen Widmann, Nero-Film AG, 1931.

Macbeth. Directed by Orson Welles, performances by Roddy McDowall, Jeanette Nolan, Dan O'Herlihy, and Orson Welles, Mercury Productions, 1948.

The Magnificent Ambersons. Directed by Orson Welles, performances by Anne Baxter, Dolores Costello, Joseph Cotten, and Tim Holt, Mercury Productions, 1942.

The Major and the Minor. Directed by Billy Wilder, performances by Robert Benchley, Rita

Johnson, Ray Milland, and Ginger Rogers, Paramount Pictures, 1942.

The Maltese Falcon. Directed by John Huston, performances by Mary Astor, Humphrey Bogart, Gladys George, and Peter Lorre, Warner Bros., 1941.

The Man with the Golden Arm. Directed by Otto Preminger, performances by Kim Novak, Eleanor Parker, Frank Sinatra, and Arnold Stang, Otto Preminger Films, 1955.

The Manchurian Candidate. Directed by John Frankenheimer, performances by Laurence Harvey, Angela Lansbury, Janet Leigh, and Frank Sinatra, M.C. Productions, 1962.

The Manchurian Candidate. Directed by Jonathan Demme, performances by Liev Schreiber, Meryl Streep, Jon Voight, and Denzel Washington, Paramount Pictures, 2004.

Mank. Directed by David Fincher, performances by Lily Collins, Gary Oldman, Tom Pelphrey, and Amanda Seyfried, Netflix, 2020.

Maps to the Stars. Directed by David Cronenberg, performances by Evan Bird, John Cusack, Julianne Moore, and Mia Wasikowska, Prospero Pictures, 2014.

Mauvaise Graine (Bad Seed). Directed by Billy Wilder and Alexander Esway, performances by Danielle Darrieux, Paul Escoffier, Raymond Galle, and Pierre Mingand, Compagnie Nouvelle Commerciale, 1934.

Mean Streets. Directed by Martin Scorsese, performances by Robert De Niro, Harvey Keitel, David Proval, and Amy Robinson, Warner Bros., 1973.

Memento. Directed by Christopher Nolan, performances by Carrie-Anne Moss, Joe Pantoliano, Guy Pearce, and Stephen Tobolowsky, Newmarket Capital Group, 2000.

Menschen am Sonntag (People on Sunday). Directed by Robert Siodmak and Edgar G. Ulmer, performances by Brigitte Borchert, Christl Ehlers, Erwin Splettstober, and Wolfgang von Waltershausen, Film Studio 1929, 1930.

Metropolis. Directed by Fritz Lang, performances by Alfred Abel, Gustav Frohlich, Brigitte Helm, and Rudolf Klein-Rogge, Universum Film, 1927.

Miller's Crossing. Directed by Joel Coen and Ethan Coen, performances by Gabriel Byrne, Marcia Gay Harden, Jon Polito, and John Turturro, Circle Films, 1990.

Ministry of Fear. Directed by Fritz Lang, performances by Hillary Brooke, Carl Esmond, Ray Milland, and Marjorie Reynolds, Paramount Pictures, 1944.

Murder, My Sweet. Directed by Edward Dmytryk, performances by Otto Kruger, Dick Powell, Anne Shirley, and Claire Trevor, RKO Radio Pictures, 1944.

Murder Is My Beat. Directed by Edgar G. Ulmer, performances by Paul Langton, Barbara Payton, Selena Royle, and Robert Shayne, Masthead Productions, 1955.

The Naked Kiss. Directed by Samuel Fuller, performances by Michael Dante, Anthony Eisley, Virginia Grey, and Constance Towers, Allied Artists Pictures, 1964.

The Night of the Hunter. Directed by Charles Laughton, performances by Billy Chapin, Lillian Gish, Robert Mitchum, and Shelley Winters, Paul Gregory Productions, 1955.

Nightmare Alley. Directed by Edmund Goulding, performances by Joan Blondell, Coleen Gray, Tyrone Power, and Helen Walker, Twentieth Century Fox, 1947.

Nightmare Alley. Directed by Guillermo del Toro, performances by Cate Blanchett, Toni Collette, Bradley Cooper, and Rooney Mara, Fox Searchlight Pictures, 2021.

Notorious. Directed by Alfred Hitchcock, performances by Ingrid Bergman, Louis Calhern, Cary Grant, and Claude Rains, RKO Radio Pictures, 1946.

An Officer and a Spy. Directed by Roman Polanski, performances by Louis Garrel, Stefan Godin, Christophe Maratier, and Pierre Poirot, Legende Films, 2019.

Oleanna. Directed by David Mamet, performances by Debra Eisenstadt, William H. Macy, Diego Pineda, and Scott Zigler, Bay Kinescope, 1994.

On Dangerous Ground. Directed by Nicholas Ray, performances by Ward Bond, Charles Kemper, Ida Lupino, and Robert Ryan, RKO Radio Pictures, 1951.

Othello. Directed by Orson Welles, performances by Suzanne Cloutier, Robert Coote, Micheal MacLiammoir, and Orson Welles, Scalera Film, 1951.

Park Row. Directed by Samuel Fuller, performances by Gene Evans, Herbert Heyes, Bela Kovacs, and Mary Welch, Samuel Fuller Productions, 1952.

Phantom of the Opera. Directed by Arthur Lubin, performances by Edgar Barrier, Nelson Eddy, Susanna Foster, and Claude Rains, Universal Pictures, 1943.

The Pianist. Directed by Roman Polanski, performances by Adrien Brody, Emilia Fox, Ed Stoppard, and Michal Zebrowski, R.P. Productions, 2002.

Pickup on South Street. Directed by Samuel Fuller, performances by Jean Peters, Thelma Ritter, Richard Widmark, and Murvyn Vye, Twentieth Century Fox, 1953.

The Postman Always Rings Twice. Directed by Tay Garnett, performances by Hume Cronyn, John Garfield, Cecil Kellaway, and Lana Turner, Metro-Goldwyn-Mayer, 1946.

The Postman Always Rings Twice. Directed by Bob Rafelson, performances by John Colicos, Jessica Lang, Michael Lerner, and Jack Nicholson, CIP Filmproduktion GmbH, 1981.

Psycho. Directed by Alfred Hitchcock, performances by John Gavin, Janet Leigh, Vera Miles, and Anthony Perkins, Shamley Productions, 1960.

Public Access. Directed by Bryan Singer, performances by Leigh Hunt, Ron Marquette, John

Renshaw, and Bert Williams, Cinemabeam, 1993.

Queen Kelly. Directed by Erich von Stroheim, performances by Sylvia Ashton, Walter Byron, Seena Owen, and Gloria Swanson, Gloria Swanson Pictures, 1932.

The Razor's Edge. Directed by Edmund Goulding, performances by Anne Baxter, John Payne, Tyrone Power, and Gene Tierney, Twentieth Century Fox, 1946.

Rebel Without a Cause. Directed by Nicholas Ray, performances by Jim Backus, James Dean, Sal Mineo, and Natalie Wood, Warner Bros., 1955.

Repulsion. Directed by Roman Polanski, performances by Catherine Deneuve, John Fraser, Ian Hendry, and Yvonne Furneaux, Compton Films, 1965.

Rosemary's Baby. Directed by Roman Polanski, performances by Sidney Blackmer, John Cassavetes, Mia Farrow, and Ruth Gordon, William Castle Productions, 1968.

Ruthless. Directed by Edgar G. Ulmer, performances by Sydney Greenstreet, Louis Hayward, Diana Lynn, and Zachary Scott, Arthur S. Lyons Productions, 1948.

Samson and Delilah. Directed by Cecil B. DeMille, performances by Hedy Lamarr, Victor Mature, George Sanders, and Angela Lansbury, Paramount Pictures, 1949.

Scarface. Directed by Howard Hawks and Richard Rosson, performances by Ann Dvorak, Karen Morley, Paul Muni, and Osgood Perkins, The Caddo Company, 1932.

Scarlet Street. Directed by Fritz Lang, performances by Joan Bennett, Dan Duryea, Margaret Lindsay, and Edward G. Robinson, Fritz Lang Productions, 1945.

Sergeant York. Directed by Howard Hawks, performances by Walter Brennan, Gary Cooper, Joan Leslie, and George Tobias, Warner Bros., 1941.

Se7en. Directed by David Fincher, performances by Morgan Freeman, Gwyneth Paltrow, Brad Pitt, and Kevin Spacey, New Line Cinema, 1995.

Shadow of a Doubt. Directed by Alfred Hitchcock, performances by Macdonald Carey, Joseph Cotten, Henry Travers, and Teresa Wright, Universal Pictures, 1943.

Shock Corridor. Directed by Samuel Fuller, performances by James Best, Peter Breck, Gene Evans, and Constance Towers, Allied Artists Pictures, 1963.

Silverado. Directed by Lawrence Kasdan, performances by Kevin Costner, Scott Glenn, Danny Glover, and Kevin Kline, Columbia Pictures, 1985.

The Spanish Prisoner. Directed by David Mamet, performances by Ricky Jay, Steve Martin, Rebecca Pidgeon, and Campbell Scott, Jasmine Productions Inc., 1997.

Stagecoach. Directed by John Ford, performances by John Carradine, Andy Devine, Claire Trevor, and John Wayne, Walter Wanger Productions, 1939.

Stagecoach. Directed by Gordon Douglas, performances by Mike Connors, Alex Cord, Bing Crosby, and Ann-Margret, Twentieth Century Fox, 1966.

Star Wars: Episode V—The Empire Strikes Back. Directed by Irvin Kershner, performances by Carrie Fisher, Harrison Ford, Mark Hamill, and Billy Dee Williams, Lucasfilm, 1980.

Star Wars: Episode VI—Return of the Jedi. Directed by Richard Marquand, performances by Carrie Fisher, Harrison Ford, Mark Hamill, and Billy Dee Williams, Lucasfilm, 1983.

Strange Holiday. Directed by Arch Oboler, performances by Gloria Holden, Martin Kosleck, Claude Rains, and Bob Stebbins, Elite Pictures, 1945.

Strange Illusion. Directed by Edgar G. Ulmer, performances by Sally Eilers, Jimmy Lydon, Regis Toomey, and Warren William, Producers Releasing Corporation, 1945.

The Strange Woman. Directed by Edgar G. Ulmer, performances by Louis Hayward, Hedy Lamarr, Gene Lockhart, and George Sanders, Hunt Stromberg Productions, 1946.

The Stranger. Directed by Orson Welles, performances by Philip Merivale, Edward G. Robinson, Orson Welles, and Loretta Young, International Pictures, 1946.

Strangers on a Train. Directed by Alfred Hitchcock, performances by Leo G. Carroll, Farley Granger, Ruth Roman, and Robert Walker, Warner Bros., 1951.

Sun-Up. Directed by Edmund Goulding, performances by Sam De Grasse, Lucille La Verne, Conrad Nagel, and Pauline Starke, Metro-Goldwyn-Mayer, 1925.

Sunrise. Directed by F. W. Murnau, performances by Janet Gaynor, Margaret Livingston, George O'Brien, and Bodil Rosing, Fox Film Corporation, 1927.

Sunset Boulevard. Directed by Billy Wilder, performances by William Holden, Nancy Olson, Gloria Swanson, and Erich von Stroheim, Paramount Pictures, 1950.

Tenet. Directed by Christopher Nolan, performances by Elizabeth Debicki, Robert Pattinson, Juhan Ulfsak, and John David Washington, Warner Bros., 2020.

Tess. Directed by Roman Polanski, performances by John Collin, Peter Firth, Nastassja Kinski, and Rosemary Martin, Renn Productions, 1979.

They Call Me Mr. Tibbs! Directed by Gordon Douglas, performances by Martin Landau, Barbara McNair, Sidney Poitier, and Anthony Zerbe, The Mirisch Corporation, 1970.

They Live by Night. Directed by Nicholas Ray, performances by Howard Da Silva, Jay C. Flippen, Farley Granger, and Cathy O'Donnell, RKO Radio Pictures, 1948.

The Thing from Another World. Directed by Christian Nyby and Howard Hawks, performances by Robert Cornthwaite, Margaret Sheridan, Douglas Spencer, and Kenneth Tobey, Winchester Pictures Corporation, 1951.

3:10 to Yuma. Directed by James Mangold, performances by Christian Bale, Russell Crowe, Logan Lerman, and Dallas Roberts, Lionsgate, 2007.

The Tomb of Ligeiae. Directed by Roger Corman, performances by Derek Francis, Vincent Price, Elizabeth Shepherd, and John Westbrook, Alta Vista Productions, 1964.

Touch of Evil. Directed by Orson Welles, performances by Joseph Calleia, Charlton Heston, Janet Leigh, and Orson Welles, Universal International Pictures, 1958.

The Usual Suspects. Directed by Bryan Singer, performances by Gabriel Byrne, Chazz Palminteri, Pete Postlethwaite, and Kevin Spacey, PolyGram Filmed Entertainment, 1995.

Vertigo. Directed by Alfred Hitchcock, performances by Barbara Bel Geddes, Tom Helmore, Kim Novak, and James Stewart, Alfred J. Hitchcock Productions, 1958.

Videodrome. Directed by David Cronenberg, performances by Peter Dvorsky, Deborah Harry, Sonja Smits, and James Woods, Filmplan International, 1983.

Walk the Line. Directed by James Mangold, performances by Ginnifer Goodwin, Robert Patrick, Joaquin Phoenix, and Reese Witherspoon, Fox 2000 Pictures, 2005.

Where the Sidewalk Ends. Directed by Otto Preminger, performances by Dana Andrews, Bert Freed, Gary Merrill, and Gene Tierney, Twentieth Century Fox, 1950.

The Wolverine. Directed by James Mangold, performances by Rila Fukushima, Hugh Jackman, Will Yun Lee, and Tao Okamoto, Twentieth Century Fox, 2013.

The Woman in the Window. Directed by Fritz Lang, performances by Joan Bennett, Edmund Breon, Raymond Massey, and Edward G. Robinson, International Pictures, 1944.

Young at Heart. Directed by Gordon Douglas, performances by Ethel Barrymore, Doris Day, Frank Sinatra, and Gig Young, Arwin Productions, 1954.

Zodiac. Directed by David Fincher, performances by Robert Downey, Jr., Anthony Edwards, Jake Gyllenhaal, and Mark Ruffalo, Paramount Pictures, 2007.

Zombies on Broadway. Directed by Gordon Douglas, performances by Wally Brown, Alan Carney, Anne Jeffreys, and Bela Lugosi, RKO Radio Pictures, 1945.

Bibliography

Adams, Jeffrey. *The Cinema of the Coen Brothers: Hard-boiled Entertainments*. Wallflower Press, 2015.

Allen, William Rodney. Introduction. *The Coen Brothers: Interviews*. University Press of Mississippi, 2006, pp. ix–xxiii.

Anderson, Edward. *Thieves Like Us*. 1937. Black Curtain, 2013.

Andrew, Geoff. *The Films of Nicholas Ray: The Poet of Nightfall*. 2nd ed., British Film Institute Publishing, 2004.

Beaty, Bart. *David Cronenberg's A History of Violence*. University of Toronto Press, 2008.

Biesen, Sheri Chinen. *Blackout: World War II and the Origins of Film Noir*. The Johns Hopkins University Press, 2005.

Bliss, Michael. *The Word Made Flesh: Catholics and Conflict in the Films of Martin Scorsese*. Scarecrow Press, 1995.

Blottner, Gene. *Columbia Noir: A Complete Filmography, 1940–1962*. McFarland, 2015.

Bogdanovich, Peter. *Fritz Lang in America*. Praeger, 1969.

Brady, Frank. *Citizen Wells: A Biography of Orson Welles*. Charles Scribner's Sons, 1989.

Brodt, Zach. "Record #17—Matt Cvetic HUAC Testimony." *ULS Archives and Manuscripts @ Pitt,* University of Pittsburgh.

Brody, Richard. "The Bigger Sleep." *The New Yorker,* 15 Dec. 2014, p. 14.

Brook, Vincent. *Driven to Darkness: Jewish Émigré Directors and the Rise of Film Noir*. Rutgers University Press, 2009.

Browning, Mark. *David Fincher: Films That Scar*. Praeger, 2010.

Bumsted, J. M., ed. *The Great Awakening: The Beginnings of Evangelical Pietism in America*. Blaisdell Publishing, 1970.

Cain, James M. *Double Indemnity*. 1943. Vintage Crime/Black Lizard, 1992.

Cameron, Ian, ed. *The Book of Film Noir*. Continuum, 1992.

Casillo, Robert. *Gangster Priest: The Italian American Cinema of Martin Scorsese*. University of Toronto Press, 2006.

Caspary, Vera. *Laura*. 1942. The Feminist Press, 2005.

———. "My 'Laura' and Otto's." *The Saturday Review,* 26 June 1971, pp. 36–37.

Chandler, Raymond. *The Big Sleep*. 1939. Vintage Crime/Black Lizard, 1992.

———. "The Simple Art of Murder." 1944. *The Simple Art of Murder*. Houghton Mifflin, 1950, pp. 519–33.

Chartier, Jean-Pierre. "Americans Also Make Noir Films." Translated by Alain Silver. *Film Noir Reader 2,* edited by Alain Silver and James Ursini, Limelight Editions, 1999, pp. 21–23.

Christopher, Nicholas. *Somewhere in the Night: Film Noir and the American City*. The Free Press, 1997.

Coen, Ethan, and Joel Coen. "Blood Simple." *Collected Screenplays Volume I*. Faber & Faber, 2002, pp. 1–109.

Comito, Terry, ed. *Touch of Evil: Orson Welles, Director*. Rutgers University Press, 1985.

Condon, Richard. *The Manchurian Candidate*. 1959. Simon & Schuster, 2004.

Connelly, Marie Katheryn. *Martin Scorsese: An Analysis of His Feature Films, with a Filmography of His Entire Directorial Career*. McFarland, 1993.

Cronin, Paul, ed. *Roman Polanski: Interviews*. University Press of Mississippi, 2005.

Crowe, Cameron. *Conversations with Wilder*. Knopf, 2001.

Dick, Bernard F. *The Screen is Red: Hollywood, Communism, and the Cold War*. University Press of Mississippi, 2016.

Dimendberg, Edward. *Film Noir and the Spaces of Modernity*. Harvard University Press, 2004.

Dyer, Richard. *Seven*. British Film Institute Publishing, 1999.

"Early Los Angeles Historical Buildings (1925+)." *Water and Power Associates,* Water and Power Associates, n.d., https://waterandpower.org/museum/Early_LA_Buildings(1925+)_4_of_8.html.

Edwards, Jonathan. "Sinners in the Hands of an Angry God." 1741. *The Norton Anthology of American Literature, Volume 1*. 4th ed., edited by Nina Baym, Norton, 1994, pp. 412–23.

Ehrenstein, David. *Masters of Cinema: Roman Polanski*. Phaidon, 2012.

Eisenschitz, Bernard. *Nicholas Ray: An American Journey*. Translated by Tom Milne, Faber & Faber, 1993.

Eisner, Lotte H. *Fritz Lang*. Secker and Warburg, 1976.

Emerson, Ralph Waldo. "Compensation." *Essays: First Series.* 1841. *The Complete Essays and Other Writings of Ralph Waldo Emerson.* Random House, 1950, pp. 170–89.

Fenton, Peter. *Eying the Flash: The Education of a Carnival Con Artist.* Simon & Schuster, 2005.

Frank, Nino. "A New Kind of Police Drama: The Criminal Adventure." Translated by Alain Silver. *Film Noir Reader 2,* edited by Alain Silver and James Ursini, Limelight Editions, 1999, pp. 15–19.

Friedman, Lawrence S. *The Cinema of Martin Scorsese.* Continuum, 1997.

Fujiwara, Chris. *The World and Its Double: The Life and Work of Otto Preminger.* Faber & Faber, 2008.

Fuller, Samuel. *A Third Face: My Tale of Writing, Fighting, and Filmmaking.* Knopf, 2002.

Furby, Jacqueline, and Stuart Joy, eds. *The Cinema of Christopher Nolan: Imagining the Impossible.* Wallflower Press, 2015.

Gemünden, Gerd. *A Foreign Affair: Billy Wilder's American Films.* Berghahn Books, 2008.

Goldsmith, Martin M. *Detour.* 1939. Black Curtain, 2013.

"Graham Greene, 86, Dies; Novelist of the Soul." *The New York Times,* 4 April 1991, p. A 1.

Grant, Barry Keith. Introduction. *Fritz Lang: Interviews,* edited by Barry Keith Grant. University Press of Mississippi, 2003, pp. vii–xvi.

Greene, Graham. *The Ministry of Fear. 3 By Graham Greene.* Viking, 1943, pp. 1–175.

Gresham, William Lindsay. *Nightmare Alley.* 1946. New York Review of Books, 2010.

Grubb, Davis. *The Night of the Hunter.* 1953. Vintage Books, 2015.

Gunning, Tom. *The Films of Fritz Lang: Allegories of Vision and Modernity.* British Film Institute Publishing, 2000.

Hammett, Dashiell. *Red Harvest.* 1929. *Dashiell Hammett: Five Complete Novels.* Avenel Books, 1980.

Hare, William. *Pulp Fiction to Film Noir: The Great Depression and the Development of a Genre.* McFarland, 2012.

Harlan, David. *The Clergy and the Great Awakening in New England.* UMI Research, 1980.

Henley, William Ernest. "Invictus." *Poets.org,* Academy of American Poets, n.d.

Heylin, Clinton. *Despite the System: Orson Welles Versus the Hollywood Studios.* Chicago Review Press, 2005.

Higham, Charles, and Joel Greenberg. "Interview with Fritz Lang." *Fritz Lang: Interviews,* edited by Barry Keith Grant, University Press of Mississippi, 2003, pp. 101–26. Excerpted from *The Celluloid Muse: Hollywood Directors Speak,* by Charles Higham and Joel Greenberg, Dutton Signet, 1969.

Hinson, Al. "Bloodlines." *The Coen Brothers: Interviews,* edited by William Rodney Allen. University Press of Mississippi, 2006, pp. 3–16.

Hirsch, Foster. *The Dark Side of the Screen: Film Noir.* Barnes and Company, 1981.

_____. *Detours and Lost Highways: A Map of Neo-Noir.* Limelight Editions, 1999.

_____. *Otto Preminger: The Man Who Would Be King.* Knopf, 2007.

Horton, Robert. Introduction. *Billy Wilder: Interviews,* edited by Robert Horton, University Press of Mississippi, 2001, pp. vii–xvii.

Isenberg, Noah. *Edgar G. Ulmer: A Filmmaker at the Margins.* University of California Press, 2014.

Jameson, Fredric. *Raymond Chandler: The Detections of Totality.* Verso, 2016.

Jenkins, Philip. *The Cold War at Home: The Red Scare in Pennsylvania, 1945–1960.* The University of North Carolina Press, 1999.

Kane, Leslie, ed. *The Art of Cinema: The Plays and Films of Harold Pinter and David Mamet.* Routledge, 2004.

Kanfer, Stefan. *Tough Without a Gun: The Life and Extraordinary Afterlife of Humphrey Bogart.* Knopf, 2011.

Kasdan, Lawrence. *Body Heat: An Original Screenplay.* Screentalk, 1980, www.dailyscript.com/scripts/BodyHeat.pdf.

Keaney, Michael F. *Film Noir Guide: 745 Films of the Classic Era, 1940–1959.* McFarland, 2003.

Kelly, Mary Pat. *Martin Scorsese: A Journey.* Thunder's Mouth Press, 2004.

Kennedy, Matthew. *Edmund Goulding's Dark Victory: Hollywood's Genius Bad Boy.* The University of Wisconsin Press, 2004.

Kidd, Thomas S. *The Great Awakening: The Roots of Evangelical Christianity in Colonial America.* Yale University Press, 2007.

Knapp, Lawrence F., ed. *David Fincher: Interviews.* University Press of Mississippi, 2014.

Knight, Stephen. "'A Hard Cheerfulness': An Introduction to Raymond Chandler." *American Crime Fiction,* ed. Brian Docherty. St. Martins, 1988, pp. 71–87.

Kobler, John. "A Study of the Snyder-Gray Case." *The Trial of Ruth Snyder and Judd Gray,* edited by John Kobler. Doubleday, Doran and Company, 1938, pp. 1–67.

Konnikova, Maria. *The Confidence Game: Why We Fall for It … Every Time.* Viking, 2016.

Koszarski, Richard. *Hollywood Directors 1941–1976.* Oxford University Press, 1977.

Krutnik, Frank, Steve Neale, Brian Neve, and Peter Stanfield, eds. *"Un-American" Hollywood: Politics and Film in the Blacklist Era.* Rutgers University Press, 2007.

Lambert, Frank. *Inventing the "Great Awakening."* Princeton University Press, 1999.

Lang, Fritz. "Fritz Lang: Autobiography." In *Fritz Lang* by Lotte H. Eisner. Secker and Warburg, 1976, pp. 9–15.

Leab, Dan. *I Was a Communist for the FBI: The Unhappy Life and Times of Matt Cvetic.* The Pennsylvania State University Press, 2000.

_____. "I Was a Communist for the FBI." *The Movies as History: Visions of the Twentieth Century,* edited by David Ellwood, Sutton, 2000, pp. 85–94.

Leaming, Barbara. *Orson Welles: A Biography.* Viking, 1985.

Lewis, R. W. B. Afterword. *The Confidence-Man: His Masquerade,* by Herman Melville. Signet, 1964, pp. 261–76.

Lingeman, Richard. *The Noir Forties: The American People from Victory to Cold War.* Nation Books, 2012.

Littger, Stephen. *The Director's Cut: Picturing Hollywood in the 21st Century.* Continuum, 2006.

LoBrutto, Vincent. *Martin Scorsese: A Biography.* Praeger, 2008.

Mast, Gerald. *Howard Hawks, Storyteller.* Oxford University Press, 1982.

_____. *A Short History of the Movies.* 2nd ed., Bobbs-Merrill, 1976.

Masterson, Whit. 1956. *Badge of Evil.* Prologue Books, 2013.

Maurer, David W. *The Big Con: The Story of the Confidence Man and the Confidence Game.* 1940. Pocket Books, 1949.

Mazierska, Ewa. *Roman Polanski: The Cinema of a Cultural Traveler.* I. B. Taurus, 2007.

McCarthy, Todd. *Howard Hawks: The Grey Fox of Hollywood.* Grove, 1997.

McGilligan, Patrick. *Fritz Lang: The Nature of the Beast.* St. Martin's, 1997.

_____. *Nicholas Ray: The Glorious Failure of an American Director.* HarperCollins, 2011.

Melville, Herman. *The Confidence-Man: His Masquerade.* 1857. Signet, 1964.

Miklitsch, Robert. *I Died a Million Times: Gangster Noir in Midcentury America.* University of Illinois Press, 2021.

Moustakas, Jane. "'Down these mean streets a man must go...': Film Noir, Masculinity, and The Big Sleep." *Australian Screen Education Online,* vol. 35, 2004, pp. 105–108.

Muller, Eddie. *Dark City: The Lost World of Film Noir.* Rev. ed., Running Press Adult, 2021.

Munby, Jonathan. *Public Enemies, Public Heroes: Screening the Gangster from Little Caesar to Touch of Evil.* The University of Chicago Press, 1999.

Nadel, Ira. *David Mamet: A Life in the Theatre.* Palgrave Macmillan, 2008.

Naremore, James. *Film Noir: A Very Short Introduction.* Oxford University Press, 2019.

_____. *The Magic World of Orson Welles.* Centennial Anniversary ed., University of Illinois Press, 2015.

_____. *More Than Night: Film Noir in Its Contexts.* University of California Press, 2008.

Neve, Brian. *Film and Politics in America: A Social Tradition.* Routledge, 1992.

Nolan, Christopher. *Memento & Following.* Faber & Faber, 2001.

Nolan, Jonathan. "Memento Mori." *Esquire,* vol. 135, no. 3, March 2001, pp. 186–91.

Occhiogrosso, Peter. *Once a Catholic: Prominent Catholics and Ex-Catholics Discuss the Influence of the Church on Their Lives and Work.* Houghton Mifflin, 1987.

Pelizzon, V. Penelope, and Nancy M. West. "Multiple Indemnity: Film Noir, James M. Cain and Adaptations of a Tabloid Case." *Narrative,* vol. 13, no. 3, 2005, pp. 211–37.

Phillips, Gene D. *Exiles in Hollywood: Major European Film Directors in America.* Lehigh University Press, 1998.

_____. "Fritz Lang Remembers." *Fritz Lang: Interviews,* edited by Barry Keith Grant, University Press of Mississippi, 2003, pp. 175–87. Originally published in *Focus on Film,* vol. 20, Spring 1975, pp. 43–51.

_____. *Out of the Shadows: Expanding the Canon of Classic Film Noir.* Scarecrow Press, 2012.

Phillips, Jayne Anne. *Quiet Dell: A Novel.* Simon & Schuster, 2013.

Poe, Edgar Allan. "Diddling Considered as One of the Exact Sciences." 1845. *Edgar Allan Poe: Poetry and Tales.* Viking, 1984, pp. 607–17.

Polanski, Roman. *Roman by Polanski.* William Morrow, 1984.

Preminger, Otto. *Preminger: An Autobiography.* Doubleday, 1977.

Rausch, Andrew J. *The Films of Martin Scorsese and Robert De Niro.* Scarecrow Press, 2010.

Raymond, Marc. *Hollywood's New Yorker: The Making of Martin Scorsese.* State University of New York Press, 2013.

Rosenbaum, Jonathan, ed. *This is Orson Welles: Orson Welles and Peter Bogdanovich.* HarperCollins, 1992.

Rybin, Steven, and Will Scheibel, eds. *Lonely Places, Dangerous Ground: Nicholas Ray in American Cinema.* State University of New York Press, 2014.

Salisbury, Mark. "Seventh Hell." *Empire,* Feb. 1996, pp. 78–85, 87.

Sandford, Christopher. *Polanski: A Biography.* Palgrave MacMillan, 2008.

Sarat, Austin, and Martha Merrill Umphrey. "The Justice of Jurisdiction: The Policing and Breaching of Boundaries in Orson Welles' *Touch of Evil.*" *English Language Notes,* vol. 48, no. 2, 2010, pp. 111–28.

Sayer, Nora. *Running Time: Films of the Cold War.* Dial, 1982.

Sbardellati, John. *J. Edgar Hoover Goes to the Movies: The FBI and the Origins of Hollywood's Cold War.* Cornell University Press, 2012.

Schickel, Richard. *Conversations with Scorsese.* Knopf, 2011.

Schwartz, Ronald. *Film Noir, Now and Then: Film Noir Originals and Remakes (1944–1999).* Greenwood, 2001.

_____. *Houses of Noir: Dark Visions from Thirteen Film Studios.* McFarland, 2014.

Scorsese, Martin. Foreword. *A Third Face: My Tale of Writing, Fighting, and Filmmaking,* by Samuel Fuller, Knopf, 2002, pp. ix–x.

Server, Lee. *Sam Fuller, Film Is a Battleground: A Critical Study, with Interviews, a Filmography and a Bibliography.* McFarland, 1994.

Sikov, Ed. *On Sunset Boulevard: The Life and Times*

of Billy Wilder. University Press of Mississippi, 2017.

Silver, Alain, and James Ursini. *American Neo-Noir: The Movie Never Ends.* Applause Theatre and Cinema Books, 2015.

Silver, Alain, and James Ursini, eds. *Film Noir: The Directors.* Limelight Editions, 2012.

Smedley, Nick. *A Divided World: Hollywood Cinema and Émigré Directors in the Era of Roosevelt and Hitler, 1933–1948.* Intellect, 2011.

Smith, Ella. *Starring Miss Barbara Stanwyck.* Crown, 1974.

Soister, John T. *Claude Rains: A Comprehensive Illustrated Reference to His Work in Film, Stage, Radio, Television and Recordings.* McFarland, 1999.

Spicer, Andrew, and Helen Hanson, eds. *A Companion to Film Noir.* Wiley Blackwell, 2013.

Staggs, Sam. *Close-up on Sunset Boulevard: Billy Wilder, Norma Desmond, and the Dark Hollywood Dream.* St. Martin's, 2002.

Stubbs, John C. "The Evolution of Orson Welles's 'Touch of Evil' from Novel to Film." *Cinema Journal,* vol. 24, no. 2, 1985, pp. 19–39.

Taylor, Eugene. *Shadow Culture: Psychology and Spirituality in America.* Counterpoint, 1999.

Thompson, David, and Ian Christie, eds. *Scorsese on Scorsese.* Faber & Faber, 1996.

Thornton, T. D. *My Adventures with Your Money: George Graham Rice and the Golden Age of the Con Artist.* St. Martin's, 2015.

Tosches, Nick. Introduction. *Nightmare Alley,* by William Lindsay Gresham, New York Review of Books, 1974, pp. vii–xiii.

Tratner, Michael. *Crowd Scenes: Movies and Mass Politics.* Fordham University Press, 2008. e-Book Collection (EBSCOhost).

Trivas, Victor. *The Stranger (1946): Shooting Script.* Alexander Street Press, 2003. e-Book Collection (EBSCOhost).

Tzioumakis, Yannis. *The Spanish Prisoner.* Edinburgh University Press, 2009.

Wagner, John, and Vince Locke. *A History of Violence.* Vertigo, 1997.

Wallis, J. H. *The Woman in the Window (Once Off Guard).* 1942. World Publishing Company, 1945.

Wernblad, Annette. *The Passion of Martin Scorsese: A Critical Study of the Films.* McFarland, 2011.

Whitfield, Stephen J. *The Culture of the Cold War.* 2nd ed., The Johns Hopkins University Press, 1996.

Williams, Catharine. *Fall River: An Authentic Narrative.* 1833. Edited by Patricia Caldwell, Oxford University Press, 1993.

Williams, Tom. *A Mysterious Something in the Light: The Life of Raymond Chandler.* Aurum, 2012.

Willis, Donald C. *The Films of Howard Hawks.* Scarecrow Press, 1975.

Wood, Robin. *Howard Hawks.* Doubleday, 1968.

Index

Numbers in **bold italics** indicate pages with illustrations

Adams, Dorothy 34
Adrian, Iris 190
The Age of Innocence 174
Agee, James 164, 169
Alfred Hitchcock Presents 104
Alien 3 175
Alonzo, John 41
American Beauty 29
Amis, Suzy 151
Anatomy of a Murder 40
Andelman, Juli 171
Anderson, Edward 4, 5, 74, 75, 78
Anderson, Judith 32
Andrews, Dana 30, 31, *36*, 40, 115
Angel Face 40
The Apartment 28

Bacall, Lauren 49, 67
Badge of Evil 5, 78–80
Baldwin, Stephen 151
Barbary Coast 70
Barlow, Joy 69
Barnett, Griff 99
Barr, Byron 15
Barry, John 58
Barton Fink 63
Bate, Barbara 98
Batman Begins 193
Beach, Guy 76
Beddoe, Don 166
Belafonte, Henry 40
Bell, Jeannie 172
Bello, Maria 194
Bennett, Joan 187, *188*
Beranger, George 143
Betrayal 190
Beyond a Reasonable Doubt 85
The Big Chill 58
The Big Heat 85, 174
The Big Lebowski 63
The Big Sleep (film) 5, 41, 64, 67–71, 74
The Big Sleep (novel) 5, 64–70
Birdman of Alcatraz 127
The Black Cat 133
Black Mask 65
Blake, Robert 186
Blanchett, Cate 149
Blondell, Joan 143, *144*
Blood Simple 5, 9, 58–63

The Blue Gardenia 85
Blue Velvet 81
Bluebeard's Eighth Wife 10
Body Heat 5, 9, 48–58, 59
Bogart, Humphrey 5, 58, 67, *68*, 70
Bogdanovich, Peter 81
Bohemian Rhapsody 149
Bombers B-52 119
Bonnie and Clyde 4, 74
The Border Sheriff 132
Brach, Gerard 41
Brackett, Charles 10, 28
Brackett, Leigh 70
Bradbury, Robert N. 132
Bradford, David 102
Brahm, John 30
Brando, Jocelyn 174
Breen, Joseph I. 138, 141, 142
Breon, Edmund 187
Bringing Up Baby 70
The Brood 198
Brooke, Hillary 86, 89
Bruce, Sally Jane 167
Bryk, Greg 195
The Bubble 104
Burke, James 144
Burr, Fritzi 43
Burt, Donald Graham 175
Busey, Jake 200
Bwana Devil 104
Byrne, Gabriel 151

Cain, James M. 4, 9, 10, 11, 12, 15, 18, 20, 58
Calleia, Joseph 82
Cameron, Carol 186
Carmen Jones 40
Carradine, David 171
Carradine, Robert 171
Casablanca 97, 149
Caspary, Vera 5, 29, 30, 31, 32, 34, 40
Castillo, Gloria 168
Chandler, Raymond 5, 10, 11, 21, 41, 58, 59, 64, 65, 67, 68, 69, 70
Chapin, Billy 167
Chartier, Jean-Pierre 4, 9, 10
Chinatown 5, 9, 40–48, 59
Christie, Agatha 64

Citizen Kane 78, 175
Clunie, Michelle 151
Coen, Ethan 5, 58, 60, 63
Coen, Joel 5, 58, 60, 63
Cold War 1, 3, 84, 86, 115, 122, 127, 128
Cole, Gordon 24
Collins, Wilkie 30, 31
Condon, Richard 6, 119, 120, 121, 124, 125, 126, 127
The Confidence-Man: His Masquerade 6, 129, 130
Cook, Elisha, Jr. 70
Cook, Tommy 99
Cooney, Michael 199, 200, 202, 204
Cooper, Bradley 149
Cooper, Chris 29
Cop Land 199
Corman, Roger 173
Corrigan, Lloyd 121
Cortez, Stanley 7, 41, 167
Cosmopolis 199
Cotten, Joseph 181
Craig, Helen 76
Crane, Bill R. 142
Crenna, Richard 51
Cronenberg, David 8, 149, 193, 194, 198, 199
Cul-de-sac 41
"The Curtain" 65
Cusack, John 200
Cvetic, Matt 6, 115, 119

Dandridge, Dorothy 40
A Dangerous Method 199
Danova, Cesare 172
Danson, Ted 54
The Dark Knight 193
The Dark Knight Rises 193
Darrin, Sonia 68, *68*
Da Silva, Howard 75
The Dawn Patrol 143
Dawson, Frank 187
Dean, Julia 145
Death and the Maiden 48
Del Toro, Benicio 151
Del Toro, Guillermo 149
DeMille, Cecil B. 21, 24–25, 27, 28
Demme, Jonathan 6, 127

De Mornay, Rebecca 200
De Niro, Robert 171
Detour (1945 film) 3, 6, 129, 132, 133, 134–141
Detour (1992 film) 142
Detour (novel) 6, 133–134, 135, 136–137, 138–140, 141–142
De Vargas, Valentin *82*
Dexter, John 33
Dhiegh, Khigh 120
"Diddling Considered as One of the Exact Sciences" 130–131
Dietrich, Marlene 83
Dmytryk, Edward 9
Dos Passos, John 74
Double Indemnity (film) 4, 9, 10, 11–20, 48, 58, 61, 159
Double Indemnity (novel) 4, 9–10, 11, 15, 16, 18, 20, 58
Douglas, Carole 68
Douglas, Gordon 6, 115, 119
Drake, Claudia 135
Drakeford, Deborah 195
Dunaway, Faye 42
Dunkirk 193
Duryea, Dan 86, 89, 189
DuVall, Clea 200

Eastern Promises 199
Edwards, James 121
Edwards, Jonathan 161, 162–163
Elise, Kimberly 127
Eltz, Theodore von 67
Ermey, R. Lee 178
Esmond, Carl 89
Esposito, Giancarlo 150
The Eternal Jew 85
eXistenZ 198

Fall River: An Authentic Narrative 179
Fallen Angel 40
Farewell My Lovely 65
Fargo 63
Farrington, Betty 12
Fassbender, Michael 199
Faulkner, William 70
Field, Mary 89
Fight Club 175
Fincher, David 4, 7, 175, *178*
Fincher, Jack 175
Finney, Edward 97
Flipper, Jay C. 75
The Fly 198
Fool for Love 190
Ford, Glenn 174
Foster, Susanna 142
Foulger, Byron 89
Fox, Jorja 193
Frank, Nino 4, 9, 10, 12
Frankenheimer, John 3, 6, 119, 120, 121, 122–123, 124, 126, 127
Frazier, Charlie 74
Freeman, Morgan 175
French Connection II 127
French Kiss 58
Fujikawa, Jerry 45

Fuller, Samuel 3, 5, 64, 71, 72, 73, 74
Furthman, Jules 70, 149
Fury (film) 143
Fury (novel) 143

Gangs of New York 174
Garnett, Tay 10
Gazzara, Ben 155
Gentlemen Prefer Blondes 70
Georgaris, Dean 127
German Expressionism 1, 4, 12, 63, 133, 166
Getz, John 59
The Girl with the Dragon Tattoo 175
Gish, Lillian 165
Gleason, James 168
Gliese, Rochus 133
Goetz, William 29, 30
Goldsmith, Martin M. 6, 132, 133, 134, 135, 136, 137, 138, 139, 140, 141, 142
Gone Girl 175
Goodfellas 174
Goulding, Edmund 3, 6, 132, 142–143
Grand Canyon 58
Grand Hotel 143
Granger, Farley 53, 74
Graves, Peter 164
Gray, Coleen 144
Gray, Judd 4, 11–12
Great Awakening 4, 7, 161–164, 179
Great Depression 4, 5, 74, 133, 164
Greene, Graham 5, 84, 85–86, 87, 89, 92, 93, 94, 95, 96
Greene, Peter 151
Gregory, James 120
Gresham, William Lindsay 7, 142, 143, 145, 146, 147, 149
Grubb, Davis 4, 7, 164, 165, 166, 168, 169, 170
Guerra, Castulo 152
Guitry, Sacha 10

Hackel, A.W. 97
Hagerthy, Ron 118
Hall, Porter 16
Hammett, Dashiell 5, 58, 59, 60, 62, 64
Harris, Ed 195
Harris, Harriet Sansom 191
Hart, Dorothy 117
Harvey, Laurence 120, *125*
Hawkes, John 201
Hawks, Howard 3, 5, 41, 64, 68, 69, 70, 71
Hawthorne, Nathaniel 129, 179
Hayes, Heidi 194
Hays Code 5, 40, 69, 133, 139; *see also* Production Code Administration
Hearst, William Randolph 119
Heart of Darkness 78
Heather, Jean 15
Hedaya, Dan 59, 150

Heist 160
Heston, Charlton 81
Hillerman, John 42
Hilton, Paul 98
A History of Violence (film) 8, 9, 181, 193–198, 199, 204
A History of Violence (graphic novel) 8, 193–194, 197–198, 199
Hitchcock, Alfred 53, 62, 71, 81, 104, 157, 159, 181, 200
Hoffenstein, Sam 31
Holden, Larry 192
Holden, William 20, 27
Holmes, Ashton 194
Holmes, Taylor 146
Hong, James 45
Hopper, Hedda 28
House, Billy 108
House of Games 160
House Un-American Activities Committee (HUAC) 84, 115, 118
Huffman, Felicity 156
Hull, Roger C. 142
Hungry Men 74
Hunter, Edward 126
Hunter, Morgan 150
Hurt, William 48, *50*, 51, 58, 63, 197
Huston, John 9, 42, 44, 104

I Was a Communist for the F.B.I. 6, 115–119
The Iceman Cometh 127
Identity 8, 9, 181, 199–204
In a Lonely Place 78
In Like Flint 119
In the Meantime, Darling 30
Inception 193
Indiana Jones and the Temple of Doom 175
Insomnia 193
Interstellar 193
The Invisible Man 97
The Island of Dr. Moreau 127

Jackson, Thomas E. 189
Jay, Ricky 155
Jenson, Roy 43
Johnson, Nunnally 182
Johnson, Roy 74
Jones, Thaddeus 100
Junior, Mark Boone 191

Kafka, Franz 159
Kammerspiel film 132
Karloff, Boris 133
Kasdan, Lawrence 5, 48, 51, 52, 58
Kate & Leopold 199
Keaton, Buster 22
Keitel, Harvey 170, *172*
Keith, Byron 106
Keith, Ian 143
Kibbee, Milton 99
Kidnapped 29
Kiley, Richard 72, *73*
"Killer in the Rain" 64
King, Henry 143

King, Max 97
Kleeb, Helen 120
Kline, Benjamin 132
Kline, Richard H. 50
Knife in the Water 41
Knudsen, Peggy 67
Kosleck, Martin 100

Ladd, Diane 41
The Lady from Shanghai 115
Laemmle, Carl 132
Lang, Fritz 3, 4, 5, 7, 84, 85, 86, 87, 88, 89, 90, 91, 92, 93, 94, 95, 96, 97, 174, 181, 184, 186, 189, 190
Lang, Walter 30
Lansbury, Angela 120, 122, 124, *125*, 126
The Last Temptation of Christ 7, 170
Laughton, Charles 4, 7, 164, 169, 170
Laura (film) 4–5, 9, 29, 30–40
Laura (novel) 5, 29, 30, 31, 32, 34–35, 36, 37, 40
Lavish, Lea 142
Lee, Will 75
Lehane, Dennis 174
Leigh, Janet 81, *82*, 121
LeMaire, Rufus 30
LePore, Richard 120
Levin, Ira 41
Lewis, Matthew Gregory 179
Liotta, Ray 150
Littleton, Carol 48
Locke, Vince 8, 193
Loehr, Bret 200
Loft, Arthur 187
Long, Richard 106
Lopez, Perry 42
The Lost Weekend 10, 28
Louden, Thomas 91
Lovejoy, Frank 116
Lowell, Tom 121
Lubitsch, Ernst 10
Lugosi, Bela 133
Lukas, George 48
Lynch, David 81, 83
Lyon, Bernice Maxine 137
Lyon, Priscilla 102

M 84, 85
Macbeth 78, 83
MacDonald, Edmund 135
Mack, Helen 99
MacMurray, Fred 11, 12, *13*, 63
MacNeill, Peter 196
The Magnificent Ambersons 115
Maher, Wally 99
The Major and the Minor 10
Malone, Dorothy 68
The Maltese Falcon 3, 9, 44
Mamet, David 3, 7, 154, 155, 156, 157, 159, 160
Mamoulian, Rouben 30, 32
The Man with the Golden Arm 40
The Manchurian Candidate (1962 film) 3, 6, 119–127
The Manchurian Candidate

(novel) 6, 120, 121, 122, 124, 125–126, 127
The Manchurian Candidate (2004 film) 6, 127
Mangold, James 8, 199, 200, 202, 204
Mank 175
Mankiewicz, Herman J. 175
Mantell, Joe 42
Maps to the Stars 199
Mara, Rooney 149
Marshman, D.M., Jr. 28
Martin, Steve 155
Martinez, Claudio 42
Massey, Raymond 186
Masterson, Whit 5, 78
Matsushita, Takeo 159
Matthews, Lester 88
Mauvaise Graine (*Bad Seed*) 10
Mazurki, Mike 144
McCambridge, Mercedes 81
McDormand, Frances 59
McGiver, John 122
McGrane, Erin 142
McGuinness, Carola 51
McHattie, Stephen 195
McQuarrie, Christopher 149, 150, 154
Mean Streets 4, 7, 161, 170–174, 175
Meehan, John 27
Melville, Herman 6, 129, 130
Memento 8, 9, 181, 190–193, 204
"Memento Mori" 190
Mendes, Sam 29
Menschen am Sonntag (*People on Sunday*) 133
Merivale, Philip 106
Messerschmidt, Erik 175
Metropolis 84, 85
Mildred Pierce 11
Milestone, Lewis 30
Millan, Victor 81
Milland, Ray 87
Miller, Bill 79
Miller, John "Skins" 24
Miller, Lorraine 69
Miller, Seton I. 86, 93
Miller's Crossing 63
Millican, James 116
Mills, Mort 83
"The Minister's Black Veil" 179
Ministry of Fear 3, 5, 84, 85, 86–96, 97
The Ministry of Fear 5, 85, 86–89, 92–93, 94, 95, 96
Das Mirakel (*The Miracle*) 132
Mister Smith Goes to Washington 97
Mitchum, Robert 40, 164, 165, *166*, 167
Molina, Alfred 201
Monash, Paul 78, 79, 80
The Monk 179
Mooney, Martin 133
Moorehead, Agnes 105
Moorhouse, Bert 24
Morris, Errol 126

Mortensen, Viggo 194, *196*, 197, 199
Moss, Carrie-Anne 191
Murder Is My Beat 132
Murder, My Sweet 9, 10
Murnau, F.W. 133

The Naked Kiss 73
Napier, Alan 89
Neal, Tom 134, *140*, 142
Neal, Tom, Jr. 142
Nebenzahl, Heinrich 133
Nicholson, Jack 41, 42, 63
The Niece of Abraham Pein 184
The Night of the Hunter (film) 4, 7, 161, 164, 165–170, 176
The Night of the Hunter (novel) 4, 7, 164, 165, 166, 168–169
Nightmare Alley (1947 film) 3, 6–7, 129, 131, 132, 142, 143–149
Nightmare Alley (novel) 7, 143, 145, 146, 147, 149
Nightmare Alley (2021 film) 149
Nilsson, Anna Q. 22
Nims, Ernest 105
Nolan, Christopher 8, 190, 193
Nolan, Jonathan 190
Northup, Harry 171
Notorious 104
Novak, Kim 181

Oboler, Arch 3, 6, 97, 98, 103, 104
O'Donnell, Cathy 74
An Officer and a Spy 48
Oleanna 160
Olson, Josh 193
Olson, Nancy 23
On Dangerous Ground 78
Once Off Guard 7, 182
Othello 115

Palmer, Belinda 46
Palminteri, Chazz 150
Paltrow, Gwyneth 176
Pantoliano, Joe 191
Park Row 73
Parrish, Leslie 122
Parsons, Louella 119
Pascale, Jan 175
Payne, Shelby 69
Pearce, Guy 191
Peet, Amanda 200
Peters, Jean 71, *73*
Peterson, Dorothy 186
Phantom of the Opera 97, 142
Phillips, Jayne Anne 164–165
The Pianist 48
Picerni, Paul 117
Pickup on South Street 3, 5, 64, 70, 71–73, 74
Pidgeon, Rebecca 154, *155*
Pinocchio 121
Pinter, Harold 190
Pitt, Brad 175
Poe, Edgar Allan 129, 130, 131, 204
Polanski, Roman 5, 40, 41, 42, 43, 48

Pollack, Kevin 151
Portnow, Richard 175
Postlethwaite, Pete 151
The Postman Always Rings Twice (film) 10, 59
The Postman Always Rings Twice (novel) 11, 58
Power, Tyrone 143, *144*, 148
Powers, Harry F. 4, 164–165
Powers, Tom 15
Preminger, Otto 3, 4, 5, 9, 29, 30, 31, 32, 33, 34, 35, 40, 132
Preston, J.A. 54
Price, Vincent 32, 173
Production Code Administration 40, 138, 149; *see also* Hays Code
Proval, David 171
Psycho 59, 81, 200, 201, 202
Public Access 149
Pyne, Daniel 127

Queen Kelly 22
Quiet Dell 165
Quigley, Gerry 194
Quo, Beulah 45

Rains, Claude 6, 97, 102, 104, 175
Raksin, David 32
Ray, Nicholas 3, 4, 5, 64, 74, 75, 76, 77, 78
The Razor's Edge 143
Rebel Without a Cause 74, 78
Red Harvest 60, 62–63
Reinhardt, Betty 31
Reinhardt, Max 132
Rennie, Callum Keith 191
Repulsion 41
Reynolds, Marjorie 86, 89
Ridgely, John 67
Ritter, Thelma 72
Roberts, Roy 117, 148
Robinson, Amy 171
Robinson, Edward G. 15, 105, 186, *188*, 189
Rocca, Peter 152
Le Roman d'un Tricheur (The Story of a Cheat) 10
Romanus, Richard 171
Rosemary's Baby 41
Rourke, Mickey 52
Rudin, Scott 127
Ruthless 132
Ryan, Michael 53

Samson and Delilah 24
Sanders, Hugh 118
Sanford, Erskin 88
Sargent, Michael *82*
Saunders, Lanna 54
Savage, Ann 137, *140*
Sayers, Dorothy 64
Scarface 70
The Scarlet Letter 179
Scarlet Street 85
Schenck, Joseph 29
Schmid, Kyle 194
Schreiber, Liev 127

Scorsese, Catherine 173
Scorsese, Martin 4, 7, 71, 149, 170, 171, 173, 174
Scott, Campbell 154, *155*
Scott, William Lee 200
Seitz, John 12
Sergeant York 70
Se7en 4, 7, 161, 175–179
Shadow of a Doubt 181
Shayne, Konstantin 105, 116
Shephard, Sam 190
Shock Corridor 73
Shutter Island 174
Sigel, Newton Thomas 152
Silva, Henry 121
Silverado 58
Simmons, Jean 40
"The Simple Art of Murder" 64
Sinatra, Frank 40, 120, 127
Sinatra, Tina 127
Singer, Bryan 3, 7, 149–150, 151, 152, 154
"Sinners in the Hands of an Angry God" 162–163
Siodmak, Robert 133
Sklar, George 29
Snyder, Ruth 4, 11–12, 31
Some Like It Hot 28
Spacey, Kevin 29, 150, 175
The Spanish Prisoner 3, 7, 129, 131, 154–159
Spiegal, Sam 105
Spielberg, Steven 149
Spillane, Mickey 71
Stagecoach 119
Stanwyck, Barbara 11, 12, *13*
Star Wars: Episode V—The Empire Strikes Back 48
Star Wars: Episode VI—Return of the Jedi 175
Stebbins, Bob 98
Steele, Bob 67
Stewart, James 181
Strange Holiday 3, 6, 97–104
Strange Illusion 132
The Strange Woman 132
The Stranger 3, 6, 83, 104–115
Strangers on a Train 53, 157
Streep, Meryl 127
street films 132
Stroheim, Erich von 21, 22
Sun-Up 143
Sunrise 133
Sunset Boulevard 3, 4, 9, 10, 20–28, 29, 58, 132
Swanson, Gloria 21, 22

Tamiroff, Akim 81
Tenet 193
Tess 48
They Call Me Mr. Tibbs! 119
They Live by Night 4, 5, 64, 74–77
Thieves Like Us 4, 5, 74, 75, 77–78
The Thing from Another World 4
This Precious Freedom 97
Thompson, Jim 71
Thornton, Roy 74
3:10 to Yuma 199

Tierney, Gene 32, 33, *36*, 40
Tobolowsky, Stephen 191
The Tomb of Ligeia 173
Toomey, Regis 67
Touch of Evil 5, 64, 70, 74, 78–83
Towne, Robert 41, 48
Trivas, Victor 104
Turner, Kathleen 49, *50*

Ulmer, Edgar G. 3, 4, 6, 132–133, 134, 135, 136, 137, 138, 139, 140, 141, 142
U.S.A. 74–75
The Usual Suspects 3, 7, 129, 131, 149

Varden, Evelyn 165
Veiller, Anthony 104
Vertigo 181
Vickers, Martha 67
Videodrome 198
Vince, Pruitt Taylor 199, *202*
Voight, Jon 127
Von Harbou, Thea 85

Wade, Robert Allison 78–79
Wagner, John 8, 193
Waldron, Charles 71
Walk the Line 199
Walker, Andrew Kevin 179
Walker, Helen 145
Walker, Robert 53
Wallace, Dan 70
Wallis, J.H. 7, 181, 182, 183, 184
Walsh, M. Emmet 58
Waram, Percy 86, *90*, 93
Warner, H.B. 22
Washington, Denzel 127
Weaver, Dennis 81
Webb, Clifton 30, *36*
Webb, Jack 23
Webb, Richard 117
Weir, Peter 149
Welles, Orson 3, 5, 6, 64, 78, 80–81, 83, 104, 105, 106, 107, 108, 109, 111, 112, 113, 114, *114*, 115, 175
Wentworth, Martha 112
Whale, James 97
Wharton, Edith 174
Wheeler, Lyle 73
Where the Sidewalk Ends 40
White, Walter, Jr. 99
Whitefield, George 161, 162, 163–164
Widmark, Richard 71
Wilbur, Crane 115
Wilder, Billy 3, 4, 9, 10, 11, 12, 16, 17, 18, 20, 21, 22, 27, 28, 29, 58, 132, 159
Williams, Catharine 179
Williams, Samm-Art 60
Williams, Wade 142
Winters, Shelley 164, *166*, 167
The Wizard of Oz 190
The Wolf of Wall Street 174
Wolfe, Ian 75
The Wolverine 199

The Woman in the Window 7, 89, 95, 181, 186–190
The Woman in the Window (Once Off Guard) 182–186
The Woman in White 30
World War II 1, 16, 41, 84, 86, 97, 99, 105, 109, 126, 127, 184
Wright, Teresa 181

Wright, Will 75
Wyatt, Eustace 88

Yoshida, Seiko 159
Young, Burt 41
Young, Loretta 105
Young at Heart 119

Zanuck, Darryl 29, 30
Zimmer, Kim 50
Zodiac 175
Zombies on Broadway 119
Zwerling, Darrell 41